Data Science

This book covers the topic of data science in a comprehensive manner and synthesizes both fundamental and advanced topics of a research area that has now reached its maturity. The book starts with the basic concepts of data science. It highlights the types of data and their use and importance, followed by a discussion on a wide range of applications of data science and widely used techniques in data science.

Key Features

- Provides an internationally respected collection of scientific research methods, technologies and applications in the area of data science.
- Presents predictive outcomes by applying data science techniques to real-life applications.
- Provides readers with the tools, techniques and cases required to excel with modern artificial intelligence methods.
- Gives the reader a variety of intelligent applications that can be designed using data science and its allied fields.

The book is aimed primarily at advanced undergraduates and graduates studying machine learning and data science. Researchers and professionals will also find this book useful.

Data Science
Techniques and Intelligent Applications

Edited by
Pallavi Vijay Chavan
Parikshit N Mahalle
Ramchandra Mangrulkar
Idongesit Williams

CRC Press
Taylor & Francis Group
Boca Raton London New York

CRC Press is an imprint of the
Taylor & Francis Group, an **informa** business

A CHAPMAN & HALL BOOK

First edition published 2023
by CRC Press
6000 Broken Sound Parkway NW, Suite 300, Boca Raton, FL 33487-2742

and by CRC Press
4 Park Square, Milton Park, Abingdon, Oxon, OX14 4RN

CRC Press is an imprint of Taylor & Francis Group, LLC

© 2023 selection and editorial matter, [Pallavi Vijay Chavan, Parikshit N Mahalle, Ramchandra Sharad Mangrulkar and Idongesit Williams]; individual chapters, the contributors

Library of Congress Cataloging-in-Publication Data
Names: Chavan, Pallavi, editor. | Mahalle, Parikshit N, editor. | Mangrulkar, Ramchandra, editor. |
Williams, Idongesit, editor.
Title: Data science : techniques and intelligent applications / edited by
Pallavi Vijay Chavan, Parikshit N Mahalle, Ramchandra Mangrulkar, Idongesit Williams.
Description: First edition. | Boca Raton, FL : Chapman & Hall/CRC Press, 2023. |
Includes bibliographical references and index. |
Summary: "The proposed book covers the topic of data science in a very comprehensive manner and synthesizes both fundamental and advanced topics of a research area that has now reached maturity. The book starts from the basic concepts of data science; it highlights the types of data, its use and its importance, followed by discussion on a wide range of applications of data science and widely used techniques in data science.
Key features: provides an internationally respected collection of scientific research methods, technologies and applications in the area of data science, presents predictive outcomes by applying data science techniques on real life applications, provides readers with the tools, techniques and cases required to excel with modern artificial intelligence methods, and gives the reader variety of intelligent applications that can be designed using data science and its allied fields. The book is aimed primarily at advanced undergraduates and graduates studying machine learning and data science. Researchers and professionals will also find this book useful"— Provided by publisher.
Identifiers: LCCN 2022002189 (print) | LCCN 2022002190 (ebook) |
ISBN 9781032254494 (hbk) | ISBN 9781032254517 (pbk) | ISBN 9781003283249 (ebk)
Subjects: LCSH: Big data. | Electronic data processing. | Information technology. | Information science.
Classification: LCC QA76.9.B45 D394 2023 (print) | LCC QA76.9.B45 (ebook) | DDC 005.7—dc23/eng/20220416
LC record available at https://lccn.loc.gov/2022002189
LC ebook record available at https://lccn.loc.gov/2022002190

ISBN: 978-1-032-25449-4 (hbk)
ISBN: 978-1-032-25451-7 (pbk)
ISBN: 978-1-003-28324-9 (ebk)

DOI: 10.1201/9781003283249

Typeset in Palatino
by codeMantra

Contents

Preface

We are in the data-driven age, and the data science field has gained attention of people not only from the technical field but also from all the areas of society. There has been tremendous growth in data every day, and we are equipping ourselves with the best set of tools and technologies to handle those data. Data science has become a core capability everywhere, more specifically in the industrial sector. Many e-commerce businesses are data driven. Every day, these e-commerce businesses collect a huge amount of data, analyze the data and decide on some policy to improve the business. The fourth industrial revolution we are observing all over the globe is based on data science and its allied fields. Machine learning, deep learning and artificial intelligence are the key elements in data science. Data science with its scientific methods gives conclusions and analysis, while machine learning and deep learning algorithms help to have predictive models. There are several algorithms available with machine learning such as supervised learning, reinforcement learning and unsupervised learning. Classification is the most popular category of machine learning algorithms. The researchers and practitioners use machine learning and deep learning algorithms as per their requirements and suitability of the algorithms to their problem statement. Deep learning techniques also play a crucial role in the design of intelligent applications. Deep learning algorithms are a family of artificial neural networks. These networks learn themselves and get trained for a given set of data. Validation testing in deep learning exhibits accuracy in learning. Artificial intelligence also plays a significant role in the design of intelligent applications with data science. Artificial intelligence helps in designing rule-based systems. Such rule-based systems include facts and rules of inferences. On the other side, there are the technologies such as soft computing, fuzzy logic and genetic algorithm. These technologies have a significant contribution to the development of intelligent applications. Today, intelligent applications are used almost in all the sectors such as healthcare, education, agriculture, finance, games and sports, and entertainment. Intelligent applications in healthcare include diabetic retinopathy, diabetes detection, expert systems for medical diagnosis and many more. In the agriculture field, the popular intelligent applications includes the prediction of rain, weather forecasting, crop prediction, and soil quality determination and prediction. In finance, applications like stock price prediction and gold rate prediction are most popular. This book aims to provide a platform for researchers to promote intelligent applications and their design for the betterment of the technology and the society in turn.

This volume comprises 18 chapters. The technical contents begin with the data science fundamentals; the book further includes the chapters based on tools, methods and the techniques used in data science. The chapters focus on the fundamentals of data science and the applications from domains such as agriculture, finance, healthcare, real estate and crime. Chapter 1 states the basic building blocks of data science with different tools and techniques used in data analysis. Chapter 2 discusses the role of statistical methods in data science. These methods are important in analytical processing. Chapter 3 describes broad application areas of data science in the real world. Some of them are agriculture, healthcare, education, entertainment, etc. Chapter 4 discusses a smart Handwritten Devanagari Word Recognition system using Deep ResNet based on the Scan Profile method. This chapter exhibits the analysis of different classifiers for speech-based emotion recognition systems using linear and nonlinear features. Chapter 5 presents an intelligent application to data science stating safe social distance monitoring and face mask detection mechanism to control the COVID-19 spread. Chapter 6 presents another intelligent application of data science that describes real-time virtual fitness tracker and exercise posture correction. This mechanism implements the concept of machine learning. Chapter 7 discusses the role of data science in revolutionizing the healthcare sector, yet another intelligent application of data science. Chapter 8 presents another intelligent application of data science stating the early-stage detection of chronic kidney disease. For development of this application, artificial intelligence techniques are experimented. Multi-optimal deep learning technique for detection and classification of breast cancer from histopathological images is presented in Chapter 9. Chapter 10 talks about influence of lifestyle on pregnancy complications. This is conducted in real-world environment, and the results are presented. Chapter 11 proposes a research paper recommendation system. Chapter 12 shows an analysis and prediction of crime rate against women using classification and regression. Chapter 13 talks about data analysis for technical business incubation performance improvement. Chapter 14 shows satellite imagery-based wildfire detection. This chapter demonstrates the usage of deep learning techniques with image data for detection. Chapter 15 demonstrates low resource language document summarization. Chapter 16 describes eclectic analysis of classifiers for fake news detection. Chapter 17 talks about data science and machine learning applications for mental health. Finally, Chapter 18 presents the contribution by authors in artificial intelligence stating analysis of ancient and modern meditation techniques on human mind and body and its effectiveness in the COVID-19 pandemic.

We would like to express our sincere thanks and gratitude to the authors for their outstanding contributions. Without their contributions, it would have become very difficult to submit this proposal. As the editors, we hope that this book will help and stimulate the researchers to pursue research in this domain. Also, we expect that the researchers will get benefited from the huge set of applications stated in this book. Special thanks go to our publisher, CRC Press/Taylor and Francis group.

We hope that this book will present promising ideas and outstanding research contributions and support further development of data science and intelligent application.

Editors

Dr. Pallavi Vijay Chavan is Associate Professor at Ramrao Adik Institute of Technology, D Y Patil Deemed to be University, Navi Mumbai, Maharashtra, India. She has been in academic for 16 years, working in the area of data science and network security. In her academic journey, she published research work in the data science and security domain with reputable publishers including Springer, Elsevier, CRC Press and Inderscience. She has published 1 book, 7+ book chapters, 10+ international journal papers and 30+ international conference papers. Presently she is guiding five Ph.D. research scholars working in a similar domain. She completed her Ph.D. from Rashtrasant Tukadoji Maharaj Nagpur University, Nagpur, Maharashtra, India, in 2017. She secured the first merit position at Nagpur University for the degree of B.E. in Computer Engineering in 2003. She is the recipient of research grants from UGC, CSIR and the University of Mumbai. She is a reviewer for Elsevier and Inderscience journals. Her firm belief is "Teaching is a mission".

Dr. Parikshit N Mahalle is a senior member of IEEE and a Professor and Head of the Department of Artificial Intelligence and Data Science at Vishwakarma Institute of Information Technology, Pune, India. He completed his Ph.D. from Aalborg University, Denmark, and continued as a postdoctoral researcher. He has 21+ years of teaching and research experience. He is a member of Board of Studies in Computer Engineering, Savitri Bai Phule University and various universities. He has 9 patents and 200+ research publications (citations: 1830, H-index:18) and authored/edited 30+ books with Springer, CRC Press, Cambridge University Press, etc. He is editor-in-chief for IGI Global – *International Journal of Rough Sets and Data Analysis*, Associate Editor for IGI Global – *International Journal of Synthetic Emotions*, Inter-science – *International Journal of Grid and Utility Computing*, and member of Editorial Review Board for IGI Global – *International Journal of Ambient Computing and Intelligence*. His research interests are Algorithms, Internet of Things, Identity Management and Security. He has delivered more than 200 lectures at national and international levels.

Dr. Ramchandra Mangrulkar, a post-graduate from the National Institute of Technology, Rourkela, received his Ph.D. in computer science and engineering from SGB Amravati University, Amravati in 2016. At present, he is working as an Associate Professor in the Department of Computer Engineering at SVKM's Dwarkadas J. Sanghvi College of Engineering, Mumbai (autonomous college affiliated to the University of Mumbai), Maharashtra, India. Dr. Ramchandra Mangrulkar has published 50 papers and 24 book chapters with Taylor and Francis, Springer and IGI Global in the field of interest. He has presented 54 papers in national and international conferences. He has also edited five books with CRC Press, Taylor and Francis Series. He has also worked as a reviewer in many international journals and also reviewed many book proposals submitted to publishers of an international reputation. He has also chaired many sessions in national and international conferences. He has also shown keen interest in conducting and organizing workshops on Artificial Intelligence Bot in Education, Network Simulator 2, Innovative tools for Research and LaTeX & Overleaf. He has also received certification of appreciation from DIG Special Crime Branch Pune and Superintendent of Police and broadcasting media gives wide publicity for the project work guided by him on the topic "Face Recognition System". He has also received a grant-in-aid of rupees three lacs and fifty thousand under the Research Promotion Scheme of AICTE, New Delhi for the project "Secured Energy Efficient Routing Protocol for Delay Tolerant Hybrid Network". He is also working as an internal thesis advisor at NMIMS's MPSTE Mumbai and DY Patil's RAIT, Navi Mumbai. He also worked as an external referee for Ph.D. thesis evaluation at SGB Amravati University and RTM Nagpur University. He is an active member of the Board of Studies in various universities and autonomous institutes in India.

Dr. Idongesit Williams is an Assistant Professor at Aalborg University Copenhagen. He holds a bachelor's degree in Physics, a master's degree in Information and Communications Technologies and a Ph.D. His research areas are socio-economic, socio-technical related to Information and Communications Technologies. His research areas include the following. The facilitation of telecom and ICT infrastructure using public–private partnerships; the development and the sustenance of community-based networks, e-government implementation; science and technology studies; gender adoption of ICTs; organizational adoption of ICTs; and user experience with ICTs and organizational learning. He has authored more than 60 research publications, including journal papers, books, book chapters, conference papers and magazine articles. He is the co-editor of the book *The African Mobile Story*. He has delivered presentations at conferences and also helped in organizing conferences such as the CMI annual conference and the CMI/GTUC conferences.

Contributors

Pallavi Vijay Chavan
Department of Information Technology
Ramrao Adik Institute of Technology
D Y Patil Deemed to be University
Navi Mumbai, India

Shalaka Prasad Deore
Department of Computer Engineering
M.E.S. College of Engineering, Pune, S.P.
  Pune University
Pune, India

Himani Deshpande
Department of Computer Engineering
Ramrao Adik Institute of Technology
D Y Patil Deemed to be University
Navi Mumbai, India

Pranjali Deshpande
Department of Computer Engineering
MKSSS's Cummins College of Engineering
  for Women
Pune, India

Prarthana Dhok
Department of Information Technology
Ramrao Adik Institute of Technology
Navi Mumbai, India

Sunil Dhore
Department of Computer Engineering
Army Institute of Technology
Pune, India

Yash Goda
Computer Engineering Department
Dwarkadas J. Sanghvi College of
  Engineering
Mumbai, India

Nitin Goje
Webster University
Tashkent, Uzbekistan

Vijay S. Gulhane
Department of Information Technology
Sipna College of Engineering &
  Technology
Amravati, India

Baisa L. Gunjal
Department of Information Technology
Amrutvahini College of Engineering
Sangamner, India

Nikhil Ingale
Department of Information Technology
Ramrao Adik Institute of Technology
D Y Patil Deemed to be University
Navi Mumbai, India

Sunita Jahirabadkar
Department of Computer Engineering
MKSSS's Cummins College of Engineering
  for Women
Pune, India

Pruthav Jhaveri
Computer Engineering Department
Dwarkadas J. Sanghvi College of
  Engineering
Mumbai, India

Tejas Kachare
Department of Information Technology
Vishwakarma Institute of Technology
Pune, India

Piyush Kadam
Department of Information Technology
Ramrao Adik Institute of Technology
D Y Patil Deemed to be University
Navi Mumbai, India

Aryan Kakade
Department of Computer Science
Sinhgad College of Engineering
Pune, India

Siddharth Kakade
Department of Computer Science
Vishwakarma Institute of Technology
Pune, India

Anant Kaulage
Army Institute of Technology
Pune, India

Anindita A. Khade
Department of Computer Engineering
Ramrao Adik Institute of Technology
D Y Patil Deemed to be University
Navi Mumbai, India
and
SIES Graduate School of Technology
Navi Mumbai, India

Vatsal Khandor
Computer Engineering Department
Dwarkadas J. Sanghvi College of
    Engineering
Mumbai, India

Dhruvi Khankhoje
Computer Engineering Department
Dwarkadas J. Sanghvi College of
    Engineering
Mumbai, India

Prateek Koul
Department of Information Technology
Ramrao Adik Institute of Technology
Navi Mumbai, India

Pankaj Kulkarni
Application Architect
Deloitte Service LLP
Franklin, Tennessee

Pournima Kulkarni
Lead Quality Analyst
Healthstream, Inc.
Nashville, Tennessee

Jyoti Kundale
Department of Information Technology
Ramrao Adik Institute of Technology
D Y Patil Deemed to be University
Navi Mumbai, India

Abhijeet Kushwah
Department of Information Technology
Ramrao Adik Institute of Technology
Navi Mumbai, India

Pravin Malve
Department of Computer Engineering
Government Polytechnic
Wardha, India

Deepa Mane
IT Department
Smt. Kashibai Navale College of Engineering
Pune, India

Ramchandra Mangrulkar
Computer Engineering Department
Dwarkadas J. Sanghvi College of
    Engineering
Mumbai, India

Yashsingh Manral
Department of Information Technology
Ramrao Adik Institute of Technology
Navi Mumbai, India

Siddharth Nigade
Department of Computer Science
Vishwakarma Institute of Technology
Pune, India

Tirth Pandya
Department of Information Technology
Ramrao Adik Institute of Technology
Navi Mumbai, India

Leena Ragha
Department of Computer Engineering
Ramrao Adik Institute of Technology
D Y Patil Deemed to be University
Navi Mumbai, India

Onkar Rane
Department of Information Technology
Ramrao Adik Institute of Technology
D Y Patil Deemed to be University
Navi Mumbai, India

Sagar Rane
Army Institute of Technology
Pune, India

Naitik Rathod
Computer Engineering Department
Dwarkadas J. Sanghvi College of
    Engineering
Mumbai, India

Priyali Sakhare
Department of Information Technology
Ramrao Adik Institute of Technology
D Y Patil Deemed to be University
Navi Mumbai, India

Ashwini Sarode
Department of Applied Computer Science
SRH Heidelberg University
Heidelberg, Germany

Krutik Shah
Computer Engineering Department
Dwarkadas J. Sanghvi College of
    Engineering
Mumbai, India

Nemil Shah
Computer Engineering Department
Dwarkadas J. Sanghvi College of
    Engineering
Mumbai, India

Yashvi Shah
Computer Engineering Department
Dwarkadas J. Sanghvi College of
    Engineering
Mumbai, India

Nitin Shekapure
Production Engineering Department
All India Shri Shivaji Memorial Society
    College of Engineering
Pune, India

Swati Shekapure
Computer Engineering Department
Marathwada Mitra Mandal's College of
    Engineering
Pune, India

Narendra M. Shekokar
Computer Engineering Department
Dwarkadas J. Sanghvi College of
    Engineering
Mumbai, India

Sachin Shelke
IT Department
Pune Institute of Computer Technology
Pune, India

Vishal Shrivastava
CRG Solutions Singapore Pte Ltd.
Bangalore, India

Vivek Kumar Singh
Department of CSE
Bharat Institute of Engineering and
    Technology
Hyderabad, India

Manisha Sinha
Department of Electronics and
    Communication Engineering
University of Engineering and
    Management Jaipur
Jaipur, India

P. Tamilarasi
Department of Computer Science
Sri Sarada College for Women
    (Autonomous)
Salem, India

R. Uma Rani
Sri Sarada College for Women
    (Autonomous)
Salem, India

Siddhesh Unhavane
University of Illinois at
    Urbana-Champaign
School of Information Sciences
Champaign, Illinois
and
Department of Information Technology
Ramrao Adik Institute of Technology
Navi Mumbai, India

Amarsinh V. Vidhate
Department of Computer Engineering
Ramrao Adik Institute of Technology
D Y Patil Deemed to be University
Navi Mumbai, India

Shreeraj Vijayan
PublicisSapient
Toronto, Canada

1

Instigation and Development of Data Science

Priyali Sakhare and Pallavi Vijay Chavan
Ramrao Adik Institute of Technology, D.Y. Patil Deemed to be University Nerul, Navi Mumbai

Pournima Kulkarni
Healthstream, Inc.

Ashwini Sarode
SRH Heidelberg University

CONTENTS

1.1 Data Science

Data is the basis or groundwork of data science; it is the matter on which all the analyses are based on processing. In the context of data science, data can be bifurcated into two types: traditional and big data.

DOI: 10.1201/9781003283249-1

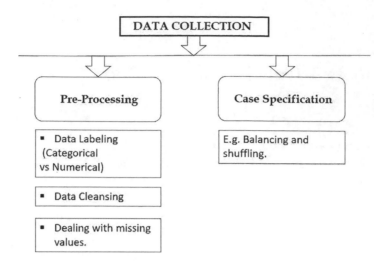

FIGURE 1.1
Traditional data processing.

Traditional Data: In the context of data science, traditional data is in a structured format and can be stored in databases. It is mainly maintained by all types of businesses starting from very small to big organizations. Traditional data is stored in relational database management systems (Figure 1.1).

For traditional data to be processed, all data goes through the preprocessing stage. This operation is necessary where the raw data is converted into a format which is more understandable. Few processes are undertaken for traditional data. They are as follows:

i. Collection of raw data and storing it on a server
ii. Class labeling
iii. Data cleansing
iv. Data balancing
v. Data shuffling

Big Data: In the context of data science, big data is larger than traditional data where it deals with complex datasets which is difficult to be managed in traditional data. Big data is usually distributed across a large network which varies by variety (number, text, audio, video), velocity (retrieved, computed), and volume (tera-, peta-, exabytes) (Figure 1.2).

In big data, as the complexity of the data is very large, the preprocessing stage becomes crucial. Some of the stages of big data are quite similar to the traditional data [1,2]. The process for big data is as follows:

i. Collection of the data
ii. Class labeling
iii. Data cleansing
iv. Data masking

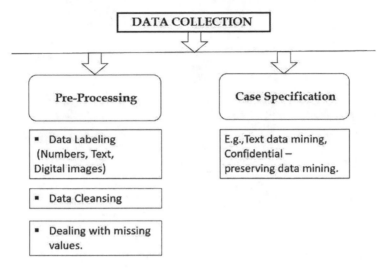

FIGURE 1.2
Big data processing.

In data science, the term "science" means the knowledge which is gained through systematic study. Basically, it is a systematic plan that builds and organizes the knowledge which is in a form that is easily testable in explanations and predictions [3].

1.1.1 Existence of Data Science

Data science is a combination of two or more fields that uses different kinds of math and statistics, scientific methods, specialized programming, artificial intelligence, data analysis, algorithms, and systems for the extraction of knowledge from the data. The data can be structured and unstructured. The data science field prepares data for analysis, expands data science problems, makes data-driven solutions, analyzes data, and searches the high-level decisions in a broad range of application domains. Data science also is related to big data, machine learning, data mining, etc. It is a study of the massive amount of data that includes extraction of meaningful insight from structured and unstructured data which is completed using different algorithms and scientific methods [4].

Figure 1.3 shows the diagram of data science. Data science is the discovery of knowledge through the analysis of data which is the statistics extension that is capable of dealing with huge amounts of data. In data science, the past data is being analyzed for prediction of future analysis. Data science usually works with dynamic unstructured data. The skills required for data science are statistics, visualization, and machine learning. Data science has several current viewpoints. They are as follows:

  i. Data science is about studying scientific and business data.
  ii. Data science is an integration of computing technology, statistics, and artificial intelligence.
  iii. The purpose of data science is to solve scientific as well as business problems by the extraction of knowledge from data [5,6].

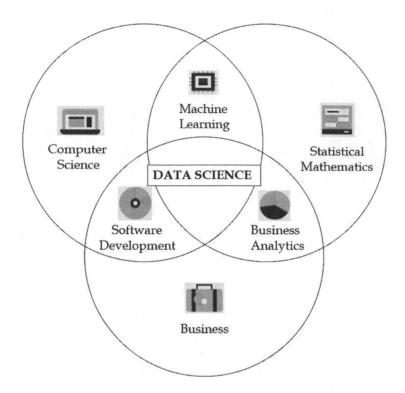

FIGURE 1.3
Existence of data science.

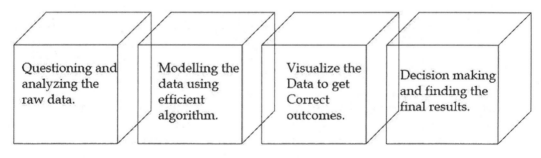

FIGURE 1.4
Simple steps of data science.

Data science uses powerful hardware, programming systems, and desired algorithms to solve the issues that arise in data. Data can be analyzed in a simple form. Refer to Figure 1.4 for a few simple steps of data science.

In short, data science is all about:

   i. Analyzing and questioning the raw data.
   ii. Modeling the data using the desired algorithm.
   iii. Visualize the data to achieve correct outcomes.
   iv. Decision-making and finding the final results [7].

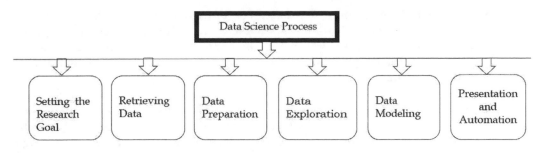

FIGURE 1.5
Process of data science.

1.1.2 Data Science Process

Data science is a multidisciplinary field, and it allows us to extract information from both structured and unstructured data. Data science helps us to raise the chances of success in data science projects at the lowest price by using the standard approach. It also makes it possible to take a project by making teams, with each team member focusing on a particular center of interest areas [8].

The data science process passes through various phases. The data science process consists of six important steps (Figure 1.5).

This summarizes the process of data science and the following list is a short introduction to the process, each step will be discussed in depth further:

i. **Setting the Research Goal**: The first phase of the process is setting a research goal. The main aim of this is to make sure that all the people of the company understand the purpose of the project.

ii. **Retrieving Data**: The second phase of data science is used for retrieving data where data is available for analysis purposes, and it also includes searching for suitable data and getting access to data from the owner of the data. The data will be in the raw form which needs to be polished and transformed before it becomes usable.

iii. **Data Preparation**: After processing the data in the second phase, i.e., retrieving data, we get raw data, so it's time to prepare it. In the third phase of data science, data preparation is undertaken for processing this raw data. This includes the transformation of raw data into data that would be directly usable. For achieving the usable form of data, we have to detect and correct various errors of data and combine data from different data sources. Then it transforms those data. Once the data preparation is successfully completed, one can progress to data visualization and modeling.

iv. **Data Exploration**: The fourth phase of the data science process is data exploration where data is explored in a deep understandable form. This phase will enable us to start the modeling phase.

v. **Data Modeling:** The fifth phase of the data science process is data modeling which is also known as model building. Here, we have to select a technique from different fields like machine learning, statistics, and operation search. Data modeling is the iterative process which involves a selection of different variables for a model, execution of the model, and diagnosis of the model.

vi. **Presentation and Automation:** The last phase of the data science process is presentation and automation. This phase is processed, only if needed. The importance of this step is more clearly visible or understood in projects on a tactical and strategic scale. Some projects need to be performed again so that automating the project will save time [9].

Following these six steps pays off, higher project success rate and also increased research results. This process makes sure that we have a well-designed research plan, clear deliverables, and a good understanding of the business query before you even start looking at data. Now, we will look into the process in detail.

1.1.2.1 Setting the Research Goal

Every project starts by understanding the purpose of why, what, and how the project is established. Refer to Figure 1.6 for understanding the setting of the research goal.

For defining research goals and creating a project charter, we need to understand what does the company expects from us? And why does management place such a value on research? And is it part of a bigger picture of a project originating from an opportunity someone detected? So, answering these what, why, and how is the goal of the first phase of the process.

This phase aims to have a clear research goal, a good understanding of contents, and proper planning of action with a timetable. This can help to create the project charter. Creating a project charter refers to the short formal document with a clear objective statement of the project.

1.1.2.1.1 Spend Time Understanding the Goals of Research

Understanding the research goals is an essential outcome which usually states the purpose of the project in a focused and clear manner. This would be slightly critical for the success of the project. Constantly querying until the doubts are resolved and until the expectations of the project are cleared, it takes months' time to resolve the research problems.

1.1.2.1.2 Creation of Project Charter

In the project charter, clients (users) want to know about what they are paying for, so we need to efficiently understand the problem and need to try to get an agreement on the deliverables. The project charter is mandatory for creating any project.

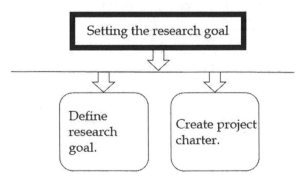

FIGURE 1.6
Setting the research goal.

A project charter needs teamwork and the inputs should consist of the following points:

  i. Research goal should be clear.
  ii. Project mission should be clear.
  iii. What resources are going to be used?
  iv. How is the project going to be analyzed?
  v. Project should be deliverable and successful.
  vi. Project should be completed in the timeline.

Clients can use all of this information so that they can make the estimation of cost for the project and the people who are specialized are required for that project to make it successful.

1.1.2.2 Retrieving Data

After setting the research goals, we need to collect the data. In this phase, we have to ensure whether there is sufficient quality of data and there is proper access to the data for further use of it. The data can be in various forms, i.e., it can be from an excel spreadsheet to many different types of databases.

Figure 1.7 shows the retrieval of data.

In this phase, the required data is retrieved for processing. Occasionally, we need to design the collection of data by ourselves, but mostly we won't get involved in this phase. Many companies already have collections of the data that are stored for us, but in rare cases if data is not available then it can be bought from third parties.

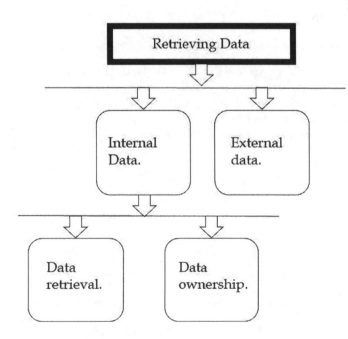

FIGURE 1.7
Retrieving data.

1.1.2.2.1 Data Stored within the Company

Firstly, we need to check whether there is access for the data to the company. Then, we have to check the quality of the data that is available in the company. Many companies have the habit of keeping the key data, so cleaning of data can be already done. Mainly, the data can be stored in data warehouses, data marts, databases, etc. Data warehouse is a system where it combines the data from different sources into a central repository to store the data and support data mining, machine learning, and business intelligence. Data mart is a subset of a data warehouse where it focuses on a specific area which only allows the authorized user to quickly access critical data without wasting time over finding through an entire data warehouse. A database is used to store the data.

Sometimes finding the data within the company becomes more challenging. As the company grows, the data gets scattered in many different places. Due to changes in the position of people in the company, many of them leave the company, so the knowledge of data may disappear. So, we need to develop some skills to recover the lost data. Another difficult task is to get proper access to data. To get access to the data is time-consuming, and company politics are also involved in it.

1.1.2.2.2 Don't Be Afraid of Buying Outside Data

If the data is not available in the company, one can look outside your organization for buying it. The outside data can be of absolute quality, and it relies on the organization that creates and manages it. There are many open-data providers, as shown in Table 1.1.

1.1.2.2.3 Check the Quality of Data to Avoid Problems

The retrieval of data is the first time where data is seen in the process of data science. Most errors are encountered while gathering information and are easily spotted. But it may take many hours to solve these errors. So, checking the quality of data is very important for avoiding problems.

1.1.2.3 Data Preparation

In the data preparation phase, we will look at how the data quality is enhanced for further processing.

The data preparation phase is divided into three sub-phases: data cleansing, data integration, and data transformation (Figure 1.8).

Similar actions have been taken during the data cleansing, transformation, and integration phases (Figure 1.9). This looks a bit abstract to understand, but it is easier to learn once we will see each in detail. Now, we will learn detailed information about these sub-phases.

TABLE 1.1

Open-Data Providers

Open Data Site	Information
Freebase.org	An open database that retrieves its information from sites like Wikipedia and MusicBrainz.
Aiddata.org	Open data for international development.
open-data.europa.eu	The home of the European Commission's open data.

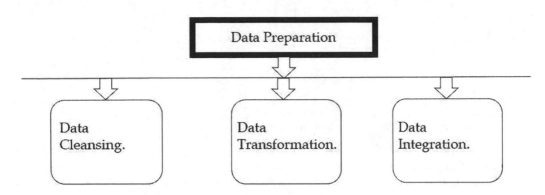

FIGURE 1.8
Data preparation.

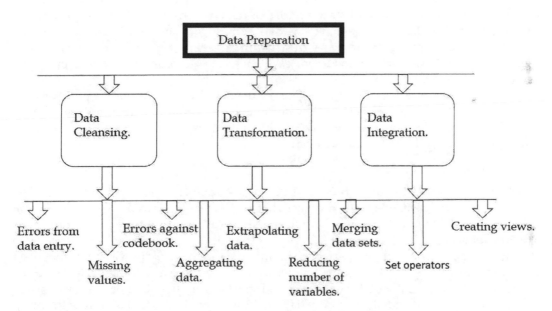

FIGURE 1.9
Common actions taken during data cleansing, data transformation, and data integration.

1.1.2.3.1 Data Cleansing

Data cleansing is a sub-process of the data preparation phase in the process of data science which focuses on removing the errors from the data that becomes a consistent and true representation of the process from which it originated. Errors are generated in two types: interpretation error and inconsistency error. Interpretation error occurs when we take the value of data for granted, whereas inconsistency error occurs when there are many inconsistencies between the data sources or against the company's standard value.

Different types of errors can be detected by an easy check method. Table 1.2 represents the overview of common errors which are detected commonly. We need to solve the problem as soon as possible in the acquisition chain or else we need to fix it in the program. Later on, it will cause issues during further execution.

TABLE 1.2

Overview of Common Errors

Error Description	Possible Solution
Errors Pointing to False Values within Single Data Set	
Impossible values	Manual overrules
Missing values	Remove values
Redundant white space	Usage of string functions
Errors Pointing to Inconsistencies between Data Sets	
Different units of measurements	Recalculation
Different levels aggregation	The same level of measurement by aggregation or extrapolation

1.1.2.3.2 Data Integration

Data integration is the process of merging various data from different sources into a single source for efficient data management. The data comes from several places and are integrated into one source. Data may vary in structure, size, and type ranging from various excel files and databases to text documents. We can create views and can also set operators in it.

There are different ways of combining data. Two majorly used combine operations are joining and tacking. The first is joining which allows us to combine the information from one table with the information that we find in another table. The second is appending effectively adding observations from one table to another table.

1.1.2.3.3 Data Transformation

Some models require the data to be in different shapes. Now, as we have well-cleaned and integrated the data, this is the next task that we have to perform. Data transformation helps us in transforming the data so that it can take a suitable form for modeling the data.

For transforming the data, we need to reduce the number of variables and we can also turn the variables into dummy variables. Many times we have many variables that need to be reduced as they don't add any new information. If there are many variables in the model, it will become difficult for handling, and some techniques don't perform well when they are overloaded with many input variables. So, it is very important to reduce the number of variables. Meanwhile, we can also turn the variables into dummy variables where we can assign dummy values as 1 or 0, i.e., true=1 and false=0. Turning variables into dummies splits a variable that has multiple classes into multiple variables.

1.1.2.4 Data Exploration

Data exploration is the fourth phase of the data science process. It is all about building a deep understanding of the data. It helps us to understand the interaction of variables within each other. For achieving this, we need to use visual techniques and statistics. Exploratory data analysis is another name for data exploration.

During data exploratory, we take a deep look into the data (Figure 1.10).

We usually understand the information when it is in the picture or image form. Therefore, we use graphical techniques for understanding the data and the interactions between variables. The visualization techniques we can use are simple graphs or combined graphs represented by connections between them.

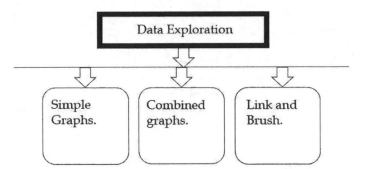

FIGURE 1.10
Data exploration.

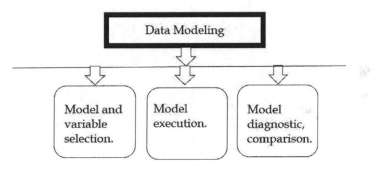

FIGURE 1.11
Data modeling.

1.1.2.5 Data Modeling

Data modeling is the fifth phase in the data science process which uses domain knowledge about the data that is found performing previous phases. In this phase, we have to choose a technique from the fields of operations research, machine learning, and statistics. Building a model is an iterative process which includes selecting a variable for the model then executing it and finally diagnosing the model.

As per Figure 1.11, data modeling is further divided into the following ways:

  i. Model and variable selection
  ii. Model execution
  iii. Model diagnostic and model comparison

1.1.2.5.1 Model and Variable Selection

Here, we need to choose the variable that we want to add to the model. There are many modeling techniques available, so choosing the right model is up to us. We have to consider the model performance and whether the project also meets all the requirements for the model.

1.1.2.5.2 Model Execution

Once we have selected the model and suitable variables for it, we will have to execute it. So, model execution is done for implementation of the code. Different software platforms can be used for execution of the code. We can use python, R programming, and various suitable programming languages for implementation of models.

1.1.2.5.3 Model Diagnostic and Model Comparison

In this, we will be making multiple models from which we can then select the best one based on multiple criteria. Many various models make high assumptions for freedom of the inputs, and we have to verify that these assumptions meet the expectations. This is known as model diagnostics.

1.1.2.6 Presentation and Automation

After successful analysis of data and building a well-performing model, the project is ready to be presented in front of the external people.

Presentation and automation are the last stages of the data science process where the soft skills are most useful and are extremely important for the presentation of the project (Figure 1.12). Automating data analysis is used for automating the projects that are needed to be executed again and again [9].

1.1.3 Life Cycle – Data Science

Life cycle of data science is also known as the data science pipeline. Life cycle of data science consists of five important stages.

Figure 1.13 shows the different stages of the life cycle of data science as follows:

  i. **Capture:** The structured and unstructured data which are raw are gathered from all the relevant sources to capture data from devices in real time.
 ii. **Prepare and Maintain:** This stage inculcates the raw data into the format which is consistent for machine learning and analytics.
iii. **Process:** Data scientist examines the patterns and range of values within the data to determine whether the data is sustainable for use with machine learning or predictive analytics.
 iv. **Analyze:** Discovery is done in this stage where the data scientist does the actual performance of machine learning, regression, and deep learning algorithms from the well-prepared data.

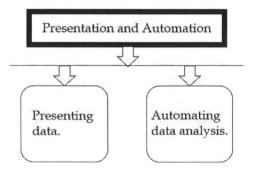

FIGURE 1.12
Presentation and automation.

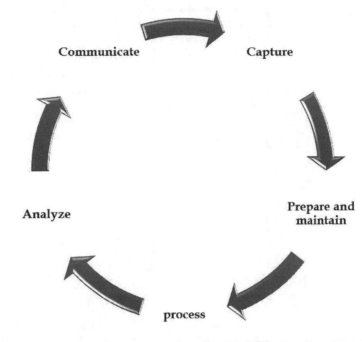

FIGURE 1.13
Life cycle of data science.

v. **Communicate:** Finally, the projects are presented as charts, reports, and in the form of other data visualizations, which is easy for decision-makers to understand [10].

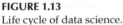

1.2 Relation between Data Science and Machine Learning

Machine learning gives the ability to computers without being explicitly programmed. It is also referred to as a process in which a computer can work accurately, as it collects and learns from the data it is given.

Data science and machine learning are related to each other but have different goals and functionalities. Machine learning is a critical part of data science where it effectively uses different statistical algorithms for analyzing the data from multiple resources [9,11].

1.2.1 Where Do We See Machine Learning in Data Science?

Although machine learning is mainly linked to the data-modeling step of the data science process, it can be also used in most of the steps in the data science process (Figure 1.14).

Machine learning is used in the data science process. The data-modeling phase cannot be started until we understand the qualitative raw data. But before that, the data preparation phase have significant benefits through machine learning. If we take an example for cleansing the text strings, machine learning helps group the same strings so that it can become easy to correct spelling errors.

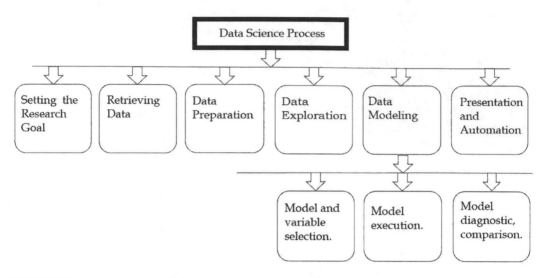

FIGURE 1.14
Machine learning used in process of data science.

Machine learning is also helpful in exploring the data. Algorithms can recognize the underlined patterns in the data and are represented through various visualization tools including pie charts, box plots, histograms, density plots, bar charts and line graphs [9].

1.2.2 Which Machine Algorithms are used in Data Science?

Data scientists should be mandatorily aware of machine learning and its algorithms as many machine learning algorithms are broadly used in data science. Following are the names of machine learning algorithms that are mostly used in data science:

   i. Linear regression algorithm
  ii. Decision tree
 iii. K-means clustering

1.2.2.1 Linear Regression Algorithm

Linear regression algorithm is a popular algorithm that is used in machine learning which is based on supervised learning. This algorithm is mostly used for prediction and forecasting purposes. Linear regression algorithm works on simple regression. Regression is the method of modeling the target values which is based on independent variables. It helps in representing the linear equation, which has the connection between the input set and predictive output. Since it determines the linear relationship between input/output variables, it is known as linear regression.

As per Figure 1.15, equation for linear regression is

$$Y = mx + c,$$

where Y is the dependent variable, x is the independent variable, m is the slope, and c is the intercept.

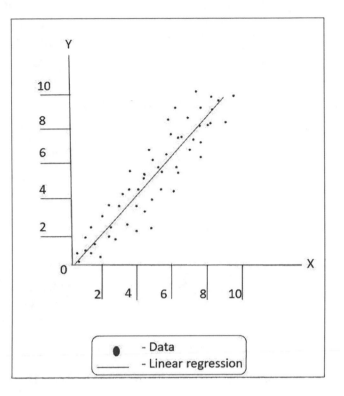

FIGURE 1.15
Linear regression algorithm.

1.2.2.2 Decision Tree

Decision tree is based on supervised learning. This machine learning algorithm is well-known because it can be used in both classification and regression problems.

In the decision tree algorithm, we can resolve the issue by using tree representation in which each node represents features, each branch shows a decision, and each leaf represents the outcomes (Figure 1.16). In the decision tree, we start searching from the root node of the tree and compare the values of root with the record attribute. We continue comparing the nodes and lastly, we come to the outcome that is to the leaf node.

1.2.2.3 K-Means Clustering

K-means clustering is the machine learning algorithm which belongs to the unsupervised learning algorithm. K-means clustering solves the problems related to the clustering. Clustering is referred to as a small set of data which are formed by breaking a large dataset. This small set of data is known as clusters. The main aim of this algorithm is to minimize the sum of distances between the clusters and data points [7,12]. Figure 1.17 shows k-means clustering.

1.2.3 Application of Machine Learning in Data Science

Machine learning algorithms have wide range of applications with data science, some of the application domains are listed below [9]:

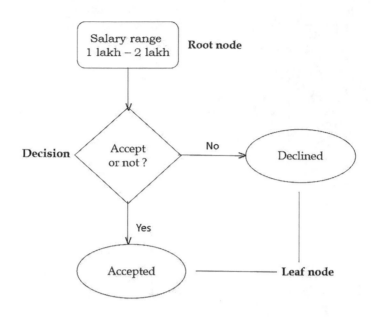

FIGURE 1.16
Decision tree.

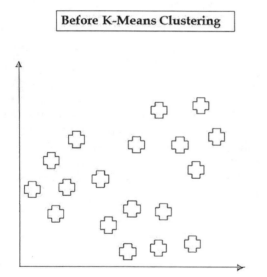

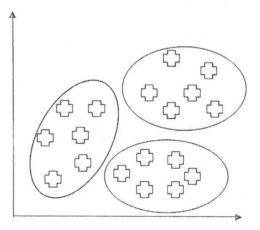

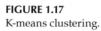

FIGURE 1.17
K-means clustering.

    i. Automation and control

   ii. Education

  iii. Finance industry

  iv. Computer vision and Intelligence

   v. Customer segmentation

vi. Weather forecasting

vii. Disease prediction mechanism

viii. Price predictions in real estate

1.3 Tools for Data science

Data scientists use many various types of tools for performing data science. Data scientists should build and run code for the creation of models. There are many open-source tools available for performing these operations. Data science tools are of many different types, namely data analysis tools, data visualization tools, data warehousing, and machine learning tools. Data science has various types of tools.

i. Data analysis tools – R, Python, MATLAB, Excel, Jupyter.

ii. Data visualization tools – Tableau, Cognos.

iii. Data warehousing tools – SQL, ETL, Hadoop, AWS Redshift.

iv. Machine learning tools – Spark, Mahout [7,11].

1.3.1 R Programming

R is the data analysis tool used for performing the data science operation. R is an open-source programming language and has a suitable environment for developing graphics and computing. R is the most popularly used programming language among the data scientist community. R provides a variety of tools and libraries for creating visualizations, cleansing data, and evaluating machine learning and deep learning algorithms. R also offers multiple features for making statistical analysis of large data sets, which is easy for performing various tasks that are mentioned below:

i. Linear and non-linear modeling.

ii. Time-series analysis.

iii. Clustering.

R Language has an integrated development environment which is available in RStudio. Packages available in R language CARET, random forest, e10171, Rpart, and many more. Data science projects that uses R programming are Twitter, T-Mobile, Google Analytics, etc.

1.3.2 Python

Python is an open-source, object-oriented, high-level, and interpreted programming language that emphasizes code readability. It is the data analysis tool which is used in data science. Python helps in developing strong data applications. The main reason why python is widely used in the scientific and research communities is that it's easy to use and there is quite a simple syntax to adapt for people who do not have an idea or are not from an engineering background.

A large number of python libraries support data science tasks, including Pandas for data manipulation, NumPy for handling large dimensional arrays, Matplotlib for building data visualizations, and SciPy for providing functionalities for mathematics and computing [13].

1.4 Benefits and Applications

  i. Data science helps drive innovation by enabling teams to share results, codes, and reports, and reduces redundancy.
 ii. It helps us to understand the project in an efficient and easy manner.
iii. It makes data scientists more productive by helping them to accelerate and deliver models extra faster with less error.
 iv. It facilitates data scientists to work with large volumes and large varieties of data [11,14,15].

The following are the trending applications:

  i. Data science is used for image and speech recognition (e.g., Siri, Alexa, Cortana).
 ii. Data science is used in healthcare for detection of tumors, medical image analysis, and recognizing other diseases.
iii. Data science is also used for detection of risk in finance industries.
 iv. Data science is used for designing self-driving cars where automation is done within the car so that there would be a reduction in the number of accidents [7,16].

1.5 Conclusion

The aim of this chapter is to understand the deep theory of data science. The authors have explained the process of data science with respect to setting the goals, retrieving data, data preparation, data exploration, data modeling, presentation, and automation. Further, the data science life cycle is described, and this life cycle is also known as the data science pipeline. In the data science lifeline, there are six stages: capture, prepare, maintain, process, analyze, and communicate. The authors have also introduced the relationship between data science and machine learning. Machine learning is used in the process for solving data science problems in different ways by using certain algorithms. The authors have also given detailed information about tools that are used for performing data science operations. Finally, the author has explained large benefits of data science in various manners and applications of data science.

References

1. https://www.kdnuggets.com/2018/06/what-where-how-data-science.html.

2. Haruki Nakamura. Big data science at AMED-BINDS. *Japan Biophysical Review*, 12(2): 221–224. 2020. doi: 10.1007/s12551-020-00628-1.
3. https://cacm.acm.org/magazines/2013/12/169933-data-science-and-prediction/fulltext.
4. Dataflair Team. (2019). What is data science? Complete data science tutorial for beginners. Retrieved 8.10.2019.
5. Alisa Bilal. Data Science: Fundamental Principles, Croatia, 2019.
6. Yangyong Zhu and Yun Xiong. Defining Data Science. *Beyond the Study of the Rules of the Natural World as Reflected by Data*, School of Computer Science, Fudan University, Shanghai, China Shanghai Key Laboratory of Data Science, Fudan University, China.
7. https://www.javatpoint.com/data-science. What is Data Science: Tutorial, Components, Life cycle.
8. Wikipedia. https://en.wikipedia.org/wiki/Data_science.
9. Davy Cielen, Arno D. B. Meysman, Mohamed Ali. Introducing Data Science. *Big Data, Machine Learning, and More, Using Python Tools*. Manning Publications.
10. https://www.ibm.com/cloud/learn/data-science-introduction. IBM Cloud Learn Hub.
11. https://www.oracle.com/in/data-science/what-is-data-science/. Oracle India.
12. Mine Çetinkaya-Rundel, Victoria Ellison. A Fresh Look at Introductory Data Science. *Journal of Statistics and Data Science Education*, 29(sup1), 2021.
13. Analysis of US Population using Data Analytics and Data Science Tools. *Computer Science and Information Technology*, 9(7), 2020.
14. Steven Perkins, Hazel Davis, Valerie du Preez. "Practical Data Science for Actuarial Task". A practical example of data science considerations by Modelling, Analytics and Insights in Data working party – New approaches to current actuarial work. 2020.
15. Harshil Jhaveri, Himanshu Ashar and Ramchandra Mangrulkar. Leveraging Data Science in Cyber Physical Systems to Overcome Covid-19. *Journal of University of Shanghai for Science and Technology*, 22(10): 1993–2015, 2020.
16. Sanyukta Shrestha. A Deep Dissertation of Data Science: Related Issues and its Applications. Department of Information Technology, Amity University Uttar Pradesh, Noida, IEEE, 2019.

2

Role of Statistical Methods in Data Science

Deepa Mane and Sachin Shelke
SPPU

CONTENTS

2.1 Introduction

Data science as a research-oriented discipline is majorly impacted by IR, computer science, mathematics, statistics, operations research, and the applied sciences too. Though data science was derived by statisticians, the significance of computer science and its role in business applications is often much more elaborated, particularly in the century of big data. John Tukey already changed the focus of statistics entirely from mathematics, statistical testing, to deriving hypotheses from data that try to understand the data before getting hypotheses. One more data mining technique is Knowledge Discovery in Databases (KDD) with its subtypes in data mining which is the knowledge data discovery combines

DOI: 10.1201/9781003283249-2

together many different approaches to knowledge edge discovery. So, KDD promotes the interaction between different fields for identifying underlying knowledge in data [1–3]. Maths and statistics for data science are essential because these disciplines build the base for all the machine learning algorithms. In fact, mathematics exists around us, starting from shapes, patterns, and colors, to the count of colors in the diagram. Mathematics is embedded in each part of our lives. Math, data science, and statistics are the building blocks of machine learning algorithms. Now the question is, what statistics is and how to use it? [4].

Statistics is a basic building block for mathematical science that pertains to data extraction, data collection, data analysis, data interpretation, and data presentation. Statistics is used to solve the complex problems in the actual world around us so that data scientists [5–7] and business people can get insights from this which can lead to meaningful trends and patterns in data. Statistics can be used to extract underlying important information from the data by applying mathematical computations to it.

Python is very popular for this kind of analysis and possesses a large number of standard libraries which can help in analyzing and representing the data. Data scientists need to work on big amounts of data. With little knowledge about Python, anybody can build better analytical tools which will help in developing machine learning, big data, clustering, artificial intelligence, etc.

Several statistical methods and techniques are executed to analyze raw data, model statistical analysis [8,9], and reach the result. The field of statistics has touched every part of life, such as weather forecasting, life sciences, e-commerce, retail, insurance, and education [10,11].

2.2 Data Science and Statistics Terminologies

We must be aware of some of the important statistical terminologies while dealing with statistics and data science. Following are the terminologies in statistics:

1. Population is something from where data is collected.
2. A sample – a subset of the population.
3. A variable – quantity or number that is countable.
   or you can say data item.
4. A statistical parameter is a number that guides probability distributions, such as mean, median, mode, correlation, and covariance of the population.

2.3 Types of Statistics

Statistical data analysis is broadly categorized into two main groups: descriptive statistics and inferential statistics. The first category talks about the description of data including central tendency, the variation in data and the dispersion in data. While, the inferential statistics talks about the inferences and the conclusions extracted from the data.

2.3.1 Descriptive

Descriptive statistics is the use of the data to describe data among the population through numerous computations, reports, or graphs [12]. Descriptive statistics organizes the data and highlights the qualities of data that provides different attributes to be considered.

2.3.2 Inferential

It generates predictions and inferences about a given population of the data based on sample data taken from the population [13]. It infers from a large dataset and applies probability theory to extract results based on statistics and generates the model based on it.

2.4 How to Describe a Single Set of Data

It is easy to produce a single set of data. Here the problem is how to describe this data. One of the obvious ways is to describe any dataset is simply the data itself:

```
test = [65, 12, 78, 43, 32
#... and so on
]
```

Small datasets are easy to describe. But for large datasets, this is clumsy and probably smeared. So statistics is used to refine and communicate characteristics of the data. The following is the sample code to generate random values:

```
my_counter = Counter()
test = [100, 49, 41, 40, 25]
for _ in range(1000):
value = randint(0, 100)
test.append(value)
counts = Counter(test)
print(counts)
x1 = range(101) # this the largest value it can take
y1= [counts[x] for x in x1]
plotting bar chart for (x1, y1)
plotting for [0, 80, 0, 24]
plotting the.title that is "Histogram of number Counts"
plotting label x as "test"
plotting label y as " data"
```

at the end, it generates the histogram. This will generate a histogram as shown in Figure 2.1.
   Probably, the simple statistics will be the number of data points:

```
num_points = len(test)
```

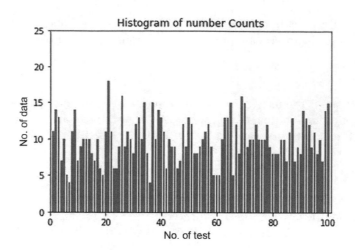

FIGURE 2.1
Histogram of number counts.

The largest and smallest values can be computed by:

```
largest_value = max(test)
100
smallest_value = min(test)
1
```

2.5 Statistical Analysis

In order to perform statistical analysis, we use standard methods that analyze the quality of data as well as the quantity of data. There are set of tools in statistics to analyze the quantity of data. On the similar note, there are the tools to measure the quality of data.

2.5.1 Quantitative Analysis

It is the statistical analysis in which quantities are taken into consideration. Quantitative measures such as numbers and graphs are used to find underlined patterns and trends [14].

2.5.2 Qualitative Analysis

It is a statistical analysis which uses qualitative measures such as color, intensity, and good parameters. Let us consider the following example:

If you have apples in the basket, they are small, medium, and big. This tells us the quality of the apple and it falls under qualitative analysis. Whereas how many small, medium and big apples are there this tells us quantitative analysis.

2.5.3 Measures of the Central Tendency

Mean: It is a statistical way of calculating an average of all data point values in a dataset under consideration. Generally, we use the mean for this. It is sum of the values of all data points divided by the count of data points. If two data points are there, then the mean will be half of the sum of their values. As you go on adding more data points, the mean gets changed, depending on the value of each data point. The following is the function to calculate the mean in Python:

```
def mean(x1):
return sum(x1) / len(x1)
mean(test)
ans. 50.842786069651744
```

Median: Median divides the data points into two halves. It is value of central data point if odd number of data points are there and average of the two middle data points if the number of data points are is even. Median function is a bit more complicated mostly in the case of the "even" data points.

Use def function to define median(v):

```
number = len(v)
sort = sorted(v)
mid = number// 2
if number % 2 == 1:
return sort[mid]
else:
low = mid -1
high = mid
return (sort[low] + sort[high]) / 2
median(test)
```

Mode: It is the value of most repeating data point in the dataset.

```
def mode(x1):
count = Counter(x1)
maximum_count = maximum(count.values())
return [x for x count in counts.iteritems()
if count == maximum _count]
mode(test)
ans. Result=array[21], count=array[18]
```

With the help of descriptive analysis, we can analyze each of the variables in the dataset.

2.5.4 Measures of Dispersion

As we have measures of central tendency, the same way we have measures to calculate the spread of data points as follows:

Range: It is the measure that represents data points distributed in a dataset are statistics whose value is near zero denotes no spread at all on other hand big value signifies very much spread of data points [15,16]. At this point range is an easy measure, it is the subtraction of the biggest and lowest data point values.

```
def data_range(x1):
return max(x1) - min(x1)
data_range(test).
```

Interquartile Range: Uneven spread of data points is the interquartile range, it is based on dividing a dataset into quartiles [17].

   Variance: It gives us how much is the value data point differs from its value. It requires following computations.
   The deviation is the difference between values of each data element from the mean of data points in the dataset.
   Variance measures population and is the average calculated by taking squares of Deviation.

```
n = len(x1)
deviations = mean(x1)
return sumofsquares(deviations) / (n -1)
variance(test)
ans. 853.0877215910497
```

Standard Deviation: It computes dispersion of a set of data values from the statistical mean of data points. Whatever parameters our data have (e.g., "test"), the following is the function to calculate standard deviation in Python:

```
def std_dev(x1):
return math.sqrt(variance(x1))
std_dev(test)
ans. 29.207665459448307
```

2.6 Tools to Measure Relationships

Covariance and the correlation are the most common tools used to measure the relationship between the data points. The relationship between the data points is measured as follows:

2.6.1 Covariance

Covariance is the measure of the variance between two random variables. If the variance is positive, then variables move in the same direction; if it is negative, then they move in opposite direction; and if it is zero, they have no relation with each other.

```
def covariance(x1, y1):
number = len(x1)
return (mean(x1), mean(y1)) / (n -1)
covariance(test1, test2)
```

2.6.2 Correlation

Correlation is the measure of association of two random variables that range from minus one to positive one; it is a normalized version of covariance. Generally, a correlation of ±0.7 shows a stronger association and ±0.3 shows no association between variables. Although the purpose of both the covariance and correlation are used to analyze to generate outputs, quantitative analysis provides a clear picture and hence it is critical in the analysis.

2.7 Probability Distribution Function

Probability density function is a probability function for continuous data where the values of data at any point can be calculated as sample space providing a relative likelihood that the value of the random variable would close to that sample.

```
def uniformpdf(x1):
return 1 if (0=< x1< 1) else 0
def normalpdf(x1):
x1 = [x / 11.0 for x (-100, 100)]
plt.plot(x1,[normalpdf(x, sigma=1) for x in x1], '-',
label='mu=0,sigma=1')
plt.plot(x1,[normalpdf(x, sigma=2) for x in x1], '--',
label='mu=0,sigma=2')
plt.plot(x1,[normalpdf(x, sigma=0.5) for x in x1], ':',
label='mu=0,sigma=0.5')
plt.plot(x1,[normalpdf(x, mu=-1) for x in x1], '-.',
label='mu=-1,sigma=1')
plt.title("Various Normal pdfs")
plt.show()
```

We can see the graph of the probability distribution function in Figure 2.2.

2.7.1 Cumulative Density Function

It is a probability function that tells us the probability of a random variable is less than a particular value, which is the integral of the probability density function.

```
def uniformcdf(x1):
if x1 < 0: return 0
elif x1 < 1: return x1
else: return 1
```

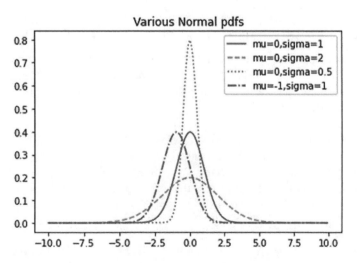

FIGURE 2.2
Normal probability density function.

$$y = \frac{1}{\sigma\sqrt{2\pi}}e^{-\frac{(x-\mu)^2}{2\sigma^2}}$$

$$\mu = \text{Mean}$$
$$\sigma = \text{Standard Deviation}$$
$$\pi \approx 3.14159\cdots$$
$$e \approx 2.71828\cdots$$

FIGURE 2.3
Normal distribution.

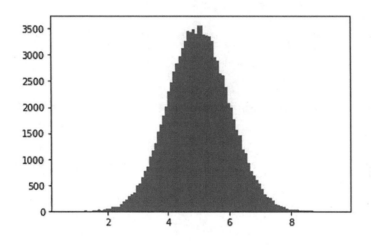

FIGURE 2.4
Normal distribution of number values.

2.7.2 Continuous Data Distributions

It is also called uniform distribution, a probability distribution in which all outcomes are equally distributed [1]. It comes out to be a bell shape and is associated with the central limit theorem has a mean zero a delta that is standard deviation of 1. Figure 2.3 represents the graph of normal distribution.

The normal distribution with several values is plotted in Figure 2.4. Probability is the likelihood of an event to occur. Data science will not be complete without using some probability and mathematics. The universal set of data consists of all likely answers and a subset of these answers is an event. We'll use probability theory to evaluate models [7].

2.7.3 Conditional Probability

[Prob(A|B)] is the probability chance of an event will occur, which depends on the occurrence of an earlier event.

```
def random_num_generator():
return random.choice(["b", "g"])
random.seed(100)
for j in range (1000):
y = random_num_generator()
o = random_num_generator()
if o == "g":
og += 1
if (o == "g") and (y == "g"):
bg += 1
if o == "g" or y == "g":
eg += 1
print("P(both | older):", bg / og)
print("P(both | either): ", bg / eg)
ans. P(both | older): 0.5007089325501317
P(both | either): 0.3311897106109325
```

Independent events are the events whose outcomes are not dependent on the possibility of the outcome of other event Prob(X|Y)=Prob(X). Mutually exclusive events are events that cannot occur simultaneously; Prob(X|Y)=0.

2.7.4 Bayes' Theorem

Bayes' theorem is an important mathematical formula to determine conditional probability [18]. The value of P(X|Y) is equal to P(Y |X) times the P(X) over the P(Y).

2.8 Hypothesis Testing

Hypothesis testing is statistics in which a statistician considers the assumption to analyze some of the parameters of the dataset. There exists two standard methods, null hypothesis and the alternative hypothesis:

1. **Null Hypothesis**: It is the hypothesis in which the data are retrieved truly based on the chance.
2. **Alternative Hypothesis**: It is the hypothesis in which data under consideration are impacted by some extraneous variables.

Statistical Significance
P-value: It is the statistical significance probability derived from the experimental outputs of a test by considering that correct null hypothesis. If the p-value is smaller, it denotes that there is much possibility that an alternative hypothesis will be accepted.

Alpha: It is the significance level that denotes the possibility of declining the null hypothesis though it is rightly called type 1 error that means the null hypothesis is rejected when it is to be accepted.

Beta: It is a type 2 error denoting the possibility of accepting the null hypothesis when is to be rejected.

Following are the steps carried out for hypothesis:

1. Specify the null and alternative hypotheses
2. Compute sample space and size of the test
3. Calculate the test statistics and probability
4. Compare the observations to either accept or reject the null hypothesis.

2.9 Conclusion

The role of statistics in data science has always been given less importance as compared to other fields like computer science. In the domains of data possession, analysis, and advanced modeling are needed for prediction. Statisticians are acquainted to carry out their tasks in this latest and highly appreciated domain of data science. By making use of mathematical models with statistics, particularly in big data, data mining, machine learning will give rise to scientific outputs depending on suitable methods. Completely balanced use of mathematics, informatics, and statistics will lead to good solutions to the problems in data science.

In this chapter, we reviewed the basics of statistical analysis and the features of Python which enriches the field of data science to extract the desired knowledge from the data available. This is possible because of Python's vast library which makes it easy and fast to collect and analyze data.

References

1. Claus Weihs, Katja Ickstadt. Data science: the impact of statistics. *International Journal of Data Science and Analytics* (2018).
2. Weihs, C. Big data classification — aspects of many features. In: Michaelis, S., Piatkowski, N., Stolpe, M. (eds.) *Solving Large Scale Learning Tasks: Challenges and Algorithms*, Springer Lecture Notes in Artificial Intelligence, vol. 9580, pp. 139–147 (2016).
3. Martin, R., Nagathil, A. Digital filters and spectral analysis, chap 4. In: Weihs, C., Jannach, D., Vatolkin, I., Rudolph, G. (eds.) *Music Data Analysis—Foundations and Applications*, pp. 111–143. CRC Press, Boca Raton (2017).
4. Bhattacharyya, G. K., Johnson, R. A. *Statistical Concepts and Methods*, John Wiley and Sons, New York (1997).
5. Joel Grus, *Data Science from Scratch First Principles with Python*. O'Reilly Media, Inc., Sebastopol, CA (2015).
6. Randy Paffenroth, Xiangnan Kong, Python in Data Science Research and Education. *Proceedings of the 14th Python in Science Conference* 2015.
7. Ramchandra Sharad Mangrulkar, Antonis Michalas, Pallavi Chavan. Design of intelligent applications using machine learning and deep learning techniques, 2021.

8. Gregory Pietatsky. *Python Eats Away at R: Top Software for Analytics, Data Science, Machine Learning in 2018: Trends and Analysis*, KDnuggets, 2018.

9. Gabriel Moreira: Python for Data Science, *The Developers Conference* 2015.

10. Bischl, B., Schiffner, J., Weihs, C. Benchmarking local classification methods. *Computational Statistics* 28(6), 2599–2619 (2013) Press, G.: A Very Short History of Data Science. 2017.

11. Dyk, D.V., Fuentes, M., Jordan, M.I., Newton, M., Ray, B.K., Lang, D.T., Wickham, H. ASA Statement on the Role of Statistics in Data Science. http://magazine.amstat.org/blog/2015/10/01/asastatement-on-the-role-of-statistics-in-data-science/ (2015).

12. Nilanjan Dey, Sanjeev Wagh, Parikshit N. Mahalle. *Applied Machine Learning for Smart Data Analysis*, 2019.

13. https://www.edureka.co/blog/statistics-and-probability.

14. Shapiro, S. S. and Wilk, M. B. An analysis of variance test for normality (complete samples). *Biometrika* 52, 591–611 (1965).

15. Brown, M.S. *Data Mining for Dummies*. Wiley, London (2014).

16. Kallol Bosu Roy Choudhuri, Ramchandra S. Mangrulkar, "Data Acquisition and Preparation for Artificial Intelligence and Machine Learning Applications", in Design of Intelligent Applications Using Machine Learning and Deep Learning Techniques, CRC Press. https://www.taylorfrancis.com/chapters/edit/10.1201/9781003133681-1/data-acquisition-preparation-artificial-intelligence-machine-learning-applications-kallol-bosu-roy-choudhuri-ramchandra-mangrulkar.

17. Maruti Techlabs: Is Python the most popular language for data science? 2018.

18. Waller, R. A., Duncan, D. B. A Bayes rule for the symmetric multiple comparison problem. *Journal of the American Statistical Association* 64(1969).

3

Real-World Applications of Data Science

Baisa L. Gunjal

Amrutvahini College of Engineering

CONTENTS

DOI: 10.1201/9781003283249-3

3.1 Banking and Finance

3.1.1 Customer Data Management

The customer's data is an invaluable asset for banking and finance-related sectors in the digital era. Banks utilize customer data to enhance their productivity/services. Banking sectors use unstructured data from social media to publish their brand services and need customers' views about their services. Data science helps banks in their transaction processing and segmenting of huge banking data as well as customer feedback obtained through social media platforms.

3.1.2 Real-Time Analytics

Predictive analysis is an important part of the banking and financial sectors. Stock/share markets' decision-making process is based on real-time analysis in the finance industry. The companies make their decision-making about their money investment based on the current market scenario. They can analyze the state of the market and possible risks, predict profit, and accordingly plan their relevant buying and selling business strategies [1].

3.1.3 Algorithmic Trading

Algorithmic trading is a process that facilitates transaction decision-making in financial markets using advanced mathematical tools. It utilizes automated and preprogrammed trading instructions to account for finance applications. Algorithmic trading is capable of capturing profit-making opportunities happening in the market much before other human traders can even spot them. Algorithmic trading provides the following benefits:

   i. Trades are executed for the best possible and profitable market prices.
  ii. They provide automated checks on multiple market conditions.
 iii. This system reduces transaction costs.
  iv. It reduces the risk of manual errors while placing trades.
   v. It reduces possible emotional and psychological factors that happen by mistakes.

3.1.4 Providing Personalized Services

Banking sectors and other financial companies use data science and machine learning for process automation, stronger levels of overall security, and social media interactions with customers. The other personalized services may include [2]:

   i. Daily/frequent transactions.
  ii. Customer's past details.
 iii. Debit/credit details.
  iv. Past/present loans details.
   v. Bank details.

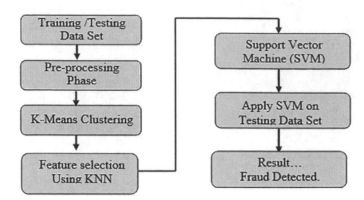

FIGURE 3.1
Basic fraud detection process.

3.1.5 Fraud Detection

There is a rapid increase in online transactions in the digital era. It invites several unethical activities. Hence, various tools are developed using data science integrating them with business software to keep track of customer transactions and their history. Frauds can be detected with such intelligent software/tools. This makes financial transactions more secure and productive. The basic fraud detection process is shown in Figure 3.1. Intelligent business software integrated with data science makes them more effective.

3.2 E-commerce and Retail Industry

3.2.1 Potential Customer Analysis

E-commerce involves business transactions that are carried out through electronic networks such as the internet. While retail refers to the sales of goods/items from a single point such as supermarts, departmental stores, and malls to the customer in small quantities. The e-commerce and retail industry needs data science to improve the ability to target their customers. The past/present customer data provides insights into customers' needs, choices, and preferences. Online transaction processing reflects various actions and decisions made by the customers in their past transactions. Such a type of data and its analysis brings efficient, fast, high-performance, and decision-making processes to e-commerce and retailing.

3.2.2 Customer Sentiment Analysis

The sentiment analysis algorithms with data science are used for customer sentiment analysis in the e-commerce and retail industry. The sentiment analysis is a sort of artificial intelligence (AI) with natural language processing. It can be carried out through social media. The overall web to know client support and understand what clients think about their brand and products. Using this analysis companies can do advertisements for their products.

3.2.3 Optimizing Prices

Selling a product at the right price is an important task for retailers or manufacturers and purchasing a product at the right price is also an important task for customers. The machine learning algorithms along with data science analyze many parameters such as flexibility of prices considering the location, attitudes of an individual customer, and competitive pricing. E-commerce websites such as Amazon, Flipkart, Alibaba, and eBay use data science to make better user-friendly services for their customers. While searching items for purchasing on e-commerce websites, similar choices with optimizing prices are recommended for customers. The recommendation includes the most rated, most searched with optimum prices are displayed based on viewers' data profiles. The retail sector also performs several tasks with the help of data science tools/algorithms for product recommendations with optimum prices.

3.2.4 Inventory Management

Inventory management is a systematic process of sourcing, storing, and selling inventory of raw materials and products. In e-commerce or retailing, inventory management focuses on proper stock, level, place, time, and cost. Inventory management should be right such that with a sudden spike in sales, supply remains unaffected. In order to achieve the same stock, supply chains should properly analyze and manage the data. Powerful machine learning algorithms with data sciences are used to provide proper inventory management. Data science along with intelligent machine learning algorithms is used to perform various tasks. The sample inventory management tasks are shown in Figure 3.2.

3.2.5 Lifetime Value Prediction

A prediction is a statement about the things that will happen in the future. Customer lifetime value is the total monetary value of purchases made by a customer to the company during his entire lifetime. In other words, customer lifetime value is the total value of the customer's profit to the company over the entire customer–business relationship. Thus, customer lifetime value gives the amount of revenue a customer can provide to the company throughout his lifetime. It is difficult to predict how much a customer will buy

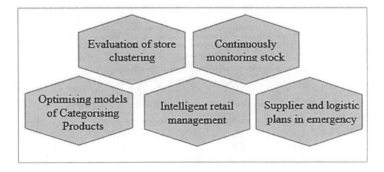

FIGURE 3.2
Various inventory management tasks.

in the future based on past transaction history. Hence intelligent data science software/ tools/e-commerce websites or mobile applications are designed and developed for predicting customer lifetime value. Data science uses past/present data statistical parameters of a customer's buying patterns to make predictions. The statistical parameters include the size of frequency of purchase, the size of repeated orders, the time interval between two orders, and discount factors [3,4].

3.3 Digital Marketing

3.3.1 Smarter Planning for Online Marketing

Digital marketing allows us to connect with potential customers using the internet and other forms of digital communication such as email, social media, web-based advertisement, text and multimedia messages. The entire digital marketing spectrum is one of the most important applications of data science and machine learning. The use of data science in digital marketing is beneficial for quicker and easier planning of your campaigns. Different tasks of planning for online marketing are depicted in Figure 3.3.

3.3.2 Business Intelligence with Smarter Decision-Making

The smarter decision-making system is the backbone of intelligent business strategy. The dynamic decision-making process includes the following:

   i. Understanding nature of the problem to be solved.
  ii. Exploring and quantifying the quality of data used.
 iii. Using the right algorithm/tools to acquire solutions.
  iv. Translating insights for a better understanding of teams.

The overall business decision-making process is depicted in Figure 3.4.

This business decision-making process needs intelligent algorithms integrated with data science.

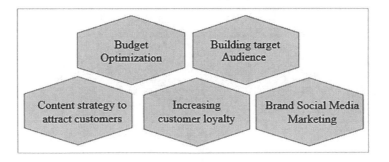

FIGURE 3.3
Different tasks of planning for online marketing are depicted.

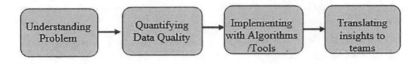

FIGURE 3.4
Business decision-making process.

3.3.3 Managing Business Efficiently

Online business management helps to operate the business more efficiently. From account to social media are involved in running a business with full speed. Data science and data scientist play very important roles in business management in the following ways:

i. Direct actions based on current market trends.

ii. Trends staff to adopt best practices in business management and related issues.

iii. Identify opportunities in business.

iv. Detecting risks and frauds.

v. Identifying and redefining the target audience in the current scenario.

3.3.4 Automating Recruitment Process

Various tools can be developed for the online recruitment process. Automated tools using data science integrated with AI are used for automating the online recruitment process. Automated tools such as AI-powered chatbots can be used efficiently for automating recruitment processes. A chatbot is an AI-based computer program that simulates human conversations with a user in natural language through messaging applications, websites, mobile applications, or phones.

The benefits of automated recruitment are listed below [5]:

i. The overall recruitment process is easy.

ii. The vast number of audiences can be included in the talent search.

iii. Recruitment process is much quicker than the traditional recruitment process.

iv. It's a low-budget recruitment process.

v. It's easy for job advertisements in the automated recruitment process.

vi. The overall process management is easy.

vii. Maintaining confidentiality is easy.

3.4 Healthcare and Medical Diagnosis

3.4.1 Managing and Monitoring Patient Health and Data

Advanced Internet of Things (IoT) devices are used for collecting and analyzing patient data such as heartbeat, temperature and blood pressure, and other medical parameters of the patient. Data Science plays an important role in IoT. The patient's collected data is analyzed with the help of data science. Along with wearable monitoring sensors, doctors can monitor a patient's health through home devices. There are several systems that track a patient's movements, monitor their physical parameters, and analyze the patterns from data. It is possible to use real-time analytics to predict if a patient is facing some health problem at present. The doctors take the necessary decisions based on a patient's condition.

3.4.2 Medical Image Analysis

Medical imaging refers to a patient's diagnosis, therapy planning, and intraoperative and post-operative monitoring. The data science algorithms are used to evaluate and learn from healthcare data. Data science algorithms integrated with AI enable the system to process images and video in a human-like manner to detect and identify objects or regions of interest for medical diagnosis. Medical images with a region of interest are used in a patient's diagnosis as shown in Figure 3.5.

The population imaging, medical image data, and other measurements are obtained from large and over a longer period of data typically more than a thousand. Intelligent data science algorithms along with AI algorithms are used in medical imaging [6].

3.4.3 Drug Research and Creation

Data science with neural networks is used by healthcare organizations in drug testing by creating virtual models to evaluate how different drugs interact in particular disease viruses and find the best cure. Data science with AI is used in prime use cases such as detection of pneumonia from lung X-rays, detection of stroke using physiological conditions, and detection of risks of other pathologies using different CT scans. Nowadays, data science techniques are applied faster and more accurately for clinical trials of cancer drugs and doses for various patients and speeding new drug development. AI algorithms along with data science and life sciences are used to build an automated process for analyzing data in clinical trials research on cancer patients. Thus, data science is used effectively in fast-track cancer drug development. Pharmaceutical companies are using data science with data analytics for drug research and creation in different ways as shown in Figure 3.6.

3.4.4 Patient Diagnosis and Preventing Diseases

Data science plays an important role to enhance the quality of healthcare applications in the diagnosis of diseases, medical imaging, faster drug discovery, and handling complex hospital operations in rural areas. This is applicable for critical diagnosis of diseases such as AIDS, cancer, and Ebola. Data science integrated with machine learning algorithms and neural networks is used to process a huge amount of data and create models for symptom

FIGURE 3.5
Medical images with a region of interest used in patients' diagnosis.

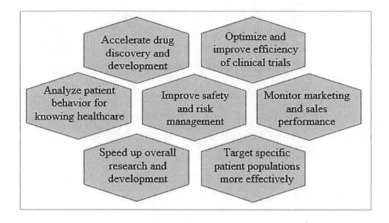

FIGURE 3.6
Data science in pharmaceutical companies for data analytics.

analysis and clinical decisions. Data science has been introduced using powerful predictive analytical tools to detect chronic diseases at an early stage. Data science with AI-based methods is used to detect viruses to prevent further complications.

3.4.5 Providing Medical Virtual Assistance

Medical virtual assistants are well-equipped to schedule daily tasks, coordinate them and take follow-ups to assist medical professionals. By using data science, comprehensive virtual platforms called expert systems have been developed that provide assistance to the patients. Using such expert systems, the patients enter details of their symptoms as input, the expert system performs diagnosis. The patients get details about their diseases. After diagnosis of particular diseases, the expert system suggests treatments for the patients [7].

3.5 Manufacturing Industry

3.5.1 Automating Product Design and Development

Product design is a process in which design decisions are based on product data and further sets of functional requirements are converted into specific product development. The manufacturers perform design customization using various permutations of the product based on performance metrics. Automation in data science is used to develop new products or to improve the existing ones. Automated data management tools are used to optimize the operational aspects of the distribution chain. Processing customer feedback and feeding this data to product marketers contribute to the idea generation stage. This is applied to strengthen the decision-making process in the manufacturing industry.

3.5.2 Inventory Management and Demand Forecasting

Inventory management is the operational activity of sourcing, storing, and selling inventory of raw materials and products. In inventory management, data science is used for analyzing and predicting customer demands. This helps in decision-making about managing supply chain and production. It prevents unnecessary production and congestion of orders. This helps to understand manufacturing company requirements and customers' needs. Data science plays an important role in demand forecasting as follows:

  i. To reduce the requirement of unnecessary storage.
  ii. To perform data analysis in inventory management.
  iii. To improve the credibility between supplier and manufacturer.
  iv. To maintain regulation in supply chain.

3.5.3 Monitoring of Manufacturing Units

Supply chain management optimization is an important factor in the manufacturing industry. Supply chain management allows manufacturers to reduce their direct sales and overhead costs by decreasing distribution at the right time. Supply chain management affects manufacturing companies in different ways such as availability of inputs required for production processes, company infrastructure, costs and profits of manufactured products, and interaction of companies with their suppliers and customers.

The supply chain management of the manufacturing industry is shown in Figure 3.7.

Data science provides a way for automation in overall monitoring of supply chain management along with automation in planning warehouse management and overall analysis of product distribution process.

3.5.4 Real-Time Data of Performance and Quality

Real-time monitoring provides new insights into how manufacturing equipment and machinery lifespans can be improved. Data science provides a way for collecting and analyzing real-time data of manufacturing units. Further, by combining real-time data with predictive analytics and machine learning, it's possible to determine when a machine will need repairing. Using real-time data with proper analysis provides the following benefits to manufacturing units:

  i. To enhance product quality continually.
  ii. To improve production plan performance.
  iii. To improve equipment effectiveness.
  iv. To prolong the life of equipment, machinery, and tools.
  v. To gain accuracy, quality, precision, and speed.
  vi. To achieve better management and optimization against constraints [8].

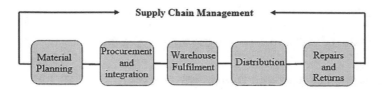

FIGURE 3.7
Supply chain management of the manufacturing industry.

3.6 Education System

3.6.1 Monitoring Students' and Teachers' Requirements

Using data analytics tools, teachers can analyze the student's requirements based on performance and results reviews. By performing statistical analysis of collected data, teachers can provide appropriate responses and update their teaching methodologies to meet student expectations. Data science with analytics is used to find student dropouts. The online education system needs to maintain large data, analyze it and report the conclusions. Data science algorithms are used for data analytics, report generation, and communication to stakeholders of the education system.

3.6.2 Measuring Students' and Teachers' Performance

For measuring students' as well as teachers' performance, the feedback/ reviews are used, and based on analysis of the same the improvement is suggested. Student reviews about teachers' performance, and analysis of the same are useful to quantify teachers' performance. Similarly, web-based business intelligence tools such as IBM Cognos are used for reporting, analyzing, and monitoring students' events through interactive visualizations.

3.6.3 Innovating the Curriculum

The education system needs innovative teaching methodologies and upgraded curriculum and skills as per industry requirements to increase the employability opportunities for students studying in educational institutions/universities. Data science along with augmented reality (AR)-based software/tools can be used to increase students' interest in learning. AR enables teachers to show virtual examples of concepts and add gaming elements to provide textbook material support for creating more realistic modeling.

3.6.4 Automating Outcome-Based Teaching and Learning Process

The worldwide education system follows outcome-based education where internal assessment tools and external assessment tools are required to evaluate course attainments. The internal assessment includes the tools used by institutions for calculating internal evaluation while external assessment tools are used for other than internal assessment. Data science with data analytical tools is developed for automation of the outcome-based teaching and learning process [9].

3.7 Entertainment Industry

3.7.1 Predictive Analytics in the Film Industry

Predictive analytics tells what is likely to happen. In each stage of a movie data analytics is used, those stages are: post-production and distribution,. The film production companies do their strategic decision-making and predict viewers' trends using predictive analytics. The factors influencing audience engagement in movies are shown in Figure 3.8.

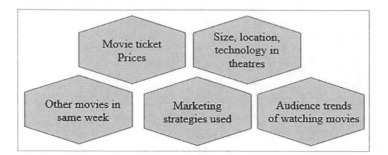

FIGURE 3.8
Factors influence audience engagement in movies.

As a part of business, film industries need to ensure that their audiences continue to revisit theaters. The data science algorithms with predictive analytics are used to predict audience response and the success of movies.

3.7.2 Tracking Progress of Movies

The process of filmmaking has three distinct stages:

  i. **Development and Pre-Production**: planning of film and getting it ready.
  ii. **Production**: filming or film shooting.
  iii. **Post-Production**: editing film and making it ready for marketing and distribution.

All the stages include many resources and past data related to every distinct stage. The best example of how data science is used in filmmaking is Netflix, Inc. It is an American content platform and production company. The primary business of Netflix is to provide a subscription-based online streaming service offering a library of films and television series. The data science algorithms are used for analysis, reporting, and predictions based on feedback from stakeholders of movies, records of movie IDs, records about films were watched, rating of the films and other related details.

3.7.3 Generate Movie Revenue

Film revenue sources include theatrical box office, i.e., ticket price revenue, home video, video on demand, television broadcast, streaming and selling rights, etc. Data science can help in revenue generation of movies. Using natural language processing and trends in social media, data scientists can analyze the best time of the year when release of films will be beneficial. The movie budget includes all costs required for resources in different phases such as movie production, development, marketing, and advertising. Data science helps film production companies to find the best budget using data analytics based on past movies, related movie features, and resources.

3.7.4 Improve Post-production of Movies

Post-production is the editing of audio and visual materials to create a film and make it ready for marketing and distribution. An editor assembles proper footage shot by shot, adds quality original or licensed music, and incorporates other visual and sound effects. The whole process uses dedicated data science-based software/tools to make the movie more effective in a technical sense. Netflix-like subscription-based online streaming services are developed for post-production of movies [10].

3.8 Logistic Delivery and Transportation Units

3.8.1 Reducing Shipping Costs through Delivery Path Optimization

The movement of goods from one location to another is a complex task, and it should be carried out with safety and efficiency. Data science with data analytics allows us to moderate the costs and save money through efficient route optimization required in logistic delivery and transportation units. By selecting an optimal route for delivering the shipments, it reduces the requirement for the number of vehicles, fuel cost, man-hours, and overall usage of vehicles. This results in optimization of overall budgeting of logistic delivery and transportation units.

3.8.2 Monitoring Traffic and Weather Data from Sensors

By using data science and equipping IoT sensors on delivery trucks and tracking weather conditions, it is also possible to take necessary precautions during transportation. Data science helps in the development of sensor-based intelligent systems for traffic data collection. Intelligent data science algorithms integrated with telecommunications are used for traffic monitoring. GPS, modern microchips, and radio frequency identification are used for smart traffic control. IoT sensing and networked systems for intelligent vehicle technologies with proper data analytics make proper support for logistic delivery and transportation units.

3.9 Shipping Sensitive Goods with Higher Quality

3.9.1 Automation of Warehouses and the Supply Chain

Warehouse automation focuses on automation of the movement of inventory within warehouses and out of warehouses to their customers with the help of automation systems or tools. For example, an autonomous mobile robot is used to move inventory from one end of the warehouse to the shipping zone and support the supply chain. The automated system, i.e., software records those movements along with past shipping references. These result in improvement in speed, efficiency, reliability, and overall accuracy in the warehouse [11]. The components of automation of warehouses and the supply chain are shown in Figure 3.9.

3.10 Digital Advertising Systems

3.10.1 Price Comparison Websites

Price comparison algorithms use data as input, extract and update this data using price comparison engines. Main challenges of price comparison websites include use of proper

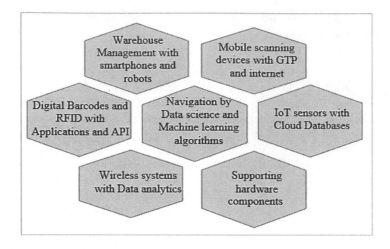

FIGURE 3.9
Components of automation of warehouses and the supply chain.

comparison technology and a huge volume of data. These price comparison engines use data science with statistical data analytics. Google Shopping, Shopping.com, Shopzilla, and PriceGrabber are a few examples of price comparison websites.

3.10.2 Website Recommendation

Website recommendation engines are developed to improve the user experience. For example, Amazon, Google Play, Twitter, LinkedIn, and Netflix websites use such engines. When use is searching for some product with certain specifications, website recommendation engines suggest relevant products from billions of products available with them. Data science with data analytics is used to develop such types of website recommendation engines. Use of such engines gives lots of information for the product with the same specifications, cost and gets multiple and better choices.

3.11 Internet Search Engines

3.11.1 Proper Filtering

A search engine is a software system designed to carry out internet searches. It means it provides a systematic way to search for particular information on the World Wide Web. Most used search engines are Google, Yahoo, YouTube, Bing, Ask, America Online, etc. However, to get specific information as per the interest of the user based on certain keywords specified in the search query search engine applies proper filtering. As shown in Figure 3.10, generalized query without proper filtering produces huge results.

Thereby, proper filtering is applied by internet search engines. Data science plays an important role to get searches faster and helps to deliver the best result for our searched query. When we search "system programming" on the internet, we get GeeksforGeeks and Wikipedia listed first. This is because these websites are visited most to get information about system programming. [12]

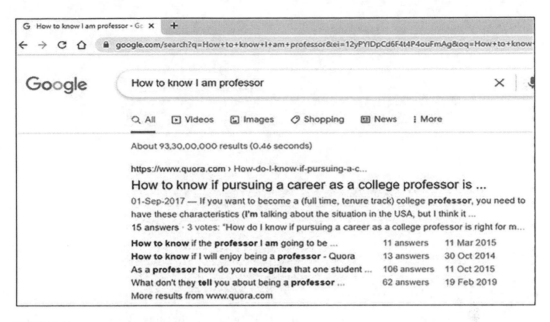

FIGURE 3.10
Hugh result generated without proper filtering.

FIGURE 3.11
Example autocomplete with the Google search engine.

3.11.2 Autocomplete

Autocomplete is a pattern used to display query suggestions that are useful in searching with internet search engines. Just go to Google and begin typing, and predictions will automatically appear. For example, when we type "Amrutvahini", it automatically completes the rest of the query and provides suggestions. An example of autocomplete with the Google search engine is shown in Figure 3.11.

Autocomplete reduces typing by about 25% on average. Such type of predictive search is important because it produces better search results and improves the user experience. Autocomplete used in internet search engines is the outcome of smart algorithms from a combination of AI with data science.

FIGURE 3.12
Benefits of recommendation-based system.

3.11.3 Recommendation Engines

The recommendation engines are software that help product-based companies to recommend the right product or service to their customers based on the history of the customer. Data science with data analytics is used in recommendation systems that predict and show the products that a user would like to purchase. The recommendation engines use collaborative, content-based, or hybrid recommendation systems. The benefits of recommendation-based systems are shown in Figure 3.12.

3.12 Airline Routing Planning

3.12.1 Predicting Flight Delays

A flight delay occurs when a flight landing or take-off happens later than its scheduled time. Airlines systems use data science along with AI-based machine learning algorithms for the collection and analysis of flight data. This data includes details about each route distance, passengers, altitudes, aircraft type, weight, halts, weather, fuel needed for a flight, etc. In case of unexpected circumstances, late flights arriving will trigger a reverse ripple impact measured over time and communicated to airports and other time-lined flights' airports. It affects all other dependent schedules including departure time of dependent flights, taxi out, taxi in, arrival time, passengers waiting time at dependent flights in airports, security delays, etc. Providing information about flight delays to their passengers and other stakeholders in advance is one of the essential services of airlines [13].

3.12.2 Decide Route of Flight In Case of Emergency

Sometimes emergency or abnormal situations may arise due to reasons such as a fire in an aircraft, failure of any component of aircraft like engine, shortage of essential fuel or any other consumable substance, abrupt extreme weather conditions, pilots inability due to illness, aircraft damage due to bird strike or worst weather conditions, and illegal activity like aircraft hijacking or bomb threat. In such emergency situations, immediate actions are needed. The immediate actions include the following step-by-step subtasks:

i. **Aviation**: The pilot ensures the safe flight path and condition of the aircraft with checklist drills.

ii. **Navigation**: Now, carry out an emergency action just to place the aircraft in a safe flying position. It will require coordination with air traffic control and other parties.

iii. **Communication**: Pilots facing an emergency situation should declare an emergency immediately. The pilot decides to change the route of the flight by communicating with the control room.

Data science and machine learning algorithms are used during handling such emergencies to evaluate optional routes considering aircraft ground handling, fueling, etc.

3.12.3 Running Customer Loyalty Programs Effectively

The term "loyalty" is used to describe a customers' willingness to continue with a firm over a long term. Airline loyalty programs are offered to keep their customers loyal to them. The entire ecosystem of air travel is designed to incorporate other facilities such as hotel chains, airport stores, car rentals, living rooms, taxis, restaurants, and travel credit cards. Customer loyalty programs work on simple logic:

i. Through customer loyalty programs, airlines retain their customers.

ii. More the customers are retained, the more they like your airline services.

iii. As they like your airline services, the more they will fly with your airline.

iv. The cycle continues.

The loyalty program of the airline industry is an important tool for customer retention. Obviously, customer loyalty programs help airline industries to generate a huge chunk of revenue. Data science with data analytics is used to run loyalty programs in the airline industry.

3.13 Image and Speech Recognition Systems

3.13.1 Image Recognition Systems

Image recognition is one of the important applications of data science with machine learning. For example, while uploading the image, Facebook gives suggestions to include a tag about the image. Once a tag is added to one profile on Facebook, if the same face is matched in a friend's profile picture, Facebook suggests auto-tagging. Similarly, while using web WhatsApp, you scan a barcode in the web browser using a mobile phone. Additionally, Google offers the option to search images by uploading them. This is implemented using image recognition algorithms and image searching techniques.

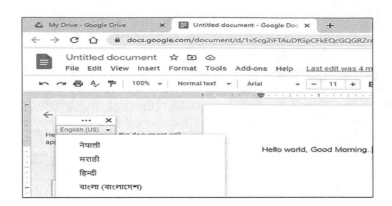

FIGURE 3.13
Voice typing with Google forms using Google drive.

3.13.2 Speech Recognition Systems

Google Voice, Cortana system for windows, Apple Siri, and Amazon Alexa are some of the examples where speech recognition systems are used. These systems are effectively used for audio waves into text conversion. For example, typing reports and news in English or regional languages line by line was a time-consuming task. However, with speech recognition systems, voice typing facilities are provided. Simply speak out the text you want to type and your voice will be automatically converted into text. These systems are useful for newspaper editors or printing presses where a large volume of data typing is required daily either in English or in regional languages. The voice typing with Google forms using Google drive is shown in Figure 3.13.

Data science with advanced classification algorithms and AI are used in speech recognition systems [14].

3.14 Gaming/Sports

3.14.1 Use Previous Gaming Experience to the Next Level

There are many games like Chess, Tic Tac Toe, Electronic Arts sports, and video games that use data science with machine learning algorithms. Apart from training and working hard, an athlete or sportsperson should know about their strengths and weaknesses to improve. Data analytics provide such analysis. Data science with data analytics provides the following benefits:

   i. It boosts revenue generation in sports.

   ii. It provides help in monitoring and performance improvement.

   iii. It enhances fan engagement.

   iv. It identifies player potential and past victories to attract crowds.

Team managers, players, coaches, and fans rely on sports analytics in decision-making and developing strategies for winning the game. Sports analytics helps for statistics about players, weather conditions, team's recent winning or losing records, etc. This helps to predict filling the stadium seats, television contracts, parking, sponsorships, etc.

3.14.2 Improve Player Moves Up to Higher Level

The computer games, the user plays with a computer opponent and uses data science with machine learning in gaming. In many games, the past data is used to improve themselves as the player moves to a higher level. In football, GPS data is recorded in training as well as in actual matches then data science with machine learning algorithms is used to detect patterns. This gives how to avoid moves so that players will avoid injuries in playing. In motion gaming, the opponent investigates your past moves and then shapes up his moves accordingly. Data science is not only important in sports to fuel competition between professional players but also it helps to improve game quality and player safety up to a higher level.

3.15 Social Life and Social Networking

3.15.1 Building and Maintaining Social Relationship

Building and maintaining social relationships essentially requires good and regular communication. Such a communication network is built by sharing thoughts/feelings with family, trusted colleagues, and family members. Human beings are social animals. Social network sites such as Facebook, Twitter, and Linked provide a platform to build your social relationship. The COVID-19 pandemic has already illustrated the significance of social networking. Data science algorithms with data analytics are used in social networking.

3.15.2 Maintaining Friend Circles through Social Media

For real-world network analysis, graph data science along with AI and machine learning algorithms are effectively used. Graph analytics and graph data science are also used for maintaining friend circles through social media. The following are some of the objectives of maintaining friend circles through social media:

   i. To clarify purpose building network.
   ii. To connect the right people for the right cause.
   iii. To cultivate trust not control.
   iv. To coordinate actions avoiding duplication of efforts.
   v. To collaborate generously with frequent communication.

3.15.3 Building Human Network for Social Causes

Human networks built for social causes have a very large-scale social impact. Many social media groups deal with issues related to human lives.
   The human network may be built for the following sample social causes:

   i. To connect a network of similar organizations.
   ii. To connect with donors for social causes.

iii. To promote social events.

iv. To gather feedback on social events.

Data science with data analytics algorithms is used in communication and social networks. Data scientists not only work for technology and research but also work on effective methods of collaboration to share information related to social causes with the general public.

3.16 Augmented Reality

3.16.1 Operation Room Augmented with Remote Presence

AR is somewhat related to virtual reality and it uses artificial digital objects to create a live experience through the use of digital technology. For example, using AR in the education field, the model of the human body will look as if it is actually present in front of us as a live object to study various parts of the body. AR is used on Google glass, Google street view, pitch summary in cricket, photography and editing, interior decoration, machinery maintenance, medical training, nursing assistance, medical diagnosis, neurosurgery, education, agriculture, and many more fields. The medical domain is the prime application of AR. For example, while practicing in neurosurgery, AR highlights the blocked and damaged nerves digitally and it serves as an assisting partner for doctors. This helps neurosurgeons to operate on the affected nerves easily and perfectly without affecting any damage and avoid any possibility of humans. Data science is used with AR for data collection and analysis in all the above applications.

3.16.2 Social Media with Augmented Reality

AR has become very common on social media. Facebook, Twitter, LinkedIn, and Instagram have developed their own filters and effects. For example, AR-enabled faces with filters and special effects look like just extended parts of images as shown in Figure 3.14.

Social AR filters on social media are an effective support for online marketing. These AR filters have gained huge popularity and work to drive engagement and brand awareness across multiple platforms. For example, with the expansion of Spark AR Studio on Facebook, companies or customers can create free innovative AR filters for fashion designing or other relevant product marketing. Data science is used with AR for data collection and analysis for social media-based marketing applications.

FIGURE 3.14
AR-enabled faces with filters and special effects.

FIGURE 3.15
Self-driving car system tracking other vehicles on road.

3.17 Self-Driving Cars and Robots

3.17.1 Intelligent Systems for Self-Driving Cars

Self-driving cars are AI systems that need real-time decisions based on a continuous, uninterrupted stream of data and instructions. A self-driving cars use self-navigation systems using high-resolution maps with sensors, actuators, data analytics with intelligent machine learning algorithms, and high-configuration processors to execute software. The radar sensors play an important role in monitoring the position of nearby vehicles. High-resolution video cameras can detect traffic lights, read road signs and track other vehicles on road. The self-driving car system tracks other vehicles on road, as shown in Figure 3.15.

Such a system is also automated to ensure less traffic, safer roads, and less pollution. For example, NuTonomy was spin-off technology start-up company that developed software for self-driving cars and autonomous mobile robots.

3.17.2 Robotics and Automation

Robotic process automation refers to software technology to design, develop, deploy, and manage software robots. These robots are programmed through computer programs to perform human-like actions by interacting with other digital systems and software. However, software robots perform faster than human beings and if programmed well, they work more responsive, effectively, efficiently, and without errors. Using data science analytics, and AI-based systems, robotic process automation is bringing rapid digital transformation to engineering applications. For example, in car manufacturing, robots can fit together the nuts and bolts of a vehicle and perform more accurate tasks than humans.

3.18 Email Filtering and Character Recognitions

3.18.1 Email Spam Filtering

Email filtering applies specified criteria for incoming emails to protect your network from viruses and possible attacks and avoid overloading servers from unwanted emails.

The spam filters detect unsolicited, virus-infected, unwanted emails and stop them from entering your mail inboxes. Following are some example filters that are applied to the email system to determine whether it is spam or not.

   i. **Content Filters:** review contents in the message.
  ii. **Header Filters:** review the email header.
 iii. **General Blacklist Filters:** stop emails from blacklisted spammers.
  iv. **Rules-Based Filters:** email from specific senders or specific subject allowed.
   v. **Permission Filters:** need permission for sending a message.

Data science with data analytics and clustering and classification algorithms are used to determine whether an email is spam or non-spam.

3.18.2 Optical Character Recognitions

Optical character recognition (OCR) uses technology to recognize printed or handwritten text inside images like scanned documents and photos. The optical character recognition process examines the text of a given document and translates characters into code that can be used for data processing. It is sometimes also called text recognition. In optical character recognition systems, hardware and software are used collectively to convert physical documents into machine-readable text. AI-based advanced methods of intelligent character recognition are used for identifying languages or styles of handwriting. The hardware includes an optical scanner, while software includes data analytics and AI-based advanced processing. The characters are identified using either pattern recognition or feature detection algorithms.

3.19 Genetics and Genomics Research

3.19.1 Analyzing Impact of the DNA on the Health

Virtually every cell in your body contains DNA or the genetic code. DNA contains the instructions needed for an organism necessary for growth, reproduction, and health. These instructions can be used to produce proteins that affect many different processes and functions in your body. Diseases can occur due to a defect in a single gene or a set of genes. Data science allows practical insights from large-scale data. Data science is used to understand the impact of DNA on our health and to detect biological connections between genetics, diseases, and drug response. MapReduce technique in Hadoop is effectively used in processing huge amounts of genetic data in less time.

3.19.2 Analyzing Reaction of Genes to Various Medications

Genomics is the study of genomes that consist of genes and DNAs of living beings. It is one of the important areas of study in medical science. The research on the genes of living organisms involves high-level treatments. Research in genomics includes the analysis of drug response for a particular type of DNA and its correlation to disease, symptoms, and health conditions of the human body. Thus, genomics plays an important role in drug discovery and development for different diseases. Data science with big data analytics in the context of biotechnology relates to genome sequencing and also helps for potential drug targets in the pharmaceutical industry.

3.19.3 Analyzing Set of Chromosomes in Humans, Animals

A chromosome is a long DNA molecule with part or all of the genetic material of an organism. They are thread-like structures located inside the nucleus of an animal. Each chromosome is made of protein and a single molecule of DNA. Chromosomes carry genes which contain all information needed by the cell for functioning and reproducing further cells of the next generation. In medical science, data analytics is used for analyzing sets of chromosomes in humans and animals.

References

1. Bansal, H. Feburary 5, 2020. *Top Data Science Applications.* https://becominghuman.ai/top-data-science-applications-how-data-science-bought-change-to-the-world-e215c3b25d9d (accessed April 15, 2021).
2. Mae Rice. July 23, 2019. *17 Data Science Applications and Examples.* https://builtin.com/data-science/data-science-applications-examples (accessed April 10, 2021).
3. Analytics Vidhya. September 21, 2015. *3 Amazing Applications/Uses of Data Science Today.* https://www.analyticsvidhya.com/blog/2015/09/applications-data-science/ (accessed April 25, 2021).
4. Upasana. November 25, 2020. *Top 10 Data Science Applications.* https://www.edureka.co/blog/data-science-applications/(accessed May 3, 2021).
5. Josh, S. January 30, 2019. *Top 10 Applications of Data Science.* https://www.zarantech.com/blog/top-10-applications-of-data-science/ (accessed April 23, 2021).
6. Blum, A., Hopcroft, J., Kannan, R., January 18, 2018. Foundations of Data Science. https://www.cs.cornell.edu/jeh/book.pdf.
7. Cielen, D., Arno, D., Meysman, B., Ali, M. 2016. *Introducing Data Science: Big Data, Machine Learning, and More, Using Python Tools,* Manning Shelter Island. http://bedford-computing.co.uk/learning/wp-content/uploads/2016/09/introducing-data-science-machine-learning-python.pdf.
8. Rao, C.R., Arni, S.R., Rao, S. 2021, *Handbook of statistics 44 : Data Science: Theory and Applications,* Elsevier Publications. *In text: (Rao, Rao 2021).* https://www.elsevier.com/books/data-science-theory-and-applications/rao/978-0-323-85200-5.
9. Hassanien, A.-E., Taha, M. H. N., Mahmoud, N. E. 2021. *Enabling AI Applications in Data Science.* Springer Publications. https://www.springer.com/gp/book/9783030520663.
10. Godbole, N.S., Lamb, J. 2015. Using data science & big data analytics to make healthcare green. *12th International Conference & Expo on Emerging Technologies for a Smarter World (CEWIT).* (October):1–6. https://ieeexplore.ieee.org/document/7338161.
11. Khanduja, V., Arora, A. Garg, S. May 5–6, 2017. Applications of big data in real world: It's not what you know. It's what you do with what you know. *2017 International Conference on Computing, Communication and Automation (ICCCA).* (May). https://ieeexplore.ieee.org/document/8229792.
12. Atov, I., Chen, K.-C., Kamal, A., Yu, S. January 27, 2020. Data science and artificial intelligence for communications. *IEEE Communications Magazine* (Volume: 58, Issue: 1). (January): 10–11. https://ieeexplore.ieee.org/document/8970159.

13. Kushwaha, A., Vijay Chavan, P., Singh, V.K. 2020. *COVID-19 Data Analysis and Innovative Approach in Prediction of Cases in* Big Data Analytics and Artificial Intelligence Against COVID-19: Innovation Vision and Approach. Springer Publications. (October): 91–115. https://link.springer.com/chapter/10.1007/978-3-030-55258-9_6.

14. Mangrulkar, R.S., Michalas, A., Shekokar, N., Narvekar, M., Chavan, P.V. 2021. Design of Intelligent Applications using Machine Learning and Deep Learning Techniques. https://www.routledge.com/Design-of-Intelligent-Applications-using-Machine-Learning-and-Deep-Learning/Mangrulkar-Michalas-Shekokar-Narvekar-Chavan/p/book/9780367679798.

4

HDWR_SmartNet: A Smart Handwritten Devanagari Word Recognition System Using Deep ResNet-Based on Scan Profile Method

Shalaka Prasad Deore

M.E.S College of Engineering, Pune

S.P. Pune University

CONTENTS

4.1 Introduction and Related Work

Handwritten character recognition is a very important research area in the field of pattern recognition. It has a wide range of applications and is also a challenging educational problem. Especially, documents which are written in local languages need a solution to convert into digital form. Hence, it will offer a method for automatically processing large amounts of any language data. As a result, a lot of work on various scripts is going on in this area. Devanagari is the most widely used script in India; it is the most adaptable writing system, with more than 120 languages (Pal and Chaudhuri 2004). Many languages, including Hindi, Marathi, Nepali, Sanskrit, and Gujarati, use Devanagari as their base language. Devanagari has evolved over a period of two thousand years and is highly continuous in nature. In terms of technology, the advent of GPUs and cluster architecture in the computational genre has

DOI: 10.1201/9781003283249-4

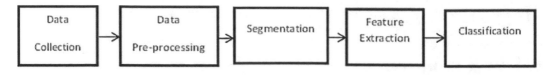

FIGURE 4.1
Text recognition phases.

resulted in significant improvements and expanded the space for performance-demanding applications. There has been a significant increase in data sources and improvements in computing capacity, allowing new methodologies for handwriting recognition in various languages to emerge. One of the methods that deal with identifying handwritten or typed words in a document is word recognition. Here, the text is scanned and then translated into a format that can be edited by machines. Nowadays, digitalization or automation is attracting the attention of researchers who want to undertake major work in the field of pattern recognition. Old documents, fragile, handwritten documents like Granthas need to be preserved. Digitization is one of the good solutions for preserving them for further research. The vast majority of Indians still choose to write in Hindi and other Devanagari-based languages. Hence there is a need for an efficient recognition system.

Many studies have been done on handwritten word recognition in various scripts, such as Japanese (Liu et al. 2002), Chinese (Su 2013), and Roman (Koerich et al. 2005; Bunke 2003). Online recognition and offline recognition (Plamondon and Srihari 2000) are two main character recognition methods. The goal of online recognition is to detect handwritten characters in a real-time environment and it usually involves drawing on the screen with an optical pen. The second method is known as offline recognition and it is used to detect text on a paper. The chapter is scanned using a digital device such as a camera or scanner, and the image is saved and later can be edited. For any text recognition, the input image goes through different phases to produce the output (Jayadevan et al. 2011). Figure 4.1 describes these various phases. The first phase is corpus creation. This process entails gathering information from different sources. Data can be gathered in one of two ways: online or offline. In this research work, the new Devanagari dataset is created which is publicly available on Kaggle. Noise is eliminated from data in the next phase called data preprocessing. Various preprocessing algorithms can be applied to raw data to get a clean dataset for training which helps to improve the overall results of the system. As described by Singh et al. (2013), standard preprocessing techniques include resizing, thresholding or binarization, thinning, and smoothing. Separating individual characters from a document is one of the most difficult stages in any handwritten character identification system. The segmentation process divides the text into sections or zones so that each section can be recognized separately. Touching handwritten characters makes segmentation extremely difficult. A projection-based methodology is presented by Mehta et al. (2021), where the input page is scanned pixel by pixel horizontally and a histogram for each line is constructed then the lines are isolated using modified local minima. This proposed method is well suited for the script where the character consists of up/down modifiers. Bansal et al. (2002) proposed the two-pass approach for segmenting touching characters. Characters in the word that are easily distinguishable from their neighbors were split into sub-images in the first pass. Subcomponents of these divided sub-images can also be separated using statistical features such as height and width. The second pass is only performed if the character image fails to remember its recognized classes, a condition known as loose coupling between segmentation and classification. The authors were able to reach an accuracy rate of 85%. Garainand and Chaudhuri (2002) present the fuzzy multifactorial approach for identifying and segmenting difficult-to-segment touching characters. Characteristics such as similarity degree and feasibility likelihood are used by authors to segment characters. The proposed method was applied to two common scripts, Bangla and Devanagari, and achieved high accuracy with fewer computations. The graph-based segmentation is explained by Kompalli et al. (2009) in which it segments overlapping characters and its modifiers into its original components. The classifier then processed these components and produced a ranking, which was then used to decide which component needed to be segmented further. For word recognition, a stochastic finite-state automaton is used, which takes into account both scores and character frequencies. Roy et al. (2016) and Bhunia et al. (2018) discussed the significance of a zonal-based method for Indic language recognition. This method divides the image into three zones: top, middle, and bottom, with each zone being recognized separately, reducing the number of compared groups. The authors discovered that using a zonal approach is more effective than using a conventional approach. Feature extraction is a crucial step in the classification process. Important features that have been extracted are often helpful in improving accuracy. Statistical, structural, local, and global categories of feature extraction with their importance are well explained by Reddy et al. (2018). However, manually extracting features from images takes more time and is a rather repetitive job. In our research, a Deep Learning (DL) approach is explored to automatically extract features, which is a faster method that works on raw pixel data to produce the best features for classification. The last phase is the classification that recognizes the input image and maps it to an output class. Here the ResNet model of the Convolutional Neural Network (CNN) is used for classification.

More than 300 million individuals use the Devanagari script for documentation in India. Being an important script in India, the work for digitizing Devanagari-based languages is comparatively less. There's considerably less research available on Indian languages compared to the amount of population interacting with it. Recognizing a handwritten script is the application of character recognition which deals with recognizing various kinds of handwritten/printed characters such as digits, cursive scripts, symbols, and touch characters and various researches have been noted.

Ren et al. (2017) present the Chinese text structure feature extractor layer by taking the motivation of the model of humans in psychology and generating the three-layer Chinese text recognition model. The new layer is then combined with the residual network to get the advantages of the proposed feature extractor as a unified feature extractor. Another feature extraction technique based on 1D moment using online data is explained in Deore and Pravin (2019). The author performed various experiments on Devanagari characters using online information and proved that 1D moments can also be used as features for online recognition where the data is not influenced by stroke. Recently for automatic feature extraction DL models are used. Pouyanfar et al. (2018) presented a survey on various DL models and their applications. The survey details many opportunities and problems in important areas of DL, such as temporal complexity, size, and power which demands priority-based attention. Various common DL networks, such as the recursive neural network, recurrent neural network, CNN, and deep generative models, are addressed in this paper. Jino et al. (2019) developed a dataset of Malayalam handwritten words and trained them using deep CNN architecture. Here the hybrid approach is implemented. CNN is used for feature extraction and a classification support vector machine (SVM) is implemented. Narang et al. (2009) performed research on the recognition of Devanagari ancient documents. The statistical features like centroid, intersection points, open endpoints, and horizontal and vertical peak extent are extracted from images and sent for classification. CNN, RBF-SVM, MLP neural network, and random forest classifiers are explored in this work and all results are compared. In Shaw et al. (2008), input images of the Devanagari word are smoothed first using a median filter and then the binarization by Otsu's (1979) thresholding method. The histogram of chain-code directions in the image is used as a feature vector with an HMM classifier and achieved 80.2% of accuracy. Bolan Su et al. (2017) proposed word-level recognition present in scenes. Basically, characters of a word are touched by each other and face a problem while recognizing. So the author used a segmentation-free approach. In this, the image is converted into a sequential signal then it is passed to the recurrent neural network for classification. The recurrent neural network technique is then combined with the Long Short-Term Memory (LSTM) technique to get a good result. But the system gives very low results when texts in scenes are severely curved or suffer from severe perspective distortion. Feature extraction plays an important role in classification. Always good features improve the recognition accuracy of the system, but it is a very time-consuming and tedious process. In a DL approach, it directly works on raw images and automatically extracts the required information from the image which helps us to improve accuracy with less time (Lee et al. 2009). The popularity of deep neural networks is increasing due to their number of applications in the area of computer vision, pattern recognition, speech recognition, natural language processing, and recommendation systems (Liu et al. 2017). In a paper by Alom et al. (2018), various deep CNNs like VGG Net, ResNet, FractalNet and DenseNet are evaluated and their performance is discussed in the application of Handwritten Bangla Character recognition. The proposed residual network by He et al. (2015) is designed using several convolutional blocks with residual calculations and feedback. Using many convolutional blocks, it is very easy to design deep convolutional models. With this concept, there is vast improvement in segmentation, detection, and classification. As per deliberated above DL techniques, the CNN architecture of the deep neural network is used for image classification and has also been effectively implemented to recognize different languages like Roman (MNIST) (Xiao and Ching 2012), Arabic (Younis 2017), and Bangla (Md. Mahbubar et al. 2015). Characters written by different persons have a lot of class variance, which makes it difficult for classifiers to do their job well. Although DL architectures have improved classification accuracy, they have also raised the computational burden of training the classifier. This is a significant challenge in the construction of an efficient handwritten character recognition system. When it comes to DL, the hyperparameter selection is the most difficult problem to solve and necessitates much research. The efficiency of the model is dependent on the proper selection of hyperparameters.

Considering this, a Devanagari word recognition system using a DL approach is proposed which would recognize handwritten Devanagari words using a variant of CNN called Residual Net. The Residual Net supports residual learning character detection.

Following are the core contributions of the work:

1. New dataset of handwritten Devanagari characters publicly available.
2. Android application for easy dataset creation.
3. New segmentation-free approaches namely, Scan Profile and Sliding Window which will recognize a word like human reading.
4. Experimentation of DL models on newly created dataset and result comparison
5. The proposed handwritten word recognition system achieves a good recognition rate as compared with other approaches found in the literature survey.

The rest of the chapter is organized as follows. In Section 4.2 characteristics of the Devanagari script are discussed. Corpus creation is deliberated in Section 4.3. The proposed work is discussed in Section 4.4. In Section 4.5 the training model and the experimental results are discussed. Finally, the conclusion of the chapter is given in Section 4.6.

4.2 Features of Devanagari Script

Devanagari is a base language, and other Indian languages such as Hindi, Marathi, and Gujarati are derived from it. Devanagari is a phonetic script, which means that each character is spoken exactly as it is written. Devanagari script follows the left to right way for writing. Each word in the Devanagari script is divided by a "Shirorekha" line, a horizontal line at the top of each word. As shown in Figure 4.2, the Devanagari script consists of 36 consonants and 12 vowels with 12 modifiers. Figure 4.2a depicts a handwritten sample of vowels and consonants and Figure 4.2b depicts modifiers. The vowels may be written as individual characters and are used as a modifier with consonants to form "Barakhadi" letters. There are also compound letters which are formed by joining characters and play a significant role in recognition as these characters are difficult to recognize. There are several other factors that contribute to the recognition system's complexity and difficulties. Various handwriting styles as shown in Figure 4.3, shapes of some characters are the same as depicted in Figure 4.4, noise present during corpus creation, etc.

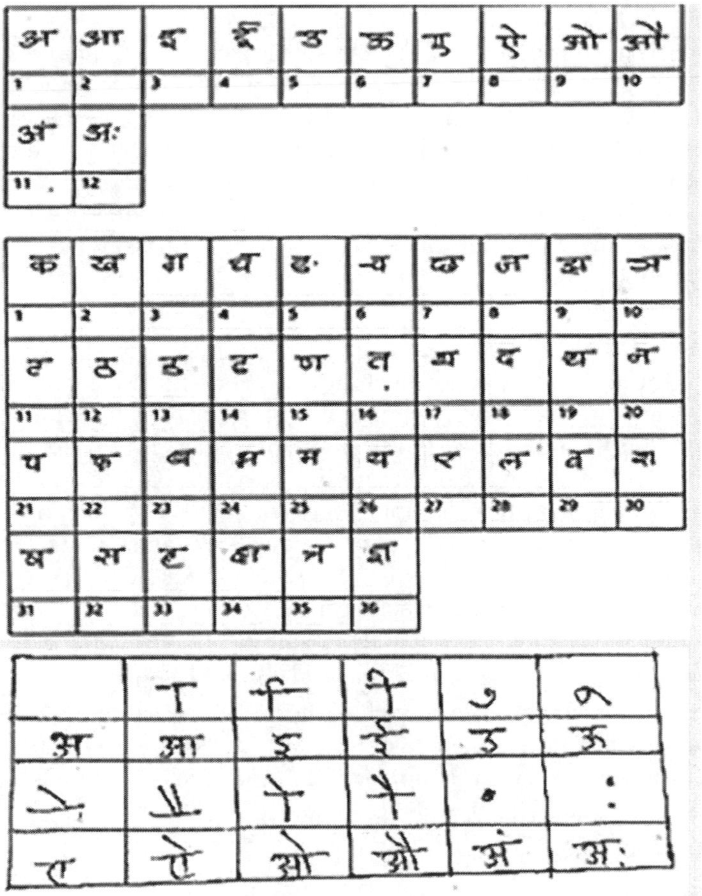

FIGURE 4.2
Handwritten sample. (a) Vowel and consonant characters. (b) Modifiers.

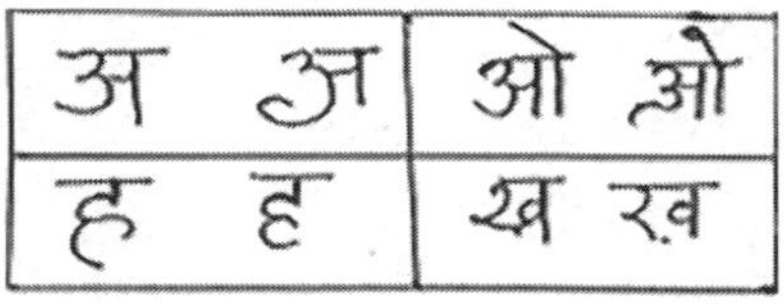

FIGURE 4.3
Different writing styles of the same character.

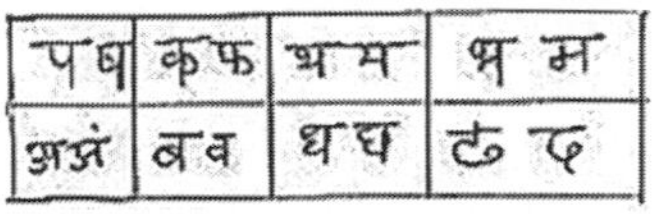

FIGURE 4.4
Similar shape characters.

4.3 Dataset Creation

In the field of pattern recognition, creating datasets is a critical challenge. Better data quality allows us to achieve greater accuracy and improves the system's recognition rate. In this chapter, the proposed system used two different datasets to train the handwritten word recognition model. The first newly dataset is created by us and the second dataset is taken from the UCI machine learning repository. The main aim of creating a new dataset is to make a contribution to the academic community in order to further research and improve the efficiency of DL models by upgrading data collection methods and introducing new data variants.

- **Our Newly Created Dataset**
  1. First is the offline collection technique where fixed-size papers were distributed to different age group peoples to write isolated characters using a ball pen and then all these handwritten characters were separately scanned. Constraints like age of a person, quality of paper, ball pen, and writing style are not kept while writing. Samples were collected from 50 people for different 58 classes. These 58 classes consist of 12 vowels, 36 consonants, and 10 numeral classes. The size of each image is 1,600×1,600 pixels which are preprocessed and saved using.jpg format. Each scanned image is labeled manually by its class name and sequence number. For example, the first image of the character "अ" of class 1 is labeled as C1_1.jpg, C1_2.jpg, and so on.
  2. In the second method, an Android application is used for data collection. Our designed application is time-consuming as well as very user-friendly. Figure 4.5 shows our designed Android application. It has the following features:
     - A white canvas of size 800×800 for drawing the character input using a black font color.
     - Functionality to save and clear the canvas.
     - The characters that have to be drawn on the canvas are displayed on the screen in the scrollable view.

FIGURE 4.5
Android application designed for data collection.

- The characters displayed are color-coded; whenever the user is writing the character, the color of the character in the scrollable view would be green; if the image is saved, then the color would be red.
- If a user wants to rewrite the character, the user can simply select the character and the color would change to yellow.
- After all the images are saved, there is a functionality to send the images to the developer by the "Send to developer" option. The images are sent to the developer through mail or any other file sharing medium in the form of a zip file.

The data was collected from 50 individuals using this application. The size of each image is 800×800 pixels and saved using a.jpg format. The total size of our created dataset is 4,800 images consisting of vowels and consonants.

- **UCI Machine Learning Repository**
  The dataset consists of 46 classes of characters including 36 consonants and 10 digits with 2,000 sample images in each class. Only Devanagari consonants and numerals are included in the dataset. Twelve vowel characters are not there in the dataset. The dataset is created by Acharya et al. (2015) and is publically available for research.

4.4 Proposed System Architecture

The architecture of the proposed Handwritten Devanagari Word Recognition (HDWR) system is depicted in Figure 4.6. A detailed explanation of the proposed HDWR system is given in the following subsections.

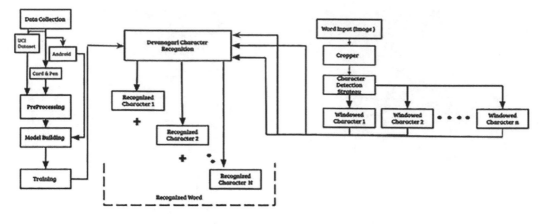

FIGURE 4.6
Architecture of proposed HDWR system.

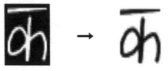

FIGURE 4.7
Preprocessing stage output.

4.4.1 Data Preprocessing and Data Augmentation

The data that was collected has inconsistencies and noise. Hence the images were pre-processed so as to convert them into a suitable form for the model. The dataset that was collected from the Android application did not need any preprocessing, this serves as an advantage where preprocessing is eliminated for the Android application dataset. The nature of the UCI dataset is that the images have a black background with Devanagari characters handwritten using the white font. Hence as the UCI is a larger dataset, a batch image processing tool called XnConvert is used. The negative filter is used to invert the image as shown in Figure 4.7.

For our created dataset, the characters were written on cards using a pen and then all images are scanned separately. No constraints like pen type, writing style, and size were kept while collecting samples hence the letters are in different fonts, colors, and styles. To make the dataset consistent in a common format a number of preprocessing operations are applied to the dataset using the XnConvert batch processing tool. One sample character is depicted in Figure 4.8. The following preprocessing operations are used in this research:

- **Resizing:** Resizing is done to adjust the base size of input images before sending them for training since the scanned images are different or larger in size. All image samples are resized to 64×64.
- **Curves:** The sample characters are defined in two states in a 2D plane with a white background and black trace of the character. Hence the character images can be best represented as a binary image. It is used to change the color channels of an image to enhance some specific features.

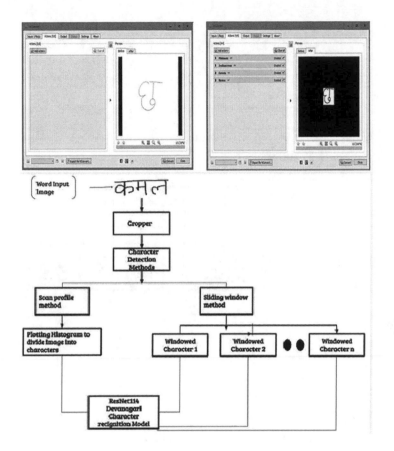

FIGURE 4.8
(a) Before preprocessing. (b) After preprocessing.

- **Minimum Filter:** It is used to increase the thickness of each character in the batch. It is also used to rejoin the broken character.

- **Zealous Crop:** It is a content-aware crop which finds the contour of an image through all boundaries until the pixel is found and then crop it.

To avoid the overfitting of a model and to get different transformations of images data augmentation is performed. Data augmentation is a technique that refers to a variety of operations for generating new training samples from existing ones. Translation, rotation, scaling, and zooming augmentation techniques are performed to enhance the existing dataset in our research. Hence all kinds of variations like different image sizes, translation, and rotated images can be operated by the model during the testing phase. Different data augmentation strategies are utilized to handle images with random changes and to improve the efficiency of our model.

4.4.2 Proposed Handwritten Devanagari Word Recognition System with Novel No-Segmentation Approach

For HDWR, the input image is taken and mapped as the Devanagari word string. A Devanagari word image written on a white background using a black font is given to the

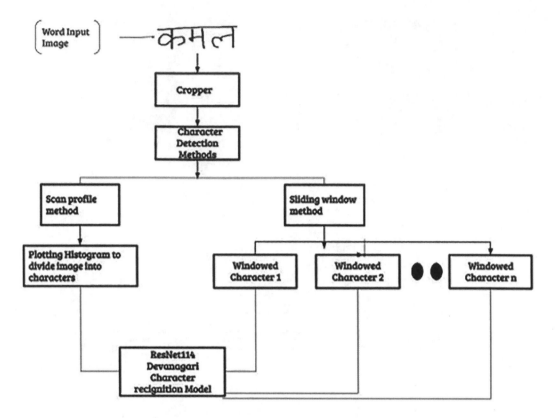

FIGURE 4.9
Flow diagram of word recognition using two different methods.

proposed system as input. Traditionally for the image to be recognized, segmentation was used. Segmentation is a content-aware mechanism for dividing the image into zones, cropping them, and individually recognizing them. While segmentation is a state-of-the-art approach, it has drawbacks. It is computationally expensive and hyperparameters are to be wisely chosen. Thereby in this work, we introduce two different methods namely the Scan Profile method and second is Sliding Window method which is without segmentation to recognize the word. The flow of the word recognition using mentioned above two methods is shown in Figure 4.9.

4.4.2.1 Cropper Method

Initially, the input word image is given to the cropper method. Devanagari word is written on a white canvas of an Android application using a black font color. On canvas, the word can be written on any part of the white canvas, as shown in Figure 4.10.

Hence need to crop the image according to the position where it is written. For this cropper, an algorithm is developed which crops only the word from the image. For cropping, four parameters (left, right, top, and bottom) of the image are calculated which will define the first black pixel from respective sides. This way the dimensions of the image are obtained, and then it is cropped as shown in Figure 4.11.

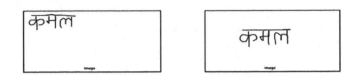

FIGURE 4.10
Word is written on a white canvas of the Android application.

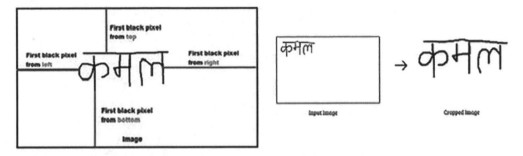

FIGURE 4.11
(a) Left, right, top, bottom parameters of the image. (b) Final cropped image.

4.4.2.2 First Approach: Sliding Window Method without Segmentation

In the first approach, the idea is to implement a scanning mechanism analogous to human reading sequentially like from left to right. For this approach, we observed the writing patterns of various writers without keeping any restrictions. Various features are as follows: (i) Basically, when a Devanagari word is written there is a very less gap present between two letters in one word. (ii) "Shirorekha" line is present until the end of the word. (iii) Writing style may vary but there is not much difference in word length and height. Based on these features the proposed Sliding Window algorithm is designed to capture a window of predefined dimension from the word image which is then passed to the classifier without knowing what is there inside that window for recognition. This window is then shifted with a stride defined based on window length. Ideally, the recognition with the highest score is considered to fit a character sufficiently. Figure 4.12 depicts the graphical representation of how the window is passed through the complete word.

A window length is predefined to accommodate each character in the word when it is fit in. After observing different collected writing patterns an equation is defined for finding window length. It is defined as:

$$\text{window\_length} = \frac{\text{word\_height}}{\text{factor\_value}} \quad \text{window\_length} = \frac{\text{word\_height}}{\text{factor\_value}} \quad \text{window\_length} = \frac{\text{word\_height}}{\text{factor\_value}}$$

(4.1)

where factor_value is a hyperparameter which is set to 1.5. It may be different for other dataset samples. The stride calculation is defined as:

$$\text{stride} = \frac{\text{window\_length}}{\text{factor}}$$

(4.2)

Where the factor parameter has an important role in deciding vital steps in a specified direction for window travel through the word. Stride value cannot be less or more. If it is

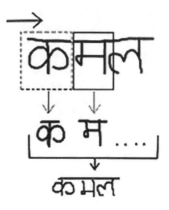

FIGURE 4.12
Sliding Window method without segmentation.

less, character will not complete in the window and when it is more, Sliding Window may skip character so the selection of factor parameters is very crucial. The algorithm for the Sliding Window method is given below.

Algorithm 1: Sliding Window Method

Input: word image, h=height of word, w=width of window, stride
Output: recognized word
Begin

    Step 1: Set window size to w=h / 1.5 // Using equation (4.1)
    Step 2: Send the image enclosed within the window to the classifier
    Step 3: Set threshold=90%
    Step 4: If prediction confidence≥threshold, then accept the window.

Else, discard window and move forward using stride // stride calculations by equation (4.2)
End

4.4.2.3 Second Approach: Scan Profile Method

The second proposed method is based on plotting a histogram. For the given input word a histogram is plotted using the black pixel count for each column of pixels. The histogram gives a graphical representation of the word. Using this graphical representation word image is scanned for its profile. This histogram is basically used to detect the location of the "Shirorekha". An almost constant set of values on the graph depicts the "Shirorekha", which can also be considered the local minima. These sections of the local minima are actually the blank spaces that are left between the characters while writing; thus, they are not required to undergo the recognition process. The size of the window is dynamically decided considering the area between two local minima. The section of the histogram within the area of the window is then sent to the model for recognition. In this way, the whole word is sent in parts or rather each character at a time to the ResNet114 classifier for further recognition. The recognition of the word is done at character level

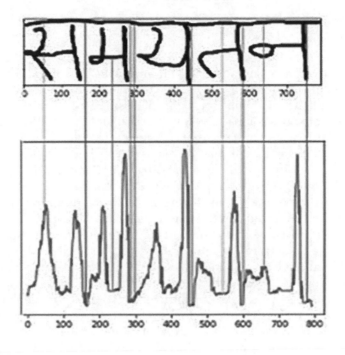

FIGURE 4.13
Scan Profile method.

by our implemented classifier which is trained on isolated Devanagari characters as shown in Figure 4.13. The red lines represent the portions of the "Shirorekha" and also the local minima of the histogram, and the green lines represent a few other sections of the word.

Algorithm 2: Scan Profile Method

Input: cropped word image
Output: recognized word
Begin

  Step 1: Find the count of non-white pixels in each column and store it in an array[]
  Step 2: Find minimum (array[]) //finding local minima, i.e., Shirorekha position
  Step 3: Calculate the range of minima between minimum count and thickness of line +10%

```
min (count) ≤ x ≤ t + (0.1xt) //t is thickness of line
```

  Step 4: Mark columns with the count in the calculated range
  Step 5: Set window to the image at marked columns
  Step 6: Resize the image of the window to 64×64
  Step 7: Feed resized window to the classifier
  Step 8: Return (output)

End

4.4.3 ResNet114 Model: Devanagari Character Recognition Model

CNN is a class of deep, feed-forward artificial neural networks, where the connection between nodes does not form a cycle. It uses a variation of multilayer perceptron designed to require minimal preprocessing. As CNN eliminates the task of feature extraction, it has been preferred for the implementation. Each of the hidden layers helps to extract various features from the text. As the number of layers increases, the complexity of extraction also increases. As CNN provides comparatively better results than the other classifiers, the use of DL classifiers is increasing in the field of computer vision and pattern recognition.

In the proposed work the ResNet classifier is used which is one of the famous architecture of CNN is explored to recognize isolated handwritten Devanagari characters. The ResNet (Residual Network) is a variant of CNN. Residual networks are easy to optimize and can achieve better accuracy from the significantly increased depth of the network (Abadi et al. 2016). ResNet introduces the concept of residual learning. In residual learning, the model is trained to learn residuals instead of learning features. Residuals are the sub-traction of features learned from the input of that layer. ResNet does this by using shortcut connections. In the traditional method, the convolution layers are just stacked one after the other, directly feeding the output of the previous layer to the input of the following layer. However, in shortcut or skip connections the existing structure is used and with this, the input of the previous layer is directly fed to the output of the following layer as well. Thus skipping connections helps to reduce the problem of vanishing gradient and also allows the model to learn an identity function which ensures that the higher layer works at least as good as the lower layer. ResNet consists of 114 layers which are as follows: input layer, zero padding, convolution layer, ReLU activation layer, max pooling, average pooling, and batch normalization. Here 3×3 convolution with fixed (64, 128, 256, and 512) feature map was performed. Input reduction between layers is obtained by using the increasing size of the stride from one to two. The first step of ResNet before inflowing into usual layer behavior is blocked which consists of convolution, batch normalization, and max pooling operations. In convolution operation, we used the kernel of size 7 with a 64 dimension feature map. In batch normalization, there is no need to change the size of our volume because the batch normalization operation is performed element-wise. Next 3×3 max pooling with stride 2 is performed. Like this, in our system, five blocks are there. ReLU non-linear activation function is applied to an input. The ReLU activation function is defined as:

$$f(y) = \max(0, y) \tag{4.3}$$

The function $f(y)$ returns 0, if it gets any negative input, and for any positive value y, it returns that value. The reason for using it instead of the widely used popular non-linear functions like sigmoid and hyperbolic tangent (Tanh) is because training with gradient-descent is comparatively much faster using ReLU than other nonlinear functions and ReLU doesn't face gradient vanishing problem also. ReLU activation function is less computationally costly than Tanh and sigmoid because it contains easy mathematical operations. The Softmax function is used to map the output of a network to predicted output classes. It uses the Softmax loss function to compute cross-entropy loss which is defined as:

$$\text{Li} = -\log\log\left(\frac{e^{f_{yi}}}{\sum_j e^{f_j}}\right) \tag{4.4}$$

The main goal of the network is to minimize the cross-entropy to reduce loss between the estimated output and target output. Many advantages our model achieved using ResNet architecture are given below:

  i. It speeds up the process of learning.
  ii. Higher accuracy of character recognition.
  iii. ResNet model reduces inconsistencies.
  iv. Other deeper networks are very difficult to optimize but the ResNet model is easy to optimize with shortcut (skip) connections that perform identity mapping and their outputs are added to the outputs of the stacked layers.

The model was compiled using Adam (adaptive moment optimization) optimizer. The optimizer is used to optimize the results and update weights. It is an extension of the stochastic gradient algorithm. It is simple, straightforward, and computationally efficient, and has fewer memory requirements. It basically gives us first and second order moments of gradients. These moments are calculated using the following formula:

$$X_t = \beta_1 X_{t-1} - (1 - \beta_1) \times G_t \tag{4.5}$$

$$Y_t = \beta_2 Y_{t-1} - (1 - \beta_2) \times G_t^2 \tag{4.6}$$

where X_t and Y_t are first- and second-order moments of gradients, and β_1 and β_2 are hyperparameters and their default values are set to 0.9 and 0.99, respectively.

4.5 Experiments, Results, and Discussion

4.5.1 Network Training Parameters

Our proposed framework was assessed on our own new handwritten Devanagari characters dataset plus a dataset taken from UCI machine learning repository. For training, the ResNet model required a large dataset hence combined our created new dataset with the UCI machine learning dataset and trained our model on 36 consonant classes. After combining two datasets, there are a total of 2,100 images of 36 classes each. Hence the dataset consists of a total of 75,600 images. Out of these, 1,800 images and 300 images per class were used for training and testing purposes respectively. The selection of training and testing samples is done randomly. The statistics of the dataset used for experiments are shown in Table 4.1. All character samples are resized to [64×64].

To solve the overfitting problem that occurs in model training, a global average pooling layer is added. No need to add a dropout layer to solve overfitting when global average pooling is used because with this layer very fewer parameters are left in our dense layers. Hence adding this layer our model becomes more generalized. This, of course, helps in preventing overfitting, and overall these layers help make very generalizable models. The training parameters of the proposed ResNet model are listed below:

- **Optimizer**: An adaptive Adam optimizer
- **Learning Rate**: 0.001

TABLE 4.1

Experimental Data Statistics

Datasets	Number of Training Samples/Class	Number of Testing Samples/Class	Total Number of Samples/Class
Our new Devanagari Character Dataset (Considered only Consonants)	80/36	20/36	100/36
UCI Machine Learning Repository (Considered only Consonants)	1720/36	280/36	2000/36
Total	1800/36	300/36	2100/36

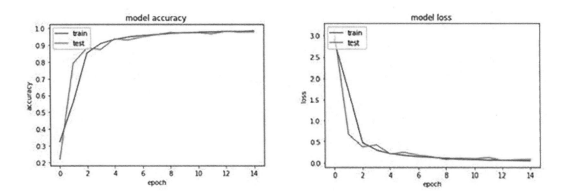

FIGURE 4.14
(a) ResNet model accuracy per epoch. (b) ResNet model loss per epoch.

- **Number of Epochs**: 15
- **Steps per Epoch**: 100

4.5.2 Experiment Results

The proposed model was implemented using Keras and TensorFlow framework and using GPU runtime. One of the advantages of using Keras is that it provides fast prototyping for DL applications and also helps in selecting the best hyperparameters based on predefined guidelines. TensorFlow is very flexible to develop training and inference algorithms required for deep neural network models and it also allows researchers to experiment with novel optimizations and training algorithms (Abadi et al. 2016). In the first step of the handwritten word recognition, the ResNet model is trained and tested on isolated character samples. The obtained accuracy of our model is depicted in Figure 4.14. Then in the testing phase, the handwritten word is given to two different proposed methods called the Sliding Window method or Scan Profile method. Each method sends a window which is enclosed with an image to the classifier for recognition. The recognition of the word is done on a character level as our model is trained on isolated characters.

The accuracy graph shows the correctness of prediction on training and testing datasets. The accuracy curve increases gradually as the number of epochs increases. The accuracy obtained by our model is 98.35% with a 5.3% loss in the training and testing phase accuracy rate is 97.7% with an 8.3% loss in 15 epochs. The loss graph represents the rate of incorrect predictions made by the model. The aim of the model is to reduce the loss and increase accuracy as much as possible. The number of epochs is an important factor that affect loss accuracy. As we can observe from the graph the loss of accuracy remains constant after a certain point. This point represents the appropriate number of epochs up to which the model should be trained. If the two curves plotted start to depart consistently it is a sign to stop training the model at an earlier epoch. Initially, network designing started with a simple sequential CNN model with seven layers. Then modifications including increasing the number of layers, changing optimizers were done in the model. VGG16, as well as VGG19, are also explored. Finally, ResNet with 114 layers gives us a good performance. The obtained testing results of various experiments are depicted in Table 4.2.

In the testing phase, 100 images out of these some samples are shown in Figure 4.15, given in a sequence to the Sliding Window and Scan Profile approaches. Single character letters without using modifiers are used to test the proposed HDWR model. The length of the word can be anything but no modifiers because the model is trained on isolated consonant characters without modifiers.

Table 4.3 clearly shows that using the Scan Profile approach gets better results compared to the Sliding Window approach. The proposed Scan Profile approach increases the recognition rate approximately by 20% compared with Sliding Window. In the Scan Profile approach, local minima are used to calculate window length so it is properly fitting on

TABLE 4.2

Accuracy Results of Different Implemented Models

Model	Number of Layers	Testing Accuracy (%)
Simple Sequential Model (without **Max pooling**)	7	74.2
Simple Sequential Model (with **Max pooling**)	7	81.35
General CNN Model	9	95
VGG16	16	96.55
VGG19	19	95.9
ResNet114 Model	114	97.7

FIGURE 4.15
Sample testing word images.

TABLE 4.3

Devanagari Word Recognition Rate Using Proposed Methods

Methods	Number of Testing Samples	Accuracy Rate (%)
Sliding Window	100	65.00%
Scan Profile	100	86.00%

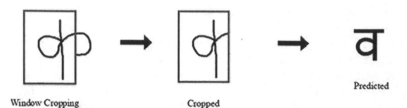

Window Cropping   Cropped   Predicted

FIGURE 4.16
Problem fetched in Sliding Window approach.

TABLE 4.4

Comparison of Testing Results of Devanagari Characters with Other Popular Work

Work Reference	Methodology	Accuracy (%)
Saha et al. (2020)	Convolutional neural network with Adam optimizer	93
Vijaya Kumar et al. (2019)	Convolutional neural network with RMSprop optimizer	97.33
Jangid et al. (2018)	DCNN	96.45
Deore et al. (2017)	Ensemble classifier (KNN+NN+SVM)	88.13
Proposed Model	ResNet 114	97.7

characters and so achieved better accuracy. Only the problem occurs in recognition when the classifier is confused with similar shape characters (Figure 4.4).

However, this method has a limitation wherein if the window captures half character it considers it as noise and gives the wrong prediction as shown in Figure 4.16. So even if one character goes wrong, whole word recognition is wrong. This method is suitable for printed word recognition where word length, gaps, and writing style are fixed.

We thought of one solution as a future scope for improvement in the Sliding Window approach. Other machine learning algorithms like SVM and KNN can be combined with features extracted by the deep network which provides a better learning to consider features such as curve, shape, and loop. Hence, it will improve the performance of the Sliding Window approach.

Comparisons with the other results of different techniques are listed in Table 4.4. First, the comparisons are done with the result of the different deep classifiers and then with the word recognition systems. The proposed ResNet 114 model gives good training accuracy ,98.4% and testing accuracy 97.7% for recognition of isolated Devanagari characters with an error rate of 5.3% for training and 8.3% for testing (Table 4.4).

Not much work is stated toward HDWR compared to printed Devanagari characters. Table 4.5 shows the results of Devanagari word recognition using a different methodology. The model proposed by us shows promising results on the Devanagari word dataset.

4.6 Conclusion and Future Work

Deep neural networks have proven superiority in pattern and script recognition for many languages with different script styles. Handwritten word recognition is a very challenging

TABLE 4.5

Comparison with Devanagari Word Recognition

Work Reference	Dataset and Size	Method	Accuracy (%)
Bhunia et al. (2018)	Devanagari Words (5k Lexicon)	HMM	71.3
Shaw et al. (2008)	Devanagari Words	LeNet (CNN)	78.87
Otsu (1979)	Devanagari Words	HMM	84.31
Proposed Model	Devanagari Words	ResNet 114(CNN)	86

task under unimpeded situations and so in recent years, many researches are going on this topic. Various approaches have been reported to solve this problem but still, there is a gap in automatic Devanagari word recognition by machines. Hence, realizing the need, we attempted to implement a system for HDWR. In this chapter, a newly created Devanagari handwritten character dataset is introduced which is publicly available.

Compared with state-of-the-art techniques, our proposed method is able to recognize the word images with no-segmentation technique. The system includes two major steps: First, the input word is passed as input to proposed no-segmentation approaches where the window is defined using different methods. Secondly, each window is passed to the classifier for recognition purposes and the result is saved. Here no need to wait to segment the complete image. Immediately the window is recognized without knowing what is there in the window automatically by our designed classifier like human reading. After one window recognition, the window moves next by the calculated stride to read the complete word. Like this, the word is recognized at the character level by our designed ResNet model. Implemented ResNet 114 layer model to recognize characters is giving a good recognition rate of 97.7%. Out of the proposed two techniques, the Scan Profile method achieved good performance. The system was developed successfully to recognize Devanagari words with an accuracy of 86% using the Scan Profile method.

The proposed Sliding Window approach has the limitation of the recognition of half-captured images. For future work, we want to work on this approach to improve the performance of the system.

Dataset Accessibility Link

https://www.kaggle.com/shalakadeore/handwritten-marathi-devanagari-characters.

References

Abadi, M., Agarwal A. et al. 2016. Tensorflow: Large-scale machine learning on heterogeneous distributed systems. arXiv:1603.04467 [cs.DC].

Acharya, S., A. Pant and P. Gyawali. 2015. Deep Learning Based Large Scale Handwritten Devanagari Character Recognition. In *Proceedings of the 9th International Conference on Software, Knowledge, Information Management and Applications (SKIMA)*, pp. 121–126. Kathmandu.

Alom, M. Z., P. Sidike, T. M. Taha, and V. K. Asari. 2018. Handwritten Bangla character recognition using the state-of-the-art deep convolutional neural networks. *Computational Intelligence and Neuroscience* 2018:1–13. doi: 10.1155/2018/6747098.

Bansal, V., and R. M. K. Sinha. 2002. Segmentation of touching and fused Devanagari characters. *Pattern Recognition*, 35(4):875–93. doi: 10.1016/S0031-3203(01)00081-4.

Bhunia, A. K., P. P. Roy, A. O. Mohta, and U. Pal. 2018. Cross-language framework for word recognition and spotting of indic scripts. *Pattern Recognition* 79:12–31. doi: 10.1016/j.patcog.2018.01.034.

Bolan, S., and L. Shijian. 2017. Accurate recognition of words in scenes without character segmentation using recurrent neural network. *Pattern Recognition* 63:397–405. doi: 10.1016/j.patcog.2016.10.016.

Bunke, H. 2003. Recognition of cursive roman handwriting- past, present and future. In *Proceedings of 7th International Conference on Document Analysis and Recognition (ICDAR)*, 1:448–59 Edinburgh, UK. doi: 10.1109/ICDAR.2003.1227707.

Deore, S., and A. Pravin. 2017. Ensembling: Model of histogram of oriented gradient based handwritten Devanagari character recognition system. *Traitement du Signal* 34(1–2):7–20.

Deore, S. P., and A. Pravin. 2019. On-line devanagari handwritten character recognition using moments features. In *Recent Trends in Image Processing and Pattern Recognition, Communications in Computer and Information Science*, ed. K. Santosh and R. Hegadi, 1037:37–48 Singapore, Springer. doi: 10.1007/978-981-13-9187-3_4.P.J.

Garainand, U., and B. B. Chaudhuri. 2002. Segmentation of touching characters in printed Devnagari and Bangla scripts using fuzzy multifactorial analysis. *IEEE Transaction on Systems, Man, and Cybernetics-Part C: Applications and Reviews* 32(4):449–59. doi: 10.1109/TSMCC.2002.807272.

He, K., X. Zhang, S. Ren, and J. Sun. 2015. Deep residual learning for image recognition. In CVPR. arXiv:1512.03385[cs.CV].

Jangid, M., and S. Srivastava. 2018. Handwritten Devanagari character recognition using layer-wise training of deep convolutional neural networks and adaptive gradient methods. *Journal of Imaging* 4(2):1–14. doi: 10.3390/jimaging4020041.

Jayadevan, R., S. R. Kolhe, P. M. Patil and U. Pal. 2011. Offline recognition of Devanagari script: A survey. *IEEE Transactions on Systems, Man, and Cybernetics-Part C: Applications and Reviews* 41(6): 782–96. doi: 10.1109/TSMCC.2010.2095841.

Jino, K., U. Bhattacharya. 2019. Offline Handwritten Malayalam Word Recognition Using a Deep Architecture. In: *Soft Computing for Problem Solving, Advances in Intelligent Systems and Computing*, ed. J. Bansal, K. Das, A. Nagar, K. Deep, and A. Ojha, Vol 816. Springer, Singapore.

Koerich, L., R. Sabourin, and C. Y. Suen. 2005. Recognition and verification of unconstrained handwritten words. *IEEE Transaction on Pattern Analysis and Machine Intelligence (TPAMI)* 27(10):1509–22. doi: 10.1109/TPAMI.2005.207.

Kompalli, S., S. Setlur, and V. Govindaraju. 2009. Devanagari OCR using a recognition driven segmentation framework and stochastic language models. *International Journal on Document Analysis and Recognition* 12:123–38. doi: 10.1007/s10032-009-0086-8.

Lee, H., R. Grosse, R. Ranganath, and A. Y. Ng. 2009. Convolutional deep belief networks for scalable unsupervised learning of hierarchical representations. In *Proceedings of the 26th Annual International Conference on Machine Learning*, ACM 609–16. New York. doi: 10.1145/1553374.1553453.

Liu, C. L., M. Koga, and H. Fujisawa. 2002. Lexicon driven segmentation and recognition of handwritten character strings for Japanese address reading. *IEEE Transaction on Pattern Analysis and Machine Intelligence (TPAMI)* 24(11):1425–37. doi: 10.1109/TPAMI.2002.1046151.

Liu, W., Z. Wang, X. Liu, N. Zeng, Y. Liu, and F. E. Alsaadi. 2017. A survey of deep neural network architectures and their applications. *Neurocomputing* 234:11–26. doi: 10.1016/j.neucom.2016.12.038.

Md. Mahbubar, R., M. A. H. Akhand, S. Islam, P. C. Shill, and Md. R. Hafizur. 2015. Bangla Handwritten character recognition using convolutional neural network. *International Journal of Image, Graphics and Signal Processing* 8:52–59. doi: 10.5815/ijigsp.2015.08.06.

Mehta, N. and J. Doshi. 2021. Text line segmentation for medieval Devnagari manuscript. In *Proceedings of International Conference on Communication and Computational Technologies*, 405–412, Springer, Singapore.

Narang, S., M. K. Jindal, and M. Kumar. 2009. Devanagari ancient documents recognition using statistical feature extraction techniques. *Sādhanā* 44(141):1–8. doi: 10.1007/s12046-019-1126-9.

Otsu, N. 1979. A threshold selection method from gray-level histograms. *IEEE Transactions on Systems, Man, and Cybernetics* 9(1):62–66. doi: 10.1109/TSMC.1979.4310076.

Pal, U., and B. B. Chaudhuri. 2004. Indian script character recognition: A survey. *Pattern Recognition* 37(9):1887–99. doi: 10.1016/j.patcog.2004.02.003.

Plamondon, R., and S. N. Srihari. 2000. Online and off-line handwriting recognition: A comprehensive survey. *IEEE Transactions on Pattern Analysis and Machine Intelligence* 22(1):63–84. doi: 10.1109/34.824821.

Pouyanfar, S. et al. 2018. A survey on deep learning: Algorithms, techniques, and applications. *ACM Computing Survey*, 51(5):1–36.

Reddy, S. and P. Deshpande. 2018. Review of feature extraction techniques for character recognition. *IETE Journal of Research* 64(2):280–95.

Ren, X., Y. Zhou, Z. Huang, J. Sun, X. Yang, and K. Chen. 2017. A novel text structure feature extractor for chinese scene text detection and recognition. *IEEE Access* 5:3193–204. doi: 10.1109/ACCESS.2017.2676158.

Roy, P., A. Bhunia, A. Das, P. Dey, and U. Pal. 2016. HMM-based Indic handwritten word recognition using zone segmentation. *Pattern Recognition* 60:1057–75. doi: 10.1016/j.patcog.2016.04.012.

Saha, P. and A. Jaiswal. 2020. Handwriting Recognition Using Active Contour. In *Proceeding of the Artificial Intelligence and Evolutionary Computations in Engineering Systems. Advances in Intelligent Systems and Computing*. Springer, Singapore. 1056:505–14.

Shaw, B., S. K. Parui, and M. Shridhar. 2008. Off-line handwritten Devanagari word recognition: A holistic approach based on directional chain code feature and HMM. In *Proceeding of the International Conference on Information Technology* 203–8. Bhubaneswar. doi: 10.1109/ICIT.2008.33.

Singh, V., B. Kumar and T. Patnaik. 2013. Feature extraction techniques for handwritten text in various scripts: a survey. *International Journal of Soft Computing and Engineering* (IJSCE) 3(1):238–41.

Su, T. 2013. *Chinese Handwriting Recognition: An Algorithmic Perspective*. Springer Science & Business Media, Berlin, Heidelberg.

Vijaya Kumar, R. and U. Babu. 2019. Handwritten Hindi character recognition using deep learning techniques. *International Journal of Computer Sciences and Engineering*. 7(2):1–7.

Xiao, N., and Y. Ching. 2012. A novel hybrid CNN–SVM classifier for recognizing handwritten digits. *Pattern Recognition* 45 (4):1318–25.

Younis, K. 2017. Arabic handwritten character recognition based on deep convolutional neural networks. *Jordanian Journal of Computers and Information Technology (JJCIT)* 3 (3):186–200.

5

Safe Social Distance Monitoring and Face Mask Detection for Controlling COVID-19 Spread

Nikhil Ingale, Onkar Rane, and Piyush Kadam
RAIT

Vivek Kumar Singh
BIET

CONTENTS

5.1 Introduction

The current COVID-19 pandemic has wreaked havoc across the globe and has brought the world to its knees, plunging the global economy into a recession, with several countries observing a massive contraction in their GDPs, stock markets witnessing record falls, job losses, businesses going bankrupt, billions under lockdown, millions dead, and has severely affected the everyday life of an average human being. The disease is caused due to a virus named severe acute respiratory syndrome coronavirus 2. The disease first broke out in the city of Wuhan in Hubei province, China in December 2019 and eventually made its way to other countries, before it was declared a pandemic by the World Health Organization (WHO) on March 11, 2020. The disease has spread to more than 180 countries and has infected millions, with over 99 million confirmed cases along with over 2.1 million deaths globally, according to the WHO, as of January 25, 2021 [12]. Several pharmaceutical firms and educational institutes like Pfizer and Oxford-AstraZeneca have developed vaccines with high effectiveness. However, its mass production and subsequent vaccination of the masses will take several months, especially in developing and highly populated countries like India. Till then, the prudent course of action would be to maintain social distance and wear face masks to control

DOI: 10.1201/9781003283249-5

the spread of the disease. As per the guidelines issued by the WHO, people should wear face masks and a distance of at least 2 m must be maintained between adjacent persons.

During the pandemic, digital technologies like artificial intelligence, Internet of Things, machine learning, and deep learning have been at the forefront of public response to the pandemic, with several applications being developed based on these technologies. Several machine learning-based models have been developed to analyze and predict the future growth of the pandemic. Artificial intelligence is being used in applications like early detection and diagnosis of the infection, monitoring treatment, and contact tracing apps like Aarogya Setu, whereas Internet of Things has found applications in Remote Patient Monitoring, Vaccine cold chain monitoring, low-cost ventilators, and Healthcare delivery drones. Inspired by this, this chapter proposes a deep learning-based model for monitoring social distancing and face mask detection in surveillance videos.

The proposed real-time, YOLO v3 [13]-based model will monitor social distancing in a live video feed provided by a surveillance camera, and detect social distance violations if any. YOLO is a clever, real-time, object detection model, which uses a different approach, as compared to its peer like Convolutional Neural Network (CNN) and Recurrent Convolutional Neural Network (RCNN). The algorithm takes an image as an input, divides the image into regions called grids, and predicts bounding boxes and probabilities for each region. The algorithm then applies image classification and location on each grid and then predicts bounding boxes and their class probabilities. Finally, non-max suppression (a process to select the best bounding box) is applied to output the final image with detected objects and their respective bounding boxes. YOLO has gained popularity in recent times due to its high accuracy and its ability to detect objects in a real-time video feed.

The model will also perform the task of monitoring whether the people in the frame are wearing a face mask or not. The face detection model is based on MobileNetv2 [3] architecture. The face mask detection model will be based on MobileNetV2 architecture. MobileNetV2 is an upgraded version of MobileNetV1 [3] and is used in several mobile vision applications. It is a part of the Tensorflow library. It retains some of the features of MobileNetV2 and also incorporates new features, which makes it faster and more accurate than its predecessor. Due to its high accuracy and speed, MobileNetV2 can be used in various visual recognition-based applications.

This chapter is organized as follows. The following section presents the literature survey. In the next section, we describe the methodology for our methods. After that, the results are presented, followed by the conclusion, and finally, the references.

5.2 Literature Survey

This pandemic situation has been taking drastic turns nowadays. There are many guidelines provided by WHO like social distancing and wearing face masks. To monitor whether these guidelines are being followed or not, various systems have been proposed. A survey of some of such systems is provided below.

In [1,2] a face mask detection model has been developed by them. In [1], they have used ResNet50 and Yolo v2. ResNet-50 performs the task of extracting features and YOLO performs mask detection. They have merged two datasets: Face Mask Dataset and Medical Mask Dataset to create a single dataset. This model has an accuracy of 81%. In [2], they have used a MAFA dataset which consists of various images of people wearing and not wearing a mask. The model uses a combination of Local Linear Embedding and CNN for detection. This model has an accuracy of 76.4%.

Research reported in [3,4] has put forth a system to detect whether people are wearing masks or not. Both the systems are using MobileNetV2 architecture for object detection. They have used OpenCV and Tensorflow to train the model and SSD Multibox Detector for high-quality image classification which provides an accuracy of 76.8%. In [4] image preprocessing is done using Pytorch transforms and OpenCV. Then the face mask classifier is trained and generated using Pytorch. Then the MobileNet V2 classifier is applied to test data for results. To detect face masks Bosheng Qin et al. [5] have also proposed a model with high accuracy up to 99% using SrcNet. For this model, they have used a Medical Mask Dataset consisting of more than 3,500 images of people wearing, not wearing, and incorrectly wearing masks.

Another system as proposed in [6,7] utilized OpenCV and deep learning techniques to detect the crowd with the help of object detection and the Euclidean distance is computed to keep track of social distancing guidelines. This system provides an accuracy of 90%. The latter system tries to detect a person and estimates its pose and on that basis, they have drawn a circle for detecting that person and divided the circle into four spaces – intimate space, personal space, social space, and public space. They have set a threshold and found that the distance between two persons and the accuracy provided by this model is 86%. Rinkal et al. [8] is also checking if social distancing guidelines are followed or not. Here, they have developed a model named SocialdistancingNet-19 for detecting the frame of a person. Along with that, they have also used a reduced ResNet-50, MobileNet-V2, and ResNet-18 architecture. Here, they are working on images and video feeds. In images, they are displaying labels and showing safe/unsafe based on the distance between them. In video feeds, they are displaying the number of violations. The accuracy of their model is 92.8%.

From the literature review, we have found that still there are many challenges to controlling the pandemic. One of the challenges is to develop a system to monitor public places and gatherings for social distance violations and face mask detection simultaneously. It is still a challenge to increase the accuracy of the solution system keeping in mind the guidelines set by WHO. Therefore our objective is to develop a solution that can function efficiently while providing useful insights, reducing the man-work required to monitor public places. It is also considered to design a solution that is not system heavy and can function effortlessly on most of the systems.

5.3 Proposed Methodology

The proposed system helps in remotely inspecting the public gatherings for monitoring social distancing violations and facemask detection. This section outlines the solution system architecture and design of proposed system to function automatically to curb the spread of this infectious coronavirus (Figure 5.1).

As shown in Figure 5.1, the proposed system is divided into two modules: the social distance monitoring module and the facemask detection module. The CCTV camera footage is provided as input to both of these modules. Further details and working information of these models are as follows.

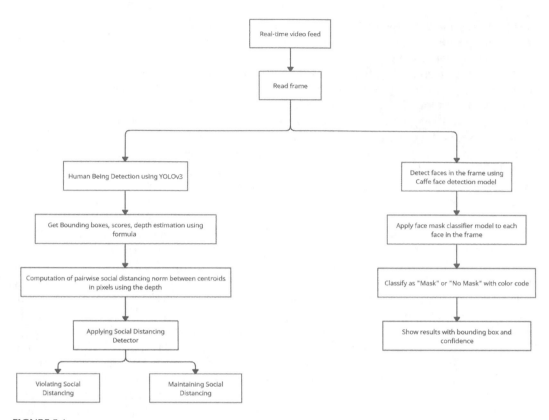

FIGURE 5.1
System workflow.

5.3.1 Social Distance Monitoring Model

In this model, Yolo version 3 is used for detecting humans in the live video feed. Yolo V3 is an object detection model with a balanced performance of FPS and mAP score [13], where FPS is frames per second and mAP score refers to mean average precision. Yolo v3 [13] provides the output in the form of type and location of the object and it does so in a single iteration. It models the problem of detecting objects as a regression problem to predict the class probability of the detected boxes. Yolo v3 has only one convolutional neural network which detects multiple objects at a time and provides bounding boxes around them along with the class probability of that particular object. Currently, there are three versions released by Yolo: Yolo v1, Yolo v2, and Yolo v3. The first version of Yolo was referred to from GoogleNet which is also an Inception network and was developed for object detection and classification in an image frame. The GoogleNet uses 14 and two fully connected layers while on the other hand a simple reduction layer is used by YoloV1 which is followed by CNN layers. The second version of Yolo, i.e. Yolo v2, was introduced to improve the accuracy and speed of the model for detecting objects in the provided input. It has Darknet-19 [14] at the core of its network which has 19 convolution layers, five max-pooling layers, and an output softmax layer for classifying various objects. It shows remarkable enhancement in mAP, FPS, and object classification score over Yolo v1. The purpose behind the development of Yolo v3 was to introduce multi-object detection and classification. Yolo v3 does so by using logistic classifiers rather than softmax as used in Yolo versions 1 and 2. In Yolo v3, Darknet-53 [13] is used as its core architecture which extricates feature maps for categorization. Darknet-53 uses short connections having up-sampling layers for concatenating and adding accuracy and depth to the network. Yolo version 3 gives the output in the form of three variables which predict spatial location on various scales in an image frame, which in turn increases the accuracy of detecting objects which are small in size. Every predicted object is tracked by classification scores, computing objectness, and boundary box regressor.

To track the detected individuals present in the surveillance footage, the deep sort technique [13] is utilized. This technique uses patterns from the bounding boxes of the detected objects in the images which are then concatenated with the temporal information for anticipating the linked trajectories of that particular object in the frame. For further statistical analysis, each object is considered and monitored by mapping unique identi-fiers of that object. This deep sort technique also helps in eliminating the various issues and challenges related to multiple viewpoints, occlusion, annotating training data, and non-stationary cameras.

The bounding boxes around the detected human beings achieved by object detection and tracking using YOLO v3 and Deepsort techniques are then used to calculate the norm of social distance for that particular frame of reference. It also efficiently computes the vectorized representation for detecting and identifying the groups of people who are vio-lating the social distancing rule. Along with this, to create the result in the live stream, each individual gets surrounded by a color-coded circle at the base, where the green color of the circle indicates that the particular individual is safe and following the social dis-tancing norm, while the red color of the circle indicates that the individual is too close to another individual. Each frame is also accompanied by the count of the number of people in the frame and the number of people violating the social distancing norm. Our workflow model for social distancing is given in Figure 5.2.

Following is the stepwise description of the model:

1. Feeding the surveillance footage to the trained object detection model to iden-tify and track the detected person in the footage. This model will surround each detected individual with a bounding box of rectangular shape.

2. Each of these bounding boxes will have three-dimensional feature space as (x, y, d), where x and y denote the coordinates of the centroid box and d corresponds to the distance/depth between the detected individual and the CCTV camera [3]. The distance is calculated using equation (5.1):

$$d = ((2*3:14*180)/(w+h*360)*1000+3) \qquad (5.1)$$

where w and h are the width and height of the bounding box, respectively.

3. The norm of social distance will then be computed for every pair of bounding boxes using equation (5.2):

$$|D|_2 = \sqrt{\sum_{i=1}^{n}(p_i - q_i)^2} \qquad (5.2)$$

where p and q are the coordinates of the bounding box.

4. The matrix of social distancing norms is then used to allocate the neighbors for each bounding box that falls under the defined closeness range. This closeness is

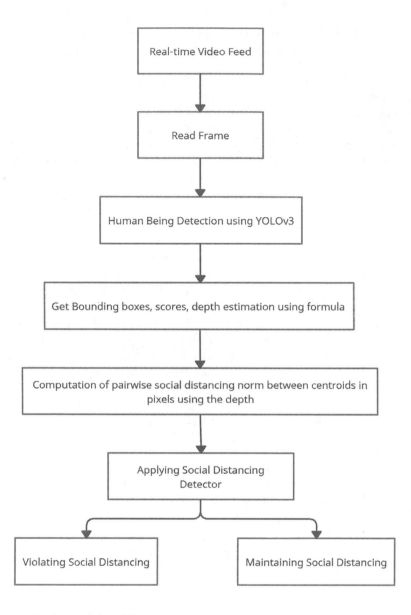

FIGURE 5.2
Social distance monitoring model workflow.

dynamically updated in accordance with the spatial location of the individual in a video frame ranging between 90 and 170 pixels.

5. Based on this range, the resultant color is assigned to the individual.

The above-mentioned steps describe the detailed working of the social distancing model.

5.3.2 Face Mask Detection Model

This model focuses on how to determine whether the individual detected in the video frame is wearing a face mask or not. It does so with the help of computer vision and deep learning algorithms by using the OpenCV, Tensor flow, Keras, Pytorch library, and MobileNetV2. The aim is to classify whether the person in the real-time video stream is wearing a mask or not.

The model is designed in two phases:

   i. Training face mask detector into classifier model using the dataset.
   ii. Detecting faces in the video stream and applying a classifier model to each face.

The detected face will then be classified as "No Mask" and "Mask" with an accuracy percentage beside it. The flow of the model is shown in Figure 5.3.

Face Mask Dataset: For extracting face and region of interest from the video frame, Open CV's Caffe Face Detector is used which is trained using an 800 image dataset. Further to identify the face mask, the model considers a dataset of size 978 images which consist of 659 images of people wearing a mask and 319 images of people not wearing masks. The dataset consists of images that are of different resolutions and sizes and are extracted from various sources or cameras of dissimilar resolutions.

Phase 1: This is the training phase wherein the Face Mask Dataset is loaded into the system and the model is trained on this dataset using MobileNetV2 deep learning classifier. MobileNetV2 is a state-of-the-art for mobile visual recognition including classification, object detection, and semantic segmentation. This classifier uses depth-wise separable convolution which is introduced to dramatically reduce the complexity cost and model size of the network and hence is suitable for mobile devices, or devices that have low computational power.

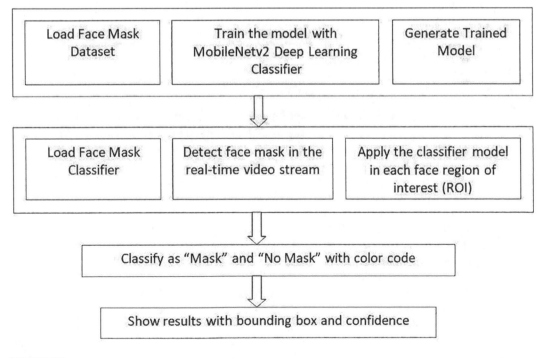

FIGURE 5.3
Face mask detection model workflow.

The layers of MobilenetV2 architecture are as follows:

i. Average pooling layer with 7×7 weights
ii. Linear layer with ReLu activation function
iii. Dropout layer
iv. Linear layer with softmax activation function with the result of two values. The ultimate layer of softmax function generates the result in probability for classifying the face into "Mask" or "No Mask".

Phase 2: The second phase demonstrates the working of the model in real time where the surveillance footage is provided as input to the system and the face mask classifier model is loaded. After this, the region of interest, i.e. faces, is detected in real-time video frame using the Caffe face detector model which is a pre-trained model in the OpenCV framework, and the classifier is applied to each face. The system provides the output using color codes such as red for "No Mask" and green for "Mask" with confidence.

5.4 Results

The proposed face mask and social distancing models were implemented on a video stream from a surveillance camera. On implementation, it was found that the face mask detection model achieved an accuracy of 93%, whereas the social distancing model provided an accuracy of 92%. The proposed face mask detection model performed better than the model in the surveyed paper, the latter providing an accuracy of 81%. Similarly, the social distancing model performed better than its counterpart, which provided an accuracy of 90%.

5.4.1 For Social Distancing Monitoring Model

The proposed YOLOv3 model was implemented on a system having an NVIDIA 150MX with a 2GB graphics card. The dataset used for training the model was provided by the Open Images dataset. Various images with a class label as Person were downloaded via the OIDv4 toolkit. This dataset comprises eight hundred images which are filtered by manually sorting to contain only the true samples and avoiding all the false ones. The training and testing data is obtained by further dividing the dataset into two parts 80% and 20%, where 80% of images are used for training the model and the remaining 20% are used for testing the model for accuracy. Then the preprocessing of the images was performed by scaling all of the images to a fixed dimension value of 416 pixels.

The model performance is constantly monitored in the training phase using parameters like mAP score along with classification, localization, and an overall loss in the result as shown in Figure 5.4. It was observed that YOLO v3 achieves decent and acceptable results. It achieved a good balance in FPS score, mAP score, and training time. This model achieved a mAP score of 0.85, FPS of 23 frames/second, total loss of 0.87, and 7,560 NoI (Number of Iterations). This trained model of Yolo V3 is then used to track and monitor the social distancing norm in the CCTV surveillance footage. The model achieved an accuracy of 92%.

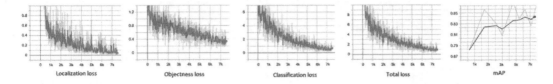

FIGURE 5.4
Social distancing model performance.

TABLE 5.1

Comparison of Proposed Social Distancing Model with Other Models

Model	Accuracy (%)
Shashi Yadav et al. [10]	91
Liu et al. [12] (SSD300)	74.3
Liu et al. [12] (SSD512)	76.8
YOLO v3-based social distancing model (proposed model)	92

The social distance model can be further subdivided into two tasks. First detecting a person and another is to check whether there is 3 feet (1 m) distance between two persons or not. For this model, we have used OpenCV and YoloV3. We have preferred Yolo version 3 over previous versions because YOLO v3 gives the output in the form of three variable predictions for every spatial location using different scales in the frame, which increases the accuracy of distance between the camera and the detected human and also detects the small objects more accurately and efficiently.

As seen in Table 5.1, the social distancing model developed by Shashi Yadav et al. [3] provides an accuracy of 91%, whereas the two models proposed by Liu et al. [9], with the former based on SSD300 and the latter based on SSD512, provide accuracies of 74.3% and 76.8%, respectively. In comparison, the proposed YOLOv3 model fares better, providing an accuracy of 92%.

5.4.2 For Face Mask Detection Model

The proposed face mask detection model is based on MobileNetv2 architecture and uses technologies like Tensorflow, Keras, OpenCV, and Caffe. The model follows a two-step process for face mask detection. The first step involves detecting faces using a pre-trained model by OpenCV named Caffe. The model was trained using a web images dataset. The latter step performs the important task of identifying whether the person is wearing a mask or not, using MobileNetv2. The model uses a dataset consisting of 978 images belonging to two classes:

- with_mask: 659 images
- without_mask: 319 images

The images used were images of people wearing and not wearing masks. The images were collected from sources like Kaggle dataset, RMFD dataset, and Bing Search API. The model was trained via TensorFlow-gpu==2.0.0. After training and implementation on test data, the model gave an accuracy of 93%.

TABLE 5.2

Facemask Detection Model Performance

	Precision	Recall	F1-Score	Support
with_mask	0.99	0.86	0.92	383
without_mask	0.88	0.99	0.93	384
accuracy			0.93	767
macro avg	0.93	0.93	0.93	767
weighted avg	0.93	0.93	0.93	767

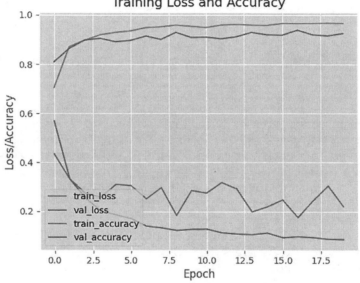

FIGURE 5.5
Training loss and accuracy graph.

As seen in Table 5.2, the model achieved a precision score of 0.99, recall score of 0.86, and F1-score of 0.92 for the with_mask test set, whereas for without_mask, it achieved a precision score of 0.88, recall score of 0.99 and F1-score of 0.93. The model achieved a macro average score of 0.93 and a weighted average score of 0.93. We got the accuracy/loss training curve plot as shown in Figure 5.5.

For our face mask detection model, we have used OpenCV, Tensor Flow, Keras, Caffe, and MobileNetV2 frameworks. The accuracy obtained in this model was 93%. For face-mask detection, we have a dataset of 659 images wearing masks and 319 images without wearing masks. The challenge that we faced was if poor quality video is presented then detection was not proper as the dataset we had was limited. The detection can be further enhanced by increasing the dataset.

As seen in Table 5.3, the face mask detection model developed by Ching et al. [10] exhibits an accuracy of 91.9%, whereas the model proposed by Mingjie Jiang et al. [11] provides an accuracy of 82.3%. In comparison to both, the proposed MobileNetv2-based model fares better, providing an accuracy of 93%.

TABLE 5.3

Comparison of Proposed Face Mask Detection Model with Other Models

Model	Accuracy (%)
Chiang et al. [13]	91.9
Mingjie Jiang et al. [14]	82.3
Face mask detection model (proposed model)	93

5.5 Conclusion

The proposed system in this project which is based on computer vision and deep learning is being developed to help the local police and COVID workers in minimizing their physical surveillance work in public areas and containment zones where surveillance is performed by means of CCTV camera footage in real time. This system will play a very crucial role in maintaining a secure environment and will ensure individual protection by monitoring public areas to contain and avoid the spread of the COVID-19 virus. Thus, the proposed system will be fruitful and efficient in the current scenario where the lockdown is being eased and containment of the virus is the primary task for the government. According to the COVID preventive measures provided by WHO, the proposed system has addressed social distance monitoring and identification of face masks that will help to contain the spread of the virus. The implementation of this system was successfully tested on a real-time webcam feed and the system performed well with an accuracy of 92%. This system has the potential ability to significantly reduce the number of violations by real-time monitoring of the public areas to improve public safety by saving time and helping to reduce the spread of coronavirus. The proposed solution can be deployed at various places like shopping malls, railway stations, bus stations, airports, and temples.

References

1. Loey, M., Manogaran, G., Taha, M., Khalifa, N.E. 2020. Fighting against COVID-19: A novel deep learning model based on YOLO-v2 with ResNet-50 for medical face mask detection. *Sustainable Cities and Society.* doi: 10.1016/j.scs.2020.102600.

2. Ge, S., Li, J., Ye, Q., Luo, Z. 2017. Detecting Masked Faces in the Wild with LLE-CNNs. *2017 IEEE Conference on Computer Vision and Pattern Recognition (CVPR)*, Honolulu, HI, pp. 426–434, doi: 10.1109/CVPR.2017.53.

3. Yadav, S. 2020. Deep learning based safe social distinctive and face mask detection in public areas for COVID-19 safety guidelines adherence. *International Journal for Research in Applied Science and Engineering Technology* 8: 1368–1375. doi: 10.22214/ijraset.2020.30560.

4. Vinitha, V. 2020. COVID-19 facemask detection with deep learning and computer vision. *International Research Journal of Engineering and Technology (IRJET)* 7(8): 3127–3132.

5. Qin, B., Li, D. 2020. Identifying facemask-wearing condition using image super-resolution with classification network to prevent COVID-19. Available: https://doi.org/10.21203/rs.3.rs-28668/v1.

6. Visal, R., Theurkar, A., Shukla, B. 2020. Monitoring social distancing for Covid-19 using OpenCV and deep learning. *International Research Journal of Engineering and Technology (IRJET)* 7(6): 2258–2260.

7. Cristani, M., ADBLue, V., Murino, F. S., Vinciarelli, A. 2020. The visual social distancing problem. IEEE Access 8: 126876–126886. doi: 10.1109/ACCESS.2020.3008370.

8. Keniya, R., Mehendale, N. 2020. Real-time social distancing detector using social distancing Net-19 deep learning network. *SSRN Electronic Journal*. doi: 10.2139/ssrn.3669311.

9. Liu, W., Anguelov, D., Erhan, D., Szegedy, C., Reed, S., Fu, C.-Y., Berg, A. 2016. SSD: Single Shot MultiBox Detector. *Computer Vision – ECCV* 9905. 21–37. doi: 10.1007/978-3-319-46448-0_2

10. Chiang, D. 2020. Detecting faces and determining whether people are wearing masks. https://github.com/AIZOOTech/FaceMaskDetection.

11. Jiang, M., Fan, X., Yan, H. 2020. RetinaMask: A Face Mask detector. arXiv.org. [Online]. Available: https://arxiv.org/abs/2005.03950.2020.

12. https://www.pharmaceutical-technology.com/special-focus/covid-19/international-update-global-covid-infections-approach-100-million-as-daily-case-count-averages-650000/.

13. https://medium.com/syncedreview/the-yolov3-object-detection-network-is-fast-fcceae0ab650.

14. https://amrokamal-47691.medium.com/yolo-yolov2-and-yolov3-all-you-want-to-know-7e3e92dc4899.

6

Real-Time Virtual Fitness Tracker and Exercise Posture Correction

Tejas Kachare
Vishwakarma Institute of Technology

Manisha Sinha
University of Engineering and Management Jaipur

Siddharth Kakade
Vishwakarma Institute of Technology

Aryan Kakade
Sinhgad College of Engineering

Siddharth Nigade
Pune Institute of Computer Technology

CONTENTS

6.1 Introduction

As per the reports of the World Health Organization, exercising regularly is a key strategy in preventing major diseases. This can forestall conditions like weight, hypertension, and helpless cholesterol levels, which can prompt cardiovascular failure and stroke. When all

DOI: 10.1201/9781003283249-6

is set and done, as an individual's age, actually they become less dynamic. Be that as it may, as we become more established, we need more customary exercise, not less. In 2019, the National Center for Health Statistics found that around one out of three grown-ups who'd visited a specialist in the previous year had been encouraged to begin or proceed with an activity program. More seasoned grown-ups matured 45–85 were bound to be prompted by their primary care physicians to work out. Among grown-ups who matured 85 years and were more established, the rate of accepting counsel to practice almost multiplied over the previous decade [1]. Active work forestalls bone misfortune, increases muscle strength, and improves coordination and equilibrium. Studies have demonstrated that expanded degrees of actual work diminish the danger of many maturing-related infections, including cardiovascular sickness.

The major barriers stated by AARP's survey paper for people to perform exercise are lack of time and motivation, expensive gym membership, self-consciousness, lack of knowledge of doing exercise, and health problems. Among these, around two of the four people, i.e., almost 50% of adults, avoid exercise because of not having the time or the gyms are just too expensive [2].

In this chapter, we present a reliable and efficient two-stage approach to analyzing exercise postures. The system will provide the repetition count and also suggestions to correct exercise postures. We have focused on developing a real-time body tracking algorithm and a robust statistical algorithm to process the body key points obtained from the first stage for a few basic exercises like squats, push-ups, plank, and skipping. The first stage compress of this model for body tracking, resulting in a total of 21 body key points. The statistical algorithm at stage two is a phase-based model wherein the correctness of exercise is based on the deviation in the angle between significant body key points and an ideal exercise posture.

6.2 Literature Review

Amit Nagarkoti et al. [3] intend to facilitate people to perform these workouts independently. The model in real-time multi-person 2D posture estimation with Part Affinity Fields was used. Then, using the Lucas–Kanade method as implemented in OpenCV for Optical Flow tracking, the Optical Flow tracking mechanism is utilized to recognize body components from nearby frames. The only fault in the system was that then the user has to provide the video of the trainer first, with which the algorithm will compare.

Up to four meters from the camera, the author in the paper [4] exhibited perfect real-time object identification and tracking, but at eight meters away, only 60% of the motions were effective. They used Haar feature-based cascade classifier to detect and focus on the user and TraceBodyObject to trace each body part.

Alexander Toshev et al. [5] presented a deep neural network-based approach for estimating human posture. They demonstrated a cascade of deep neural network regressors that produce high-precision posture estimations. A comprehensive examination of state-of-the-art performance on four academic benchmarks of various real-world images was also given in the research.

Alex Kendall et al. [6] present a strong and real-time monocled six degrees of the freedom localization system. Without any further engineering or graph optimization, the system is trained as a convolutional neural network to regress the 6-DOF camera posture. Their algorithm can run in real-time both indoors and outdoors, and it only takes 5 ms/frame to compute. For large-scale outdoor scenes, it achieves roughly 2 m and 6-degree precision, and 0.5 m and 10-degree accuracy indoors.

In [7], the research conducted into image filtering as a preprocessing stage for the Lucas–Kanade Optical Flow computing framework. They also discovered that the Gaussian filter outperforms other filters in their research.

6.2.1 Motivation for the Research

As per the review reports of AARP, the thinking for physical inactiveness inside individuals is sub-sorted into four kinds of what else is going on in their lives, as many as 33% of non-exercisers claim that medical difficulties prevent them from exercising. For a couple (8%), the chance of conceivably getting harmed is also a huge inspiration driving them to do wrong workouts currently. The subsequent one is that time limitations over individuals deprive them of doing any sort of activity. People expressed that finding an opportunity to rehearse when you are feeling like the test is a huge issue for a few. Thirty-seven percent state they are too depleted or lacking the energy to work out, the most broadly perceived clarification Americans 50–79 give for not participating in proactive errands. One out of four (26%) essentially says the individual being referred to needs additional time. This is especially an issue for the working professionals so far, diverged from the people who are not (39% versus 16%). The third classification of issues looked at by individuals being helpless area or environmental factors. Having a good spot to rehearse that is secured and affordable—and having someone to rehearse with—are also huge reasons why people aged 50 and over don't work out. The outline says that practically one in every three (33.33%) individuals don't rehearse because the cooperation with gym instructors via online mediums is exorbitantly expensive, posing as the obvious reason for the individual not working out. Additionally, thirteen percent regard not having anyone to rehearse with as their primary reason for missing workouts. The last and fourth sub-class is freshness or absence of information. Experts expressed that exercise can moreover be a staggering task for those not used to the activity. Around one of every eight (13%), people allude to feeling uncertain as a critical inspiration posing for the reason why the individual doesn't work out. Additionally, just around one of every 20 (6%) cases says there is an exorbitant measure of the individual would have to sort out some way to start working out.

6.3 Methodology

6.3.1 Brief Overview of Need for the System

The proposed architecture is based on two key elements, a 2D human body tracking model and a statistical algorithm providing repetition count, suggestions for the wrong posture, and also a complete exercise report as shown in Figure 6.1. As operating the model in real-time is the key aspect of the research, the 2D human body tracking model is enhanced using the Lucas–Kanade algorithm, and details are presented in Section 6.3.2. The body key coordinates extracted from the body tracking model are further fed to statistical algorithm presented in Section 6.3.3, which out-turn in the repetition count, real-time suggestions for the correctness in exercise posture and also providing the detailed exercise report.

FIGURE 6.1
Overall proposed architecture.

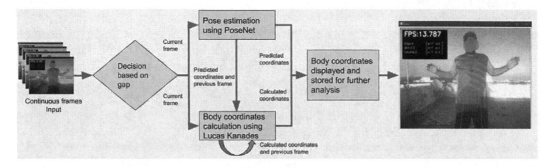

FIGURE 6.2
Overall architecture of the system.

6.3.2 Enhancing 2D Body Tracking Performance

The strategy that we contrived with the end goal of human movement following endeavors three primary parts: body movement recognition, include following, and strong assessment. As demonstrated in Figure 6.2, the detection mechanism is done using a cutting-edge algorithm called PoseNet. The overall system takes an input frame, and then the pose estimation and the Lucas–Kanade algorithm are executed for alternate frames or depending upon the gap.

It runs over the Gaussian pyramid of images as shown in Figure 6.3. The pyramid approach is adapted to track the larger object movement or object moving with a larger speed [8].

6.3.2.1 Initial Body Pose Detection Using PoseNet

Body-centric issues present are at first recognized with OpenPose, which yields 21 2D body points. Given an info picture, OpenPose gauges the area of the key points of the relative multitude of bodies found in the scene and while it gauges the probability of each central issue being associated with different ones [9]. Because OpenPose is a locator, it does not rely on previous casing data or the movement of the focuses. It simply uses a deep convolutional neural network architecture to locate the body tracking points in an RGB image, and then it connects them using a heuristic computation. Operation likewise discharges a proportion of certainty (going from 0 to 1) for each recognized key point and traditionally sets to (0,0,0) any undetected purpose of a body [10].

6.3.2.2 Feature Tracking Using the Lucas–Kanade Algorithm

Once OpenPose has recognized the critical spots, the Lucas–Kanade (LK) tracker may be used to locate them in the following frames. By analyzing the fluctuation of pixel intensity

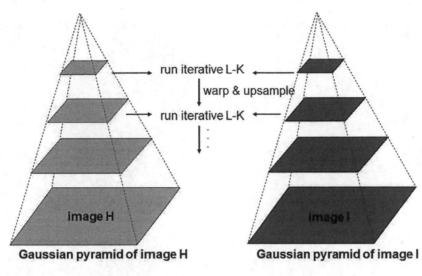

FIGURE 6.3
Pyramid structure in the Lucas–Kanade algorithm.

in a region, the Lucas–Kanade algorithm approximates the displacement value of a pixel in two neighboring frames [11]. Taking u as the movement with respect to x and v as the movement w.r.t. y and $I(x, y)$ the pixel intensity at pixel (x, y) LK as shown in equation 6.1.

$$\frac{dI}{dx}(x,y,t).u + \frac{dI}{dy}(x,y,t).v = -\frac{dI}{dt}(x,y,t)\frac{dI}{dx}(x,y,t).u + \frac{dI}{dy}(x,y,t).v = -\frac{dI}{dt}(x,y,t) \quad (6.1)$$

A neighborhood of pixels is anticipated to contain more conditions than an arbitrary pixel, which has two questions (u, v) and one condition. In this manner, the model becomes over decided and LK proposes the least-squares arrangement that midpoints the optical stream surmises over the area. LK is built over Optical Flow vectors that are computed according to the following algorithm [12].

1. **Step 1:** Compute Image x and Image y derivatives.
2. **Step 2:** Compute the difference Image It=Image 1 – Image 2.
3. **Step 3:** Smoothen the image components Ix, ly, and It.
4. **Step 4:** Solve the Linear Equations for each pixel and calculate the Eigenvalues.
5. **Step 5:** Depending on the Eigenvalues obtained, solve the equations using Cramer's rule.
6. **Step 6:** Plot the Optical Flow vectors.

This algorithm is a lot quicker than the recognition one since its unpredictability is just subject to the number of followed focuses and not on the number of pixels in the picture. The principal issue with this tracker, likewise with all the trackers dependent on visual highlights, is that it can't deal with impediments. The mix of the central issues indicator with the LK tracker permits to help the speed of the posture assessor; however, it doesn't ensure a liquid reproduction of human movement.

(a) Simple Body Tracking

(b) Tracking with proposed architecture and gap: 2

(c) Tracking with proposed architecture and gap: 3

(d) Tracking with proposed architecture and gap: 4

FIGURE 6.4
Results with and without proposed architecture.

As shown in Figure 6.4, the experimentation was carried out in a real-time paradigm, altering the gap after an instance. During the experimentation, the gap was altered as 1, 2, and 3. The respective FPS obtained by increasing the gap can be seen in Figure 6.4.

6.3.3 Statistical Model of Proposed Model

The statistical model is proposed to process the 2D body coordinates obtained from Section 3.2 and generate the repetition count and suggestions for the wrong posture. Figure 6.5 shows the algorithm for counting repetitions. As shown in the figure, the following are the steps of the algorithm in detail.

Step 1: Take the stream of 2D body coordinates from the proposed model in Section 3.2 for the current frame.

Step 2: Drop all the unnecessary key points and store all the necessary key points in a dictionary. Also, check for all necessary key points, if the confidence of all points is above a threshold or not as shown in equation 6.2.

$$\forall x, \text{Confidence of } x \geq T \forall x, \text{Confidence of } x \geq \text{Threshold Confidence} \qquad (6.2)$$

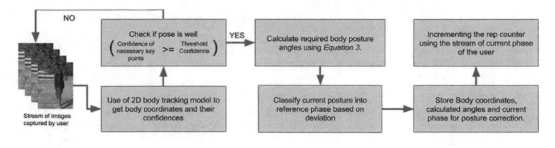

FIGURE 6.5
Architecture of proposed statistical model.

> where x is necessary to the key point.
>
> For example, for exercise class squats, body key points are nose, shoulder, hip, knee, and ankle.

Step 3: Calculate the angles using filtered key points from the previous step using equation 6.3.

$$a = \left(p1 \cdot x - p2 \cdot x, \; p1 \cdot y - p2 \cdot y \right)$$

$$b = \left(p1 \cdot x - p3 \cdot x, \; p1 \cdot y - p3 \cdot y \right)$$

$$\theta = \cos^{-1}\left(\frac{a \cdot b}{|a| \cdot |b|} \right) \theta = \cos^{-1}\left(\frac{a \cdot b}{|a| \cdot |b|} \right) \tag{6.3}$$

> where $p1$, $p2$, and $p3$ are three key points, a and b are two vectors, and θ is the angle between those two vectors.

Step 4: Calculate the deviation of angles with the reference pose angle and classify the current posture into one of the reference phases.

Step 5: Furthermore, store the body coordinates, calculated angles, and current phase for posture correction suggestions.

Step 6: Increment the repetition counter using the stream of current phases, i.e., a phase pattern like 0,0,0,1,1,2,3,3,2,2,2,1,0 means to increment the counter by 1.

6.4 Results and Discussion

6.4.1 Real-Time 2D Pose Estimation

Figure 6.6 represents the execution time plots with varying gaps from 1 to 6, giving avg fps up to 25.6. The execution time of PoseNet is greater than 0.2s while for the frames with the Lucas–Kanade algorithm is nearly equal to 0.05. Hence avg execution time can be determined using equation 6.4. Hence the best-obtained execution time for the proposed model is 0.0783 s.

$$\text{Avg Execution Time} = \frac{\text{Posenet Execution Time} + (\text{Gap} - 1) * \text{LK Execution Time}}{\text{Gap}} \tag{6.4}$$

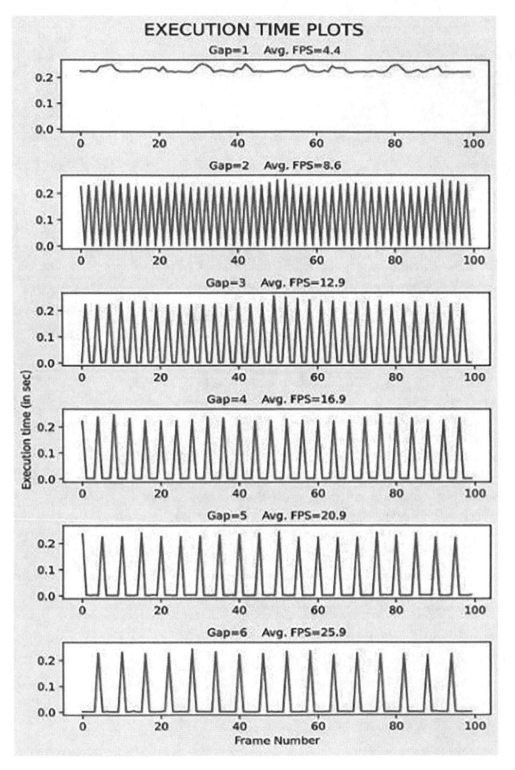

FIGURE 6.6
Execution time graph of proposed body tracking model.

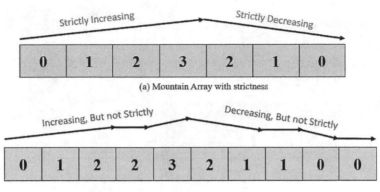

FIGURE 6.7
Phase list pattern for updating repetition counter.

6.4.2 Repetition Counter Mechanism

The repetition counter mechanism works on basis of the obtained phases stream. The phase list is initially empty, and the corresponding posture is added to the phase list after each phase categorization. For each update in the list, call the function "UpdateCounter" to check whether to update the counter or not. The counter update depends on the following two factors:

1. **Min-Max-Min Phase Pattern**: It checks if the phase list pattern is present in the form of 0-3-0 as a min-max-min phase.
2. **Mountain Array Pattern:** It checks whether the list is in the mountain array format as shown in Figure 6.7. Both the mountain array with strictness and without strictness pattern is acceptable for the UpdateCounter.

6.4.3 User Feedback and Posture Correction Mechanism

The most deviated frame per phase is chosen from each phase using the stored body coordinate angles. Furthermore, these frames are compared to reference frames, with erroneous angles being highlighted in red. For better understanding, the incorrect frames and corresponding correct postures are shown as an output as shown in Figure 6.8, at the end of exercise or if the user performs incorrect posture multiple times.

6.5 Conclusion

This research accomplished all of the major goals for a virtual gym trainer. The suggested model is a stable method that addresses a virtual gym trainer's shortcomings. It continually analyses a user's form and provides real-time feedback and comprehensive suggestions throughout exercises. With frame rates up to 25.6 frames per second and a frame execution time of 0.783 s, perfect real-time object detection and tracking was accomplished.

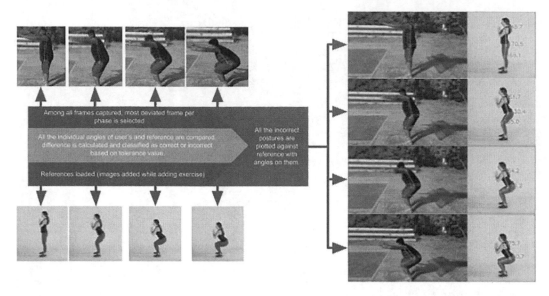

FIGURE 6.8
Incorrect posture suggestion.

The identification and tracking method are a valuable addition that may be used in other systems as well. The system as a whole seems promising, and it may be expanded for further capabilities in the future.

References

1. https://www.heart.org/HEARTORG/HealthyLiving/PhysicalActivity/StartWalking/The-Price-of-Inactivity_UCM_307974_Article.jsp#.WUBgGxMrKb-.
2. Exercise Attitudes and Behaviors: A Survey of Adults | Conducted by Roper ASW Report Prepared by RoperASW | https://assets.aarp.org/rgcenter/health/exercise.pdf
3. A. Nagarkoti, R. Teotia, A. K. Mahale and P. K. Das. 2019. Realtime indoor workout analysis using machine learning & computer vision. *41st Annual International Conference of the IEEE Engineering in Medicine and Biology Society (EMBC)*, pp. 1440–1443, doi: 10.1109/EMBC.2019.8856547. URL: https://ieeexplore.ieee.org/abstract/document/8856547.
4. D. Brown, M. Ndleve. 2019. Virtual Gym Instructor. URL: https://www.researchgate.net/publication/335378603_Virtual_Gym_Instructor.
5. A. Toshev, C. Szegedy. 2013. DeepPose: Human Pose Estimation via Deep Neural Networks. *Proceedings of the IEEE Computer Society Conference on Computer Vision and Pattern Recognition.* 10.1109/CVPR.2014.214. URL: https://www.researchgate.net/publication/259335300_Deep Pose_Human_Pose_Estimation_via_Deep_Neural_Networks.
6. A. Kendall, M. Grimes, R. Cipolla. 2015. Convolutional networks for real-time 6-DOF camera relocalization. URL: https://www.researchgate.net/publication/277334078_Convolutional_networks_for_real-time_6-DOF_camera_relocalization.
7. N. Sharmin, R. Brad. 2012. Optimal filter estimation for Lucas-Kanade Optical Flow. *Sensors (Basel, Switzerland).* 12: 12694–12709. 10.3390/s120912694. URL: https://www.researchgate.net/publication/232742482_Optimal_Filter_Estimation_for_Lucas-Kanade_Optical_Flow.

8. J.-Y. Bouguet. 1999. Pyramidal implementation of the lucas kanade feature tracker.

9. G. Gkioxari, B. Hariharan, R. Girshick and J. Malik. 2014. Using k-Poselets for Detecting People and Localizing Their Keypoints. *IEEE Conference on Computer Vision and Pattern Recognition*, pp. 3582–3589. doi: 10.1109/CVPR.2014.458. URL: https://ieeexplore.ieee.org/document/6909853.

10. M. Sun, P. Kohli and J. Shotton. 2012. Conditional regression forests for human pose estimation. *IEEE Conference on Computer Vision and Pattern Recognition*, pp. 3394–3401. doi: 10.1109/ CVPR.2012.6248079. URL: https://ieeexplore.ieee.org/document/6248079.

11. L. Y. Siong, S. S. Mokri, A. Hussain, N. Ibrahim and M. M. Mustafa. 2009. Motion detection using Lucas Kanade algorithm and application enhancement. *International Conference on Electrical Engineering and Informatics*, Selangor, pp. 537–542, doi: 10.1109/ICEEI.2009.5254757.

12. S. Oron, A. Bar-Hille, S. Avidan. 2014. Extended Lucas-Kanade tracking. In: Fleet D., Pajdla T., Schiele B., Tuytelaars T. (eds) *Computer Vision – ECCV 2014. ECCV 2014.* Lecture Notes in Computer Science, vol 8693. Springer, Cham. https://doi.org/10.1007/978-3-319-10602-1_10 URL: https://link.springer.com/chapter/10.1007/978-3-319-10602-1_10.

7

Role of Data Science in Revolutionizing Healthcare

Yashsingh Manral
University of Mumbai

Siddhesh Unhavane
University of Illinois at Urbana-Champaign

Jyoti Kundale
Ramrao Adik Institute of Technology, D.Y. Patil Deemed to be University

CONTENTS

7.1 Introduction

The art of extracting significant insights and trends from data has existed since prehistoric times. The ancient Egyptians, for example, employed statistical data to improve tax collection efficiency, and guess what? Every year, they prophesied that the Nile River would flood. Since then, many of us in the data science area have carved out a unique and distinct field for our work. Data science is the name of the field. Since then, many of us in the data science area have carved out a unique and distinct field for our work.

Today, data science is fast expanding to encompass all businesses. Healthcare is one of these unique industries. Today with healthcare, businesses are transitioning from volume-based to value-based business models, which necessitates doctors and nurses to work longer hours in order to be more productive and efficient. This will enhance healthcare through changing people with lifestyles and encouraging them to live longer lives, as well as preventing diseases, illnesses, and infections.

Healthcare firms, like every other industry, generate a significant amount of data, which brings both opportunities and challenges. It is now feasible to detect the symptoms of a disease at a very early stage because of data science applications in healthcare.

Healthcare data has become more complex over the last few years as a result of the vast amount of data that has just become available, as well as the quick change of technologies

DOI: 10.1201/9781003283249-7

and mobile applications, and the discovery of new diseases. As a result, healthcare organizations think that healthcare data analytics technologies are critical for managing vast amounts of complicated data, strengthening healthcare organizations, and assisting medical practices in achieving high levels of efficiency and workflow accuracy.

We'll learn how data science is transforming the healthcare industry in this chapter. The coronavirus pandemic has shown us that medicine and healthcare are two of the most vital aspects of our existence.

This chapter will give you a comprehensive idea of data science in healthcare as well as its benefits in the healthcare sector. Moreover, this chapter will discuss some of the real-world cases of data science in diabetes detection.

In the healthcare industry, data plays a crucial role in bringing improvisation and innovation. The healthcare data generate avenues for several discoveries. It inspires to run the evaluation and produce simpler drugs. It establishes better communication between patients and doctors. It improves the general quality of healthcare giving a deeper insight into a patient's health report and the way a selected drug is responding.

As the healthcare industry progresses, the utilization of data science has increased and is considered the foremost important aspect of innovation. With the collection of knowledge through many devices and tools that patients are using, researchers, scientists, and doctors are becoming conscious of the healthcare challenges and digging for solutions to supply efficient patient care.

According to a study, every physical body generates 2 terabytes of data per day. This information covers brain activities, stress levels, pulses, sugar levels, and much more. We now have more advanced technology to handle such massive amounts of data, one of which is data science. It uses recorded data to assist in the monitoring of a patient's health.

It is now feasible to recognize the symptoms of a disease at an early stage because of the application of data science in healthcare. In addition, with the introduction of a variety of modern instruments and technology, doctors are now able to monitor patient health from afar.

Doctors and hospital administrators were not prepared in the past to handle large groups of patients at the same time. The patient's problems will not worsen as a result of the lack of effective therapy. In 2019, the global artificial intelligence in the healthcare market was worth USD 3.39 billion. From 2019 to 2027, the market is predicted to increase at a compound annual growth rate of 43.6%, with a market size of USD 61.69 billion in 2027. The predicted difference is significant, which is why we have written this chapter. We've given you a better idea of how data science can be used in healthcare. However, the situation has suddenly altered. Doctors are frequently updated about the health status of patients through wearable devices, thanks to the development of data science and machine learning applications. The hospital's management can then dispatch junior doctors, assistants, or nurses to the homes of those patients.

Doctors are frequently updated about the health status of patients through wearable devices, thanks to the development of data science and machine learning applications. The hospital's management can then dispatch junior doctors, assistants, or nurses to the homes of those patients. Hospitals can also install various diagnostic equipment and devices for those patients. These gadgets, which are based on knowledge science, may collect data from patients such as their pulse, vital signs, blood temperature, and so on. Updates and notifications in mobile applications provide doctors with real-time data and the current status of a patient's health. They will then diagnose the illnesses and aid junior doctors or nurses in providing appropriate therapies to the patient's reception. This is frequently how data science aids in the technology-assisted care of patients. Data science is changing the healthcare industry in many ways by improving medical image analysis, providing predictive medication, and creating a global database of medical records, drug discovery, bioinformatics, and virtual assistants. And that's just the beginning! Who knows where this integration of the field of data science and healthcare may lead in the future.

7.2 Applications of Data Science

Data science applications have not evolved overnight. One should be thankful for faster computing techniques and cheaper storage frameworks; we can now predict outcomes in minutes, which could take us several human hours to process. Data science may be a career field that stems from multiple disciplines. There is no industry within the world today that doesn't use data. Data has become the necessity of industries and thus, data science features a sizable amount of applications. The field of data science includes a variety of applications that are outspread in numerous industries. In this chapter, we'll look at a few of the most important data science applications and how they're affecting the world's industries today.

So, here may be a list of top data science applications.

1. **Finance:** Customer segmentation, strategic decision making, algorithmic trading, and risk analytics.
2. **Healthcare:** Medical image analysis, drug discovery, bioinformatics, and virtual assistants.
3. **E-commerce:** Identifying consumers, recommending products, and analyzing reviews.
4. **Manufacturing:** Predicting potential problems, monitoring systems, automating manufacturing units, maintenance schedules, and anomaly detection
5. **Transport:** Self-driving cars, car monitoring system, enhanced driving experience, and enhancing the safety of passengers

In the healthcare industry, data plays a crucial role in bringing improvisation and innovation. Healthcare data generates avenues for many discoveries. It inspires to run the evaluation and produce simpler drugs. It establishes better communication between patients and doctors. It improves the general quality of healthcare giving a deeper insight into a patient's health report and the way a selected drug is responding.

As the healthcare industry advances, the usage and implementation of the field of data science have increased and are taken into account as one of the important and foremost aspects of innovation. With the emerging collection of data through many devices and tools that patients are using, researchers, scientists, and doctors are becoming conscious of the healthcare challenges and digging for solutions to provide efficient patient care.

Healthcare stores data related to practices like clinical trials, electronic medical records, genetic information, care management databases, billing, internet research, and social media data. Patients used tools like Babylon, DocPlanner, and TataHealth to determine communication between the health professionals and to book appointments, through the synchronization of those tools it becomes easier to manage customer data. One of the major examples of this generation that we have is the COVID-19 pandemic.

The COVID-19 pandemic has become unprecedented and experts say that there are so many unknowns—the virus is moving quite fast, and it's seemingly unpredictable. The urgency of these diseases is that we cannot believe only traditional methods to understand how the disease works and therefore the way it'll spread—we must utilize all data and advanced tools at our disposal, broadly within various companies and across universities. The vaccine program is being pushed forward by a range of data sources, methodologies, and cross-functional viewpoints. Data science has helped us in this pandemic in the following ways:

1. Using data collected to trace the pandemic and forecast hotspots
2. Harnessing data to find out more about who might be most at risk of getting infected
3. Leveraging data insights to assist inform decisions about returning to the workplace

As per the U.S. emerging jobs report, the sector of data science has expanded up to 350% since the year 2012 and is expected to grow extensively in the future.

7.3 Data Science Technique Used for Diabetes Detection

Diabetes is a body condition in which the blood sugar level of the individual is in very high concentration. Most of the food that we consume is broken down to glucose which is a form of sugar. This sugar is dissolved in the blood and circulated throughout the body, and when this sugar content is high in the blood, then that individual is said to be diabetic. Insulin is a body fluid that is created by the pancreas. Insulin helps in breaking down sugar present in the blood which provides energy to the human body. Diabetes occurs when either the pancreas does not make enough insulin or the insulin is ineffective in breaking down the sugar present in the blood. Diabetes affected 30.3 million persons in the United States in 2015, accounting for 9.4% of the population. More than one-fourth of them were unaware that they had the condition. One in four people over the age of 65 has diabetes. In adults, type 2 diabetes accounts for 90%–95%of occurrences. One may think that an increase in sugar concentration is not as harmful to the human body but the reality is the opposite. Diabetes is associated with many harmful body conditions like heart disease, vision loss, kidney disease, eye problems, dental problems, nerve damage, foot problems, and stroke. The cure for diabetes is yet to be developed by scientists and researchers around the world but scientists believe losing weight, eating healthy meals, and being active can help in alleviating the diabetic conditions of a person [1].

Hesy-Ra, an Egyptian physician, noted frequent urination as an indication of a strange ailment that also produced emaciation in 1552 B.C., which was the first known mention of diabetic symptoms. Those known as "water tasters" were used to diagnose diabetes by tasting the urine of people suspected of having diabetes centuries later. Diabetes was diagnosed if the urine tasted sweet. Scientists were unable to establish any chemical assays to detect the presence of sugar in the urine until the 1800s.

Type 1 and type 2 diabetes are the two forms of diabetes that exist today. The glycated hemoglobin (A1C) test is the first to detect them. If the A1C test isn't available, or if a patient has specific factors that could cause the A1C test to be erroneous, such as pregnancy or an unusual form of hemoglobin, the doctor may employ tests like the random blood sugar test and the fasting blood sugar test. To forecast diabetes, a blood sample is taken at various intervals of these tests, which vary from test to test. The oral glucose tolerance test and the screening test are two additional tests that many clinicians recommend for the diagnosis of type 2 diabetes. When a person is diagnosed with diabetes, a blood test can be performed to detect autoantibodies, which are common in type 1 diabetes. When doctors are unsure whether they have type 1 or type 2 diabetes, these tests can help them distinguish between the two [2,3].

Prescribed exercise, mainly horseback riding, was supposed to decrease excessive urine and was the first diabetic treatment to be proven. Insulin and metformin are still the principal treatments for type 1 and type 2 diabetes, respectively; other drugs to assist manage blood glucose levels have also been created. Diabetic patients can now test their blood glucose levels at home, as well as make dietary adjustments, exercise regularly, and use insulin and other medications to more accurately control their blood glucose levels, lowering their risk of health issues [4–6].

Diabetes is a very common chronic disease that is of rising concern. According to the World Health Organization, it is estimated that approximately 422 million people worldwide suffer from diabetes. By 2040, the number of people suffering from diabetes is estimated to increase to approximately 642 million. Due to diabetes, one person dies every six seconds (five million a year) which is more than HIV, tuberculosis, and malaria combined and 1.6 million deaths are due to diabetes every year. In the previous part, we have covered some of the traditional ways of diabetes prediction.

The use of machine learning applications in this disease can reform the approach to its diagnosis and management. Various machine learning models have been used for predicting the risks of developing diabetes or consequent complications related to this disease. The care of patients, healthcare professionals, and healthcare systems has been facilitated using artificial intelligence and machine learning. Clinically case-based reasoning, deep learning, and neural networks enable predictive population risks, enhanced decision making, and self-management of individuals.

Support vector machines, logistics regression, k-nearest neighbor, and decision tree algorithms were used to identify the model. These techniques are more suitable to detect early signs of diabetes based on nine important parameters. Accuracy, F-measure, recall, precision, and receiver operating curve measures are used to define the performance of the different machine learning techniques.

One of the most important real-world chronic medical problems is the early detection of diabetes in patients. With the development and advent of artificial intelligence and machine learning approaches, patients can be empowered to manage their diabetes, generate data/parameters, and become health experts. Awareness and knowledge of early signs will be useful in the management of diabetes in patients and especially in pregnant women. The technical advances in the domain of diabetes care include health care professionals, patients, diabetes care, management center, data science, and enthusiasts. Artificial Intelligence and machine learning approaches have introduced a quantum of change in health care systems especially in diabetes care and will continue to evolve. In the future, experience generated from the system developed with help to improvise the system further in terms of functionality and utility in diabetes care using concepts of enforcement learning and will be used on a larger scale across the world [7,8].

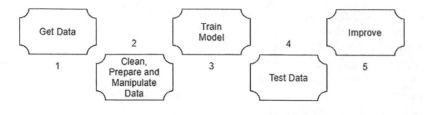

FIGURE 7.1

Diagrammatic representation of workflow of any generic machine learning project.

7.4 Methodology and Proposed Framework for Diabetes Detection

Machine learning as the name is means getting machines to train and learn to act and make decisions like humans. Machine learning has come a long way and has strengthened its roots in all walks of life. Data science and machine learning are being used in every field to make better data-driven decisions. Figure 7.1 diagrammatically explains the generic workflow of any machine learning project.

A generic machine learning workflow always involves five key steps which are as follows:

1. **Get Data:** Getting data means gathering data from various sources that are available. The data gathered in this step should have all the characteristics that the project requires. The data can be open source and free or can be from a paid source. Many websites like Kaggle and GitHub provide free datasets to facilitate the community. Governments of various countries have also been involved in this data-centric revolution and have made various datasets available to the public free of cost. These datasets are easily accessible and can be used in a wide variety of projects.

2. **Clean, Prepare and Manipulate Data:** We often see data in tabular form and it seems as if data is well organized and can be used as it is after gathering it. But in reality, this is not the case. Data exists with attached impurities, imperfections, and discrepancies which can lead to inaccuracy of the results and ultimately the failure of the project. Hence the data needs to be cleaned by removing outliers and not available values. Dataset when sourced from a website may not always have the necessary structure that is required for the project. In some cases, the dataset may have some extra columns or in other cases, new columns have to be derived from existing columns. This process is called preparing and manipulating the data and it helps in structuring data as per the problem statement [9].

3. **Train Model:** As it is clear from the earlier section that machine learning means getting machines to train and learn to make decisions like humans, this step trains the machine to make human-like decisions which are commonly referred to as predictions. Before training, an appropriate model is selected based on multiple attributes. The selected model is then trained with a part of the dataset called training data. This enables the machine to initiate the training phase. Initially, the accuracy of the predictions made by the machine may not be high but it gradually increases as the iterations and the training data size increase.

4. **Test Model:** In this phase, the model is tested with the remaining part of the dataset commonly referred to as the testing dataset. The model is not familiar with the

testing dataset and that is why the testing dataset is employed in knowing the actual accuracy of the dataset. The accuracy of the model obtained with the testing dataset is a close estimate of how the model will perform in the real-world scenario [10].

5. **Improve:** As we have discussed earlier, models are not always accurate. Even if they are accurate in the training phase, they might not be accurate in the testing phase. These models have some attributes of their own which can be changed as per the need. In an improved phase, if the accuracy of the model is not up to the desired accuracy, then some tweaks and adjustments are made to the model to increase the accuracy. In some cases, the size of the dataset used in the training phase increases, which leads to more iterations and ultimately more accuracy .

These are generic five key steps that are involved in every machine learning project and are iterated over and over again until desired results are obtained. This process is generally referred to as hyper-parameterization in technical terms.

The basic diabetes detection algorithm follows the same workflow that was discussed earlier. The framework remains the same with some changes in the model selection and improvement phase. In the data-gathering stage, the data is obtained from a wide number of sources as many datasets are available for educational purposes. The cleaning and preparing are done as per the requirement. The dataset obtained is not clean and has a lot of missing values which are replaced by a predefined value. Then some outliers are eliminated and the discrepancies are resolved to make the dataset more usable. The dataset has many health-related indicators and the irrelevant indicators are filtered out to prepare the dataset for training and testing of the model.

One of the major reasons for diabetes is variation in glucose levels. Insulin is used for balancing the blood glucose level in the body, its deficiency of which can cause diabetes. A wide array of models are used for diabetes detection, out of which the one with maximum efficiency and accuracy is chosen. The chosen model is then trained with a training dataset and tested with a testing dataset and the overall accuracy is calculated. The model is then fine-tuned to achieve maximum accuracy [11]. We can use any of them to predict the disease, or we can investigate strategies for employing a hybrid methodology to increase accuracy over a single one.

Researchers and scientists have employed a variety of different algorithms for diabetes detection over some time. Some have developed their hybrid algorithm to overcome the accuracy bottleneck and increase efficiency. Currently, the researchers are using a single classification algorithm to predict diabetic conditions with an accuracy of 70%-80% [12–14].

Some of the commonly used algorithms for diabetes detection are as follows:

1. **Naïve Bayes classifier:** Naïve Bayes classifier is an algorithm that classifies or labels the outcome with the desired label as per the features that are reflected by that instance. This is also called the Generative Learning model. The Naïve Bayes classifier assumes that all the variables are independent of each other and hence this classifier works best with data that have unbalancing problems and missing values. At its core, the Naïve Bayes classifier uses theBayes theorem to calculate the label. This classification technique works well with huge datasets and is simple to implement [15].

2. **Logistic Regression:** Regression is a technique that means establishing a relationship between an independent and a dependent variable. In logistic regression, the scale used to fit the model is a logistic function, and hence, this regression is called

logistic regression. The goal of this classification technique is to establish a link between the dichotomous category and the predictor factors. The main reason why logistic regression is used in diabetes detection is that logistic regression is majorly used when the outcome variable is binary. Meaning the outcome variable must have only two values like yes or no, male or female, etc. This requirement fits perfectly in diabetes detection and the majority of other healthcare use cases where a disease is detected or not detected. Hence, logistic regression fits perfectly with the diabetes detection problem and hence gives the maximum accuracy [15,16].

3. **Decision Tree:** A decision tree is a classifier-based machine learning algorithm that falls under the category of supervised machine learning. A decision tree follows a flowchart-like structure where a branch means an outcome of a test or condition and the node means the test or the condition. The main reason why a decision tree is used in the prediction of the target variable in the case of diabetes detection is that the algorithm can build up the rules and take the necessary conditions along with the required variables by itself with the help of previous data and the labels. In each iteration, the highest information gain is used as the criteria for choosing the node in that particular iteration. Due to their ease of use, auto-generation of rules, and efficient handling of all kinds of data, decision trees are one of the most popular tools for the classification and prediction of a variable. We can also call this the best predictor [15,17].

4. **Random Forest:** We have already discussed decision trees in detail and their uses in classification and prediction. A forest is formed when numerous trees are grouped. Similarly, a random forest classifier is formed by grouping multiple decision tree classifiers together. Similar to the decision trees, the random forest classifier is also a supervised machine learning algorithm that is used for classification and prediction. The random forest has multiple applications like image classification, feature selection, recommendation engine, fraud detection, and disease prediction. The random forest generally employs multiple decision trees in parallel and stores all the outcomes. To choose the most optimal outcome out of all multiple outcomes, it uses the process of voting. This classifier accuracy for decision trees practice of overfitting the training dataset. The whole workflow of the random forest can be seen in Figure 7.2.

   Through this voting process, the final output is chosen as the prediction of the random forest classifier [3,15,18].

5. **Neural Network:** A neural network is a network of neurons or circuits that are interconnected to each other and form a network. A basic neural network contains an input layer, several hidden layers, and an output layer. A basic neural network can be seen in Figure 7.3.

The overall neural network can be made more complex by adding more hidden layers and various filters and complex intermediate layers to make the neural network more efficient and accurate. There is a term called an activation function that is used quite frequently when talking about neural networks. An activation function is simply a mathematical function that defines how the input can be converted into output over the layers that are present in that particular neural network. Many libraries and tools are available which provide easy creation of complex neural networks with few lines of code like Keras and TensorFlow. Once a basic neural network is designed, it is up to the user to make it as easy or as complicated as he or she wishes as per the accuracy. However, because the previous

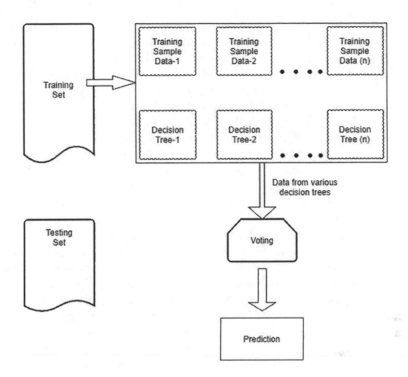

FIGURE 7.2
Random forest classifier.

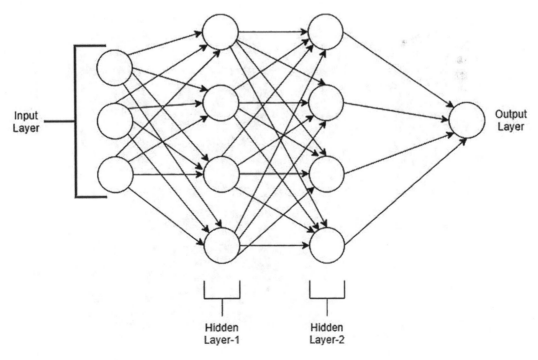

FIGURE 7.3
Generalized neural network.

layer receives no feedback, the signals flowing through the neurons and layers are given a weighting, and these signals are then put into a training phase, resulting in a network that can handle any situation [15,19].

All the above-said algorithms can be easily implemented using the python programming language along with some libraries that are available for free.

All of the machine learning classification methods and approaches used to predict the disease have already been covered. Following the completion of this survey, we propose combining more than one classification algorithm with any of the learning methodologies to boost disease prediction accuracy by more than 80%. To get the needed accuracy, it is beneficial to combine more than two classifiers.

Figure 7.4 explains the proposed work. The suggested system consists of two key stages that will collaborate to achieve the desired outcomes. The first step is to prepare the data, and the second is to classify it. The PIMA dataset is used in the framework to compare and derive the results. The National Institute of Diabetes and Digestive and Kidney Diseases developed this dataset. The primary goal of the dataset is to make diagnostic measurements easier to determine whether or not a person has diabetes. Multiple diagnostic measurement variables are included in the dataset, including the number of pregnancies, glucose, blood pressure, skin thickness, insulin, body mass index, diabetes pedigree function, and age. The major goal is to enhance classification accuracy and identify the data as diabetes or non-diabetic. The bigger the number of samples picked for various classification problems, the lower the classification accuracy. In many circumstances, the algorithm's performance is excellent in terms of speed, but the accuracy of data classification is poor. The outcome is in an outcome column which is the target variable of the whole study. The outcome variable is a binary variable that has 1 and 0 as its values. If the outcome for a particular row is 1, then the person has diabetes and if the outcome is 0 and then the person does not have

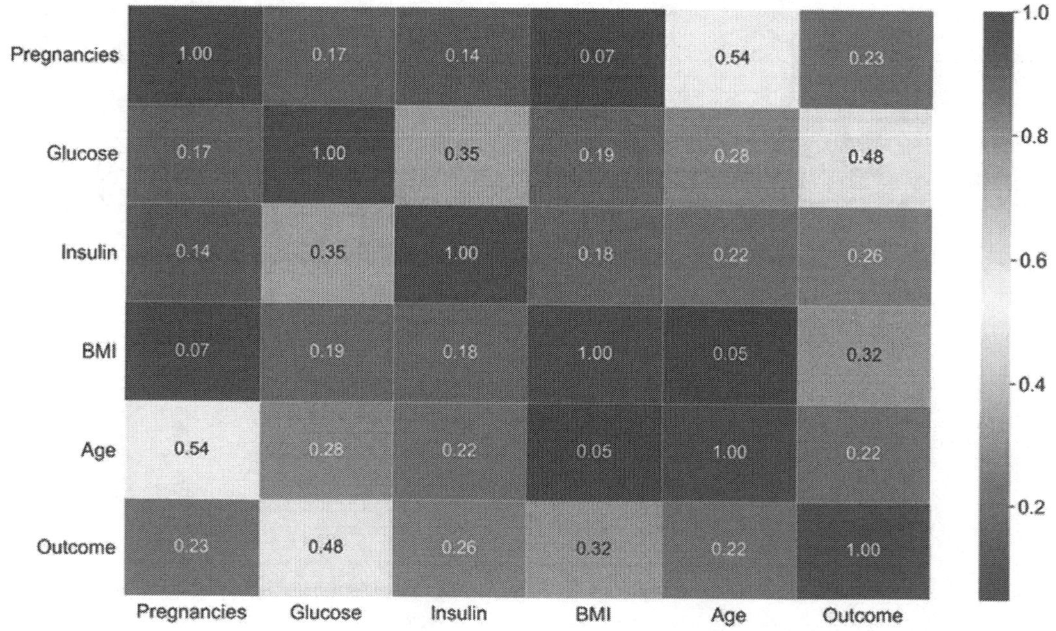

FIGURE 7.4
Proposed framework.

diabetes. Then exploratory data analysis is done to figure out the overall structure and central tendencies of the various columns. The data is then cleaned and prepared for training and testing. The training is carried out with an 80:20 split denoting that 80% of the whole dataset will act as a training dataset and the remaining 20% will act as a testing dataset. Since this study is about making people aware of the use of data science and machine learning in healthcare, especially diabetes detection, we decided to put forth a comparative study based on the above five algorithms. This will not only help in understanding the importance of data science in healthcare but will also present a more complete picture of how data science is revolutionizing the healthcare industry. The machine learning algorithms are already explained above. Following that, we employ a mixture of classifiers to get our desired result, which is referred to as a hybrid approach to data testing. In this strategy, we propose to utilize a combination of two classifiers. A classifier is an algorithm that translates input data to a certain category. There are various types of classifiers. The various classifiers that can be employed to attain high accuracy have already been identified and described. The most crucial step after training the model is to evaluate the classifier to ensure its accuracy. We advise combining more than one classifier to acquire our correct results after thoroughly comprehending and analyzing each classifier.

7.5 Results

The executed algorithms show respectable accuracies ranging from 75% to more than 90%. But the main result to be noted is that one cannot say one algorithm is superior to all of the other existing algorithms. This is because each algorithm has its specific use case and is used either when the type of dataset available in hand, that is the structure of the dataset is favorable according to the model or a certain kind of output is required. Thus, accuracy is not the parameter through which we can decide whether one algorithm is superior to that other or not. All the algorithms can fairly classify whether the person is diabetic or not. So, all the executed models can predict whether the person is diabetic or not with a respectable accuracy of more than 85% accuracy in all cases. This will lead to the detection of diabetes or borderline diabetes in a person's body before the situation is out of hand and the person can take all the necessary precautions to ensure that diabetes is kept under check.

We all know data science is a field of performing operations on a huge amount of data to extract useful information or knowledge from it and use that knowledge for various applications. Generally, the knowledge extracted from the dataset is not readable to a common person who does not know how to read the model summary or the prediction results. Hence, the knowledge obtained from the dataset must be presented in such a manner that every person will be able to understand and draw conclusions. This process is called data visualization. Data visualization is a part of every data science project and involves several kinds of charts to represent knowledge efficiently. In the same way, their visualization was obtained while doing the comparative study of the diabetes system as well [20].

The first visualization that we will be looking into is a correlation plot. Correlation means that one variable has a relationship with another variable. The correlation may be positive or negative. A correlation of 0.7 or greater is considered to be a strong correlation. Figure 7.5 denotes a general correlation plot that all the individuals use to get to know the important or relevant variables that affect the outcome variable.

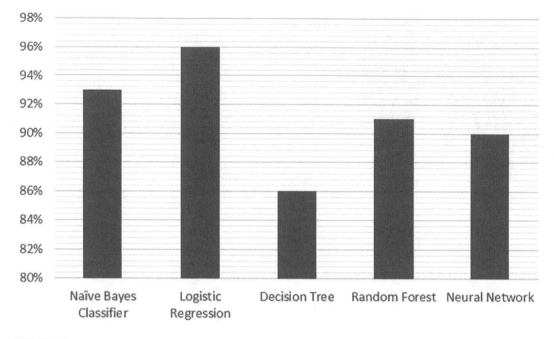

FIGURE 7.5
Correlation plot.

The basic overview of the correlation plot in Figure 7.6 is that the X-axes and Y-axes denote the variables that are present in the PIMA dataset. On the rightmost side, we can see a scale that shows the color according to the correlation. The numbers that are present in the individual cells denote the correlation in a numerical format and the cell color denotes the correlation in a graphical format. From the correlation plot in Figure 7.3, there is no strong correlation present in the dataset as no variable shows a correlation of 0.7 and more. So this is the conclusion that can be drawn from Figure 7.6.

After applying the five algorithms which are Naïve Bayes classifier, logistic regression, decision tree, random forest, and neural network, the accuracy of all the algorithms is calculated based on the testing dataset as the testing dataset represents the real-life accuracy of the model. Table 7.1. denotes all the accuracies of the mentioned models. This table or the comparison of the algorithm by no means shows the superiority of one algorithm over the other. The accuracy mentioned in the table only denotes the performance of the models with the PIMA dataset which contains data from Indian patients.

As we can see, the logistic regression outperforms every other selected algorithm with 96% accuracy on the PIMA dataset. A more complex form of neural networks can also be used for building a diabetes detection framework. Talking about the predictions made by the logistic regression model, 93 people were predicted as diabetic and they turned out to be diabetic, 5 people were predicted to be diabetic but they were non-diabetic, 4 people non-diabetic but were classified as diabetic, and 138 were non-diabetic and were correctly predicted as non-diabetic by the logistic regression model. This number establishes the efficacy of the logistic regression model in predicting whether the person is diabetic or not by using the PIMA dataset. Hence the logistic regression model can be fed with the inputs of a person and the model will be successfully able to predict whether the person has diabetes or not.

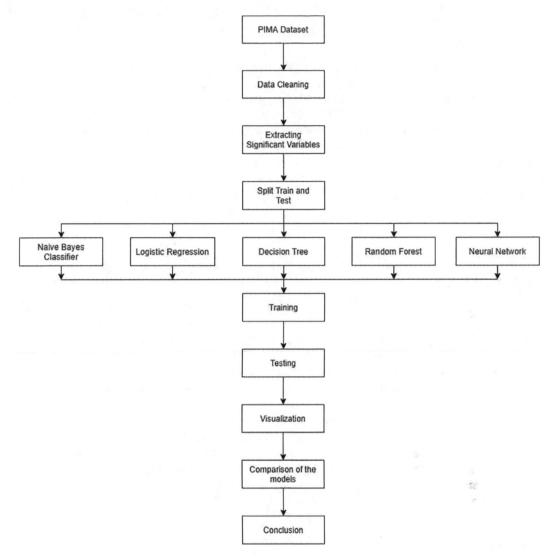

FIGURE 7.6
Accuracy chart.

TABLE 7.1

Accuracy Table

Algorithms	Accuracy (%)
Naïve Bayes classifier	93
Logistic regression	96
Decision tree	86
Random forest	91
Neural network	90

7.6 Conclusion

Hence, we have successfully gone through the journey of how a generic machine learning project works with the basic steps that are involved in every machine learning project. Through these steps and their concise yet accurate definitions, people can implement a basic machine learning project with the concepts discussed in the chapter. The algorithms that we have taken into the study to present a comparison successfully predict whether the person is diabetic or not. For the prediction to be made accurate, the person is required to fill in all the measures and the person can obtain the prediction about his or her diabetic condition well before the symptoms start to show. In this way, the diabetic condition can be mitigated well in advance and the body can be kept out of risk efficiently.

7.7 Future Scope

As we all know, technology, change, and advancement are interleaved with each other. All three things go hand in hand. Many technology leaders like Google, Amazon, and Apple are already working on diabetes detection systems. These giants have realized the importance of data science and the opportunities that are available in the healthcare sector. For example, Apple is trying to implement glucose monitoring built into the iwatch so that the user can be notified of the fluctuation in the glucose level. Alphabet, which is the parent company of Google, is also trying to integrate a model with a web interface and provide this product to many healthcare providers for the self-assessment of diabetes in patients. Many major healthcare providers are also working with such tech giants to improve the system and implement it efficiently. They are also collaborating with these companies to provide real-time data from their patients directly to these companies to train and increase the overall accuracy of the system.

References

1. Centers for Disease Control and Prevention. National diabetes statistics report, 2017. Centers for Disease Control and Prevention website. www.cdc.gov/diabetes/pdfs/data/statistics/national-diabetes-statistics-report.pdf External link (PDF, 1.3 MB) Updated July 18, 2017. Accessed August 1, 2017.
2. Patil, K., Sawarkar, S. D., & Narwane, S. 2019. Designing a model to detect diabetes using machine learning. *International Journal of Engineering Research & Technology (IJERT)* 8(11), 333–340.
3. Patil, R., & Tamane, S. 2018. A comparative analysis on the evaluation of classification algorithms in the prediction of diabetes. *International Journal of Electrical and Computer Engineering* 8(5), 3966.
4. Joshi, R., & Alehegn, M. 2017. Analysis and prediction of diabetes diseases using machine learning algorithm: Ensemble approach. *International Research Journal of Engineering and Technology* 4(10), 426–436.
5. Singh, D. A. A. G., Leavline, E. J., & Baig, B. S. 2017. Diabetes prediction using medical data. *Journal of Computational Intelligence in Bioinformatics* 10(1), 1–8.

6. Zia, U. A., & Khan, N. 2017. Predicting diabetes in medical datasets using machine learning techniques. *International Journal of Scientific & Engineering Research Volume* 8, 1538–1551.

7. Naqvi, B., Ali, A., Hashmi, M. A., & Atif, M. 2018. Prediction techniques for diagnosis of diabetic disease: A comparative study. *International Journal of Computer Science and Network Security* 18(8), 118–124.

8. Dash, S., Shakyawar, S. K., Sharma, M., & Kaushik, S. 2018. Big data in healthcare: Management, analysis and future prospects. *Journal of Big Data 6*, Article Number: 54. SpringerOpen.

9. Kathiroli, R., RajaKumari, R., & Gokulprasanth, P. 2018. Diagnosis of diabetes using cascade correlation and artificial neural network. *Tenth International Conference on Advanced Computing (ICoAC).*

10. Sisodia, D., & Sisodia, D. S. 2018. Prediction of diabetes using classification algorithms. *Procedia Computer Science* Elsevier, 132, 1578–1585.

11. Kaur, H., & Kumari, V. 2018. Predictive modelling and analytics for diabetes using a machine learning approach. *Applied Computing and Informatics* 18 (1/2), 92–102.

12. Barik, R. K., Priyadarshini, R., Dubey, H., Kumar, V., & Yadav, S. 2018. Leveraging machine learning in mist computing telemonitoring system for diabetes prediction. In: Mohan L. Kolhe, Munesh C. Trivedi, Shailesh Tiwari, & Vikash Kumar Singh (Eds.), *Advances in Data and Information Sciences* (pp. 95–104). Springer, Singapore.

13. Nachabe, L., Raiyee, R., Falou, O., Girod-Genet, M., & ElHassan, B. 2020. Diabetes mobile application as a part of semantic multi-agent system for EHealth. *IEEE 5th Middle East and Africa Conference on Biomedical Engineering (MECBME).*

14. Samant, P., & Agarwal, R. 2017. Diagnosis of diabetes using computer methods: Soft computing methods for diabetes detection using iris. *Threshold 8*, 9.

15. Yadav, B., Sharma, S., & Kalra, A. 2018. Supervised Learning Technique for Prediction of Diseases. In: Rajesh Singh, S. Choudhury, & Anita Gehlot (Eds.), *Intelligent Communication, Control and Devices* (pp. 357–369). Springer, Singapore.

16. Dagliati, A., Marini, S., Sacchi, L., Cogni, G., Teliti, M., Tibollo, V.,..., and Bellazzi, R. 2018. Machine learning methods to predict diabetes complications. *Journal of Diabetes Science and Technology* 12(2), 295–302.

17. Kavakiotis, I., Tsave, O., Salifoglou, A., Maglaveras, N., Vlahavas, I., & Chouvarda, I. 2017. Machine learning and data mining methods in diabetes research. *Computational and Structural Biotechnology Journal* 15, 104–116.

18. Choudhury, A., & Gupta, D. 2019. A survey on medical diagnosis of diabetes using machine learning techniques. In: Janusz Kacprzyk (Ed.), *Recent Developments in Machine Learning and Data Analytics* (pp. 67–78). Springer, Singapore.

19. Carter, J. A., Long, C. S., Smith, B. P., Smith, T. L., & Donati, G. L. 2019. Combining elemental analysis of toenails and machine learning techniques as a non-invasive diagnostic tool for the robust classification of type-2 diabetes. *Expert Systems with Applications* 115, 245–255.

20. Khanam, J. J., & Foo, S. Y. 2021. *A Comparison of Machine Learning Algorithms for Diabetes Prediction.* ICT Express – Elsevier, New York.

8

Application of Artificial Intelligence Techniques in the Early-Stage Detection of Chronic Kidney Disease

Anindita A. Khade

Ramrao Adik Institute of Technology
DY Patil Deemed to be University
SIES Graduate School of Technology

Amarsinh V. Vidhate

Ramrao Adik Institute of Technology
DY Patil Deemed to be University

CONTENTS

8.1 Introduction

Because of its rising prevalence, chronic kidney disease (CKD) is among some of the gravest health issues usually affecting the population of Asian countries. It is a chronic disorder linked to higher morbidity and mortality, as well as a higher risk of many other illnesses, such as heart diseases along with elevated health care costs. Therefore, early detection, monitoring, and prevention of CKD are somewhere critical [1]. The key challenge comes

DOI: 10.1201/9781003283249-8

TABLE 8.1

CKD Stages

Stage	Description	Glomerular Filtration Rate (mL/min)	Percent Kidney Function
1	Normal to highly functioning kidney	>90	>90
2	Mild decrease in kidney function	60–89	60–89
3A	Tolerable decrease in function of kidney	45–59	45–59
3B	Tolerable decrease in function of kidney	30–44	30–44
4	Acute decrease in function of kidney	15–29	15–29
5	Kidney failure	<15	<15%

from the lack of clear signs in the early stages of CKD. As a result, determining the disease stage is critical since it provides many indicators that aid in the selection of necessary interventions and treatments. To determine how well kidneys function, a blood test is performed to detect urea, other waste products, and creatinine in the blood. The factor which measures the amount of damage done to kidneys' is known as glomerular filtration rate (GFR). In a non-CKD patient, this is normally 100 mL/min. Any CKD patient generally, must go through five stages in terms of kidney damage (Table 8.1).

Table 8.1 describes the various stages of CKD. If the GFR value for a person is <60 ml/min for more than 3 months, he/she is detected to have CKD. It has been observed, from previous studies, that till stage 3 patients usually do not get any symptoms. As a result, early prediction of the disease becomes a challenge. Detection of CKD in its early stages will aid patients in receiving successful care and preventing the progression of the disease to end-stage renal disease [1]. As a result, the primary goal may be to develop a model that can accurately predict CKD faster and use the fewest number of predictors possible [4].

8.2 Literature Review

Until now, a variety of intelligent techniques have been used to detect CKD in its early stages. In the study, presentation, and comprehension of complicated medical and health care data, artificial intelligence (AI) is a broad aspect that refers to the use of various machine learning (ML) algorithms and software to emulate human perception. The following table will describe a few techniques implemented by different authors and their findings. It is divided into ML supervised techniques and deep learning (DL) techniques. This leads to the conclusion of which kind of AI techniques should be used for prediction. Table 8.2.1 gives a brief idea of implemented algorithms under ML category. It also reflects their findings. Table 8.2.2 gives an idea of the DL algorithms implemented.

Table 8.2.1 Based on Supervised Machine Learning Algorithms

Algorithms Used	Authors	Conclusions	Major Findings
Random forest, logistic regression	Gunarathne W.H.S.D, Perera K.D.M et al. [1]	RF has a prediction accuracy of 93%, while logistic regression has a prediction accuracy of 92%.	It is possible to incorporate more algorithms with higher accuracy.

(Continued)

Algorithms Used	Authors	Conclusions	Major Findings
Neural networks and support vector machines	Njoud Abdullah Almansour, Hajra Fahim Syed [2]	SVM showed an accuracy of 89.25%, while ANN had a performance accuracy of 90.75% using the optimized features.	The prediction time for the ANN classifier had a markedly longer execution time than SVM.
Decision tree	I.A. Pasadana, D. Hartama, M. Zarlis, et al. [3]	The project has a near-perfect accuracy rate of nearly 92%.	The work isn't based on recent evidence. In addition, only one algorithm has been investigated.
Naive Bayes, decision tree, KNN	Olayinka Ayodele Jongbo, Adebayo Olusola Adetunmbi [4]	Each of these algorithms has a near-perfect accuracy rate of 90%.	The KNN algorithm takes longer to train a model. When compared to KNN, Naive Bayes has less precision.

Table 8.2.2 Based on Deep Learning Techniques

Algorithms Used	Authors	Conclusions	Major Findings
Autoencoder network	Aditya Khamparia1 & Gurinder Sainil [5]	With a precision of 100 %, the model outperformed other models in the literature. Furthermore, the model provides a high level of precision and recall, with both being 100%.	The accuracy of a simulated network is 100% It has only been tested on data from 100 patients.
Neural networks	Chalumuru Suresh, B. Chakra Pani, C. Swatisri et al. [6]	The accuracy achieved is 91%.	Only 60 patients are included in the data. Hemoglobin was chosen as the main attribute.
Probabilistic neural networks	Ayman S. Anwar, El-Houssainy A. Rady [7]	The PNN algorithm improves classification accuracy and prediction efficiency by about 93 % when predicting the stages of CKD patients.	The current research used a clinical dataset of almost 361 patients to apply the PNN algorithm. This accuracy is where stage-by-stage classification is handled.
SVM+CNN	Guozhen chen, Chenguang ding, Yang li, et al. [8]	Ultrasonography photographs of the kidney are considered in hospitals. Along with CNN, SVM is used to pick features.	As opposed to a single algorithm, a hybrid of SVM and CNN offers better accuracy.
CNN	Charumathi Sabanayagam, Dejiang Xu, Daniel S W Ting et al. [9]	Has been put to the test on the Singaporean population. The changes in the retina that the AI is detecting are most likely the result of several shared mechanisms contributing to the early detection of CKD [9].	For Asian countries, it must be enforced.
CNN	N Bhaskar, M Sucheta [10]	Instead of convolution, the correlation operation is used in the CNN model. When combined with a classifier like SVM, classification efficiency improves.	The accuracy of the model is greater than 93%. Time taken to train the model is more.

8.3 Methodology Used

In this chapter, we have implemented ML as well as DL algorithms and tried to compare their results. We have implemented five ML algorithms (SVM, KNN, decision tree, random forest, and XGBoost) and three DL algorithms (artificial neural networks, multilayer perceptron, and recurrent neural networks). ANN is a computer system component that models how the human brain processes and interprets data.

The dataset was collected from the University of California, Irvine's ML repository [7]. It consisted of 400 records. We combined this dataset with the 200 pilot records received in real time from DY Patil University, School of Medical Sciences. The classification variable shows whether a patient has CKD or no. There are 25 attributes total, with 24 clinical characteristics and one goal attribute. Medical history, physical examination, and lab tests are the three sections of the features. The goal attribute is defined as non-CKD or CKD based on the properties of the attributes. Table 8.2 explains the different parameters of blood which need to be investigated for CKD.

Figure 8.1 represents a snapshot of the dataset taken into consideration. It includes 600 cases in total, 350 of which are patients with CKD and the remaining 250 are not.

A brief idea about the above-mentioned algorithms has been discussed below.

TABLE 8.2

Attributes

Name	Type Units/Values
Age	Measured in years
Blood pressure	Measured in mm/Hg
Specific gravity	Nominal attribute
Albumin	0–5
Sugar	0–5
Red blood cells	OK/NOTOK
Puss cell	OK/NOTOK
Puss cell clumps	Present/Absent
Bacteria	Present/Absent
Blood glucose	Measured in mg/dL
Blood urea	Measured in mg/dL
Serum Creatinine	Measured in mg/dL
Sodium	Measured in mEq/L
Potassium	Measured in mEq/L
Hemoglobin	Measured in g
Packed cell volume	Any number
White blood cell count	Measured in cells/cumm
Red blood cell count	Measured in millions
Hypertension	Have/Don't Have
Diabetes mellitus	Have/Don't Have
Coronary artery disease	Have/Don't Have
Appetite	OK/NOT OK
Pedal edema	Have/Don't Have
Anemia	Have/Don't Have
Class	Positive/Negative

	age	bp	sg	al	su	rbc	pc	pcc	ba	bgr	bu
0	48	80	1.02	1	0	1	1	0	0	121	36
1	7	50	1.02	4	0	1	1	0	0	99	18
2	62	80	1.01	2	3	1	1	0	0	423	53
3	48	70	1.005	4	0	1	0	1	0	117	56
4	51	80	1.01	2	0	1	1	0	0	106	26
5	60	90	1.015	3	0	1	1	0	0	74	25
6	68	70	1.01	0	0	1	1	0	0	100	54
7	24	80	1.015	2	4	1	0	0	0	410	31
8	52	100	1.015	3	0	1	0	1	0	138	60
9	53	90	1.02	2	0	0	0	1	0	70	107
10	50	60	1.01	2	4	1	0	1	0	490	55
11	63	70	1.01	3	0	0	0	1	0	380	60
12	68	70	1.015	3	1	1	1	1	0	208	72
13	68	70	1.02	0	0	1	1	0	0	98	86
14	68	80	1.01	3	2	1	0	1	1	157	90
15	40	80	1.015	3	0	1	1	0	0	76	162
16	47	70	1.015	2	0	1	1	0	0	99	46
17	47	80	1.02	0	0	1	1	0	0	114	87
18	60	100	1.025	0	3	1	1	0	0	263	27
19	62	60	1.015	1	0	1	0	1	0	100	31

FIGURE 8.1
Dataset.

8.3.1 Machine Learning (ML) Methods

ML is an important component of the rapidly growing field of data science. In data mining projects, algorithms are taught to provide classifications or predictions using statistical methodologies, exposing key insights. Following that, these insights influence application and decision-making.

8.3.1.1 Support Vector Machine (SVM)

The purpose of the SVM algorithm is to discover a hyper-plane that distinguishes between data points in a multi-dimensional space which has multiple features. There are several hyper-planes from which to choose. Our goal is to find the plane with the largest margin, or interval between data points from both classes. By increasing the margin difference, it becomes easier to distinguish possible data points.

8.3.1.2 K-Nearest Neighbors (KNN)

KNN is a simple method that categorizes data using a similarity score (e.g., distance functions). Distance is calculated based on

$$d = \sqrt{[(x2 - x1)^2 + (y2 - y1)^2]}$$

8.3.1.2.1 Choosing the Right Value of K

We run the KNN algorithm multiple times with different values to discover the K that minimizes errors while keeping the system's capacity to correctly anticipate data it hasn't seen before.

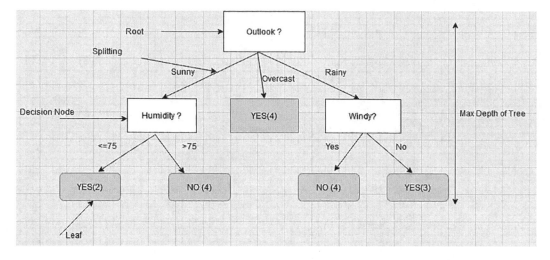

FIGURE 8.2
Decision tree source [12].

8.3.1.3 Decision Tree Classifier

One of the efficient prediction models used in analytics, ML, and data mining is decision tree learning. It goes from observations about an item (represented in the branches) to inferences about the item's goal value using a decision tree (as a forecasting model) (represented in the leaves). In these tree structures, leaves indicate class labels, and branches indicate key factors that lead to specific class labels [11]. Classification trees illustrate models in which the parameter might take several values.

Regression trees are decision trees with a target variable that can take on any value. Figure 8.2 represents the structure of the decision tree.

8.3.1.4 Random Forest (RF)

RF algorithms are an ensemble learning strategy for classification, regression, and other problems that work by training a large number of decision trees and then producing a class that is the average prediction (regression) of all the trees [13].

The potential of decision trees to overfit their training data is addressed by random decision forests [14]. In most circumstances, RF outperforms the performance of decision trees, but they are less precise than the gradient-enhanced trees. On the other hand, data characteristics may have an impact on their efficiency.

8.3.1.5 XGBoost

XGBoost is a distributed gradient boosting toolkit that has been tuned for efficiency, flexibility, and portability. It uses the gradient boosting framework to create ML algorithms.

8.3.2 Deep Learning (DL) Methods

DL architectures have been used in speech recognition, computer vision, NLP, bioinformatics, machine translation, material inspection, medical image analysis, drug discovery, and board game programs. The term "deep" in DL refers to the usage of multiple layers in the network. A linear perceptron cannot be utilized as a universal classifier, according to early research, but a network with a nonpolynomial activation function and one unbounded width hidden layer can. DL is a very recent variant that utilizes an unbounded number of layers to allow for practical application and optimizations specifically.

8.3.2.1 Artificial Neural Networks (ANN)

ANN is made up of nodes which connect many artificial neurons also named as processing units. Input and output are parts of the processing units. Based on any aforementioned scheme, the input units collect various forms of information, and the neural network attempts to learn about the information supplied in order to provide a meaningful output. Backpropagation, or backward propagation of error, is a set of learning rules used by ANNs to improve their performance results, much like people need rules and instructions to produce a result or output (Figure 8.3).

8.3.2.2 Multilayer Perceptron (MLP)

A multilayer perceptron (MLP) ANN is a type of feedforward ANN. The name MLP can be applied to any feedforward ANN, but it is mostly used to describe networks composed of many layers of threshold-activated perceptrons. There are three node layers in an MLP. For training, MLP employs backpropagation as a supervised learning approach [2,3].

MLP is distinguished from a linear perceptron by its nonlinear activation and several layers.

8.3.2.3 Recurrent Neural Network (RNN)

A recurrent neural network (RNN) is a sort of ANN in which nodes are connected in a directed graph in a temporal order. This allows it to respond in a time-dependent manner.

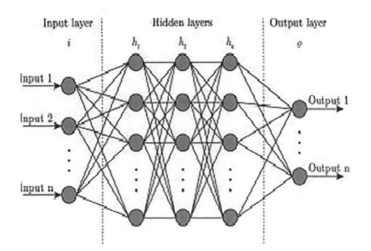

FIGURE 8.3
Artificial neural networks source [15].

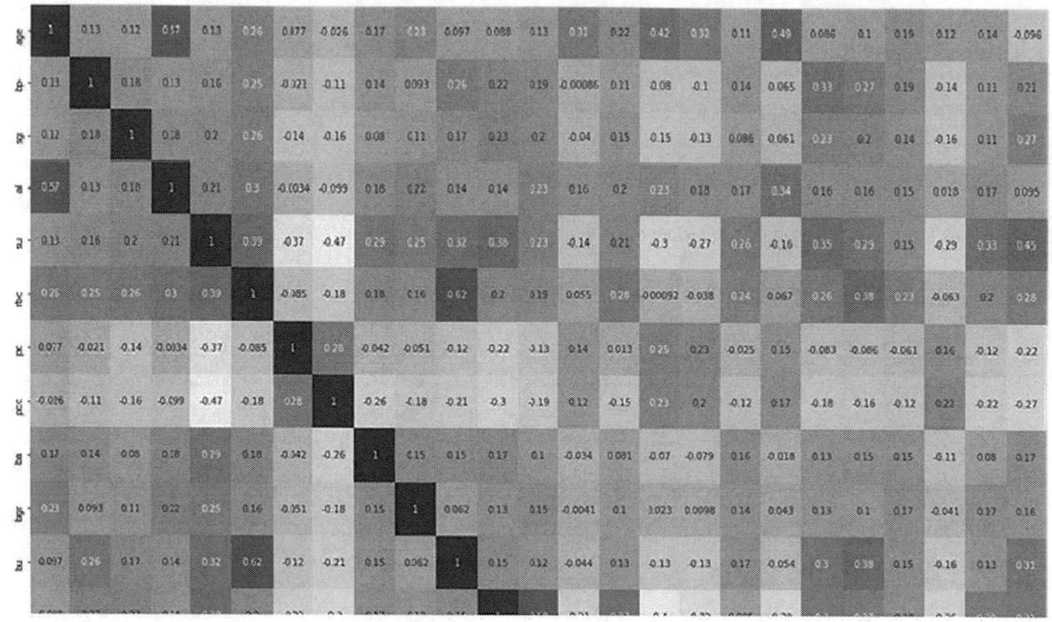

FIGURE 8.4
Correlation between different parameters.

Every piece of information is remembered by an RNN over time. It is usually used in time series prediction tasks since it can remember previous inputs. This is sometimes called a long short-term memory.

Data preprocessing techniques have been applied to the above mentioned dataset. The data consisted of many missing fields. They were taken care of by computing the mean and median of non-missing observations [16].

Figure 8.4 shows the correlation between different parameters using the heatmap. This shows that hemoglobin and specific gravity have a better correlation.

8.4 Results and Discussion

The graphs in Figure 8.5 depict the performance of all the above-discussed ML and DL algorithms.

These algorithms are compared based on precision, recall, F1 score, and accuracy. The above analysis helped us in finding our candidate algorithms. We have also considered prediction time as an important factor in the selection of candidate algorithms (Figure 8.6).

RNN is useful for applications that handle temporally changing data. As a result, although RNN provides good accuracy, we rule out this for our analysis. The time taken to predict each of these algorithms is also taken into consideration. We found out that RF, XGBoost, and ANN were giving the best performances with the combined dataset. Figure 8.7 shows our analysis of the three above said algorithms on 400 as well as 600 records.

As discussed above, we have also considered the prediction time of the algorithms to figure out the best among the three selected (Table 8.3).

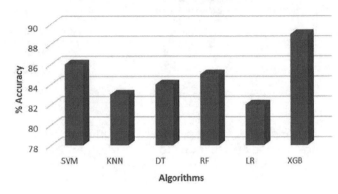

FIGURE 8.5
Performance of ML algorithms.

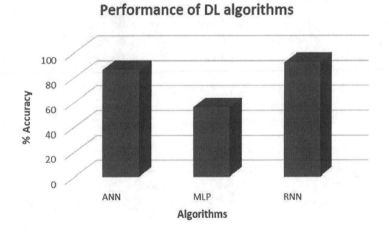

FIGURE 8.6
Performance of DL algorithms.

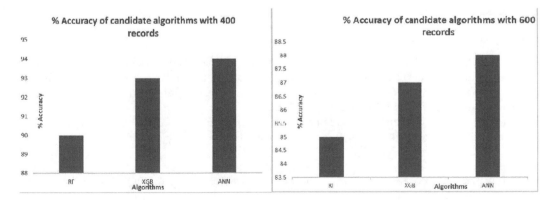

FIGURE 8.7
Comparison of candidate algorithms based on performance.

TABLE 8.3

Prediction Time of Candidate Algorithms

Algorithm	Accuracy (%)	Prediction Time (ms)
Random forest	88	13.05
Artificial neural networks	90	10.02
XGBoost	87	8.06

However, we are exploring more recent parameters in addition to the existing 24 parameters which may reduce accuracy further due to diversification. Hence, we further need to investigate the above-mentioned algorithms to modify parameters to increase accuracy.

8.5 Conclusion and Future Work

Based on the information presented above, we conclude that DL techniques provide better performance as compared to basic ML techniques. DL algorithms like ANN provide self-learning capabilities, due to which we tend to get better accuracy. Although the processing time for DL techniques is slightly high as compared to ML algorithms, this can be taken care of by the availability of high-performance computing infrastructures. Undoubtedly, there have been a lot of AI algorithms which have been implemented for the early prediction of CKD. But, there is a lot of scope for improvement in the prediction process. We have trained our models on multiple sets of data. We have observed that when we merged diversified data, the accuracy was drastically reduced. Optimization measures need to be applied to reduce the prediction time in case DL algorithms get involved. Non-invasive or minimally invasive techniques need to be developed with the help of other biomarkers which will ease the task of lab technicians. Finally, the proposed system will be an aid to nephrologists in detecting and minimizing the rate of CKD in the Indian population.

References

1. Gunarathne, W.H.S.D., Perera, K.D.M., Performance evaluation on machine learning classification techniques for disease classification and forecasting through data analytics for Chronic Kidney Disease (CKD), 2018, IEEE 17th International Conference on Bioinformatics and Bioengineering (BIBE), 2018, DOI: 10.1109/BIBE.2018.00-39.
2. Al Janab, S., Al Sourabji, I., et.al.. Survey of main challenges (security and privacy) in wireless body area networks for healthcare applications. *Egyptian Informatics Journal* 18(2), 2018, 113–122.
3. Pasadana, I.A., Hartama, D., Zarlis, M., et al., Chronic Kidney Disease prediction by using different decision tree techniques. *Journal of PhysicsConference Series*, 2019, DOI: 10.1088/1742–6596/1255/1/012024.
4. Jongbo, O.A., Adetunmbi, A.O., Development of an ensemble approach to chronic kidney disease diagnosis. *Scientific African Journal*, Elsevier 2020, DOI: 10.1016/j.sciaf.2020.e00456.

5. Khamparia, A., Saini, G., KDSAE: Chronic kidney disease classification with multimedia data learning using deep stacked autoencoder network. *Book on Multimedia Tools and Applications*, Borko Furht (Ed.), Springer, New York, pp. 35425–35440.

6. Suresh, C., Chakra Pani, B., Swatisri, C., et al. A neural network based model for predicting Chronic Kidney Diseases. 2020 Second International Conference on Inventive Research in Computing Applications (ICIRCA), IEEE, 2020, DOI: 10.1109/ICIRCA48905.2020.9183318.

7. Rady, S.A., Anwar, A.S. *Prediction of kidney disease stages using data mining algorithms. Informatics in Medicine Unlocked* 15, 2019, 100178, DOI: https://doi.org/10.1016/j.imu.2019.10017.

8. Chen, G., Ding, C., Li, Y., et al. Prediction of Chronic Kidney Disease using adaptive hybridized deep convolutional neural network on the internet of medical things platform. Book on Deep Learning Algorithms for Internet of Medical Things, IEEE 2020, pp. 100497–100508, DOI: 10.1109/ACCESS.2020.2995310.

9. Sabanayagam, C., Xu, D., Ting, D.S.W. et al., A deep learning algorithm to detect chronic kidney disease from retinal photographs in community-based populations. *Lancet Digital Health* Elsevier 2020, DOI: 10.1016/S2589-7500(20)30063-7.

10. Bhaskar, A.N., Sucheta, M. An computationally efficient correlational neural network for automated prediction of Chronic Kidney disease. *IRBM Journal-Science Direct* 2020, DOI 10.1016/j.irbm.2020.07.002.

11. Yang, Y., Li, Y., Chen, R., et al., Risk prediction of renal failure for chronic disease population based on electronic health record big data. *Big Data Research* 25, 2021, 32–37

12. https://www.vebuso.com/2020/01/decision-tree-intuition-from-concept-to-application/.

13. Pontillo, C., Zhang, Z.-Y., Schanstra, J.P. Prediction of Chronic Kidney Disease stage 3 by CKD273, a urinary proteomic biomarker. *KI Reports* 2(6), 2017, 1066–1075.

14. Le, S., Allen, A., Calvert, J. et al., Convolutional neural network model for intensive care unit acute kidney injury prediction. *KI Reports* 6(5), 2021, 1289–1298.

15. Bre, F., Gimenez, J., Fachinotti, V. Prediction of wind pressure coefficients on building surfaces using Artificial Neural Networks. *Energy and Buildings* 7, 2017, 158–169. DOI: 10.1016/j.enbuild.2017.11.045.

16. Almansour, N.A., Syed, H.F., Khayat, N.R. Neural network and support vector machine for the prediction of chronic kidney disease: A comparative study. *Computers in Biology and Medicine* 4, 2019, 108–111.

9

Multi-Optimal Deep Learning Technique for Detection and Classification of Breast Cancer

Pravin Malve

Government Polytechnic, Arvi

Dr. Vijay S. Gulhane

Sipna College of Engineering & Technology, Amravati

CONTENTS

9.1 Introduction

The cases of breast cancer have increased tremendously in the last two decades. The survey states that it's the second most common cause of death, next to lung cancer. It is also observed that 90% of breast cancer is benign; the tissue lumps are easily diagnosed at an earlier stage. Depending on tumors classification, the breast cancer cells are classified into benign (or) malignant. World Cancer Research Fund, 2018 [1], estimated that approximately 626,679 deaths were encountered over recorded 2 million new cases. Around 24.2% of women suffer from cancer of which 11.6% from breast cancers. Women visit an oncologist in order to diagnose breast cancer. Physical tests are carried out based on medical history and also monitor the swelling (or) hardening of any lymph nodes near the armpit. Manual analysis of detecting breast cancer increased the death risk rate of women [1,2].

Detecting cancer at an earlier stage is a cumbersome task due to the selection of features during the training stage. The adequate feature selection and classification process

DOI: 10.1201/9781003283249-9

are difficult to design for earlier detection of cancer. The machine learning techniques have advanced significantly through microscopic learning of dataset attributes and suitably documenting the behavior of variables resulting in a wider range of applications [3]. Learning models are developed from a variety of statistical, probabilistic, and optimization techniques that works based on past models from large, noisy, and complex datasets. Most of the multiple variables were used for defining the medical applications. Nowadays, machine learning is being incorporated into other domains and become the intrinsic part of computer vision. The learning theories without explicit programming, identification of stochastic behavior, dynamics of input variables, and pattern identification can be performed with minimal computational requirements [3,4]. Machine learning technologies have made it feasible to diagnose breast cancer at an earlier stage. Machine learning is frequently used in cancer research to not only detect and diagnose cancer but also in prognosis and disease progression. The performance evaluation matrixes provide a regular check on the model's accuracy and applicability in cancer detection. The large size of the patient record creates a better dataset for application of machine learning approaches and produces accurate results for the detection of disease. The early detection of ailment would aid in the supply of proper treatment procedures and drastically reduces the death rates [5].

9.2 Literature Review

Several researchers work on the histopathology images to classify the dataset into different classes for the estimation and early diagnostics of breast cancer [4, 6–9]. Kassani et al. [4] developed and demonstrated the model to diagnose breast cancer using a deep convolutional neural network (DCNN) descriptor and pooling operation. To improve the model performance and operation, several data pre-processing and feature selection techniques were applied. The author compared several models and observed that the deep convolution neural network model developed using the pre-trained Xception model performed exceptionally with an accuracy of 92.5% compared to other DCNN models. However, it is further assumed that the model classification performance could be enhanced using the combination of different deep learning or machine learning techniques and an appropriate selection of data correction and enhancement techniques.

Golatkar et al. [6] develop a model for the recoloring and adequate arrangement of hematoxylin and eosin tissue. When compared to random or grid sampling, the author discards regions of the photos that are not useful. The image is categorized into specific classes based on the presence of high nuclear density patches. It is decided what class the entire image belongs to by employing a majority vote over the various nuclear classes. Xu et al. [9] demonstrated a critical step in automatic nuclei detection as an evaluation of bosom malignant growth tissue examples. Stacked sparse autoencoders were acquainted with distinguishing the high-goal histopathological pictures of bosom malignant growth. The author worked on a set of 537 hematoxylin and eosin-stained histopathological images. Based on generated ground truth details, metrics such as precision, recall, and F-measure were evaluated. The autoencoders have achieved 78% accuracy compared with other models. The complexity and smaller window size are the major limitations of sensitivity analysis [10]. Wang et al. [11] investigated a bosom CAD technique reliant on the combination with a convolutional neural network (CNN), where features like morphology, texture, and density were selected and fused. Then, it was classified as benign (or) malignant using the ELM classifier. They have worked with 400 mammograms that contain 200 malignant and 200 benign images along with the performance metrics, such as detection and diagnosis metrics. Detection metrics like misclassified error, area over-covered metrics, area over-segmentation metrics, and under-segmentation metrics and comprehensive metrics, whereas diagnostics metrics such as accuracy, specificity, sensitivity, and area under curves were measured and achieved with better detection and diagnostic rate. However, the challenging part is the selection of the appropriate features. The development of a feature for a fused set enhanced the complexity of the training classifier.

Saha and Chakraborty [12] observed a profound (deep) learning-based Her2Net that was created for cell layer, core location, division, and characterization. The model was developed using a five-layer structure of CNN (convolution layers, max-pooling layers, spatial pyramid pooling layers, deconvolution layers, and up-inspecting layers). The performance of long short-term memory (LSTM) has been enhanced to improve the system performance through the utilization of the Her2 image database. Patches of images are created with size 251* 251 of 2,048 pixels with 98% accuracy. However, the limitation of the system is that they have achieved an exceptionally low false-positive rate. Patch-based segmentation models should be enhanced further for decision-making systems. Using histological images, Brancati et al. [13] developed a deep learning algorithm that was used to diagnose breast invasive cancer and classify the disease-causing features in multiple classes from histological images. They investigated the use of deep learning algorithms in breast cancer images that were stained with hematoxylin and eosin and then analyzed in real time. It has been projected in two cases, namely, the presence of invasive ductal carcinoma and its lymphoma classification. FusionNet was developed from convolutional neural networks. It has been applied to public datasets, namely, Unet and Resnet.

Kumar et al. [14] proposed an approach using VGGNet16, with the combination of appropriate data pre-processing, normalization, and feature-extraction techniques for cancer detection. CMT histopathological images and human breast cancer dataset were used for study purpose. The system has achieved a 97% accuracy of the systems. Overfitting issues in defining the classifiers increased the false-positive rate. Some higher-level discriminating features have slowed down the learning models. Saha et al. [15] defined that one of the most important aspects of cancer prediction systems is the detection of mitosis. To solve the deficiencies in mitosis detection, a supervised model was created utilizing deep learning architecture. It was assessed on datasets such as MITOS-ATYPIA, ICPR-2012, and AMIDA-13. By differentiating between mitosis and non-mitosis, an increase in the detection rate is observed. The correlation index was less during mitosis prediction. The incompleteness of the histopathological images degrades the pre-processing units with enhanced computational time. Kaur et al. [16] presented the k-means clustering algorithms, multi-class SVM, and deep neural networks under decision tree models, which enhanced the accuracy of the decision systems. Ten cross-validation models were analyzed using MLP, J48+, and k-means clustering. The developed deep learning models improves the sensitivity and the region of interest produces better segmentation results.

DCNN requires a more extensive training model, where a more significant number of decision rules decrease the performance of prediction models.

On the basis of the literature review, it can be concluded that training a complicated deep network from scratch with a short dataset is a complex task. There are also no known guidelines for designing a network topology for a certain purpose [17–19], which is another problem. When attempting to classify fine-grained histological images of breast cancer, it is difficult to determine whether an image is benign, malignant, or another specific category. In order to construct a model for the identification of breast cancer using CNN, a study was carried out. The pre-processing techniques are used to improve the image quality and dataset normalize to bring uniformity to the dataset. Following the pre-processing of the dataset, the classifier models are trained to detect cancerous tissues.

9.3 Material and Methodology

A methodology has been prepared to implement the convolution neural networks for the classification of the cancerous tissue from histopathology images. The detailed steps are explained as follows.

9.3.1 Convolution Neural Network

A ConvNet is the layer grouping method, and every layer of a ConvNet tends to change one volume of activation to another by a differentiable capacity. We used three principal layers to build ConvNet structures: fully connected layers, pooling layers, and convolutional layers, and these layers are allocated accordingly to shape a full ConvNet design. The model architecture which was utilized for this work is INPUT-CONV-RELU-POOL-FC. The model structure adopted for the study is shown in Figure 9.1.

The convolution layer forms CNN, and the basic structure involves the neurons with different weights and biases located within multiple fully interconnected layers [20]. The convolution layer is the building block of the whole CNN framework, which holds extensive data. The convolution layer selects the kernel k, stride s, padding p, and image size $m \times n$ and applies the operations to generate the output [20].

The type and number of kernels operate to select the neuron's appropriate feature and field to maintain the connectivity with the other neurons of previous layers. The output O is

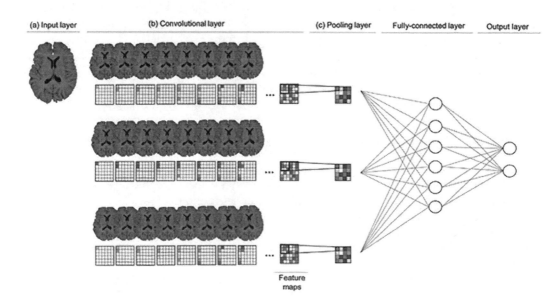

FIGURE 9.1
The five layer architecture of CNN model [22].

obtained from matrix A having size of (P, Q) and matrix B having a size of (X, Y) after performing the operations [21] in the convolution layer. The convolutional layers are followed by both the linear and non-linear layers containing activation functions like rectified linear unit and sigmoid. The rectified linear unit has overcome the disadvantages of sigmoidal and tanh activation functions and is most commonly used for deep learning operations.

9.3.2 Image Acquisition

The first step is the data collection from a publicly accessible repository and removal of irrelevant noises from the dataset before performing data pre-processing techniques. The sample images are shown in Figure 9.2.

9.3.3 Image Pre-Processing

Since the input taken is histopathological images, the color-based pre-processing models are carried out to enhance the visibility of the histology images using image point processing. Brightness and contrast of the histopathological images are enhanced. Most of the histopathological images utilize blue channels, thus, high brightness and contrast of the blue channels were selected to enhance the image visibility, as shown in Figure 9.3. The dataset is further processed as follows:

a) Processing image paths
b) Processing patient IDs

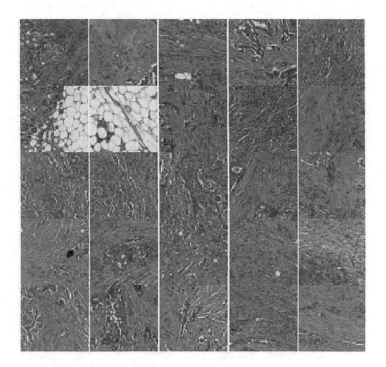

FIGURE 9.2
Raw histopathology images of breast cancer.

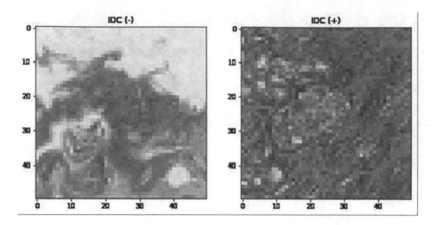

FIGURE 9.3
Histopathology images after pre-processing.

c) Processing images by changing the size of the images to a uniform threshold (50*50)

d) Fixing the size of the total dataset (90,000)

9.3.4 Image Segmentation

Once after that, image segmentation will be designed to resolve the overlap and eliminate the unwanted nuclei in each cell membrane. Here, a novel segmentation model, named, morphological-based connected component model are used for segmentation, which segments relevant nuclei and then connect those relevant nuclei for building efficient deep neural classifier [23]. The pseudo-steps of the morphological-based connected component model are as follows:

a) Selection of pink color of each pre-processed image (The selection is based on the nuclei for the segmentation process.

b) Determine area, perimeter and eccentricity of each selected nuclei through morphological operations on selected nuclei.

c) Clustering of similar values and labelling as 'component'.

d) Clustering of similar components for further process.

9.3.5 Feature Extraction

Feature extraction is a crucial stage in the development of a deep neural classifier. Since the study is on breast cancer, tissue characterization plays a vital role. In order to minimize computational requirements, it is preferable to employ the fewest number of features possible. This is because a large number of features would make it impossible to define precise decision boundaries in a vast dimensional space. The suspicious zones are subjected to statistical analysis, and statistical characteristics such as the mean, standard deviation, smoothness, third moment, uniformity, and entropy are retrieved [24]. Finally, with the help of statistical features, the characterization of tissues will be estimated. The pixel intensities were determined to extract the maximum information from the images.

9.3.6 Classification

The dataset is classified in to 'benign' (or) 'malignant' based on characterization of each image through deep neural networks [25]. The proposed model consists of five layers: convolution layers, max pooling, dense, dropout, and flatten layers. The input layer takes the input as 'tissue characterization'. The hidden layer converts the data into neuron n and then analyzes each neuron by summation functions. The benign and malignant produce the output in term of 0 and 1, respectively.

9.3.7 Detection

Phases 9.3.3–9.3.6 will be developed as 'knowledge base'. Then, the testing images will be connected to 'knowledge base' and thus detects the class of breast cancer.

9.3.8 Performance Evaluation

The CNN model developed was evaluated using different performance metrics. The performance metrics will be displayed in confusion matrix, represent data in C_{ij} where i represents the observed data point and j represents the predicted data points.

a) **Recall**: It is the true positive rate of the model, defined as the ratio of true positive cases to the summation of true positive and false negatives.

b) **Precision**: It classifies the instance of positive data points and is defined as the ratio of true positive against the summation of true positive and false-positive instances from data points.

c) **Accuracy**: It represents the correctly predicted data points from all the possible instances. It is defined as the ratio of true positive and negative to the total number of instances.

d) **F1-Score**: It is a function of precision and recall and provides a balance between the two defined as F1-score=2(Precision*Recall)/(Precision+Recall).

9.4 Results and Discussion

The pre-processing of the dataset is the primary function to be performed to enhance the image quality, which assists in obtaining good accuracy of detection. The dataset is converted into a 2D array and resized (50*50) to maintain uniformity in the images. The images of equal size also allow better visualization, uniformity, and data interpretation. A total of 90,000 images were selected for the analysis, out of which 66,025 images are class 0 and 23,975 images are class 1. The dataset rescaled in the range of 0 to 1 from 0 to 256, to make the dataset compatible with a wide variety of classification algorithms. The pixel intensities plot was designed to identify the percentage of information from each image belong to each class, as shown in Figure 9.4.

The dataset was further divided into two parts for training and testing. The training of the model was performed on 80% of the dataset, whereas the rest 20% of the data was used for testing. The division of the training and testing dataset was obtained to make the trained model less prone to overfitting. And an oversampling was performed to deal

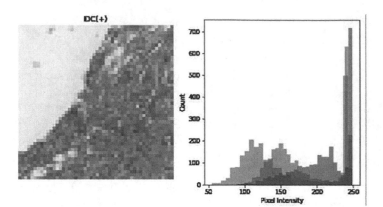

FIGURE 9.4
Plot histogram of RGB pixel intensities.

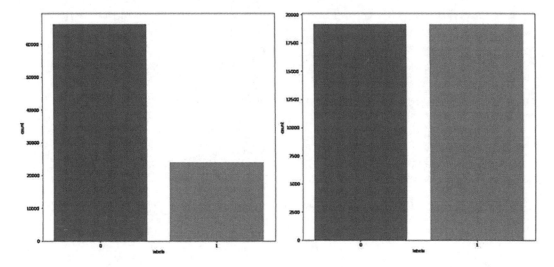

FIGURE 9.5
The imbalanced scenario. (a) Before applying ROS. (b) After applying ROS.

with the imbalanced class sizes. The dataset was trained on 72,000 images, and tested on 18,000 images. The Random Over Sampler (ROS) was applied to deal with the problems associated with an unbalanced dataset. The unbalanced dataset causes the generation of biased results. Figure 9.5 depicts the imbalanced scenario after applying ROS to the CNN architecture leads to the balancing of samples in each class.

The helper function of the Scikit library is used to perform the classification of the images. The model is configured in a batch size of 128 and classified into two classes using the following structure:

```
model = Sequential()
model.add(Conv2D(32, kernel_size=(3, 3), activation='relu', input_
shape=input_shape, strides=e))
model.add(Conv2D(64, (3, 3), activation='relu'))
```

```
model.add(MaxPooling2D(pool_size=(2, 2)))
model.add(Dropout(0.25))
model.add(Flatten())
model.add(Dense(128, activation='relu'))
model.add(Dropout(0.5))
model.add(Dense(num_classes, activation='softmax'))
model.compile(loss=keras.losses.categorical_crossentropy,
optimizer=keras.optimizers. Adadelta(), metrics=['accuracy'])
```

The results suggested the higher accuracy of the proposed model as 83.57% along with overall precision as 84%, recall as 84% and F1-score obtained as 83%. The results of analysis for benign and malignant classes are shown in Table 9.1, where IDC(–) represent the class 0 and IDC(+) represent the class 1. Figure 9.6 illustrates the confusion matrix of the proposed model depicting how accurately a proposed CNN model is working. The largest

TABLE 9.1

Confusion Matrix of CNN Model

	Precision	Recall	F1-score
IDC (–)	0.89	0.76	0.82
IDC (+)	0.79	0.91	0.85
Average	0.84	0.84	0.93

{0: 'IDC(–)', 1: 'IDC(+)'}

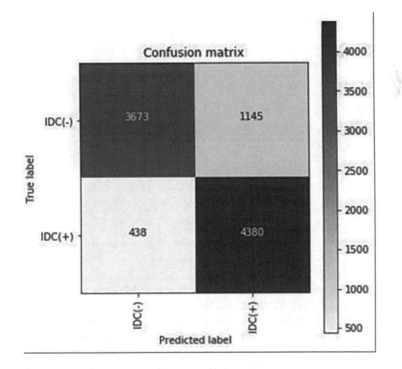

FIGURE 9.6

Confusion matrix of the proposed model.

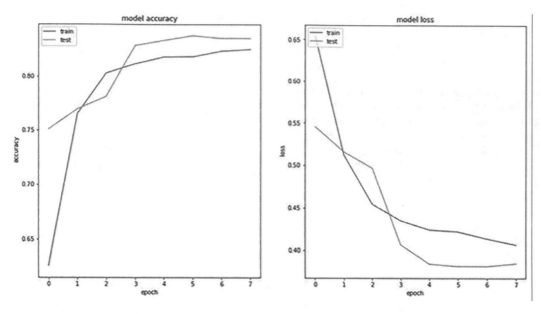

FIGURE 9.7

Graph depicting the increase in model accuracy and decrease in loss of the proposed model.

number of images was recorded in the true positive and false negative, showing the effectiveness of the model. The results obtained are comparable with the studies referred to in the literature review. Figure 9.7 depicts that there is an increase in model accuracy and a decline in the loss of the proposed model. The accuracy of the model is increasing and further loss is declining at each epoch in the case of the proposed model. The model accuracy and loss were found to stabilize at epoch 7, whereas the model was designed for 15 epochs to achieve maximum efficiency. The obtained results suggest that with the implementation of other feature-extraction techniques the model accuracy can be further increased and used for the analysis of cancer detection.

9.5 Conclusion

This study was carried out to develop a raw architecture for the classification of histopathology images for breast cancer detection at the early stage. Recently, the application of CNN has been increased exponentially for the analysis of images for dataset classification of different domains. The CNN architecture is used as a base classifier for the classification of cancerous images from other normal cases by recognizing the information from each pixel and learning the input dataset in the set of small groups. The proposed framework is designed with minimal pre-processing and feature-extraction techniques for improvising the dataset. The model performance was determined after testing at 20% of the dataset using confusion matrix, accuracy, precision, recall, and F1-score as evaluation measures. The model delivers an accuracy of 83.57% and an average F1-score of 0.93.

It has been concluded that the proposed model can extract vital information and delivers for the classification of histopathology images for the detection of cancer at an early stage. It is proposed to further improvise the model with the application of other pre-processing and feature-extraction techniques to enhance the model accuracy.

References

1. Bray, F., Ferlay, J., Soerjomataram, I., Siegel, R. L., Torre, L. A., & Jemal, A. (2018). Global cancer statistics 2018: GLOBOCAN estimates of incidence and mortality worldwide for 36 cancers in 185 countries. *CA: A Cancer Journal for Clinicians 68*(6), 394–424.
2. World Health Organization. *WHO Position Paper on Mammography Screening.* World Health Organization, 2014.
3. Nguyen, L. D., Lin, D., Lin, Z., & Cao, J. (2018, May). Deep CNNs for microscopic image classification by exploiting transfer learning and feature concatenation. In 2018 *IEEE International Symposium on Circuits and Systems (ISCAS)* (pp. 1–5). IEEE.
4. Kassani, S. H., Kassani, P. H., Wesolowski, M. J., Schneider, K. A., & Deters, R. (2019, October). Breast cancer diagnosis with transfer learning and global pooling. In *2019 International Conference on Information and Communication Technology Convergence (ICTC)* (pp. 519–524). IEEE.
5. Pan, S. J., & Yang, Q. (2009). A survey on transfer learning. *IEEE Transactions on Knowledge and Data Engineering 22*(10), 1345–1359.
6. Golatkar, A., Anand, D., & Sethi, A. (2018, June). Classification of breast cancer histology using deep learning. In *International Conference Image Analysis and Recognition* (pp. 837–844). Springer, Cham.
7. Gong, Y. (2013). Breast cancer: Pathology, cytology, and core needle biopsy methods for diagnosis. In: Shetty MK., (ed.) *Breast and Gynecological Cancers* (pp. 19–37). Springer, New York.
8. Gulzar, R., Shahid, R., & Saleem, O. (2018). Molecular subtypes of breast cancer by immunohistochemical profiling. *International Journal of Surgical Pathology 16*(2), 129–134.
9. Xu, J., Xiang, L., Liu, Q., Gilmore, H., Wu, J., Tang, J., & Madabhushi, A. (2015). Stacked sparse autoencoder (SSAE) for nuclei detection on breast cancer histopathology images. *IEEE Transactions on Medical Imaging 35*(1), 119–130.
10. Kandlikar, S. G., Perez-Raya, I., Raghupathi, P. A., Gonzalez-Hernandez, J. L., Dabydeen, D., Medeiros, L., & Phatak, P. (2017). Infrared imaging technology for breast cancer detection–Current status, protocols and new directions. *International Journal of Heat and Mass Transfer 108*, 2303–2320.
11. Wang, Z., Li, M., Wang, H., Jiang, H., Yao, Y., Zhang, H., & Xin, J. (2019). Breast cancer detection using extreme learning machine based on feature fusion with CNN deep features. *IEEE Access 7*, 105146–105158.
12. Saha, M., & Chakraborty, C. (2018). Her2net: A deep framework for semantic segmentation and classification of cell membranes and nuclei in breast cancer evaluation. *IEEE Transactions on Image Processing 27*(5), 2189–2200.
13. Brancati, N., De Pietro, G., Frucci, M., & Riccio, D. (2019). A deep learning approach for breast invasive ductal carcinoma detection and lymphoma multi-classification in histological images. *IEEE Access 7*, 44709–44720.
14. Kumar, A., Singh, S. K., Saxena, S., Lakshmanan, K., Sangaiah, A. K., Chauhan, H.,... & Singh, R. K. (2020). Deep feature learning for histopathological image classification of canine mammary tumors and human breast cancer. *Information Sciences 508*, 405–421.
15. Saha, M., Chakraborty, C., & Racoceanu, D. (2018). Efficient deep learning model for mitosis detection using breast histopathology images. *Computerized Medical Imaging and Graphics 64*, 29–40.

16. Kaur, P., Singh, G., & Kaur, P. (2019). Intellectual detection and validation of automated mammogram breast cancer images by multi-class SVM using deep learning classification. *Informatics in Medicine Unlocked 16*, 100151.

17. Qi, Q., Li, Y., Wang, J., Zheng, H., Huang, Y., Ding, X., & Rohde, G. K. (2018). Label-efficient breast cancer histopathological image classification. *IEEE Journal of Biomedical and Health Informatics 23*(5), 2108–2116.

18. Carneiro, G., Nascimento, J., & Bradley, A. P. (2017). Automated analysis of unregistered multiview mammograms with deep learning. *IEEE Transactions on Medical Imaging 36*(11), 2355–2365.

19. Saraf V., Chavan P., Jadhav A. (2020). Deep learning challenges in medical imaging. In: Vasudevan H., Michalas A., Shekokar N., Narvekar M. (eds) *Advanced Computing Technologies and Applications. Algorithms for Intelligent Systems*. Springer, Singapore. https://doi.org/10.1007/978-981-15-3242-9_28.

20. Lecun, Y., Bottou, L., Bengio, Y., & Haffner, P. (1998). Gradient based learning applied to document recognition. *Proceedings of IEEE 86*(11), 2278–2324.

21. Goodfellow, I., Bengio, Y., Courville, A., & Bengio, Y. (2016). *Deep Learning* (Vol. 1, p. 2). Cambridge: MIT press.

22. Bringas, S., Salomón, S., Duque, R., Montaña, J. L., & Lage, C. (2019). A convolutional neural network-based method for human movement patterns classification in Alzheimer's Disease. *Multidisciplinary Digital Publishing Institute Proceedings 31*(1), 72.

23. Zhang, X., Zhang, Y., Han, E. Y., Jacobs, N., Han, Q., Wang, X., & Liu, J. (2018). Classification of whole mammogram and tomosynthesis images using deep convolutional neural networks. *IEEE Transactions on Nanobioscience 17*(3), 237–242.

24. Shorten, C., & Khoshgoftaar, T. M. (2019). A survey on image data augmentation for deep learning. *Journal of Big Data 6*(1), 1–48.

25. Xie, J., Liu, R., Luttrell IV, J., & Zhang, C. (2019). Deep learning based analysis of histopathological images of breast cancer. *Frontiers in Genetics 10*, 80.

10

Realizing Mother's Features Influential on Childbirth Experience, towards Creation of a Dataset

Himani Deshpande and Leena Ragha

Ramrao Adik Institute of Technology, D Y Patil Deemed to be University

CONTENTS

10.1 Introduction

As said by Diane Mariechild, "A woman is the full circle. Within her is the power to create, nurture and transform." She is the one who is considered the most powerful creation of the almighty. A woman is always considered to be the strength behind a successful man, but now things are changing. Women today are not only strong for others but for themselves too. Her health should be on priority, to empower all dimensionalities of her personality. Although woman empowerment across the globe has been practiced from time immemorial, still there is more with regard to their health which needs to be explored. There are organizations like WHO and UNICEF which are working toward the betterment of

DOI: 10.1201/9781003283249-10

a woman's life and are seriously trying to address issues like gender equality, violence toward women, period stigma, body shaming, harassment at work, and family-related issues. There are many chanllenges faced by woman which while portraying different roles and responsibilities like a wife, sister, daughter, mother, and colleague, etc. She needs to be strong physically and mentally to stay happy herself and to carry out her responsibilities well. Women's health defines the growth and prosperity of a country. A family's well-being and contentment depend on the lady of the house, who is the key to sustainable development. Pregnancy is the phase of her life when she carries a life within herself and many changes happen within her body which are associated with the way she lives and the environment around her. Over time, doctors and researchers have revealed various observations and facts about a woman's reproduction capability, there are still many questions which remain unfolded and need to be addressed by observing the women population and their pregnancy experiences. Creating a dataset for the women population which gives a detailed insight to her lifestyle and surroundings while focusing on her pregnancy will be of great help with regards to this.

In the health domain, standard datasets are available for intense health issues like cancer, diabetes, thyroid, etc. but while looking into the research work done in the maternal domain, it was realized that there is no standard dataset available that depicts the characteristics of mothers, thus with this study we aimed at creating a dataset having detailed information about mothers with features depicting information across her reproductive age starting from her teenage to childbirth. In India, the city of Mumbai is the largest metropolis by population, as per the census of 2018, it had a population of 22.1 million. Mumbai women are considered to be strong and dynamic while dealing with the fast-paced life of the city. We have focused on the female population of Mumbai to create a standard dataset, which could be used to analyze the lifestyle effects on pregnancy. A child's health during the time of birth is considered to be the most important factor for her healthier future. It is said that the health of a baby in the mother's womb is related to the mother's health. Looking into the same, we have tried to scrutinize the way the mother has lived, by looking into different aspects of her lifestyle for creating a dataset depicting her health throughout the reproductive years of her life. The aim is to prevent pregnancy complications, thus ensuring a happy and meaningful life for the better section of society.

10.1.1 Significance of Woman's Reproductive Health

Life is never pleasant to a person of broken health, it is rightly said that a sound mind in a sound body is key to a happy life. Women, in spite of being strong in many ways, have multiple health issues, many of which are related to their reproductive health. Maternal health defines the state of a woman's health across the span of her pregnancy, childbirth experience, and the postpartum period. While motherhood is often a positive and fulfilling experience, for some women, it is associated with suffering, ill-health, and sometimes even mortality [1,2]. The reproductive age of a woman starts from her teenage, from there onward her body goes through many changes influenced by many factors. During these years a woman's lifestyle in terms of biological, social, environmental, economic, and cultural factors affects her reproductive health [3–5]. Even today, the onset of menses is celebrated as the empowerment of a woman with the reproductive capabilities and at the same time many stigmas are attached to it. This is the phase when she starts maturing in terms of accepting the transition from a child to a young girl along with accepting the norms of the society. The transition of environment, lifestyle, and health in terms of hormonal, physical, and emotional changes are a few of the factors which can have effects on the difficulties she may face during pregnancy and may influence the child's health. A woman's health during the reproductive or fertile years (between the ages of 13 and 49 years) is relevant not only to herself, but it also has an impact on the health and development of her child. A healthy woman turns into a healthy mother and gives birth to physically fit offsprings who are the future of the nation thus a woman's health plays a key role in the progress of a nation. Reproductive health needs to be given more importance as it is not just a major health issue but also a human right and is strongly associated with the development of a nation [6]. Not just the woman herself but the society as a whole needs to step up to understand the gravity of a woman's maternal health.

10.1.1.1 Maternal Health as a Global Issue

Maternal health has always been considered on high priority for nations and many initiatives are taken across the globe toward the improvement of maternal health [7,8]. Improving the health status of pregnant women and infants is an important public health issue in India and worldwide which needs to be urgently addressed because it leads to short- and long-term impacts on individuals, families, society, and the healthcare system [9–11]. The World Health Organization (WHO) has always focused on working to promote happier and healthier woman-prioritizing issues like gender equality, pleasant work environment, violence against women, and sexual and reproductive health, etc. [12] As mentioned by UNICEF on Maternal health, "Maternal mortality is considered a key health indicator and the direct causes of maternal deaths are well known and largely preventable and treatable" [13]. WHO proposed its "Millennium Development Goals", to be achieved globally by the year 2015, under which Goal 4 and Goal 5 deal with reducing childbirth mortality and improve maternal health by reducing maternal mortality and universal access to reproductive health. Both these goals are partially achieved, and WHO is still working on them [14]. A detailed guideline is communicated to all the countries to ensure a safe and healthy pregnancy experience for all women worldwide. The WHO has made recommendations regarding antenatal care, prevention and precautions during pregnancy, fetal and mother health assessment, and nutrition [15]. Improvement of maternal health of South Asian women and children is a key goal of UNICEF and they have targeted to reduce child mortality to 20.6 per 1,000 live births by the year 2021 [16]. Countries like Indonesia [17], China [18], the USA [2], and France [19] and many more have taken maternal health as a national priority.

10.1.1.2 Significance of Maternal Health in India

Indian women have shown their worth in all spheres of life and are strong-minded, efficient, hard-working, intelligent and a team player, still the literacy rate among Indian women is less than their male counterparts. As per the 2011 census, only 65.46% of Indian women are literate as compared to 82.14% of men [20]. Women are generally married young and take the responsibilities of domestic and financial support to the family, along with reproducing soon after the marriage. They know how to manage children, family, work, social relations, and many more things simultaneously. They are appreciated for carrying out their responsibilities well but their personal physical and mental health is always de-prioritized leading to various health complications during childbirth.

Women in India face various difficulties during childbirth, especially in rural areas with poor antenatal care. The targets set by the WHO for adequate antenatal care (ANC) are not met for pregnant women in India, rural women lack the basic care during pregnancy [21].

In spite of the great efforts taken in India toward reducing maternal and child morbidity and mortality, it does face various challenges associated with mother and child health.

There are many initiatives taken in India to promote the well-being of women, the Indian Council of Medical Research (ICMR)-INCLEN has taken a national initiative to engage faculty from top colleges to research maternal health and nutrition for the year 2016 to 2025 [22]. The Indian government has launched various schemes to help pregnant women and facilitate mother and child health as a principal goal toward the progress of the nation. Mentioned below are a few schemes launched in India toward maternal health.

- **Pradhan Mantri Surakshit Matrutva Abhiyaan**: This scheme was launched in 2016 by Indian Prime Minister, Shri. Narendra Modi. Under this scheme, the Ministry of Health & Family Welfare has made provision to provide free medical concealing and diagnostics with the objective to improve the quality and coverage of antenatal care to pregnant women especially the ones in the second and third trimesters of pregnancy. A mobile application and portal are designed to involve private sectors and volunteer for schemes [23].
- **Indira Gandhi Matritva Sahyog Yojana**: Indira Gandhi Matritva Sahyog Yojana is a scheme launched by the Ministry of Women and Child Development in 2010 with the objective to help women financially so that they can have enough nutrition. Both pregnant women and lactating mothers can be beneficiaries of the schemes, thus promoting the health of mother and infant [24].
- **Dr. Muthulakshmi Maternity Benefit Scheme**: This is a scheme launched by the government of Tamil Nadu, to provide financial assistance to a pregnant woman within the range of 12,000–18,000 Rs. along with a nutrition key with health mix powder. Women can avail this scheme for a total of two pregnancies [25].

In spite of many efforts taken by the government with respect to maternal health, still a lot needs to be addressed. Most of the schemes initiated are helping women financially to have nutritious food and antenatal care. With the penetration of mobile and computers in urban as well as rural areas of the country there is a need to provide computerized solutions for risk analysis of any future complication. A mobile application or website which takes the features of a woman as input and can help to give a detailed analysis of her health and pregnancy experience, and the health of newborns will be of great help to plan resources with rural as well as urban population when facilities are limited and expensive. Problematic cases can be predicted in advance and arrangements can be made to reach out to better medical facilities available in distant cities. Designing an accurate prediction model depends on the availability of the dataset. For the same reason, we have created Mother's Significant Feature (MSF) dataset with records of the Indian female population, which can be used to design machine learning-based models for timely diagnosis and prognosis for mother and child health. MSF dataset records the effect of lifestyle on pregnancy-related issues for analysis.

10.1.2 Lifestyle

Lifestyle is defined as how a person lives. It includes daily habits and is affected by many factors like economic status, social surrounding, culture, ideology, etc. The modern urban lifestyle is characterized by a high level of stress for the inhabitants. Uneven food habits, sedentary lifestyle, academic stress, workplace stress, blurring of boundaries between

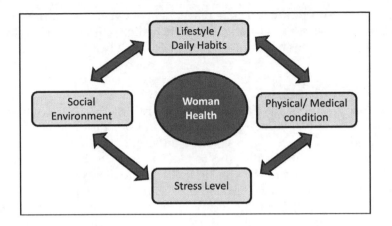

FIGURE 10.1
Factors influencing a woman's health.

home and work, gradual end of the joint family system and appearance of nuclear families, and loss of social support system are some of the several factors that are adversely affecting the health of the average urban resident. Women's reproductive health is getting adversely affected due to these detrimental changes. There are multiple diseases which are said to be rapidly increasing as a result of changing lifestyle [26–32], which affects the health of baby and mother during pregnancy and post pregnancy. Health conditions like polycyclic ovary syndrome, high blood pressure, gestational diabetes, infertility, and infections are associated with the woman and slowly start affecting the reproductive organs. It has been observed through studies that proper guidance given to women regarding lifestyle practices, would be beneficial to them in promoting healthy pregnancy experience [9,33–35].

As shown in Figure 10.1, a woman's health is a reflection of her lifestyle habits, the social environment around her, the stress she goes through, her physical body status, and medical conditions. All these factors are correlated to each other in some or the other way. Lifestyle of a woman is strongly influenced by her social surroundings. Unhealthy lifestyle is said to be the main reason behind stress and as discussed earlier many medical conditions are associated with it. One important solution to prevent health complications in the future is to ensure lifestyle awareness among the female population of the society regarding their reproductive health as well as overall well-being and to educate them about the factors that affect their general and emotional well-being, and specifically the reproductive health.

The transition to motherhood is a period of behavioral, social, psychological, and biological change in women's lives [4]. It is believed that infants' health is affected by the way mothers live through different phases of her life, thus making it important to study the lifestyle of a woman during reproductive age and especially during pregnancy. There has been work done by researchers on the maternal health of women as well as on the newborn's health, but not much research has been conducted looking into the lifestyle aspects of a woman across different phases of her life and a possible reason could be non-availability of a standard dataset for same.

As a nation we need to work toward women's reproductive health, as there are many gynecological as well as non-gynecological issues creeping in with the change in lifestyle, especially in an urban part of the country. With the MSF dataset we aim to help the women to understand and the doctors to conclude the relation between the features defining social status, physical health, stress level, and daily habits which define the lifestyle of a woman, and the pregnancy outcomes in terms of mother and child health.

10.1.3 Data in Research

Digitalization and advancement of technology have resulted in the growth of data across all domains, which are motivating researchers to analyze information toward exploring available knowledge. Researchers have relied on experimenting with relevant data to reach useful conclusions and identifying facts. Data need to be organized and categorized before being interpreted for analysis in order to find answers to unsolved problems. Data mining and machine learning have evolved as tools for identifying hidden patterns and classification using existing data and providing solutions to future incidences [36]. Research data can be qualitative or quantitative. Qualitative data describes and gives detailed information about the concerned problem associated with it and helps to investigate and provide a better understanding of the problem with significant information. Qualitative data relies on descriptive judgment using words, which are processed using content analysis. Quantitative data is numeric and has a unit and count associated, it is structured in nature and could be used directly for statistical analysis. Handling and processing of data have always been a challenge for researchers [37]. Good research needs relevant data in sufficient quantity and a strategic approach for deciding on the features and acquisition of information.

Data science enables the optimal utilization of available data using computerized tools and algorithms to predict possibilities of future complications and can alert women of any future pregnancy complications, which in turn could help in decision making and resource planning before and during childbirth. Even the best of the algorithms rely on the availability of significant data to be used as input for processing.

10.2 Study of Features Influencing Pregnancy and Childbirth Experience

Women are blessed with the divine power of the creation of life, the strength within her makes it possible to carry and nurture a life in her womb. Pregnancy is a stage in a woman's life, which is characterized by changes and is an opportune time to influence diet, surroundings, and habits toward healthier outcomes [23]. It is advised to live a healthier life which leads to a happy pregnancy and childbirth experiences. In this section, we aim at identifying the features of a woman which have an effect on her health, health of child, and childbirth experience.

Before giving birth to a child, the life of a woman constitutes mainly of three phases across her reproductive years. The first phase is her teenage when she is a young girl. The second phase is after getting married, this is the time when she joins a new family and new environment, there are different changes that she adapts after marriage. Third and the last phase is her pregnancy tenure which lasts for around nine months with few exceptions. During pregnancy, a woman's body comes across various hormonal and physical changes, which could have short- and long-term effects on her health. This section of the chapter concentrates on identifying the mother's features that have an impact on pregnancy and can directly affect the health of mother and child.

10.2.1 Phases of a Woman's Reproductive Age

Women's health during the reproductive or fertile years is relevant to women themselves, and also has an impact on the health and development of a baby. We have identified three phases of a woman's life that can affect the pregnancy and childbirth experience. These three phases are explained as follows.

1. **Teenage & Adulthood**: Teenage is a beautiful phase of life, where the body of an individual goes through many changes internally. Adolescence age plays a key role in laying the foundation for healthy adulthood [38]. On average, girls experience puberty at the age of 10–12, thereafter an important phase of their life starts, when they experience changes in many ways within their bodies. Depression, inappropriate food habits, and lack of physical activity during teenage are identified as very fatal for individual health and are found to be having long-term effects on health. Many of the health challenges during this period are ones that only young girls and women face For example, complications of pregnancy and childbirth are the leading cause of mortality in a young woman aged between 15 and 19 years in developing countries [39]. The most fundamental social changes affecting youth in Asia occur at the particular stage of transition to adulthood. Youth in their 20s to early 30s are most directly affected by social and environmental changes [40]. Adulthood is a period of optimum mental functioning when the individual's intellectual, emotional, and social capabilities are at their peak to meet the demands of social acceptance, beautiful appearance, career stability, and marriage. Because of the introduction of responsibilities and exposure at this age, there are changes in one's self, which are related to a female's emotional as well as physical aspects. Women have less time and plan to achieve a lot, which in turn could leave less time and concern for personal care and health. It is important to understand if the behavior and habits of females during this phase of life can have a long-term effect on her reproductive health and may reflect during pregnancy. Studies have shown that a proper lifestyle during adolescent age turns out to be a healthier pregnancy experience [3,34,35,41]. Researchers have always shown a keen interest in understanding the changes and behavior of women during this phase; teenage data can help them to understand if the habits during this phase of her life have a positive or negative correlation with future health conditions.

2. **After Marriage**: Marriage is a socially recognized union of two individuals through rituals that establishes various legal rights and responsibility toward each other and their families [42]. Marriage though called to be a union of two souls comes with its own set of pros and cons. In countries like India, marriage is not just the union of two souls, but it is much beyond that; it comes with many new relations in the life of both bride and groom. Though both husband and wife are considered to be equal, marriage leads to more changes in the life of a woman. She has to move to a new place and tries to adapt to new people and living conditions. As there are changes in terms of place, people, and day-to-day activities, marriage is related to the change in a woman's lifestyle and social status, and these changes affect the mental and physical health of women. There are psychological and hormonal changes observed after marriage, and fertility is said to be affected by marital aspects. The modeling and empirical literature in both economics and sociology tends to separate these two subjects, although the importance of fertility as an impetus for marriage is frequently stressed [43]. Lifestyle changes after

marriage are associated with health complications whose occurrence is primarily based on the daily habits and stress of a woman, and are a result of an inappropriate relationship of people with their environment [27] these could be linked to post-marital changes. A woman conceives a baby after marriage and data related to the mental and physical status of a woman during this time is associated with the health of child and mother. This data cap help to realize if environmental and lifestyle changes followed after marriage could have any effect on the general and reproductive health of the woman and her child.

3. **During Pregnancy**: Pregnancy is a beautiful phase of a woman's life, which needs to be handled with love and care. It is said that a child completes a woman, but the journey of these nine months when a life is formed goes through many ups and downs for a woman. A woman carries and nourishes another life within herself; this life is very delicate and frail, which makes it important to follow healthy habits throughout this phase. Other than having frequent visits to the doctor and taking advised medication, it is also advised to eat nutritious, healthy food in sufficient quantity, take proper rest, and stay away from any kind of physical and mental stress. Women are advised to be happy and moderately active during their pregnancy. It has been said that a good lifestyle followed during pregnancy results in a healthy child and mother. As discussed in Section 10.1, mother care during pregnancy is addressed as the prime health goal across all the countries of the world.

We have tried to create a dataset which could be used to analyze the physical health, stress level, social environment and lifestyle of a woman during pregnancy. Woman features are selected such that they define the behavior and habits of a woman which could be associated with a healthy childbirth experience.

10.2.2 Features Selected for Study

After identifying the important phases of a women's reproductive health next step is to identify relevant features, which gives detailed information about a woman's health and habits across the selected three phases. After consulting gynecologists and pediatricians with more than a decade of experience and reviewing the literature we have identified parameters which are assumed to influence mother and child health. All the features are divided widely into two categories: women's features and evaluation parameters. Woman feature defines the physical and mental status of a woman, while evaluation parameters help to understand the pregnancy outcomes in terms of mother and child health.

Features to describe women and pregnancy outcomes are further divided into different subcategories as shown in figure 10.2 and are explained further in this chapter. Selected woman's features are further divided into physical/health features, social circumstances, stress levels, lifestyle habits, and general information. Features selected under each of these categories are mentioned below:

1. **Physical/Health Feature**: Physical features of a woman refer to the bodily features, which could tell about the condition/age of the body. Referring to the literature, we have jotted down 23 important physical features which give relevant information about the health of a woman. These features define her external appearance and internal health of the body. Physical features selected for this study are as shown in Table 1.

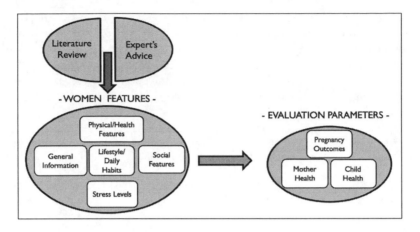

FIGURE 10.2
Category of features for MSF dataset.

Table 1

1. Age of mother	9. Infertility treatment	17. Gastric issues
2. Mother's weight before pregnancy	10. Miscarriage history	18. Cold/viral infection
3. Mother's weight after pregnancy	11. Menstrual cycle (before marriage)	19. Low amniotic fluid
4. Height	12. Menstrual cycle (after marriage)	20. High amniotic fluid
5. BMI	13. Time taken to conceive	21. No health complication during pregnancy
6. Hemoglobin	14. Thyroid	22. IVF
7. Polycyclic ovary syndrome	15. Hypertension	23. Birth parity
8. Age of father	16. Gestational diabetes	

2. **Social Features**: Social features define a mother's social circumstances and environment. It refers to her relationship with society and family and her status in society. Selected features under this category are listed in table 2.

Table 2

1. Years of marriage	8. Hobbies (visiting places)	15. Family support by (parents)
2. Does newborn have siblings	9. Hobbies (e.g., artistic things/dance/singing/painting)	16. Family support by (husband)
3. Number of newborn's siblings	10. Hobbies (shopping)	17. Women supporting the family (in-laws)
4. Mother education status	11. Hobbies (cooking/household work)	18. Women supporting the family (parents)
5. Family income	12. Hobbies (sitting alone in peace)	19. Women supporting the family (other family members)
6. Hobbies (spending time with people)	13. Working till which month of pregnancy	
7. Hobbies (eating/ foodie)	14. Family support by (in-laws)	

3. **Lifestyle/Daily Habits**: The third category of woman features consists of information about behavior and habits of the mother, which is termed her lifestyle. This includes eating habits, sleep patterns, traveling routine, job profile, intercourse details, etc. It has been observed by researchers [29–33,44] that lifestyle

has a great impact on the health of a woman. According to the WHO, 60% of factors related to individual health and quality of life are correlated to lifestyle [26]. Features are picked ranging from food habits to sleeping patterns to work environment. We have tried to leave no stone unturned to understand the lifestyle of a woman across all the three selected phases of her life. Lifestyle features selected across three phases of a woman's reproductive health are mentioned in table 3.

Table 3

1. Exercise (during teenage)	25. Diet consists of grains, vegetables, pulses, rice, salad (during teenage)	49. Sleep pattern (after marriage) (sleep more than 8 hours a day)
2. Exercise (after marriage)	26. Diet consists of more of pulses and rice (during teenage)	50. Sleep pattern (after marriage) (sleep less than 7 hours a day)
3. Exercise (during pregnancy)	27. Diet consists of more of dairy products (during teenage)	51. Sleep pattern (during pregnancy) (used to get up early in the morning)
4. Use of laptop/mobile (during teenage)	28. Diet consists of mostly snacks and high carbohydrate (during teenage)	52. Sleep patter (during pregnancy) (more of a night person, used to be awake till late night)
5. Use of laptop/mobile (after marriage)	29. Diet consists of non-vegetarian food (during teenage)	53. Sleep pattern (during pregnancy) (sleep more than 8 hours a day)
6. Use of laptop/mobile (during pregnancy)	30. Diet consists of fruits and salads (during teenage)	54. Sleep pattern (during pregnancy) (sleep less than 7 hours a day)
7. Outside food habits (during teenage)	31. Diet consists of grains, vegetables, pulses, rice, salad (after marriage)	55. Exposure to morning sunlight (during teenage)
8. Outside food habits (after marriage)	32. Diet consists of more of pulses and rice (after marriage)	56. Exposure to morning sunlight (after marriage)
9. Outside food habits (during pregnancy)	33. Diet consists of more of dairy products (after marriage)	57. Exposure to morning sunlight (during pregnancy)
10. Tea/coffee/caffeine (during teenage)	34. Diet consists of mostly snacks and high carbohydrate (after marriage)	58. Travel time (during teenage)
11. Tea/coffee/caffeine (after marriage)	35. Diet consists of non-vegetarian food (after marriage)	59. Travel time (after marriage)
12. Tea/coffee/caffeine (during pregnancy)	36. Diet consists of fruits and salads (after marriage)	60. Travel time (during pregnancy)
13. Smoking (during teenage)	37. Diet consists of grains, vegetables, pulses, rice, salad (during pregnancy)	61. Mode of commutation (during teenage)
14. Smoking (after marriage)	38. Diet consists of more of pulses and rice (during pregnancy)	62. Mode of commutation (after marriage)
15. Smoking (during pregnancy)	39. Diet consists of more of dairy products (during pregnancy)	63. Mode of commutation (during pregnancy)
16. Alcohol (during teenage)	40. Diet consists of mostly snacks and high carbohydrate (during pregnancy)	64. Works as (after marriage)
17. Alcohol (after marriage)	41. Diet consists of non-vegetarian food (during pregnancy)	65. Works as (during pregnancy)

(Continued)

18. Alcohol (during pregnancy)	42. Diet consists of fruits and salads (during pregnancy)	66. Use of contraceptive (how long)
19. Noise/air pollution (during teenage)	43. Sleep pattern (during teenage) (used to get up early in the morning)	67. Type of contraceptive used (before pregnancy)
20. Noise/air pollution (after marriage)	44. Sleep pattern (during teenage) (more of a night person, used to be awake till late night)	68. Intercourse frequency
21. Noise/air pollution (during pregnancy)	45. Sleep pattern (during teenage) (sleep more than 8 hours a day)	69. Craving for food during pregnancy
22. Health conscious (during teenage)	46. Sleep pattern (during teenage) (sleep less than 7 hours a day)	70. Mood swings during pregnancy
23. Health conscious (after marriage)	47. Sleep pattern (after marriage) (used to get up early in the morning)	71. Craving for vacation/ outing during pregnancy
24. Health conscious (during pregnancy)	48. Sleep Pattern (after marriage) (more of a night person, used to be awake till late night)	

4. **Stress Level**: Stress is referred to the mental strain a person goes through. Stress level features are selected to contribute to the MSF dataset with the thought of understanding what a woman feels from within. These features help to identify the mental stress she may be going through. We tried to collect the data by asking direct and indirect questions. Features for the same are listed in table 4.

Table 4

1. Travel time (during teenage)	5. Hours at work (during pregnancy)	9. Depression/loneliness (before pregnancy)
2. Travel time (after marriage)	6. Stress level at work/home (after marriage)	10. Depression/loneliness (during pregnancy)
3. Travel time (during pregnancy)	7. Stress Level at work/home (during pregnancy)	
4. Hours at work (after marriage)	8. Happy about arrival of baby	

5. **Evaluation Parameters/Health Complications**: Above mentioned features give detailed information about the mother. Category 5 with evaluation parameters consists of the mother's features (across selected three phases) that reflect the childbirth experience, her health, and child's health. Evaluation parameters can be termed as outcomes of the MSF dataset and are very important for any study for understanding healthy pregnancy and child birth experience. The MSF dataset consists of ten outcomes, which are mentioned in table 5.

Table 5

1. Pre-term birth	5. NICU stay requirement	9. Hours in labor before childbirth
2. Full-term birth	6. Jaundice detected in baby after birth	10. Need to induce artificial pain for labor
3. Weight of baby/babies	7. C-section delivery	
4. Number of days in hospital just after childbirth	8. Vaginal delivery	

Finding the correlation between the evaluation parameters and mother's features falling under each category is an open research question, which could be answered with MSF dataset analysis using machine learning and statistical tools.

6. **General Information**: General information about the mother consists of her name, contact number, and order details as shown in table 6. These details are not disclosed while sharing datasets for research work to hide the personal identity of an individual.

Table 6

1.	Unique identity (U_ID)	3.	Address	5.	Date of childbirth
2.	Name of mother	4.	Contact number	6.	Hospital name

Figure 10.3 shows the feature sets considered across different phases of a woman's life, which helps to understand her behavior, body, and mental state during these phases. Arrows in Figure 10.3 show the association of each phase with the feature set selected for MSF dataset creation. In this study, we intend to get data, which in turn can help the researchers to understand women and their reproductive health. MSF dataset can help to understand the health of a woman, her social environment, stress level, and lifestyle habits which could affect her health in the long go. MSF dataset is designed so that researchers can experiment with different combinations of features and outcomes to analyze mother and child health. For the creation of the MSF dataset, a survey form was prepared and sent across to women for data collection. A detailed explanation of the same is mentioned in the next section of this chapter.

10.2.3 Designing Survey Form

Once the features are selected for study, the next step was to design the questionnaire which could be used to collect data from women who have experienced childbirth. The

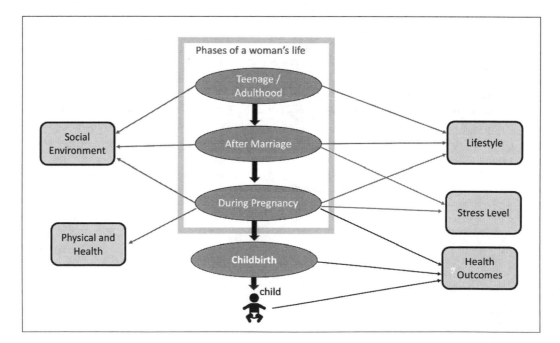

FIGURE 10.3
Phases of a woman's life and factors associated with each.

survey form used to collect data has been designed using google forms, questions were framed keeping the following points in mind:

1. While selecting the options for objective questions it is important to select relevant and sufficient number of possible answers. Options for questions have been decided after brainstorming sessions with medical experts in the field of gynecology.

2. We aimed at getting more information through less number of questions, as larger forms might look lengthy to the interviewee and they might not feel like giving more time to it. More information though limited questions helps to save the time of the interviewee and the interviewer. Figure 10.4 shows a few of the questions from the survey form. Question number 30, as shown in Figure 10.4a, asks for information about all the health conditions through a single question. Question number 11, as shown in Figure 10.4b, shows information about all her hobbies, if she has an interest in art and culture or likes to party and enjoy herself with friends, or is a self-loving person who likes to spend time with herself or she may

30. **Any of the following issues detected during pregnancy? (you can choose more then one option)**
   *

   Check all that apply.

	Thyroid	Hyper Tension	Diabetes	Gastric issues	frequent cold/cough/viral	Low amniotic fluid	High Amniotic Fluid	NONE of these
During Pregnancy	☐	☐	☐	☐	☐	☐	☐	☐

11. **Things that you love to do.**
   Mark only one oval per row.

	yes, a lot	yes, sometimes	hardly anytime / No
Visiting places	◯	◯	◯
Artistic things(Dance/singing/painting etc.)	◯	◯	◯
Shopping	◯	◯	◯
Cooking/house hold work	◯	◯	◯
Spending time with people	◯	◯	◯
Eating / Foodie	◯	◯	◯
Sitting alone in peace	◯	◯	◯

3. **Have outside/canteen food** *
   Mark only one oval per row.

	Hardly anytime	Occasionally (once or twice a week)	Often (thrice a week)	Very often (five or more times a week)
During Teenage	◯	◯	◯	◯
After Marriage	◯	◯	◯	◯
During Pregnancy	◯	◯	◯	◯

FIGURE 10.4
(a–c) Sample questions from the survey form.

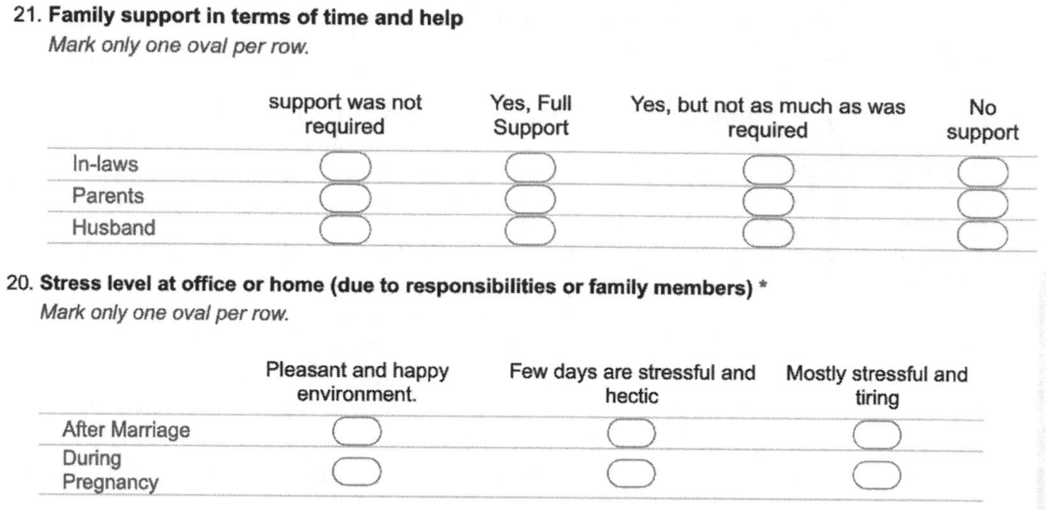

21. **Family support in terms of time and help**
Mark only one oval per row.

	support was not required	Yes, Full Support	Yes, but not as much as was required	No support
In-laws	◯	◯	◯	◯
Parents	◯	◯	◯	◯
Husband	◯	◯	◯	◯

20. **Stress level at office or home (due to responsibilities or family members)** *
Mark only one oval per row.

	Pleasant and happy environment.	Few days are stressful and hectic	Mostly stressful and tiring
After Marriage	◯	◯	◯
During Pregnancy	◯	◯	◯

FIGURE 10.5
(a and b) Sample questions from a survey form.

be liking all of these thus with one question we get enough information about her personality. All the questions related to lifestyle and daily habits have three rows as shown in Figure 10.4c; with one equation we can get information about three phases of her life.

We have tried to frame the questions such that even the more serious questions like stress due to family and in-laws are presented in a very general way, and doesn't reveal the gravity of questions so that mothers don't hesitate to give the right information as shown in Figure 10.5a. Words such as bad, very stressful, and always stressful are avoided in questions as shown in Figure 10.5b.

Figure 10.6 shows the six pages of the used survey form, Figure 10.6a is the first page of the form it consists of the basic information about the mother, while Figure 10.6b–e have questions related to lifestyle, stress and social features for mother while the last page of questionnaire Figure 10.6f consists information related to childbirth experience.

10.3 Data Collection

Data collection is a process to acquire information following a well-planned procedure. Acquiring authentic data is the first step toward reaching some useful facts about the population. In this study after understanding the relevant features, the next step was to have a well-planned strategy to acquire data. Along with the number of samples, authenticity and diversity of data are essential while creating a dataset that can help in efficient analysis using machine learning methodologies. After identifying influential features across the reproductive age of a woman and preparing the questionnaire for the same, the next step was finding target subjects of the female population.

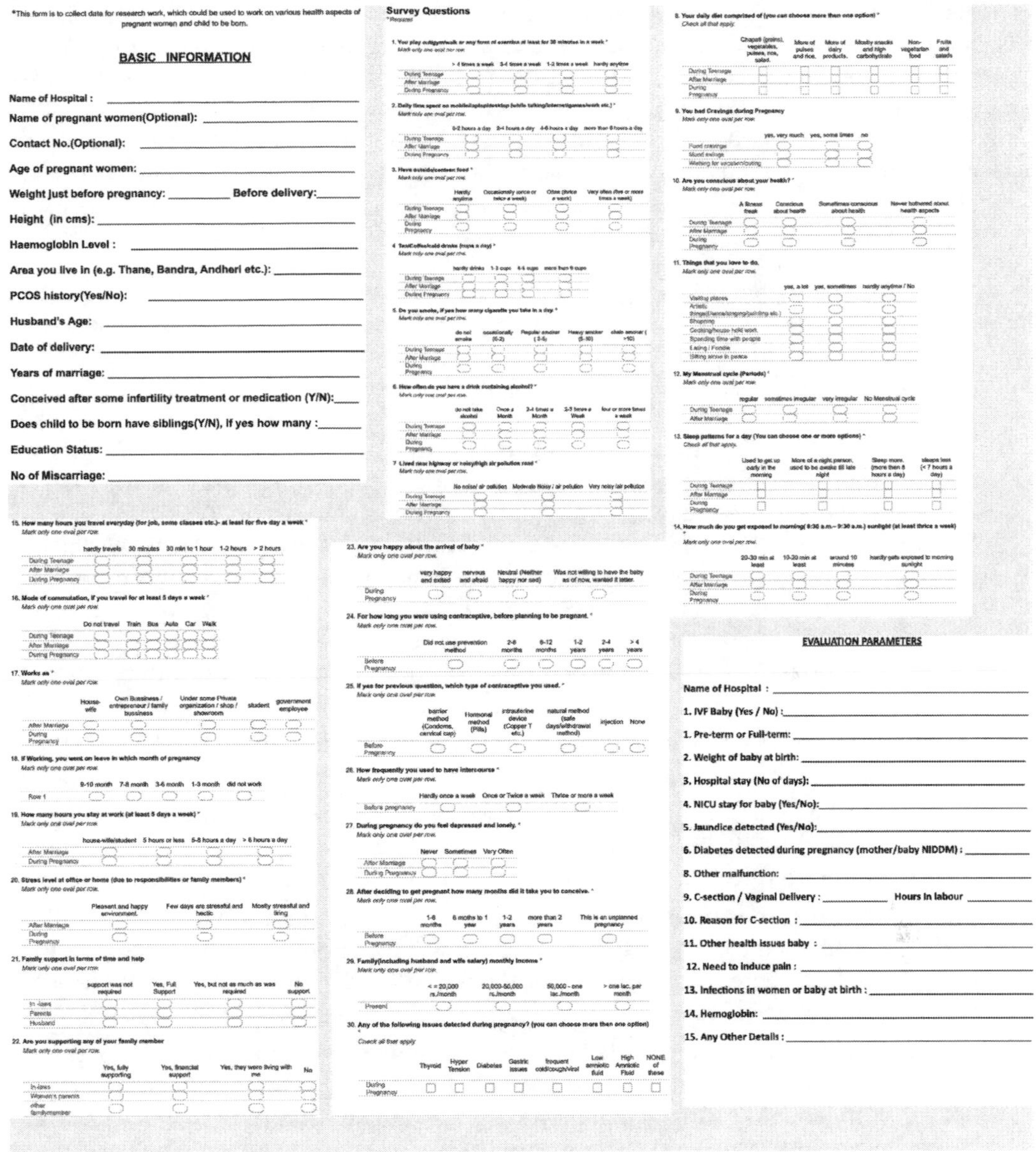

*This form is to collect data for research work, which could be used to work on various health aspects of pregnant women and child to be born.

BASIC INFORMATION

Name of Hospital : ______

Name of pregnant women(Optional): ______

Contact No.(Optional): ______

Age of pregnant women: ______

Weight just before pregnancy: ______ Before delivery: ______

Height (in cms): ______

Haemoglobin Level : ______

Area you live in (e.g. Thane, Bandra, Andheri etc.): ______

PCOS history(Yes/No): ______

Husband's Age: ______

Date of delivery: ______

Years of marriage: ______

Conceived after some infertility treatment or medication (Y/N): ______

Does child to be born have siblings(Y/N), If yes how many : ______

Education Status: ______

No of Miscarriage: ______

Survey Questions

EVALUATION PARAMETERS

Name of Hospital : ______

1. IVF Baby (Yes / No) : ______

1. Pre-term or Full-term: ______

2. Weight of baby at birth: ______

3. Hospital stay (No of days): ______

4. NICU stay for baby (Yes/No): ______

5. Jaundice detected (Yes/No): ______

6. Diabetes detected during pregnancy (mother/baby NIDDM) : ______

8. Other malfunction: ______

9. C-section / Vaginal Delivery : ______ Hours in labour ______

10. Reason for C-section : ______

11. Other health issues baby : ______

12. Need to induce pain : ______

13. Infections in women or baby at birth : ______

14. Hemoglobin: ______

15. Any Other Details : ______

FIGURE 10.6
(a–f) Survey forms used for the creation of the MSF dataset.

10.3.1 Selection of Subjects

There has been utmost care taken while selecting the individual subjects for inclusion in the research data collection process. We wanted to ensure variation in the MSF dataset across age groups, economic status, geographical locations, working status, eating habits, education status, daily schedule, family relations, etc. Subjects are selected ranging from age 18 to 52, and women from different areas of Mumbai metropolitan region, spread over 6,640 sq. km. with 9 Municipal Corporations are interviewed with different work profiles, some taken infertility treatment, and some with miscarriage history. There have been healthy women as well as a woman's suffering from medical issues like Polycystic Ovarian Disease, irregular menstrual cycle, thyroid, diabetes, and anemia. Some women carried single/twin/triplet babies, women with one or multiple birth parity. Women are under attributable stress because of the nuclear/joint family system and work commitments. We want to thank all the medical experts, who have helped us to understand and identify the possible variation in subjects, which in turn helped us to select our subjects for the creation of a meaningful dataset.

10.3.2 Reaching Out to Subjects

To acquire larger sample size, we preferred going to maternity hospitals and collecting data from women who have just delivered babies and are in hospitals under observation as a routine procedure after childbirth. Here we list a few reasons for preferring data collection at hospitals with the involvement of hospital personnel:

1. While trying to collect data, we realized that most of the women were hesitant to share their personal details for research work as there are questions like intercourse frequency, contraceptive use, family relations, and occupation details. For the same reason, they might give wrong details or don't agree to fill the form or may answer only limited questions. But when we approached the mothers through the hospital people, whom they trust, women were comfortable enough to share their details. Hospital people assured them that these details will be used for research purposes toward the betterment of mother and child health.

2. As suggested by the literature, we too realized that questionnaire without human intervention can be passive and miss out on some of the finer nuances, leaving the responses open to interpretation.

3. We designed google forms and tried to reach out to mothers through soft copy on their email, but the form looked very lengthy with many questions and women were not interested to take out the time and putting in effort to complete the form.

4. We wanted to gather data on women across different educational backgrounds and have considered uneducated women as well. Few women were not able to read and write. There were some medical terms like amniotic fluid, which are not familiar to many women.

5. In addition, there are some detailed questions which talk about women's health during pregnancy like hemoglobin levels, weight before pregnancy, weight just before delivery, infections during pregnancy, cravings during pregnancy, and working hours. To get proper answers to these questions, we targeted women who have just delivered babies, as they tend to forget details with time. So, we are sure enough to get accurate data especially for the questions which talk about pregnancy interval. We realized the importance of the lifestyle of a woman across different phases of her life: lifestyle during teenage, lifestyle before marriage, and lifestyle after marriage. As we wanted to have a detailed analysis of her lifestyle, our questionnaire consists of many questions. We feel that woman immediately after deliverey will be able to answer propoerly, the questions related to "after marriage" phase , again for the same reason, that people tends to forget details with time. Especially, as after kids, woman gets fully involved in activities with kids and have less memories about the time when they didn't have kids (after marriage).

6. There are features like a reason for C-section and hemoglobin level, which could be explained properly by a medical domain person. It's always better to refer

a patient's medical records for features like hemoglobin, weight before pregnancy, weight just before delivery, reason for cesarean birth, baby birth weight, pre-term/full-term delivery, hours in child labor, and need to induce pain.

7. Maternity hospital is the place where we can find our target subjects easily. Mothers get busy after having kids, and it will be difficult to ask them to take time and fill in the survey form. After childbirth, mother stays in the hospital under observation for around 3–7 days. We thought this is the time when they are resting in hospitals and would not mind sparing a few minutes to help us with their details.

10.3.3 Challenges while Collecting Data

After deciding on the subjects to be examined and where to reach out to them, the next challenge was to collect data. We wanted to observe the outcomes during the time of pregnancy and at the time of childbirth. For the same, we wanted to interview women who have delivered babies. Here we list a few of the issues that we faced while collecting data for the MSF dataset:

1. The first step was to meet doctors and hospital management and to convince them that we are here to work on a serious issue which in turn will help future mothers to have healthier pregnancy, childbirth, and infants. For the same, we explained our research in detail and took their feedback and suggestions. We presented the necessary documents to them to assure our credibility and intentions.

2. Hospitals were hesitant to share information about their patients, as they felt that their patients would feel disturbed and might be uncomfortable in sharing personal details, which in turn could result in compromising the hospital's reputation. Few renowned hospitals said that they have various high-profile patients and leakage of their details might have serious outcomes. Other hospitals were having a very small count of monthly deliveries, so they will not be able to help us in acquiring a sufficient number of records for the MSF dataset.

3. There were legal aspects too, because of which hospitals were reluctant in sharing the information about their patients. According to Medical Law [45], managing and protecting personal information is a serious issue, and data should be handled with utmost care.

4. There are few hospital managements that agreed to share patient details after the consent of their patients and following the legal procedure. A proper message was printed on survey forms for clarification wherever necessary, to ensure research credibility before data creation. But, here the challenge was that patients were either not in the condition to fill the form or were not willing to take the efforts to fill the forms themselves. We tried giving forms to patients, but despite giving multiple reminders during their stay in the hospital, very few filled the complete form. They were not willing to put effort in understanding the questions and answering accordingly. Most of the survey forms given to patients were left unattended or incomplete.

We decided to seek the help of hospital paramedical employees, especially nurses, who can interact with patients and can interview them for the question mentioned in the survey form. This would help to have more accurate answers and complete forms. For this job, we preferred female staff who have some knowledge about pregnancy procedures, as mothers might not be comfortable sharing their pregnancy information with males. Out of all the staff members, we thought that nurses are most appropriate for the task of interviewing mothers. But, it was not easy to convince the hospital staff to work for something which is not part of their job. In spite of getting permission from hospitals, we were not able to collect data due to lack of human resources to interview mothers. We handed over survey forms to many hospitals but without much luck.

As on-duty nurses were busy with their daily duties we didn't want to disturb the overall system of the hospital, we tried to find out nursing students who can help us with data collection at hospitals, as they can sustain the hospital environment and knows how to interact with patients. We visited nursing colleges near the hospitals where we had permission to collect data and tried to find some students who are willing to help us in data collection. We took permission from college heads and looked into it that studies are not affected for students. Finally, we met a nursing student, at a reputed nursing college in suburban Mumbai, who helped us to interview mothers after taking the requisite permission. For the same, we took permission from the hospital dean, gynecology, obstetrics head of department, and nursing head of the hospital.

10.3.4 Collection of Data

Records for the MSF dataset have been collected through mothers in different ways, which are as follows:

1. Most of the data samples are collected with one-on-one discussions with mothers. Women just after childbirth stay in hospital for a few days. This is the time when hospital people meet them for regular check-ups. After taking permission from doctors and consent from mothers, a nursing student had interviewed women with the survey questions. While interviewing, all the questions were explained properly to mothers. The interviewer continuously made note of the replies by mothers. Medical records of patients were referred for answers to questions like hemoglobin, weight before pregnancy, weight just before delivery, reason for cesarean birth, baby birth weight, and hours in child labor.

2. Women were given forms to be filled, some were handed over hard copies of forms in hospitals, they were requested to fill the forms and submit. Women who delivered babies few years back were also given hardcopy of the survey forms to be filled.

3. Online submissions were done through links to online google forms, which have been passed to women on their email IDs. They were requested to fill the forms online and submit them.

10.3.5 Limitations

MSF dataset has been created to provide detailed information about a woman, which could be used to analyze pregnancy outcome and childbirth experience in terms of the health of mother and child. There are a few limitations to the created dataset which are mentioned as follows:

1. Mother and father both contribute toward the creation of a new life. We have focused on the features of a mother but have not considered the features of a father

while creating the dataset. Information about a father's features could be helpful in analyzing the health of newborn.

2. We have considered social, stress, physical, and lifestyle features of the mother but have not looked into family history and hereditary issues in the maternal or paternal family, which can affect childbirth experience and health of newborn.

3. There could be authenticity issues with the data provided by respondents as they may not be fully truthful with some of their answers, especially for questions which are considered as social taboo in India, such as smoking and alcohol consumption habits and intercourse details. Lifestyle parameters across different phases of a woman's life are assessed through retrospective might have led to recall bias leading to wrong information.

MSF dataset is created keeping the well-being of women and newborns in mind, utilizing the advancements done in the field of data science to provide solutions to existing problems in the domain.

10.4 MSF Dataset

Childbirth is an experience which initiates a life on earth; a healthy beginning leads to a brighter future. Looking into the available health domain dataset repository it was realized that standard datasets are available for serious health conditions like cancer, diabetes, and thyroid but there are no standard datasets available which can help to analyze pregnancy and childbirth experiences. MSF dataset has been created with the aim to make data available for research toward the betterment of mother and child health.

10.4.1 Dataset Description

MSF dataset consists of a total of 130 features spread over six categories as stated in Section 10.2.2 of this chapter. Dataset is formed using records of 1,000 mothers, out of which most of the mothers have experienced childbirth between February 2018 to September 2019 at D. Y. Patil Hospital, situated in Navi Mumbai. Women right after the birth of a child were interviewed by medical personnel to contribute toward the MSF dataset creation. Features contributing to the MSF dataset are selected by looking into literature and advised by medical domain experts in the field of mother and child health. Record of each mother is divided into six sub-dataset as per the categories stated in Section 10.2.2, which are stored in Microsoft Excel format. Few records of the MSF dataset have been made publicly available on "IEEE DataPort" website [46]. Dataset consists of a total of six excel sheets which are as follows:

1. MSF_Dataset_Complete.xlsx (all the 130 features)

2. MSF_Physical&health_Fetaures.xlsx (consists of Physical and Health-related features)

3. MSF_Mother_lifestyle.xlsx (consists of mother lifestyle-related features)

4. MSF_Mother_Social.xlsx (consists of a mother's social status-related features)

5. MSF_Mother_stress.xlsx (consists of mother stress level related features)

6. MSF_HealthOutcome.xlsx (consists of outcomes associated with pregnancy, baby health)

General information about a woman like her name, contact number, and address is not made available to protect her privacy. All the excel sheets have a common primary key feature named as "Mother_UID", which is a unique identity given to each mother, Mother_UID helps to correlate the records of the same women across all the six excel files. For features with binary values, '1' denotes true/yes and '0' value denotes false/no. While collecting the data, we realized the need to add a few more questions, thus adding them subsequently to the survey form. For the same reason there are missing values in dataset for six features, quetsions for these features were added at a later stage to the survey form: mother's weight before delivery, mis- carriage history, cravings during pregnancy, family support to women, women supporting family, and hobbies. All the other features of the MSF dataset have no missing values.

10.4.2 MSF Dataset Analysis

Dataset consists of a total of 130 features, which includes the mother's physical, social, stress, lifestyle feature, and pregnancy outcomes. Age of mother, weight before pregnancy, weight before delivery, height, BMI, hemoglobin, age of father, years of married life, weight of newborn, and hours in labor pain are continuous features, whereas other features are categorical in nature. Table 10.7 depicts the average value, median, mode, standard deviation, largest value, and smallest value falling under each of the continuous features. Variable "a" in the last rows of Table 10.7 expresses how much percentage of the mean is the standard deviation. The value of variable "a" shows that there is significant variation across features like weight before pregnancy, weight after pregnancy, hemoglobin, years of marriage, weight of baby, and hours in labor, while height, age of mother, BMI, and age of father are found to have comparatively less variation from the mean value. Dataset is recorded by interviewing women just after childbirth, to get the most accurate data and avoid recall bias.

We wanted to have an even distribution across all MSF (Mother's Significant Feature) dataset features, but after collecting data it was observed that the distribution is skewed. Figure 10.7 demonstrates the spread of some of the variables used in MST dataset, in all the plots x-axis denotes frequency and y-axis denotes the range for feature, it has been identified that the data under mother's age, BMI, and hemoglobin levels are concentrated within a range. 88% of the mother's records fall under the range of 26–30 years, 65% of women have BMI between 21 and 25 kg/m^2 and 73% of the population have hemoglobin in the range of 12–13 gm/dL. Figure 10.7 shows that the father's age and years of marriage features are positively skewed, while height and weight of mother are evenly distributed across the MSF dataset.

In the medical profession, doctors while working on a health condition focus on trying to associate symptoms and behavior with the medical condition of a patient, thus realizing the relationship between features. Correlation analysis between features plays an important role with medical data, in drawing inferences [47]. Figure 10.8 shows the heat map for correlation between the features falling under the four categories, namely social, physical, lifestyle and stress; the figure depicts negative and positive correlations. Negative correlation is shown with darker shades of color, while positive correlation is shown with lighter shades.

Dataset analysis shows that the MSF dataset is a detailed dataset having 130 features for 1,000 records of women. These women have many similarities as they have gone through

TABLE 10.7

Statistical Analysis of Continuous Features

	Age of Mother	Wt. before Preg (in kg.)	Wt. before Delivery (in kg.)	Height (in cm.)	BMI	Hemoglobin	Age of Father	Years of Marriage	Baby Weight (in kg.)	Hours in Labor
Mean ($\bar{x}$)	26.61	59.53	66.31	161.15	23.17	12.05	30.85	4.05	2.14	14
Median	26	59	66	161	23	12.4	30	3	2.68	12
Mode	26	68	72	169	22	12.4	30	2	3.15	12
Standard deviation (SD)	4.24	18.78	27.55	12.45	3.19	4.6	4.77	2.78	0.6	5.53
Largest	52	95	89	189	42	17.8	52	30	6.4	28
Smallest	18	24	39	124	8	2.6	21	0	0.55	0
(SD/$\bar{x}$)*100	15.94	31.55	41.55	7.73	13.77	38.18	15.47	68.65	28.04	39.5

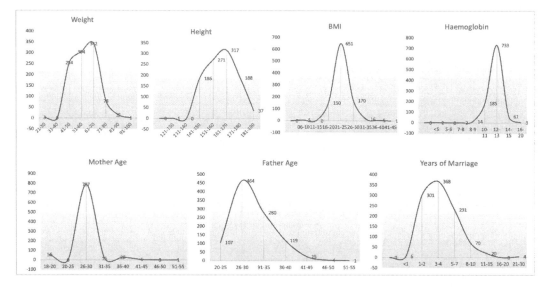

FIGURE 10.7
Data skewness for mother's continuous features.

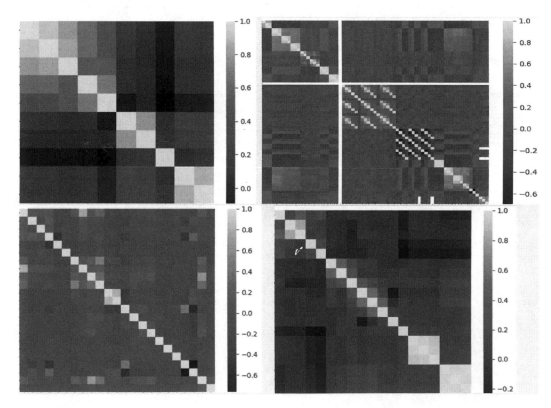

FIGURE 10.8
Heat map for correlation between features under the categories of MSF dataset: (a) social, (b) lifestyle, (c) physical, and (d) stress.

the same process of maternal maturity, pregnancy, and childbirth, while they differ in terms of their lifestyle habits, physical features, social environment, and stress levels.

10.5 Conclusion

Health of mothers and children has always been on the prime agenda across the globe. In this study, we have created the MSF (Mother's Significant Feature) dataset, with detailed information about the mother. We have considered three phases of a woman's life that can affect pregnancy: teenage, after marriage, and during pregnancy. MSF (Mother's Significant Feature) dataset consists of information across these three phases covering different aspects of a woman's life which includes physical, social, stress level, and lifestyle parameters. Creating the dataset was a continuous learning process, which helped us to understand pregnancy in various ways. Visiting hospitals and interacting with medical and paramedical personnel with decades of experience helped us in practical learning of the domain, while insights of literature helped us to explore the domain from newer implementation angels. MSF (Mother's Significant Feature) dataset is created keeping the well-being of women and newborn in mind, with the purpose to promote utilization of the advancements done in the field of data science to provide solutions to existing problems in the childbirth domain. With the use of the MSF dataset, it is possible to analyze the correlation between a mother's features and childbirth experience, thus helping women to work upon improvisation of lifestyle habits which could have a negative impact on her or child's health. There is skewness among the features of the MSF dataset which represents the spread of the Indian women population experiencing childbirth. MSF dataset can be used to research on pregnancy outcomes for the betterment of society in terms of achieving the goal of healthier women and stronger children. Exploring the patterns and facts with experimenting on the MST dataset can help women and doctors to be aware of any future complications, thus helping them to have a better resource, time, and financial management.

References

1. Liu, L., Oza, S., Hogan, D., Chu, Y., Perin, J., Zhu, J., Lawn, J.E., Cousens, S., Mathers, C. and Black, R.E., 2016. Global, regional, and national causes of under-5 mortality in 2000–15: an updated systematic analysis with implications for the Sustainable Development Goals. *The Lancet*, 388(10063), pp.3027–3035.
2. Firoz, T., Chou, D., von Dadelszen, P., Agrawal, P., Vanderkruik, R., Tunçalp, O., Magee, L.A., van Den Broek, N. and Say, L., 2013. Measuring maternal health: focus on maternal morbidity. *Bulletin of the World health Organization, 91*, pp.794–796.
3. Joshi, B.N., Chauhan, S.L., Donde, U.M., Tryambake, V.H., Gaikwad, N.S. and Bhadoria, V., 2006. Reproductive health problems and help seeking behavior among adolescents in urban India. *The Indian Journal of Pediatrics*, 73(6), pp.509–513.
4. Devine, C.M., Bove, C.F. and Olson, C.M., 2000. Continuity and change in women's weight orientations and lifestyle practices through pregnancy and the postpartum period: the influence of life course trajectories and transitional events. *Social Science & Medicine*, 50(4), pp.567–582.

5. Goossens, J., Beeckman, D., Van Hecke, A., Delbaere, I. and Verhaeghe, S., 2018. Preconception lifestyle changes in women with planned pregnancies. *Midwifery*, 56, pp.112–120.

6. Cook, R.J., Dickens, B.M. and Fathalla, M.F., 2003. *Reproductive Health and Human Rights: Integrating Medicine, Ethics, and Law*. Clarendon Press.

7. Firoz, T., Chou, D., von Dadelszen, P., Agrawal, P., Vanderkruik, R., Tunçalp, O., Magee, L.A., van Den Broek, N. and Say, L., 2013. Measuring maternal health: focus on maternal morbidity. *Bulletin of the World health Organization*, 91, pp.794–796.

8. World Health Organization, 2015. *Trends in Maternal Mortality: 1990–2015: Estimates from WHO, UNICEF, UNFPA, World Bank Group and the United Nations Population Division*. World Health Organization.

9. Hemsing, N., Greaves, L. and Poole, N., 2017. Preconception health care interventions: a scoping review. *Sexual & Reproductive Healthcare*, 14, pp.24–32.

10. Clark, A.M., Thornley, B., Tomlinson, L., Galletley, C. and Norman, R.J., 1998. Weight loss in obese infertile women results in improvement in reproductive outcome for all forms of fertility treatment. *Human Reproduction (Oxford, England)*, 13(6), pp.1502–1505.

11. Hamilton, E.A.A., Nowell, A.K., Harden, A. and Thangaratinam, S., 2018. Conduct and reporting of acceptability, attitudes, beliefs and experiences of pregnant women in randomised trials on diet and lifestyle interventions: a systematic review. *European Journal of Obstetrics & Gynecology and Reproductive Biology*, 225, pp.243–254.

12. https://www.who.int/news-room/spotlight/6-priorities-for-women-and-health.

13. https://www.unicef.org/india/what-we-do/maternal-health.

14. https://www.who.int/news-room/fact-sheets/detail/millennium-development-goals-(mdgs).

15. World Health Organization, 2016. *WHO Recommendations on Antenatal Care for a Positive Pregnancy Experience*. World Health Organization.

16. https://www.unicef.org/rosa/what-we-do/maternal-newborn-child-health.

17. Webster, P.C., 2012. Indonesia makes maternal health a national priority. *The Lancet*, 380(9858), pp.1981–1982.

18. Wu, Z., Viisainen, K., Li, X. and Hemminki, E., 2008. Maternal care in rural China: a case study from Anhui province. *BMC Health Services Research*, 8(1), pp.1–9.

19. Saurel-Cubizolles, M.J., Romito, P. and Lelong, N., 2007. Women's psychological health according to their maternal status: a study in France. *Journal of Psychosomatic Obstetrics & Gynecology*, 28(4), pp.243–249.

20. Grover, V.K., 2015. Second generation gender bias: Invisible barriers holding women back in organizations. *International Journal of Applied Research*, 1(4), pp.1–4.

21. Mugo, N.S., Mya, K.S. and Raynes-Greenow, C., 2020. Country compliance with WHO-recommended antenatal care guidelines: equity analysis of the 2015–2016 Demography and Health Survey in Myanmar. *BMJ Global Health*, 5(12), p.e002169.

22. Arora, N.K., Swaminathan, S., Mohapatra, A., Gopalan, H.S., Katoch, V.M., Bhan, M.K., Rasaily, R., Shekhar, C., Thavaraj, V., Roy, M. and Das, M.K., 2017. Research priorities in maternal, newborn, & child health & nutrition for India: an Indian Council of Medical Research-INCLEN initiative. *The Indian Journal of Medical Research*, 145(5), p.611.

23. https://pmsma.nhp.gov.in/.

24. https://niti.gov.in/writereaddata/files/document_publication/IGMSY_FinalReport.pdf.

25. https://krishnagiri.nic.in/scheme/dr-muthulakshmi-maternity-benefit-scheme/.

26. Farhud, D.D., 2015. Impact of lifestyle on health. *Iranian Journal of public Health*, 44(11), p.1442.

27. Sharma, M. and Majumdar, P.K., 2009. Occupational lifestyle diseases: An emerging issue. *Indian Journal of Occupational and Environmental Medicine*, 13(3), p.109.

28. Joshi, B., Mukherjee, S., Patil, A., Purandare, A., Chauhan, S. and Vaidya, R., 2014. A cross-sectional study of polycystic ovarian syndrome among adolescent and young girls in Mumbai, India. *Indian Journal of Endocrinology and Metabolism*, 18(3), p.317.

29. Ratner, R.E., Christophi, C.A., Metzger, B.E., Dabelea, D., Bennett, P.H., Pi-Sunyer, X., Fowler, S., Kahn, S.E. and Diabetes Prevention Program Research Group, 2008. Prevention of diabetes in women with a history of gestational diabetes: effects of metformin and lifestyle interventions. *The Journal of Clinical Endocrinology & Metabolism*, 93(12), pp.4774–4779.

30. Goossens, J., Beeckman, D., Van Hecke, A., Delbaere, I. and Verhaeghe, S., 2018. Preconception lifestyle changes in women with planned pregnancies. *Midwifery*, 56, pp.112–120.

31. Anand, A. and Shakti, D., 2015, Prediction of diabetes based on personal lifestyle indicators. *In 2015 1st International Conference on Next Generation Computing Technologies (NGCT)* (pp. 673–676). IEEE.

32. Patil, M., Lobo, V.B., Puranik, P., Pawaskar, A., Pai, A. and Mishra, R., 2018, July. A proposed model for lifestyle disease prediction using support vector machine. *In 2018 9th International Conference on Computing, Communication and Networking Technologies (ICCCNT)* (pp. 1–6). IEEE.

33. Homan, G., Litt, J. and Norman, R.J., 2012. The FAST study: Fertility Assessment and advice Targeting lifestyle choices and behaviours: a pilot study. *Human Reproduction*, 27(8), pp.2396–2404.

34. Richards, J. and Mousseau, A., 2012. Community-based participatory research to improve pre-conception health among Northern Plains American Indian adolescent women. *American Indian and Alaska Native Mental Health Research: The Journal of the National Center*, 19(1), pp.154–185.

35. Wade, G.H., Herrman, J. and McBeth-Snyder, L., 2012. A preconception care program for women in a college setting. *MCN: The American Journal of Maternal/Child Nursing*, 37(3), pp.164–170.

36. Wu, X., Kumar, V., Quinlan, J.R., Ghosh, J., Yang, Q., Motoda, H., McLachlan, G.J., Ng, A., Liu, B., Philip, S.Y. and Zhou, Z.H., 2008. Top 10 algorithms in data mining. *Knowledge and Information Systems*, 14(1), pp.1–37.

37. Yang, Q. and Wu, X., 2006. 10 challenging problems in data mining research. *International Journal of Information Technology & Decision Making*, 5(04), pp.597–604.

38. World Health Organization, 2014. WHO calls for stronger focus on adolescent health. WHO Media Centre.

39. http://www.who.int/genderwomenhealthreportfullreport20091104en.pdf.

40. Ziglio, E., Currie, C. and Rasmussen, V.B., 2004. The WHO cross-national study of health behavior in school aged children from 35 countries: findings from 2001–2002. *Journal of School Health*, 74(6), pp.204–206.

41. Sebire, N.J., Jolly, M., Harris, J.P., Wadsworth, J., Joffe, M., Beard, R.W., Regan, L. and Robinson, S., 2001. Maternal obesity and pregnancy outcome: a study of 287 213 pregnancies in London. *International Journal of Obesity*, 25(8), pp.1175–1182.

42. https://en.wikipedia.org/wiki/Marriage.

43. Michael, R.T. and Tuma, N.B., 1985. Entry into marriage and parenthood by young men and women: The influence of family background. *Demography*, 22(4), pp.515–544.

44. Lindqvist, M., Lindkvist, M., Eurenius, E., Persson, M. and Mogren, I., 2017. Change of lifestyle habits–motivation and ability reported by pregnant women in northern Sweden. *Sexual & Reproductive HealthCare*, 13, pp.83–90.

45. Stanton, C., 2018. Patient information: to share or not to share? *Medical Law Review*, 26(2), pp.328–345.

46. Himani Deshpande, Leena Ragha, April 22, 2021, Mother's significant feature (MSF) dataset. *IEEE Dataport*, doi: https://dx.doi.org/10.21227/kq5k-b784.

47. Gogtay, N.J. and Thatte, U.M., 2017. Principles of correlation analysis. *Journal of the Association of Physicians of India*, 65(3), pp.78–81.

11

BERT- and FastText-Based Research Paper Recommender System

Nemil Shah, Yash Goda, Naitik Rathod, and Vatsal Khandor
Dwarkadas Jivanlal Sanghvi College of Engineering

Pankaj Kulkarni
Deloitte Service LLP

Ramchandra Mangrulkar
Dwarkadas Jivanlal Sanghvi College of Engineering

CONTENTS

11.1 Introduction

As one of the most widespread branches of computer science, artificial intelligence (AI) has emerged with developing smart machines efficient enough to perform tasks that require human intelligence. The evolution in deep and machine learning (ML) fields are crafting an ideal change in each domain of the tech sector. 'Programs with Common Sense' was the first paper published by John McCarthy on AI. This paper consists of information regarding the development of the AI programming language Lisp' [1]. Not long enough Allen Newell and Herbert A. Simon designed the 'first artificial intelligence program' which they named 'Logic Theorist'. 'Organization of Behavior: A Neuropsychological Theory' was publicized by Donald Hebb, 1949 [2]. This proposed a theory about learning regarding neural networks based on conjectures. With the help of this, Frank Rosenblatt, 1958 [3] produced a perceptron algorithm. This algorithm is a binary classification ML algorithm. It is the simplest type of neural network. It consists of a single node or neuron that accepts a row of data as input and predicts a class label. Similarly, AI incipient computer vision in the 1960s, which was further transmogrified by the concept of neocognitron by Fukushima et al., 2004 [4].

Recent advancement in the field of AI was marked by the formation of a human-like robot Sophia as cited in Retto et al., 2017 [5]. On February 14, 2016, Sophia was first set into motion. Sophia's structure involves scripting software, OpenCog, and a chat system, and an AI system designed for general reasoning. Sophia can also emulate facial expressions and human gestures and also can answer specific questions and make basic conversations on predefined topics. Sophia also uses speech recognition technology developed by Alphabet Inc. The AI program of Sophia analyzes conversations and extricates data that allow it to respond in the future. Much growth has occurred in ML [6], an application of AI. ML provides the capacity to autonomously learn and grow through experience, without being explicitly designed. ML is divided into three parts: supervised learning, unsupervised learning, and reinforcement learning. Many advancements have been carried out in the field of reinforcement learning. Reinforcement learning is used for recommending news, music, etc., according to the user's preference. Also, there are many applications [7] of reinforcement learning in the domain of healthcare, gaming, self-driving cars, etc. Natural processing language (NLP) is a part of AI. It helps machines process and understands human language to automatically perform repetitive tasks like machine translation, classification, and summarization. NLP launched in the 1950s as the convergence of AI and linguistics. NLP was earlier discrete from text information retrieval that emphasizes the use of highly scalable statistics-based techniques for indexing and searching of large volumes of text efficiently. Currently, NLP is diversified into several fields, requiring today's NLP developers and researchers to considerably expand their mental knowledge base. Primitive approaches, for instance, machine translation like Russian to English were vanquished by homographs. Homographs are words with the same spelling but different meanings and metaphors. Due to this, sentence meanings would be highly altered resulting in deteriorating the quality of the sentence. Progress has been achieved in the domain of NLP. GPT-2 created an OpenAI which can generate a whole article based on a small input sentence.

Writing technical papers, reports, and presentations is a crucial activity for lots of people all over the world. People are always in search of a copious amount of information needed for writing something meaningful and germane. Recommender System is a section of data filtering system that looks for predicting the 'rating' and 'preference' that a user would give to an item. Although the recommender systems were earlier considered novel, they have now become quotidian in people's lives with their extensive applications. Some of the popular applications [8] are music, news, books, movies, research articles, and search queries. Recommender systems are found in many modern applications that disclose a huge collection of items to the user. The task of finding preferred data or items in the collection is made easier by these systems. Recommendation processes are entirely based on the input provided by the visitors or users. Recommender systems construct a list of recommendations in one of two ways: collaborative or content-based filtering. Collaborative and content-based filtering are the two most popular techniques for recommender systems and their hybridization is called the hybrid approach. The technique which filters the elements that a user might like based on some matching users' interests is called collaborative filtering. It examines the elements the user favors and amalgamates them for forming a categorized list of suggestions. The fundamental presumption of the collaborative filtering method is that if person 1 has the same point of view as person 2 on a topic, person 1 is highly probable of having person 2's opinion on a separate topic than that of an arbitrarily chosen person. For instance, a recommendation system containing collaborative filtering for music liking could perform filtering about the genre of music a user would like given a brief list of that user's liking. Content-based filtering uses the item features to recommend other items homogeneous to users' likes based on their past actions or direct feedback. Content-based filtering describes the items and the profile of the user's preferences. This system tries to predict the features or behaviors of a user, given the item's features. Content-based recommenders recommend the user-specific classification problem and learn a classifier based on the user's likes and dislikes.

11.2 Literature Review

Beel et al., 2016 [9] performed a research paper recommendation, content-based filtering is the predominant approach. Of the 62 reviewed approaches, 55% applied the idea of content-based filtering including Lee et al., 2013 [10] which uses a web crawler and then uses this methodology. 'Interaction' between users and items is generally viewed through authorship, downloading, reading, and browsing papers. Beel et al., 2017 [11] used mind maps that were found to be equally effective to user modeling which is often ignored. As abstracts are representative of the whole research paper these abstracts can be used to generate keywords that are representative of the whole research paper. Thus Term Frequency – Inverse Document Frequency (TF-IDF) technique is used for the generation of appropriate keywords from the abstract. Few papers have described a hybrid approach as in Gipp et al., 2009 [12] and Haruna et al., 2020 [13] has created an independent framework that customizes scholarly publications using public contextual metadata. Despite a lot of research about research paper recommender systems, ambiguity still lies in the process.

11.3 Dataset Description

The arXiv dataset consists of a subset of all the research papers digitally maintained by Cornell University. This dataset consists of the hyperlinks of research papers, the authors of the research papers as well as the date of publications. This dataset is regularly updated and is freely available on Kaggle in JSON format.

The metadata of this dataset contains the title of the research paper. Comments which include additional information like the numbers of figures and number of pages are also provided. The dataset also includes details about the journal in which the original paper was first published (journal-ref). The digital object identifier is also provided, which is a distinct alphanumeric string assigned by appropriate registration agencies to identify articles hosted on the World Wide Web. Additionally, the dataset also contains the unique arXiv ID of all the research papers. Information about the authors who submitted the research paper is also provided. The dataset also provides the abstract of all the papers as well as the various tags in the arXiv system. The version history of the research paper is also provided.

11.4 Proposed Methodology

Figure 11.1 explains the preferred approach for the research paper recommender system with the major steps discussed below.

11.4.1 Keyword Extraction

It has been identified that for performing the aforementioned task of recommendation systems, keywords that capture the essence of the abstract need to be extracted. Predominantly, statistical approaches like TF-IDF in Kim et al., 2019 [14], RAKE, YAKE! in Campos et al., 2020 [15], and Rapid Automatic Keyword Extraction in Rose et al., 2010 [16]. However, as these approaches rely on word frequency for keyword extraction, they fail to take into account the semantic nuances of the language. For this purpose, keyword extraction using state-of-the-art language models was proposed. The widely used BERT (Bidirectional Encoder Representations from Transformers) model was proposed to extract relevant keywords from the abstracts. The BERT architecture has been explained in detail below. Since 2018, BERT has powered Google's various suite of products like Google Search as well as Google Translate.

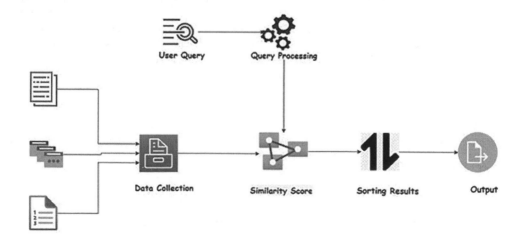

FIGURE 11.1
Proposed methodology for the recommender system.

As proposed in Devlin et al., 2018 [17], BERT is a groundbreaking innovation in the field of NLP and language representation. For pre-training of BERT, a novel bidirectional approach is used instead of a unidirectional approach (left to right) used in other language representation models like OpenAI's GPT as cited in Radford et al., 2018 [18].

The architecture of BERT is based on the Transformers architecture which was proposed in Vaswani et al., 2017 [19]. Although the transformer models were initially proposed for performing the task of machine translation, subsequently the transformer architecture was modified and widely used for language representation. The transform architecture generally comprises two main parts: encoder and decoder. However, BERT is a versatile general-purpose model which can be used for various tasks like named entity recognition, tagging the parts of speech in a sentence, next-word prediction, and calculation of similarity. As BERT performs various tasks, it doesn't have a decoder model. An output layer can be added at any time according to the required task. Although the BERT base model consists of 12 encoders whereas the BERT large model consists of 24 encoders, the number of encoders is arbitrary. The batch of sentences is provided as inputs to the stack of encoders. These sentences are broken down into a sequence of words and each word is represented as a 512-dimensional embedding. Before providing the inputs, a positional embedding is added to the word embeddings. The position of words in the sentence is represented in the form of dense vectors known as positional embeddings. The positional embeddings can adequately represent both the absolute and relative position of a word in the sentence. The positional embedding of the ith word is added to the ith word embedding and then provided as input to the encoder. All the encoder blocks comprise a multi-head attention layer, an add norm layer, a feedforward neural network, and another add norm layer.

A multi-head attention layer as in Voita et al., 2019 [20] can be described as a series of scaled dot product attention layers as cited in Shen et al., 2021 [21]. A scaled dot product attention layer is given by:

$$\text{Attention}(Q, K, V) = \text{soft max}\left(\frac{QK^T}{\sqrt{d_{\text{keys}}}}\right)V \tag{11.1}$$

In this equation, Q is a matrix which contains a single row per query. The shape of this matrix is $[n, d]$.

The number of queries is represented by n, whereas the number of dimensions of each query and each key is specified by d.

K is a matrix containing one row per key. Its shape is $[n, d]$. The total number of keys and values are represented by n.

V contains a single row per value. The shape of this matrix is $[n, d]$, where d is used to denote all the values.

QK is the matrix product of Q and KT. The shape of QK is $[n, n]$. It contains a single similarity score for each query/key pair. Then, the softmax function is computed over each row of the matrix. The output of the softmax function has the same shape, but the sum of all values of a single row adds up to 1. The final output has a shape of $[n, d]$: there is a single row per query and each row depicts the query result (a weighted sum of all the values). As the softmax function can lead to the vanishing gradients problem, the gradients are multiplied with a scaling factor to avoid this problem. Some key/value pairs can be masked out by adding a very large negative value to the corresponding similarity scores, before the computation of the softmax function. This is quite useful in the masked multi-head attention layer.

The multi-head attention layer encodes vectorized information about the words like whether the word is a verb, a noun, or an adjective, the tense of the verb. This helps the architecture to find relevant words according to the required output.

11.4.1.1 Add Norm

The add norm layer adds up all the different outputs computed by the multi-head attention layer. After summing up the outputs, layer normalization is applied to them. Layer normalization by Ba et al., 2016 [22] normalizes the inputs across the feature dimension.

11.4.1.2 Feedforward Neural Network

The feedforward neural networks as in Syozil et al., 1997 [23] are neural networks in which no information flows backward, i.e., the intermediate output isn't sent back to any layer.

11.4.1.3 Residual Connections

Residual connections as in Szegedy et al., 2017 [24] are often used for regularization in neural networks. The residual layer is a modification of skip connection as in Tong et al., 2017 [25], i.e., some intermediate output skip some hidden layers and are directly passed to the next layers as well as the same output is passed through the hidden layers and the outputs are concatenated.

This helps to alleviate the vanishing gradient problem as in Hochreiter et al., 1998 [26] as well as mitigate the problems of overfitting. However, along with the architecture, BERT also modifies the training process to produce even better results. These tweaks are discussed below.

11.4.1.4 Masked Language Model

All the words in the sentence have a 15% probability of being masked. The training of the model is done to predict the masked words. However, out of all the words to be masked, 80% of the words are masked, 10% of the words are replaced with random words to reduce discrepancies during fine-tuning and the rest 10% are left unchanged to improve model accuracy.

Next-sentence prediction: BERT has also been trained to predict whether two sentences can be consecutive or not. Such training improves the accuracy of BERT compared to other models and eases the fine-tuning of the task. This training drastically improves tasks like question answering and finding the similarity of sentences.

All these tweaks as well as the transformer architecture make BERT one of the best language models. Figure 11.2 shows the architecture of the BERT representation. For performing keyword extraction, all the candidate keywords are determined.

Stop words are excluded from candidate keywords to save computational resources. The candidates can be *n*-grams where *n* can be assigned a high value but as the aim is to find only the candidate keywords and not the keyphrases, the feature space is restricted to 1-grams, 2-grams, and 3-grams. As the neural networks are unable to process textual data directly, these keywords are then assigned a unique embedding according to BERT embeddings. A unique embedding is generated for the whole abstract. Then the cosine similarity of the candidates and the abstract embeddings is calculated. Cosine similarity calculates the similarity between two vectors. The cosine similarity is calculated based on the dot product of the vectors The cosine of the angle between two vectors is calculated

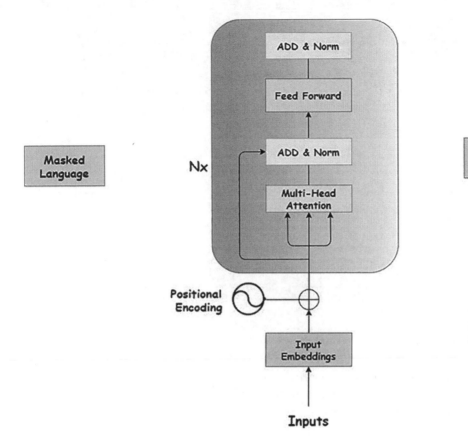

FIGURE 11.2
BERT representation.

which determines if the two vectors point in the same direction. Cosine similarity is commonly used to find the similarity of various documents. The top ten keywords having the highest similarity are then chosen. However, the keywords may be synonyms of each other and might not represent the abstract adequately. To solve this issue, the cosine similarity of each chosen keyword and other chosen candidates is calculated. If the similarity is above a chosen threshold, the candidate keyword is eliminated. This ensures that the candidate keywords are diverse. These keywords are then added to the rest of the data to build the recommendation system.

Now, the next task would be the calculation of the similarity of the query and items. The proximity is computed based on the angle using the vector space model.

In this model, each item is stored as a vector in an n-dimensional space and the angles between the vectors are used for calculating the similarity between the vectors. Subsequently, the user profile vectors are created based on his actions on previous attributes of items, and the similarity between an item and a user is also determined similarly.

11.4.2 FastText

FastText is a library created by Facebook to perform word embeddings to perform sentence classification and word representations. FastText supports continuous bag of words

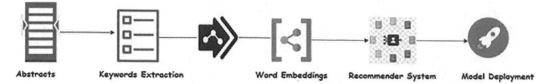

FIGURE 11.3.
Block diagram of the system.

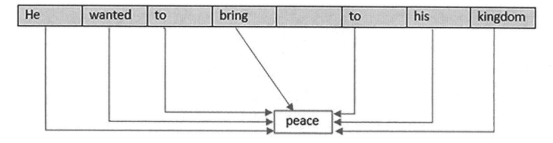

FIGURE 11.4
CBOW representation.

(CBOW) or skip-gram models using two different methods to address classification and training word representations in text: hierarchical softmax and word n-grams.

The different terminologies discussed are explained below (Figure 11.3).

11.4.2.1 Word Embeddings

While training any model, machines cannot understand words. So, they need to be converted into numbers. Some of the popular techniques include Word2Vec, FastText, Bag Of Words, Glove, TF-IDF, etc., as shown in Ge et al., 2018 [27].

11.4.2.2 CBOW

Predicting the target word from context. Context may be single or multiple words. The model tries to understand words on the basis of context and further predict words that suit the context. (Figure 11.4).

Let's demonstrate this with an example. For the following sentence: 'It has been a dull evening'. Here, the word 'dull' acts as an input neuron to the neural network. The output layer will try to predict the word 'evening'. One hot encoding is done for the input words and the error rates are measured with the target word (one hot encoded). This will help predict the output with the least error as in Birunda et al., 2021 [28].

The CBOW architecture is shown in Figure 11.5. The target word is predicted by the model by having an understanding of the context words surrounding it. Considering the same example, 'It has been a dull evening'. This model/architecture converts the sentence into pairs of words of the form (context word, target word). A window size is now needed to set up by the user. For instance, if the size set for the context word is 2, then the word pairs would be: ([it, a], is), ([is, has], been), and ([has, evening], dull). With these word pairs, the target word is predicted by the model with the help of context words surrounding it

CBOW

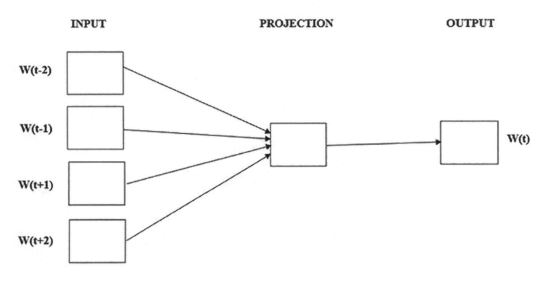

FIGURE 11.5
CBOW model architecture.

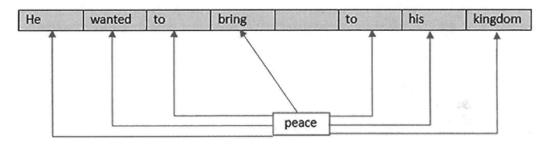

FIGURE 11.6
Skip-gram representation.

as in Jang et al., 2019 [29]. If there are 'x' context words which are for predicting a target word, then the input layer will be in the form of 'x' 1XW input vectors. The vectors of the input are passed to the hidden layers where it is multiplied by a matrix [WXN]. Finally, the output [1XN] from the hidden layer enters the sum layer where the summation is performed (element-wise) on the vectors and finally an activation is performed and the output is obtained.

11.4.2.3 *Skip-Gram*

Predicting the context words from the target.

It is the reverse of the CBOW algorithm which is shown in Figure 11.6. Here, the input is the target word and the context words are predicted as the output. Since the context word to be predicted is more than one, this problem is difficult.

SKIP-GRAM

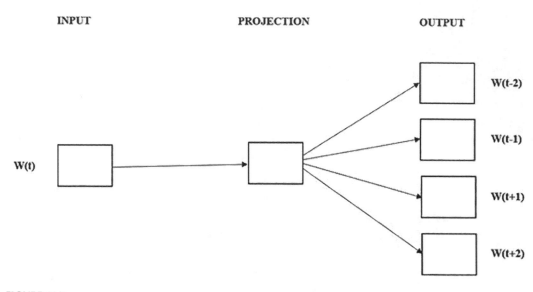

INPUT   PROJECTION   OUTPUT

FIGURE 11.7
Skip-gram model architecture.

In Figure 11.7, it is clearly seen that there is a single input $w(t)$. There is a single input hidden layer that does the calculation which is the dot product between the weight matrix and the vector which is taken as the input $w(t)$. The hidden layer requires no activation function. The computation of the dot product at the hidden layer is then passed to the output layer where the computation of the dot product between the output vector from the hidden layer and the other is the weight matrix from the output layer. Subsequently, the activation function (softmax) needs to be applied which gives the probability of words at a context location with respect to input $w(t)$.

11.4.2.4 Hierarchical Softmax

As discussed above, this is an activation function to output the probability of a given input belonging to k classes in multi-class classification problems. The probability that a given text belongs to a class is explored via a DFS along with the nodes across the different branches. Therefore, classes with low probability can be discarded away.

11.4.2.5 Word n-Grams

Using the only CBOW representation of the text leaves out crucial sequential information. FastText incorporates a bag of n-grams representation along with word vectors to preserve the relationships between words.

11.4.3 FastText Representation

Since it uses character-level information, good performance on rare words is achieved as well as in Roy et al., 2018 [30]. Each word in the sentence is represented as a bag of character n-grams (word n-grams as discussed above) and in addition to the word itself, for example, for the word lively, with $n=3$, the FastText representations for the character n-grams is ¡li, liv, ive, vel, ely, ly¿. Boundary symbols are added ('¡' and '¿') from differentiating the word and n-grams of the word. It helps preserve the meaning of shorter words that may show up as n-grams of other words. Inherently, this also helps to capture meaning for suffixes/prefixes.

Flags can be used for controlling max and min for the length of n-grams. The range of values is controlled for getting the n-grams. The bag of words model and the appearance of any character in a particular order doesn't make any difference. The most common example is ids as the words. During the update of the model, the weights are learned by FastText for each n-grams token as well as the entire word token as in Young et al., 2019 [31]. Now, a recommender system will be made using a cosine similarity score. First of all, all the stop words are filtered. Elimination of stop words is one of the first steps in all Natural Language Processing tasks. Stop words are usually removed because they are not pertinent and the words which add some meaning to the sentences are kept. Stop words are only removed in tasks where grammatical coherence isn't a necessity. Since the chapter is aimed at building a research paper recommender system, only the keywords are converted to vectors as this drastically reduces the computational power and resources.

Cosine similarity is used as a metric to compare the keywords extracted from the abstract and the user-entered query. The output of cosine similarity ranges from 0 to 1. The formula for cosine similarity is:

$$\text{similarity} = \cos\theta = \frac{b \cdot c}{\|b\|\|c\|} \tag{11.2}$$

$$\|b\|\|c\| \rightarrow \text{Product of each vector's magnitude}$$

$$b \cdot c \rightarrow \text{Dot product of two vectors}$$

The result obtained is a NumPy array and the value inside it depicts the correlation between a user-entered query and a particular paper. If the value obtained is 0, that indicates that the user-entered query is 0% similar to the particular research paper and if the value obtained is 1, that indicates that the items are 100% correlated. After calculating the cosine similarity score for a particular query, the results are sorted in descending order and only the most relevant results are displayed to the user. These results include all the relevant details about a particular research paper such as the author, title, as well as hyperlink of the research paper.

However, like all other recommender systems, this recommender system also suffers from the problem of 'cold start'. The cold start problem as in Volkovs et al., 2017 [32] occurs when new users or new items are added to the recommendation systems. During the addition of new items to the recommender systems, the new items must undergo the same training process to alleviate this problem. If a different training process is used, the results might differ from the original results leading to discrepancies. Also, newer data must be regularly added to the recommender systems so that the latest recommendations are readily available to the users.

11.4.4 Limitations

Since, the availability of the user's choice data and the research papers' citations are sparse, using a hybrid approach is not feasible. The hybrid approach is an amalgamation of both content-based and collaborative-based filtering, which provides finer results.

In the approach used in this paper, keyword extraction is performed on the abstract of the research paper. Sometimes it may provide less effective results. However, performing keywords extraction on the entire research paper is not feasible as it will increase the computation time and will provide delayed outcomes.

11.4.5 Future Scope

A hybrid approach can be used if data regarding user choice as well as the citations of research papers are made publicly available. This hybrid would be an amalgamation of both content-based and collaborative approaches and thereby producing even better results. Hybrids among the currently available systems can also get better and more accurate results.

A system that would collect the author's keywords of the publication could be a game-changer considering the accuracy that could be achieved on recommendations using those keywords will be much higher and the publications recommended would be even more relevant. Authors in this research have used just around three gigabytes of the arXiv dataset. Usage of the whole dataset that is just above one terabyte of data can get a better recommender as the larger the dataset, the better results could be achieved. All the open access books can also be included along with the large arXiv datasets so as to achieve better accuracies and wider search results. This can also be done by merging the data from different publications other than arXiv for further expansion of the dataset.

11.4.6 Conclusion

An alternative approach has been effectively proposed in this research using BERT and FastText which will fetch better results in comparison to the traditional methods of research paper recommender systems. This new methodology uses the arXiv dataset and the approach of assigning the BERT embeddings to the possible keywords in the abstract. The cosine similarity is calculated of the embeddings to ensure only similar direction keywords are kept. These are later used alongside the whole data to recommend research papers. FastText library is used for the classification of the text of the abstract using the word embeddings calculated using BERT and obtaining a vector representation for the text.

This system has the ability to retrieve accurate results for the searches which can be very handy for the research community. This proposed approach takes advantage of the more used BERT embeddings and provides a solution which is fast and accurate and provides the relevant recommendations.

11.4.7 Applications

This system can be used by any student who is in search of a particular topic and wants to delve deeper into that particular topic. It will provide the students with germane and copious information regarding their topic. This system benefits not only the students but also the teaching faculty, administrators as well as researchers who are in search of a specific topic and will obtain relevant and suitable information about their required topic.

Digital libraries generally have an extensive range of digital objects like research papers, journals, publications, projects, newspapers, and magazines. Few digital libraries also offer access to millions of such digital objects. Hence, finding a particular paper or journal won't be viable. This recommender system will help in finding the required paper or journal or any other material by providing keywords of the required material. This will make the work of obtaining the desired article easy and will also provide various other related articles. Also during this COVID situation where it is not possible to obtain hard copies of the research articles, papers, or books, a digital library along with a recommender system installed in it will ensure the availability of the research materials.

Also, a website can be hosted where details about intellectual articles or germane research papers based on the topic can be provided. This website will acquire authors' keywords and will yield not only the particular paper but also will advocate related papers.

References

1. McCarthy, John. Programs with common sense. RLE and MIT computation center, 1960. http://jmc.stanford.edu/articles/mcc59.html.
2. Hebb, Donald Olding. The organization of behavior; a neuropsycholocigal theory. *A Wiley Book in Clinical Psychology* 62 (1949): 78. https://doi.org/10.2307/1418888.
3. Rosenblatt, Frank. The perceptron: a probabilistic model for information storage and organization in the brain. *Psychological Review* 65, no. 6 (1958): 386. https://doi.org/10.1037/h0042519.
4. Fukushima, Kunihiko, and Sei Miyake. Neocognitron: A self-organizing neural network model for a mechanism of visual pattern recognition. *In Competition and Cooperation in Neural Nets*, S. Amari and M. A. Arbib (Eds.), pp. 267–285. Springer, Berlin, Heidelberg, 1982. https://doi.org/10.1007/978-3-642-46466-9-18.
5. Retto, Jesús. Sophia, first citizen robot of the world. https://www.coursehero.com/file/50766519/PDF-PAPERVIIpdf/.
6. Chavan, Pallavi, Prerna More, Neha Thorat, Shraddha Yewale, and Pallavi Dhade. ECG-Remote patient monitoring using cloud computing. *Imperial Journal of Interdisciplinary Research* 2, no. 2 (2016): 368–372.
7. S. K. Narad and P. V. Chavan, Neural network based group authentication using (n, n) secret sharing scheme. *2015 International Conference on Advances in Computer Engineering and Applications*, 2015, pp. 409–414, doi: 10.1109/ICACEA.2015.7164739. https://doi.org/10.1109/ICACEA.2015.7164739.
8. Mudia, Hinal M. and Pallavi Vijay Chavan. Fuzzy logic based image encryption for confidential data transfer using (2, 2) secret sharing scheme-review. *2015 International Conference on Advances in Computer Engineering and Applications* (2015): 404–408. https://doi.org/10.1016/j.procs.2016.02.110.
9. Beel, Joeran, Bela Gipp, Stefan Langer, and Corinna Breitinger. Paper recommender systems: a literature survey. *International Journal on Digital Libraries* 17, no. 4 (2016): 305–338. https://doi.org/10.1007/s00799-015-0156-0.
10. Lee, Joonseok, Kisung Lee, and Jennifer G. Kim. Personalized academic research paper recommendation system. arXiv preprint arXiv:1304.5457 (2013). https://arxiv.org/abs/1304.5457v1.
11. Beel, Joeran. Towards effective research-paper recommender systems and user modeling based on mind maps. arXiv preprint arXiv:1703.09109 (2017). https://arxiv.org/abs/1703.09109.
12. Gipp, Bela, J̈oran Beel, and Christian Hentschel. Scienstein: A research paper recommender system. *In Proceedings of the international conference on Emerging trends in computing (ICETiC'09)*, pp. 309–315. 2009. https://www.gipp.com/wp-content/papercite-data/pdf/gipp09.pdf.
13. Haruna, Khalid, Maizatul Akmar Ismail, Atika Qazi, Habeebah Adamu Kakudi, Mohammed Hassan, Sanah Abdullahi Muaz, and Haruna Chiroma. Research paper recommender system based on public contextual metadata. *Scientometrics* 125, no. 1 (2020): 101–114. https://doi.org/10.1007/s11192-020-03642-y.

14. JKim, Sang-Woon, and Joon-Min Gil. Research paper classification systems based on TF-IDF and LDA schemes. *Human-Centric Computing and Information Sciences* 9, no. 1 (2019): 1–21. https://doi.org/10.1186/s13673-019-0192-7.

15. Campos, Ricardo, Vítor Mangaravite, Arian Pasquali, Alipio Jorge, Célia Nunes, and Adam Jatowt. YAKE! Keyword extraction from single documents using multiple local features. *Information Sciences* 509 (2020): 257–289. https://doi.org/10.1016/j.ins.2019.09.013.

16. Rose, Stuart, Dave Engel, Nick Cramer, and Wendy Cowley. Automatic keyword extraction from individual documents. *Text Mining: Applications and Theory* 1 (2010): 1–20. https://doi.org/10.1002/9780470689646.ch1.

17. Devlin, Jacob, Ming-Wei Chang, Kenton Lee, and Kristina Toutanova. Bert: Pre-training of deep bidirectional transformers for language understanding. arXiv preprint arXiv:1810.04805 (2018). http://dx.doi.org/10.18653/v1/N19-1423.

18. Radford, Alec, Karthik Narasimhan, Tim Salimans, and Ilya Sutskever. Improving language understanding by generative pre-training. (2018). http://www.nlpir.org/wordpress/wp-content/uploads/2019/06/Improving-language-understanding-by-generative-pre-training.pdf.

19. Vaswani, Ashish, Noam Shazeer, Niki Parmar, Jakob Uszkoreit, Llion Jones, Aidan N. Gomez, Lukasz Kaiser, and Illia Polosukhin. Attention is all you need. arXiv preprint arXiv:1706.03762 (2017). https://arxiv.org/abs/1706.03762v5.

20. Voita, Elena, David Talbot, Fedor Moiseev, Rico Sennrich, and Ivan Titov. Analyzing multihead self-attention: Specialized heads do the heavy lifting, the rest can be pruned. arXiv preprint arXiv:1905.09418 (2019). http://dx.doi.org/10.18653/v1/P19-1580.

21. Shen, Zhuoran, Mingyuan Zhang, Haiyu Zhao, Shuai Yi, and Hongsheng Li. Efficient attention: Attention with linear complexities. *In Proceedings of the IEEE/CVF Winter Conference on Applications of Computer Vision*, pp. 3531–3539. 2021. https://arxiv.org/abs/1812.01243v9.

22. Ba, Jimmy Lei, Jamie Ryan Kiros, and Geoffrey E. Hinton. Layer normalization. arXiv preprint arXiv:1607.06450 (2016). https://arxiv.org/abs/1607.06450v1.

23. Svozil, Daniel, Vladimir Kvasnicka, and Jiri Pospichal. Introduction to multilayer feed-forward neural networks. *Chemometrics and Intelligent Laboratory Systems* 39, no. 1 (1997): 43–62. https://doi.org/10.1016/S0169-7439(97)00061-0.

24. Szegedy, Christian, Sergey Ioffe, Vincent Vanhoucke, and Alexander Alemi. Inception-v4, inception-resnet and the impact of residual connections on learning. *In Proceedings of the AAAI Conference on Artificial Intelligence*, vol. 31, no.1. 2017. https://ojs.aaai.org/index.php/AAAI/article/view/11231.

25. Tong, Tong, Gen Li, Xiejie Liu, and Qinquan Gao. Image super-resolution using dense skip connections. *In Proceedings of the IEEE International Conference on Computer Vision*, pp. 4799–4807. 2017. https://doi.ieeecomputersociety.org/10.1109/ICCV.2017.514.

26. Hochreiter, Sepp. The vanishing gradient problem during learning recurrent neural nets and problem solutions. International Journal of Uncertainty, Fuzziness and Knowledge-Based Systems 6, no. 02 (1998): 107–116. https://doi.org/10.1142/S0218488598000094.

27. Ge, Xingtong, Xiaofang Jin, and Ying Xu. Research on sentiment analysis of multiple classifiers based on word2vec. *In 2018 10th International Conference on Intelligent Human-Machine Systems and Cybernetics (IHMSC)*, vol. 2, pp. 230–234. IEEE, 2018. https://doi.org/10.1109/IHMSC.2018.10159.

28. Birunda, S. Selva, and R. Kanniga Devi. A review on word embedding techniques for text classification. *In Innovative Data Communication Technologies and Application*, pp. 267–281. Springer, Singapore, 2021. https://doi.org/10.1007/978-981-15-9651-3-23.

29. Jang, Beakcheol, Inhwan Kim, and Jong Wook Kim. Word2vec convolutional neural networks for classification of news articles and tweets. *PloS One* 14, no. 8 (2019): e0220976. https://doi.org/10.1371/journal.pone.0220976.

30. Roy, Dwaipayan, Debasis Ganguly, Sumit Bhatia, Srikanta Bedathur, and Mandar Mitra. Using word embeddings for information retrieval: How collection and term normalization choices affect performance. *In Proceedings of the 27th ACM International Conference on Information and Knowledge Management*, pp. 1835–1838. 2018. https://doi.org/10.1145/3269206.3269277.

31. Young, Julio Christian, and Andre Rusli. Review and visualization of Facebook's FastText pre-trained word vector model. *In 2019 International Conference on Engineering, Science, and Industrial Applications (ICESI)*, pp. 1–6. IEEE, 2019. https://doi.org/10.1109/ICESI.2019.8863015.
32. Volkovs, Maksims, Guang Wei Yu, and Tomi Poutanen. DropoutNet: Addressing Cold Start in Recommender Systems. *In NIPS*, pp. 4957–4966. 2017. https://proceedings.neurips.cc/paper/2017/file/dbd22ba3bd0df8f385bdac3e9f8be207-Paper.pdf.

12

Analysis and Prediction of Crime Rate against Women Using Classification and Regression Trees

P. Tamilarasi and R. Uma Rani

Sri Sarada College for Women (Autonomous)

CONTENTS

12.1 Introduction

Data analytics is basically utilized in logical investigation and advances in insights, computer and insights, commonsense remodel areas such as science, building, open segment, commerce, social, and way of life. In Data analytics, information is extricated and classified to recognize and analyze behavioral information, and designs. Here strategies are changing, agreeing to the organizational requirements:

1. Predictive data analytics is used for forecasting
2. Descriptive data analytics is used in business intelligence and data mining
3. Prescriptive data analytics are used in optimization and simulation
4. Diagnostic analytics is mainly used for learning about past issues.

Predictive analytics focused on predicting expected outcomes based on historical information using systematic methods like statistics and machine learning (ML). Descriptive data analytics is a statistical method used to search and summarize historical data to identify patterns or meanings. Prescriptive analytics is used to find the best actions from given

DOI: 10.1201/9781003283249-12

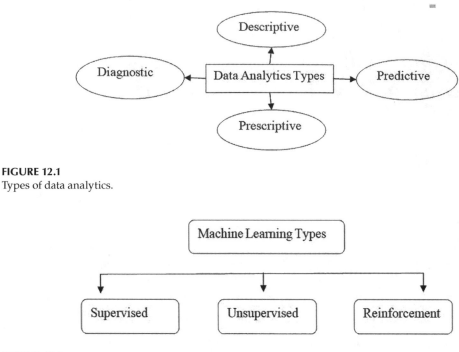

FIGURE 12.1
Types of data analytics.

FIGURE 12.2
Different types of machine learning.

data including predictive and prescriptive analytics. Diagnostic analytics is advanced analytics that focuses on explaining why something has happened based on data analysis. Figure 12.1 shows different types of data analytics.

12.1.1 Machine Learning Approach

ML is a collection of algorithms for computer programs. It can train and adapt to new data without human intrusion. It is a slice of artificial intelligence that keeps built-in algorithms. ML techniques are categorized into three main types such as supervised, unsupervised, and reinforcement. Supervised ML techniques are a very familiar model for ML. It is the very easiest to recognize and the simplest to implement. It is similar to teaching kids with the use of flashcards. The supervised learning algorithm will be able to monitor a new, never-before-seen paradigm and find a good label for it. Unsupervised learning is a conflict of supervised learning which has no labels. This algorithm reads a lot of data and is given tools to recognize the properties of data. Augmentation learning is a fragment of ML. This is discussed as the right action to maximize credit in a specific circumstance. It is used by different applications and organizations to find out the good feasible behavior or track it to get an exact situation. Augmentation learning varies from supervised learning, this way that supervised learning supports the data and has a response key within this. So the algorithm is trained up with an honest response itself whereas the reinforcement studies. If it has no response, even a reinforcement mediator decides against what is going to be present in the given work. From the lack of training datasets, it is very difficult to gain the knowledge. Figure 12.2 shows different types of ML.

12.2 Literature Survey

Crimes are a general problem that affects the quality of life and economic growth of a nation. Ahishakiye proposed decision tree algorithms for crime prediction and classification. The algorithm has given 94.25287% accuracy [1]. Esra Kahya Ozyirmidokuz implemented decision tree algorithms for prospect decisions and concluded the results based on the performance of the algorithms [2]. Lana Clara Chikhungu proposed the cluster and multinomial logistic regression ML algorithms for concluding the results maximum number of domestic violence has happened by alcohol-addicted partners [3]. Sapna Singh Kshatri proposed decision tree algorithms for categorized crimes in the different states of India and also algorithms performed with 73.33% accuracy [4]. Random forest regression techniques are implemented to predict the crime rate in Brazilian cities and also get the outcome with 97% accuracy by Luiz [5]. Prajakta Yerpude proposed some supervised and unsupervised ML techniques for finding features based on the algorithm's performance [6]. Decision tree and Naïve Bayes algorithms are proposed for finding criminal hotspots in Los Angeles, Denver, and Colorado [7]. The Researcher Concluded the results based on the newspaper information and used some statistical methods for finding crime against women in Brahmaputra Valley [8]. Ankit Agarwal proposed some supervised ML algorithms to predict the crime rate against women based on eleven crime types like rape, dowery deaths, and cruelty [9].In this paper, k-means clustering techniques are implemented to predict the crime rate against women [10].Deeksha Dayal focuses on two issues that are violence against women and femininity empowerment and concluded the results based on the correlation coefficient [11]. The author proposed k-means cluster algorithms for finding types of crimes and behaviors [12]. Jha, Gouri [13] analyzed the crime against women before and after COVID-19. Shruti S. Gosavi proposed many ML algorithms for predicting the crime rate against women; finally concluded Naïve Bayes has performed better than others [14]. In the paper [15], the author implemented many ML algorithms to predict the crime types by using python.

12.3 Proposed Methodologies

Figure 12.3 explains the workflow for the proposed methodologies.

12.3.1 Data Preprocessing

Data preprocessing is one type of data analytics technique that is mainly used to convert the data from raw format to meaningful format or machine understanding format. Data cleaning is one of the main parts of data preprocessing. It is used to handle the situation of missing and noisy information in the dataset. Missing data is handled in many ways. This is to ignore the tuples while filling the missing values. The row is eliminated from the data when repeated values are present in the dataset and missing values are filled manually by using mean and other probable values. In this chapter, the missing values are filled by using mean values.

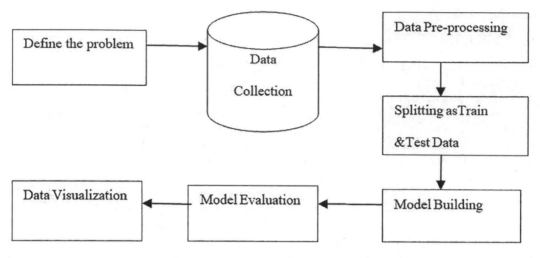

FIGURE 12.3
Work flow for the crime analysis.

Train Dataset	80%	Test DataSet
		20%

FIGURE 12.4
Train and test data values.

12.3.2 Splitting Train and Test Data

The train and test systems are used to assess the ML algorithms. This is a very quick method for estimating algorithm performance. These types of results are very helpful to judge the different types of algorithms' accuracy values. In this method, the dataset is separated into two parts that are train and test. The first piece of data mentions the train data, and the second piece of data is denoted by the test dataset. Generally, the train dataset values are used to shape the ML model, and test methods are used to assess the fit model performance. Figure 12.4 shows the train and test data.

12.3.3 Classification and Regression Trees (CART)

Classification and regression are the main techniques for decision trees. The decision tree is supervised by nonparametric algorithms of ML. It is used in both classification and regression types of problems. These types of problems are often called the CART method. The CART types of problems splitting the dataset are used by Gini impurity methods. Equations 12.1 and 12.2 explain the Gini impurity methods.

$$I_{\text{Gini}} = 1 - \sum_{i=1}^{J} P_i^2 \tag{12.1}$$

$$I_{\text{Gini}} = 1 - \left(\text{The Probabilities of "No"}\right) 2 - \left(\text{The probabilities of target "yes"}\right) \tag{12.2}$$

12.3.4 Model Evaluation

The model evaluation or accuracy is calculated by using distinguished test data values with predicted values. Here in the decision tree performance for the Salem district crime dataset is 78.53%, this is good performance and the crime against women in the Indian dataset accuracy values for decision tree is 73.66%. This is also good accuracy, but compared to the Salem district crime dataset accuracy, it is low.

12.3.5 Data Visualization

The decision tree picture has a rule that divides the data. Here the impurity of the node is measured by the Gini ratio. When every record is fit in the same class that class is called pure and also it is called a leaf node.

12.4 Result and Discussions

Figure 12.5 shows details about the crimes against women in India. It holds various types of crimes in India. Figure 12.6 illustrates the particulars of crime against women in the Salem District, Tamil Nadu. Both datasets are collected from 2003 to 2018.

Figure 12.7 proves the result of the decision tree against women in the Indian dataset.

Figure 12.8 shows the result of the decision tree from the Salem region crime against women dataset.

Figure 12.9 describes the highest crime rate in India against women. Here cruelty crimes are recorded at a high level. Figure 12.10 gives details about the maximum crime recorded per year against women from 2003 to 2014. From this figure, it is clear that elevated crimes were recorded against women in India in 2010.

Figures 12.11 and 12.12 show the highest crime types and highest crime recorded per year in the Salem region, Tamil Nadu. Here Protection of Children from Sexual Offences is the greatest crime type, and 2010 is the crime recorded year.

Table 12.1 shows the accuracy of the CART model of the Salem region dataset and India-level crime dataset. The CART model has performed well for the Salem region compared to the Indian dataset.

	RAPE	KIDNAPPING	DOWRY	ASSAULT	INSULT	CRUELTY	IMMORAL	IRWOMEN	LABEL
0	16075	14645	6851	34124	9746	49170	8796	1052	0
1	16373	14506	6822	33943	10155	49237	6598	2508	0
2	15847	13296	6208	32939	12325	50703	5510	1043	0
3	18233	15578	7026	34567	10001	58121	5748	1378	1
4	18359	15750	6787	34175	9984	58319	5908	2917	1

FIGURE 12.5
Crime against women dataset in India.

	RAPE	DOWRY	MOLESTATION	SEX	CRUELTY	KIDNAPPING	CMACT	POCSO	LABEL
0	11	3	11	13	13	8	1	8	0
1	11	9	5	27	18	4	1	8	0
2	4	6	9	9	18	10	1	8	0
3	7	6	3	24	18	13	1	8	0
4	10	2	14	21	42	21	1	8	1

FIGURE 12.6
Crime against women dataset in Salem.

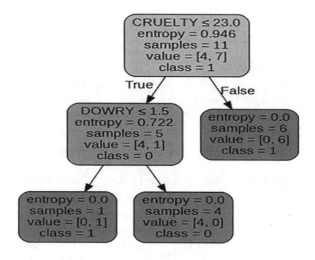

FIGURE 12.7
Decision tree results for crime against women dataset in India.

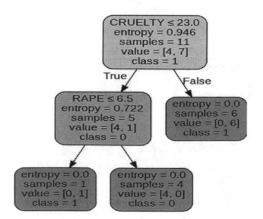

FIGURE 12.8
Decision tree results for crime against women dataset in Salem.

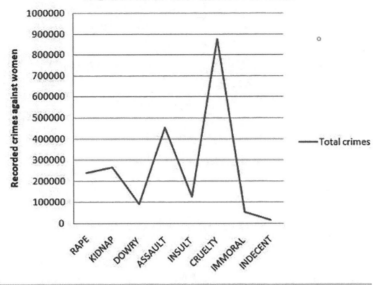

FIGURE 12.9
Highest crime type in India.

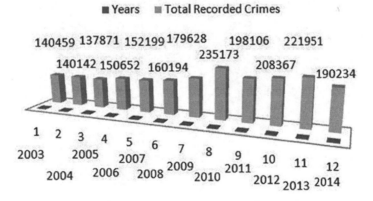

FIGURE 12.10
Year-wise crime rate in India.

12.5 Conclusion

In this chapter, the (CART) model is proposed to analyze the two crime dataset. Those are the Salem region crime dataset, it is collected from the Salem police and another one is India-level crimes against women data. The results are concluded based on the model

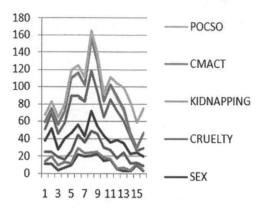

FIGURE 12.11
Salem region crime types against women.

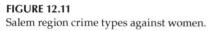

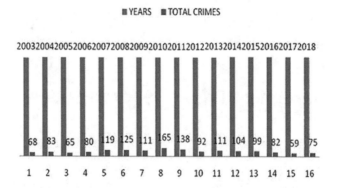

FIGURE 12.12
Year-wise Salem region crime rate against women.

TABLE 12.1

Evaluation of the CART Model.

S.No	Dataset	Model	Accuracy
1	Salem Region	CART	80%
2	All State in India	CART	50%

performance. Here the CART model is performed better for the Salem crime data than for the Indian dataset. It has given the accuracy of 80% for the Salem data. This chapter also has given detailed information about the highest crimes recorded in a year and crime types from 2003 to 2018. This result will be exceptionally supportive to the police division, for advance examining and controlling the wrongdoings against ladies within the future.

References

1. Ahishakiye, Emmanuel. Crime prediction using decision tree (J48) classification algorithm. *IJCIT*, Volume 6, Issue 3, pp. 188–195, 2017.
2. Özyirmidokuz, Esra Kahya. Decision tree induction of emotional violence against women. *Turkey Proceedings of INTCESS14- International Conference on Education and Social Sciences*, 2014.
3. Chikhungu, Lana Clara. Married women's experience of domestic violence in malawi: new evidence from a cluster and multinomial logistic regression analysis. *Journal of Interpersonal Violence*, Volume 36, Issue 17–18, pp. 8693–8714, 2019.
4. Kshatri, Sapna Singh. Analytical study of some selected classification algorithms and crime prediction. *IJEAT*, Volume 9, Issue 6, pp. 241–247, 2020.
5. Alvesa, Luiz G. A. Crime prediction through urban metrics and statistical learning. arXiv:1712.03834v2 [physics.soc-ph], 2018.
6. Yerpude, Prajakta. Predictive modelling of crime dataset using data mining. *International Journal of Data Mining & Knowledge Management Process*, Volume 7, Issue 4, pp. 43–58, 2017.
7. Almanie, Tahani. Crime prediction based on crime types and using spatial and temporal criminal hotspots. *International Journal of Data Mining & Knowledge Management Process (IJDKP)*, Volume 5, Issue 4, pp. 1–19, 2015.
8. Borah, Lekha. Crime against women in Brahmaputra valley. *Transactions of the Institute of Indian Geographers*, Volume 39, Issue 1, pp. 47–57, 2017.
9. Agarwa, Ankit. Prediction & classification of crimes against women. *International Journal of Psychosocial Rehabilitation*, Volume 24, Issue 8, pp. 2441–2451, 2020.
10. Than Win. Predicting of crime detection using K-means clustering algorithm. *IJETA*, Volume 6, Issue 3, pp. 8–12, 2019.
11. Dayal, Deeksha. Crime against women in India and declining labour force participation rate of females: a hidden correlation? *Indian Journal of Human Development*, Volume 8, Issue 2, pp. 111–119, 2014.
12. Jha, Gouri. Criminal behaviour analysis and segmentation using K-means clustering. *2020 8th International Conference on Reliability, Infocom Technologies and Optimization (Trends and Future Directions)*, 2020.
13. LaurenHoehn-Velasco. The great crime recovery: Crimes against women during, and after, the COVID-19 lockdown in Mexico. *Economics and Human Biology*, Volume 41, p. 100991, 2021.
14. S.Gosavi, Shruti. A Survey on Crime Occurrence Detection and Prediction Crimes. *International Journal of Management, Technology and Engineering*, Volume 8, Issue XII, pp. 1405–1409, 2018.
15. Teja, K. Ravi. Analysis of Crimes Against Women in India Using Machine Learning Techniques. In: Satapathy, S.C., Bhateja, V., Ramakrishna Murty, M., Gia Nhu, N., Jayasri Kotti (eds) *Communication Software and Networks. Lecture Notes in Networks and Systems*, Springer, Singapore 2021.

13

Data Analysis for Technical Business Incubation Performance Improvement

Swati Shekapure

Marathwada Mitra Mandal's College of Engineering

Nitin Shekapure

All India Shri Shivaji Memorial Society College of Engineering

CONTENTS

DOI: 10.1201/9781003283249-13

13.1 Introduction

Encouraging company growth and addressing problems of economic development in India through improving entrepreneurial base and dispersion of intellectual capital is a matter of gravity in everyone's mind. Understanding the potential of incubators to transform the local regional and national economies and giving rise to self-sustaining communities, there is perhaps a constant need for evaluation of incubation systems not just considering their goals of producing successful firms but also concentrate renewed endeavor to evaluate incubator contributions to long term incubate graduate success, but the variance in the operability and output of incubators in a developing nation such as India and abroad demands for Indian start-up centric research to leverage Indian technical entrepreneurial ecosystem. Technical business incubator models in India need to adapt to the needs of the local Indian community, economy, and academia demands not only for the social, economic, and political betterment of the nation but also for its own growth.

This paper is essentially focus on withdrawing factors from universally applicable factors which contribute to the success of technical business incubators and identify and analytically verify factors befitting Indian conditions from the set. It runs an inductive approach accumulating factors from literature in conjunction with analytical study procedures.

India, being a fast developing, rapidly progressing nation, has been moving toward achieving the goals of macro-stability, inclusive and sustainable growth with the help of small- and medium-scale industries. This has provided an impetus to establishing nurturing environments to ensure long standing successful home-grown businesses. The cultural differences have been recognized and a collection of factors contributing to the success of the incubators in the Indian context have been presented in this study.

13.2 Evolution of Business Incubators and Their Current State

The first recorded idea of business incubators trails back to the United States of America, where Student Agencies Inc., began embracing student incubate companies. The year 1946 marked the first time that an incubator outside the student community was established. A handful of Massachusetts Institute of Technology (MIT) alumni launched American Research Development to grant risk capital to entrepreneurs [1]. This was soon followed by the Batavia Industrial Center in New York which provided multi-tenant space adding a real estate element to the concept of incubators. Until the 1970s, the incubator's cornerstone was either on technology or management; it is only from here that incubators transformed [2].

In the period between the 1970s and mid-1990s, the concept of traditional or first-generation business incubators caught up as a means to tackle unemployment by producing alternative job opportunities in the time of crisis. In fact, Lalkaka [3] rightly claims that the origin of business incubators can be found in the period between the late 1970s and early 1980s in the western industrialized countries tackling the rapid rise of unemployment following the collapse of industries and economy. These business incubators which were controlled by national or local authorities expedited economic development by promoting entrepreneurship, innovation, and employment opportunities indigenously to maximize indigenous potential and make underdeveloped and lower economic classes self-sufficient. It is only here that moderately priced multi-tenant space, shared services, and an integrated package of business services were offered to start-up tenants by incubators. Educational hubs such as science technology, engineering, and mathematics, universities and science parks too had established incubators.

According to Magnus Klofsten et al [4], Korea has only 12 incubators in operation initially in the late 1990s but by early 2000 had amassed over 130 incubators, universities operating 95% of them. Germany grew from merely 10 innovation hubs to 360 in 15 years, all distributed diversely among industrial rural and urban educational centers as per Ann-Kristin Achleitner et al [5].

The second-generation incubators which existed in the late 1990s were primarily virtual as per Jeffrey [6]. They were also considered the "New Economy Incubators". These virtual incubators were, private sectors, profit driven incubators with heavy technology and internet driven, industry sector specific activities in their core unlike the first generation which had contribution to the economy and job creation as its foundational principles. These virtual incubators flourished in the early 2000s due to the expanding opportunities and myriads of possibilities offered by the internet.

Over 7,000 business incubators are operating globally. The exponential growth in the number of incubators operates globally. In the early days, incubation had to do with economic development and its charity to a community. With an abundance of empty spaces and buildings and unemployment on the rise as an aftermath of the wars, the sheer brilliance of generating jobs by using these spaces served the community. In those days incubation was about bricks and mortar. But now, incubation is about mentoring, just-in-time business development; the support and the selectivity in the front end.

13.3 Success Factors

The definition of success is volatile and changes over time setting new standards and benchmarks with evolution in time for all individuals, organizations, or incubators. For instance, the shift from incubators providing mere space for companies to essential services and assistants set a new benchmark for business incubator success in the timeline of incubators.

Critical success factors can be defined as those conducting elements that must get the current attention of management if the organization is to continue to be relevant in the competitive environment. The term success factors can be described as activities that an individual or an organizational framework should be dutifully obliged to perform in order to accomplish its mission.

Elaborating a Success Factors for productive and progressive business incubation.

13.3.1 Affiliation to Education Hubs

Smilor [7] claims proximity to research establishments having a catalytic role Affiliation to educational hubs such as universities plays the role of a catalyst in leveraging the success rate of incubators. This is important because of the ready supply of tools equipment and intellectual resources compounded with students and mentors. Teachers with multiple specializations mentor tenant companies on various topics spanning from technology specific to finance such as accounting and corporate taxes. Sheanan [8] observed that investors and venture capitalists are drawn to incubator centers affiliated to universities due to low negative cash flow since the onus of the provision of the resources for the incubator has been looked after by the institution the incubator is affiliated to. The relationship between the institution and the incubator is symbiotic in nature since the incubator receives its mentoring and inventory from the institution, while the university gets to be on the heel of new technology. Peters, Rice and Sundarajan [9] believe that incubators who have access to unique government grants and resources such as specialized research labs, seminars on campus, and a concentrated pool of talents namely the students and teachers. Tornatzy [10] believes that incubators get leverage on getting access to science and technology expertise and facilities. Wagner [11] says that supporting infrastructure and access to technical, administrative, and academic support from universities nurture young businesses. The synergy between educational centers and incubators keeps them on the heel of cutting-edge technology. Incubators in association with universities also have greater odds of securing research capital compared to other incubators.

13.3.2 Feasibility Study

A feasibility study is crucial to an incubator's success. It typically involves the following according to Wagner:

A. Market analysis

B. A mission statements

C. Funding, capitalizing, short-term and long-term investment, debt plan

D. Project timeline and benchmarks

E. Identification of leaders

F. Admission factor of tenants

G. Entry exit criteria of tenant companies

It is critical for the company to carefully inspect and scrutinize the expected outcome, and draw a timeline with benchmarks and establish the current state to enable an understanding of the feasibility of the entire operation.

Feasibility studies are important since they force one to see on the macro-scale and think in a top-down fashion to build a viable program. Richards states that feasibility study allows sponsors to test the waters before entering into business and identifying required resources and the commitments necessary to conjure a viable project.

13.3.3 Availability of Funding

Availability of capital for businesses in any form like government grants, loans, equity, and debt financing arrangements or the presence of venture capitalists or angel investors contribute to incubator success. Without seed funding or early-stage funding, no business would even get the opportunity to transform its vision into a business. Barrow [12] rightfully indicates that incubators hence also offer grants, loans, equity, and debt financing arrangements and business and tax and risk management. Even technology start-ups which are the most sought after by investors fail to take flight without sufficient early-stage seed funding.

13.3.4 Caliber of Entrepreneur

The quality of the entrepreneur affects the success rate of the incubator; the expected qualities are as follows:

A. **Open-Minded**: Ability to recognize business as well as learning opportunities.
B. **Self-Starter**: Goal setters and achievers who set the parameters and work in accordance.
C. **Persistence**: An important trait of indispensable sense.
D. **Decisive and Action Oriented**: Quick on the foot.
E. **Venture Survival Rate**: Higher if entrepreneurs have substantial knowledge and ability at the beginning few stages itself and continues to show the substantial knowledge throughout.

Big 5 model is a multidimensional approach to defining personality considering different parameters, namely openness, conscientiousness, extraversion, agreeableness, and neuroticism. These five traits have been heavily discussed by the authors.
Nelton [13] provides a few suggestions to entrepreneurs for success in their endeavor:

1. Learn from experience by serving in other ventures.
2. Hire people smarter than you.
3. Network and gain knowledge vicariously from others experiences.
4. Affiliate with organizations with concentrated knowledge and government agencies.
5. Develop a board of directors.
6. Set up an advisory board.
7. Establish friendly relations with employees.
8. Utilization of business incubators for consultation.
9. Keep aside ego and learn from different sources.
10. Pay heed to customer complaints.
11. Hone business and administration skills.

Rosa et al. [14] say that the path to a successful entrepreneurship is not just about innovativeness but is immensely opportunity driven. It is a complicated, aggregated, and comprehensive balance of multitudes of factors. Experts and researchers concur with the fact that an entrepreneur has several layers to them both intellectually, cognitively, and philosophically. Spearheading a new business is never a predictable affair and events never play according to the books, the wisdom to manage multiple things, ability to deal with unfriendly environments, identifying new opportunities and resources, efficiency in managing multiple resources are all a few distinguishable characteristics of entrepreneurs. One must agree that management and entrepreneurial skills are like two peas in a pod. Gartner and Bhatt [15] support the claim that ventures have greater odds of surviving post-graduating from an incubator if the entrepreneur was substantially well informed and educated prior to joining, and continued to demonstrate during the process of incubation.

Unlike often mentioned in orthodox management literatures many are of the thought social capital might be one of the most important factors for the social competence of an entrepreneur. The term social capital involves the reputation, reliability among the peers, employees, and the market which indirectly influence factors such as employee influence and reliability of the established brand. A few cognitive comparators for entrepreneurs' assessment of success rate would be their confidence, reasoning with counterfactual statements without getting overwhelmed, etc. Factors such as overconfidence in their own judgments, lateral thinking, and reduced tendency to engage in conditional thinking might impact the entrepreneur's success.

Innovation is possible only with divergent minds and environments that flourish among disarray and mayhem according to Hickman et al. [16]. The slowdown in progress in science, technology, engineering, and mathematics has been attributed to conservative and risk aversive researchers and a lack of venture capitalists. The characteristics that set apart an entrepreneur from an average employed person are often theoretically ascribed to the attraction-selection-attrition model.

13.4 Successful Incubates and Graduates

The metric to measure the success of incubators has for the longest been comparing the numbers of successful businesses within the portfolios according to Barrow [17]. Hence the successes of both the incubator and the tenant companies are complementary, i.e., their successes are tied. This mere fact should thrust incubators to strive for providing the best services to their tenants. Incubators also need to contribute to the companies in their portfolio to be able to attract venture capitalists and not lose them to ventures outside the incubator.

13.4.1 Supportive Government Policies

The impetus to initiate successful entrepreneurship starts from promotion and consensus on economic and industrial policies. The innovative framework of business incubators can only be truly admired if the association between entrepreneurship and economic impact is addressed. This can be viable only if the project the incubator is in pursuit of are in line with the economic goals and strategies and with the socio-cultural environment the government is in pursuit of. Developing countries like India, China, and other South-African nations might follow foreign incubator business models adopted during their growing stages which attribute to a facilitative entrepreneurial environment, government policies, and grants. A business incubator is highly successful if its goals and objectives are in line with that of the country. The success of business incubators in the United States is largely owed to the national demand for jobs, infrastructure, and services with an aim for profit by the people nationally.

13.4.2 Stakeholder Consensus

The stakeholders of a business incubator are far more in number and elusive in nature unlike the stakeholders of a company. The strategy for the framework must be in line with the needs and capacities of the community it is focused to serve for. Business incubators

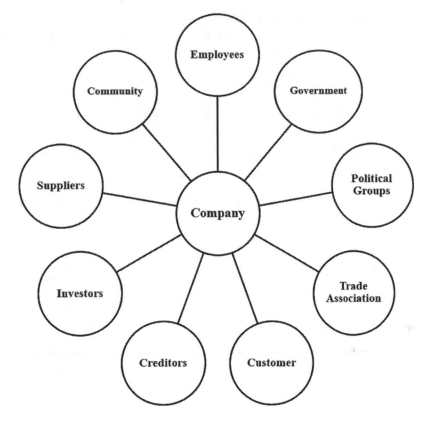

FIGURE 13.1
Company stakeholders.

work through connections and associations of myriads of stakeholders consisting of the government sponsors from the business community, and the community they themselves are serving (Figure 13.1).

13.4.3 Competent and Properly Encouraged Management Team

A management team is essential to any company to enhance the company capabilities continuously, management teams need to strive for minuscule incremental changes in company operations to improve efficiency. Several management practices have been established over the years which contribute to the companies' overall performance and its core values. Lean management and Six Sigma are some of the prevalent and widely accepted management tools that are adopted by proficient and accomplished management teams. Businesses signed up in incubators that provide valuable opportunities for networking and opportunities to the CEOs to ameliorate their skills in management have a vantage point over other businesses not under the umbrella of an incubator.

Researchers and experts often debate on the relevance of leadership over management or vice versa, but from the above points it is clear that management implements the practices of the organization, making work processes as close to efficient as possible, while a leadership help organization to grow, be motivated and inspired and aroused qualities such as loyalty dedication and accountability. The perfect blend of both the leadership and management team's demonstrations has never been more critical to success than before. Businesses need to harness passion and vision in perfect proportion with disciplined processes.

Lalkaka suggests some success benchmarks:

A. Separately functioning owners and management team
B. Freedom to the management team to award employees for performance
C. The team needs to invest its energy and resources into multiple ventures and not just one venture opportunity or goal.

Many existing studies emphasize the need for both a leader entrepreneur figure and managers to streamline organization functioning. Both have unique vital roles essential for multitudes of reasons. In several meta-analyses such as Zhao et al. [18], it is said that entrepreneurs are more open to experience, more conscientious, and less neurotic toward employees in comparison to the managers. This balance is viewed as essential in organizations.

13.4.4 An Able Advisory Board

The onus of establishing an advisory board with multiple disciplines willing to advise to contribute to building the tenant companies is on the incubators. The advisory board should disperse the experiences impartially and both to tenants and the management.

13.4.4.1 Financial Sustainability

The incubators must be practical and should generate some revenue. They might generate income by taking royalties or equities from the tenant companies. Some incubators might resort to the orthodox tradition of taking rents on subsidies. Incubators established by government and educational centers such as universities are mostly non-profit based and are willing to proceed since the tenant companies on graduating add a feather to the universities cap. The universities also get to be on the heels of cutting-edge technology.

Ultimately the best test for incubator would be to test the withstanding and longevity of its client companies' post-graduation, hence the incubator needs to be handled like a business Campbell [19] offers suggestions for potential developers as follows:

1. For financial sustainability the incubator must have a diversified portfolio with both old and young firms.
2. Well qualified team.
3. Comparing costs of renovation and new structure.
4. Explicit and flexible agreements.

13.4.5 Entry and Exit Criteria

Authors of the literature works considered all concur to the need for strict admission and retreating criteria. The incubators could add their own criteria but a few mandatory ones would be only admitting businesses with law-abiding and feasible ideas that have potential in the market. This facilitates the incubator to hold a niche market demographic and cater specifically to their needs.

Lalkaka believes examining and screening the technical, business, and market potential of the applicant is critical to an incubator's success.

13.4.6 Networking

Networking is the act of clustering and interaction between like-minded business people who identify, create, and strive for business opportunities by conducting socio-economic activities.

The presence of a network of executive champions and expert consultants has often been proven to contribute to the success of business incubators. This is so because elemental nodes of the network which constitute multiple elements such as partners, investors, allies such as fellow tenants, and vendors like service providers share knowledge and experiences for the growth of the start-ups. This basic network which is established in an incubator keeps expanding through referrals (Figure 13.2).

Networking widens market prospects for incubates and graduates. Networking isn't restricted to the residing registered country but also other nations. Incubators across the globe tie-up to provide combined and enhanced services.

Hansen et al. [20] mentioned in their literature how a well-networked incubator is equivalent to a perennial long-standing model capable of withstanding the blows from the fast volatile internet economy. Such models provide economies of scale. Strategic establishment of portfolio companies and network of potential partners is a notable feature of incubators that incubates can leverage from.

Pena et al. [21] say that assets that the organizations of inter-organizational arrangements assist companies in sustaining themselves by exploiting the benefits of venture companies from tangible and intangible assets of partner firms.

What the definition of networking fails in conveying is the need to maintain the connections as well. It has been recognized that successful businesses continually maintain bonds with each member of the network. Each network member has something to contribute and weakening ties might adversely affect reputation.

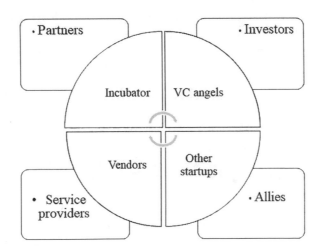

FIGURE 13.2
Networking for business incubation.

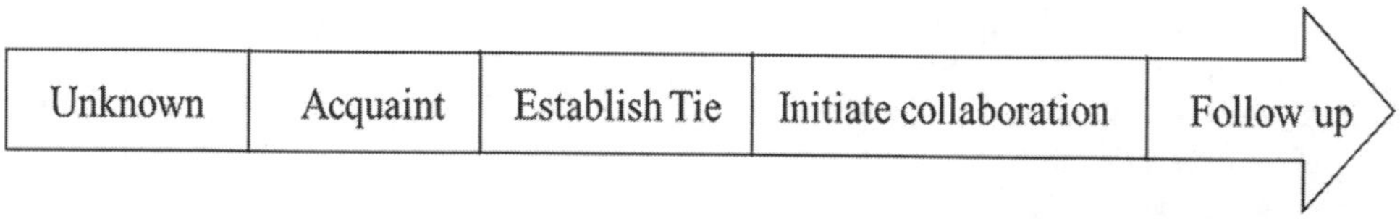

| Unknown | Acquaint | Establish Tie | Initiate collaboration | Follow up |

FIGURE 13.3
Process flow of networking.

Regularly engaging with the contacts and finding occasions to give them a hand helps to toughen the bond. Each network has insights that might help other businesses, offering solutions and ideas wisely also helps in building a reputation of an innovative thinker in the market. Expanding the network opens doors to career advancement, personal growth, wisdom, and provision to exchange the best industry-specific practices (Figure 13.3).

13.5 Services Provided by Incubator

The services provided by an incubator to its client companies can be categorized broadly into the following categories as shown in the figure below. These services provided substantially reduce the set-up cost of young businesses (Figure 13.4).

13.5.1 Community Support

The performance of an incubator attests for the community's support, reverence, and effort to diversify its economy to generate jobs and promote entrepreneurship among the masses. Incubators help indigenous companies to promote self-sustaining depressed economies.

13.5.2 Modus Operandi of Successful Business Incubations

Rice et al. have explored three principles and ten practices of business incubations with positive success rates. They can be summarized as follows.

13.5.2.1 Principles

The primary focus of an incubator should be on developing companies. All other objectives such as job creation and economic impact would automatically follow. This can be explained by the Principle of Causality where successful free-standing graduate companies result in job creation and a change in the existing economy.

Never lose sight of the fact that the incubator in itself is a venture and needs to be managed as one; the mission of the said venture is to assist young businesses to succeed. The incubator as a business itself undergoes several challenging periods.

Programmed and services offered by the incubator should be formulated having acknowledged the fact that businesses with different needs and specializing in different verticals have varying needs. The "one-size-fit-all" approach by management will lead to unsuccessful grooming and mentoring of programmers.

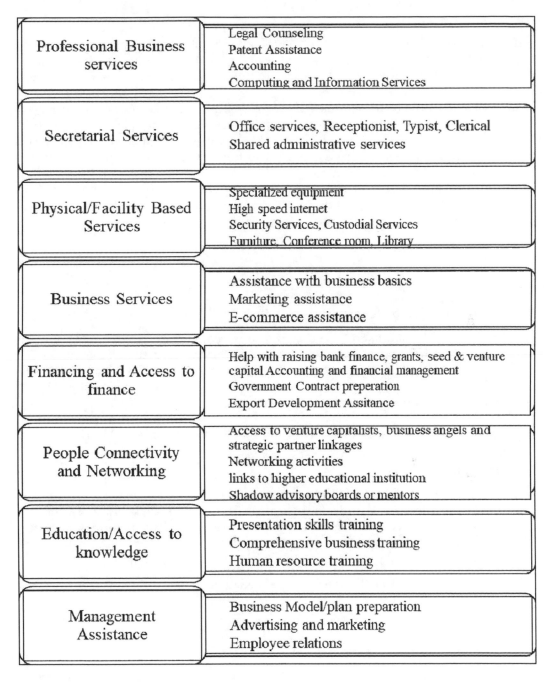

FIGURE 13.4
Services provided by incubator.

13.5.2.2 Best Practices

Dedicate to the core set of beliefs and principles of the incubation to set the agenda.

Collect data and analyses to decide feasibility of the incubator. With a provision of sponsors and capitalists the analyses help in setting the course and timeline for launching a successful program.

The incubator should be treated like a business venture. It will be observed during cost accounting that during initial phases the cost exceeds the revenues by a huge margin. Measures can be taken to bridge it and eventually a break-even point needs to be achieved. The revenues could be rental from companies, fees for services, royalties and equities, and financial backing from various sources.

Various responsibilities such as recruitment of staff of various grades need to be carried out. Keep track of the development of the incubator as it moves from one phase to the other. Keep a tab on the developmental phase of each tenant company.

13.6 Result and Factor Analysis

The discussion and examination of success factors acquired from success factors. The observed variables have been modeled to extract a covariance structure to identify underlying unobservable factors. Inferences are drawn at a significance level and biplots and hit maps have assisted to corroborate the success factors for business incubation [22]. The survey response is based on the following questions:

1. Who were the initial seed investors or sponsors? (Select all that applies.)
2. Who were the other stakeholders involved in the project? (Select all that are applicable.)
3. What roles did the stakeholders assume?
4. Was a feasibility study conducted? (Real estate/building, availability of clients, cost-benefit analysis of public opinion, i.e., in favor or not, legal requirements, tax implications, etc.)

    4.1. If yes, what were the strongest factors that gave the green light?

5. Was break-even a part of the business plan? (Gather income from multiple sources to cover operating costs.)

    5.1. If your answer to the previous question was yes, how long was it predicted to achieve break-even?

6. Are there supportive government policies?

    6.1. If your answer to the previous question was yes, please select policies of interest

7. Please rate the government policies that are the most supportive to you and your tenants on a scale of 1–5 (1 being of least impact):

    7.1. Tax exemption

    7.2. Funding support

    7.3. Mobile app registration

    7.4. Simplified exit strategy

7.5. Self-certification

7.6. Filing of patents

7.7. Public sector procurement

7.8. Incubator and infrastructure

7.9. Development

13.6.1 Table KMO and Bartlett's Test

These tests speak about the quality of the data. KMO value should be more than 0.5, and Bartlett's value should be less than 0.05 (Table 13.1).

The KMO is less than 0.5 so the results should be interpreted carefully. The relevance of results is less if KMO is less than 0.5.

Biplot: This graph graphically shows the presence of factors (Figure 13.5).

TABLE 13.1

KMO and Bartlett's Test for Section C

Kaiser–Meyer–Olkin Measure of Sampling Adequacy		0.30
Bartlett's Test of Sphericity	Chi-square value	1067.996
	Degrees of freedom	105
	P value	$< 2.22\text{e-}16$

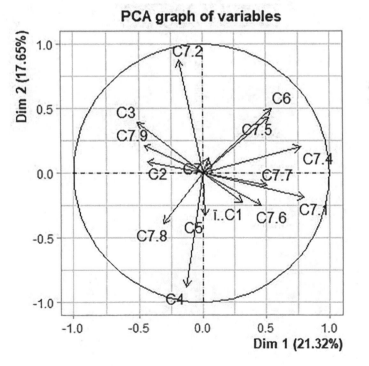

FIGURE 13.5
Biplot of Section C.

The bi-plot clearly verifies the existence of correlations between 7, 7.4, 6, 7.5, 7.7, C3 (henceforth considered Factor 4), existence of correlations between 5, 4 (henceforth considered Factor 5), 1, 7.9, 3 (henceforth considered Factor 6); and 6 (henceforth considered Factor 7), 7.8 (henceforth considered Factor 8) being standalone variables.

13.6.2 Scree Plot of Individual Variances of Dimensions

See Figure 13.6.

13.6.3 Scree Plot of Eigenvalues of Dimensions

See Figure 13.7.

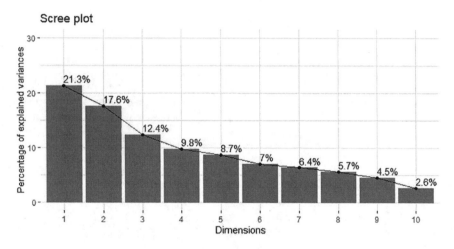

FIGURE 13.6
Scree plot of individual variances of dimensions for Section C.

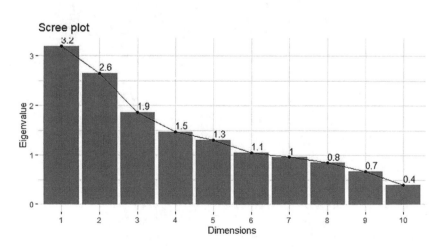

FIGURE 13.7
Scree plot of eigenvalues of dimensions.

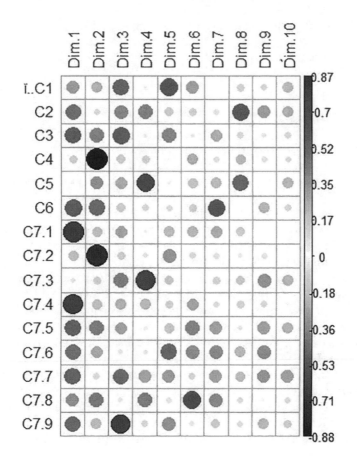

FIGURE 13.8
Correlation (C) plot.

13.6.4 Correlation Plot

A correlation plot shows factors and weights of factors or dimensions.

Using the Scree plots of individual variance of dimensions and the Scree plot of eigenvalues of dimensions, we were able to infer that the first seven principal components have eigenvalues greater than 1. These three components explain roughly 83% of the variation present within the data. Since 83% explicability of the amount of variance in data is adequate, those factors have been selected for the thesis (Figure 13.8).

The correlation heatmap which develops a matrix of the results of Pearson correlation coefficients corroborates the existence of dimensions and their correlation value signified by the colored circles. Correlation ranges from +1 to −1. Dark blue circles signify strong linear correlation; white spaces signify no correlation between the dimensions and the variables [23].

Table 13.2 shows factor loading, eigenvalue, and percentage of extraction using a principal component method based on Section B for managers.

This table provides the strength of the relationship between each variable to the underlying factor. It is evident from the table that most of the variables have high factor loadings to the factor they are correlated to; this is considered a strong association for factor analysis.

The factors identified in this section are as follows:

A. Support from the public and private sectors
B. Financial evaluation
C. Involvement of stakeholders
D. Incubator infrastructure

The government actively encourages entrepreneurship and creation of small- and medium-scale industries to fire the economy. This is done in numerous ways starting with consensus on economic and industrial policies. The public sector provides tax incentives and other monetary support to young promising companies; they ensure that projects that the technical business incubators that are seeking support are in line with the economic goals and strategies of the government. Support from the national or local government not only financially but in other ways plays a critical role to promote the success of technical business incubators. Support from the private sector catered toward providing diverse expertise is crucial too. Intellectual capital building in the form of easing patent filing, trademarking or copywriting formalities, and providing valuable assistance in rapid commercialization of new ideas, processes, services and products alike. Local or national governments addressing regulatory issues relating to estate use permissions, foreign investment proposals and environment clearances facilitates more successful technical business incubators [24].

From the data it has been found that incubators having conducted financial evaluations prior to establishment had greater prospects of being successful. Feasibility study including identifying addressable market, admission factor of clients, setting up timelines and benchmarks, and identifying the period to reach break-even tend to be more successful. From the data it was also discovered that incubators affiliated with universities did not

TABLE 13.2

Factor Loading, Eigenvalues, and Percentage of Extraction for Section C

Factor	Question	Factor Loading	Eigenvalues	% of Variance	Cumulative %
1	7.1	0.799299502	3.198316475	21.32210984	21.32210984
	7.4	0.772214036			
	6	0.547524354			
	7.5	0.522874293			
	7.7	0.512198078			
	3	−0.508569215			
2	5	−0.881674993	2.646823487	17.64548992	38.96759975
	4	0.871746483			
3	1	0.525815616	1.862273997	12.41515998	51.38275973
	7.9	−0.674176114			
	3	0.549517264			
4	7.3	0.74946203	1.472964725	9.819764832	61.20252456
	5	−0.630438517			
5	7.6	0.518406242	1.304923757	8.699491714	69.90201628
	1	0.613408282			
6	7.8	0.636377525	1.056160774	7.041071826	76.9430881
7	6	−0.542758775	0.960356143	6.402374285	83.34546239

rely on financial evaluations which could be attributed to their sheltered heavy funding from universities or the government.

The involvement of stakeholders ensures a common understanding and involvement in the decision-making process of the project. Participation of stakeholders makes the incubators accountable to the stakeholders. A majority of the respondents had stakeholders who took up financial roles and played an important role in building a cohesive vision for the future.

13.7 Conclusion

Incubators set up creates sustainable and strong entrepreneurial support infrastructure and enable entrepreneurial teams to build successful enterprises. Elements such as the space, design, network activities, partnerships and linkages, service providers, experts, and consultants promote a holistic environment of growth for nascent ventures. Collaborative spaces equipped with specialized equipment, IT infrastructure, security support, and administrative support are all essential to a successful technical business incubator.

It is noted that incubators affiliated with educational hubs or in close proximity to universities tend to tended to have the best infrastructure since the term perhaps not only encapsulates hardware but also the easily available pool of raw talent in the form of students and experienced teachers and other experts who prove to be a catalyst to innovate and create.

References

1. Massimo G. Colombo, Evila Piva, Start-ups launched by recent STEM university graduates: The impact of university education on entrepreneurial entry, *Research Policy*, Volume 49, No. 6, 98–103, 2020.
2. Jones O., Meckel P., Taylor D. (2021) Discussion: The INNOSPACE community of practice. In: *Creating Communities of Practice. International Studies in Entrepreneurship*, vol. 46. Springer, Cham. https://doi.org/10.1007/978-3-030-62962-5_8.
3. Ramchandra Sharad Mangrulkar, Antonis Michalas, Narendra Shekokar, Meera Narvekar, Pallavi Vijay Chavan. *Design of Intelligent Applications using Machine Learning and Deep Lea*. 2021, Chapman and Hall/CRC.
4. B. Bigliardi, A.I. Dormio, A. Petroni (2018) Startups and spin-offs: the role of business incubators, *ICERI2018 Proceedings*, pp. 3507–3516.
5. Magnus Klofsten, Erik Lundmark, Karl Wennberg, Nata Bank, Incubator specialization and size: Divergent paths towards operational scale. *Technological Forecasting and Social Change*, Volume 151, 129–134, 2020.
6. Ann-Kristin Achleitner, Reiner Braun, Jan Henning Behrens, Thomas Lange. Enhancing innovation in Germany by strengthening the growth finance ecosystem. *National Academy of Science and Engineering*, 1–40, 2019.
7. Jeffrey M. Shepard. When incubators evolve: new models to assist innovative entrepreneurs. *International Journal of Entrepreneurship and Innovation Management (IJEIM)*, Volume 21, No. 1/2, 86–104, 2017.

8. S. C. Bose, Dr. Ravi Kiran, Dr. Dinesh Goyal. Entry and exit policy and ties with university as critical success factors influencing agri-business incubation performance. *Global Journal of Management and Business Research*, 17–23, 2018.

9. Wulandari, S., Rendra, M., Alam, P. F., Kusumasari, T. F., Dewi, A. S., & Gustyana, T. T. The development of Pantiku application business strategy using business model canvas approach. *Indonesian Journal of Business and Entrepreneurship (IJBE)*, Volume 5, No. 3, 231–241, 2019.

10. Caren Klingbeil & Thorsten Semrau. For whom size matters – the interplay between incubator size, tenant characteristics and tenant growth. *Industry and Innovation*, Volume 24, No. 7, 735–752, 2017, DOI: 10.1080/13662716.2017.1319802.

11. Mustafa Torun, Laura Peconick, Vinicius Sobreiro, Herbert Kimura, Josep Pique, Assessing business incubation: A review on benchmarking. *International Journal of Innovation Studies*, Volume 2, No. 3, 91–100, 2018.

12. Wagner, M., Schaltegger, S., Hansen, E.G. et al. University-linked programmes for sustainable entrepreneurship and regional development: How and with what impact? *Small Business Economy*, 2019. https://doi.org/10.1007/s11187-019-00280-4.

13. Dee, N., Gill, D., Lacher, R., Livesey, F., & Minshall, T. A review of research on the role and effectiveness of business incubation for high-growth start-ups. https://doi.org/10.17863/CAM.44134.

14. Nico Kreusel, Natalie Roth, Alexander Brem European business venturing in times of digitisation - an analysis of for-profit business incubators in a triple helix context. *International Journal of Technology Management (IJTM)*, Volume 76, No. 1/2, 104–136, 2018.

15. Chu-chen Rosa Yeh and Rossana Obregon. Impact of business incubator services on performance of micro, small and medium sized enterprises in Nicaragua. *Academy of Management Global Proceedings*, Volume Tel Aviv, No. 2018.

16. Preeti Tiwari, Anil K. Bhat & Jyoti Tikoria. The role of emotional intelligence and self-efficacy on social entrepreneurial attitudes and social entrepreneurial intentions. *Journal of Social Entrepreneurship*, Volume 8, No. 2, 165–185, 2017. DOI: 10.1080/19420676.2017.1371628.

17. Hickman, L. and Akdere, M. Exploring information technology-business alignment through stakeholder theory: a review of literature. *Industrial and Commercial Training*, Volume 51, No. 4, 228–243, 2019. https://doi.org/10.1108/ICT-11-2018-0098.

18. Cosenz, F. Supporting start-up business model design through system dynamics modelling. *Management Decision*, Volume 55, No. 1, 57–80, 2017. https://doi.org/10.1108/MD-06-2016–0395.

19. Abhijeet Kushwaha, Pallavi Vijay Chavan, Vivek Kumar Singh, COVID-19 Data Analysis and Innovative Approach in Prediction of Cases. *Book Series: Studies in Big Data, 2020, COVID-19 Data Analysis and Innovative Approach in Prediction of Cases* | springerprofessional.de.

20. Hao Zhao, Gina O'Connor, Jihong Wu, G.T. Lumpkin. Age and entrepreneurial career success: A review and a meta-analysis. *Journal of Business Venturing*, Volume 36, No. 1, 08–14, 2021.

21. Shekapure S., Patil D.D. (2020) Learning preferences analysis by case-based reasoning. In: Iyer B., Deshpande P., Sharma S., Shiurkar U. (eds) *Computing in Engineering and Technology. Advances in Intelligent Systems and Computing*, vol. 1025. Springer, Singapore. https://doi.org/10.1007/978-981-32-9515-5_14.

22. Campbell, T.A. A phenomenological study of business graduates' employment experiences in the changing economy. *Journal for Labour Market Research*, Volume 52, No. 4, 265–284, 2018. https://doi.org/10.1186/s12651-018-0238-8.

23. Vaibhav Saraf, Pallavi Chavan, Ashish Jadhav. *Deep Learning Challenges in Medical Imaging*, Springer Singapore, 2020.

24. Carlo Bagnoli, Francesca Dal Mas and Maurizio Massaro. The 4th Industrial Revolution: Business Models and Evidence from the Field. *IGI Global*, 34–47, 2019.

14

Satellite Imagery-Based Wildfire Detection Using Deep Learning

Anant Kaulage, Sagar Rane, and Sunil Dhore

Dept. Of Computer Engg

Army Institute of Technology

CONTENTS

14.1 Introduction to the Proposed Chapter

Wildfire is hit or miss and uncontrolled fire that burst call at forest naturally or by act. This fire causes harm to both flora and fauna as well as human life. Every year, there are several cases of wildfire, which causes severe destruction to nature and human lives. Last year, Australia became the victim of a fire which is taken into account as the worst wildfire seen in decades. Over 28 people have died, and 3,000 homes got destroyed. A complete 17.9 million acres of land got affected which approximately costs $100 billion. The main cause of forest fires is that they are located in remote places, they are unmanaged areas with lots of trees, dry and perching woods and leaves, therefore these things are the source of wild-fires. These sources all together form a highly flammable and are the most explanation for initial oxidization and act as combustible and explosive for later stages of the fireside. The fireside ignition could also be caused by human's unthoughtful behaviors like smoking or accidentally on camp flies or by elemental reasons like heat during a hot summer day. Once oxidization starts, flammable material can easily act as a catalyst for the fire to spread which then becomes enormous, berserk, and outspread. Then this results in prey on adjoining trees as a fuel and therefore the fire flame became more berserk. For the most

DOI: 10.1201/9781003283249-14

part, at this phase, the hearth becomes obstreperous and inevitable, which leads to a large destruction to the landscape and wildlife, and this can become unrestrained and will last long, and therefore it also depends on the prevailing monsoon in that topography [1].

With the advancement in deep learning (DL) and computer vision and data collected through the satellite, it's made possible to detect wildfire and alarm the priority authority to tackle the fireside before it gets uncontrolled. With an increase in global warming, there is an increase in chances of wildfire causing harm to both human life and nature. A number of preexisting works in this field have been using non-image data based on historical incidents. With recent advancement in technology, DL and computer vision, in particular, it has become possible to detect these fires captured through satellite images at an early stage and alarm the concerned authority. In this chapter, we tend to discuss a "Satellite Imagery-Based Wildfire Detection System" in order to detect the wildfire through a convolutional neural network (CNN)-based model by using satellite images. There are lots of satellites that provide the data related to wildfire, but we are using the data provided by the Copernicus Sentinel-2 satellite. Sentinel-2 is a satellite that is placed in the sun-synchronous orbit. Sun-synchronous orbits are wont to make sure the angle of sunlight upon the surface is consistently maintained. Copernicus Sentinel-2 takes images of the land and coastal areas at a high geographical resolution within the optical zone. The main application of this satellite is to monitor cultivation, terrestrial ecosystems, forests, inland and coastal water quality, catastrophe mapping, and public security. It will be developed via CNN (DL) trained on various features such as RGB models and some additional layers. The data set will be divided into two sets: training and testing. Accuracy of the model can be determined by presenting the validation set. On completion of the model may be exposed through an API. The user can upload an image and results will be displayed in terms of "Fire" or "Not Fire". To detect the wildfires, using DL, different multiple features like vegetation index, true color, and moisture content can be extracted via the Sentinel-2 satellite (10–40 m). Our model uses only satellite imagery film's truth color with a simple sequential model of CNN for wildfire detection. The business requirement for this model is to develop an API that receives an image, processes it through machine learning (ML) models, returns the presence or absence of fire in me input image, and accordingly signals the concerned department. This model can be used by forest departments to quickly detect wildfire and take necessary actions so as to control the wildfire before it gets berserk. It can identify some of the most vulnerable places across the globe which are more prone to wildfire.

14.2 Literature Review

The literature consists of various examples of usage of numerous ML approaches for the detection of wildfire models. But most of these ML approaches predominantly use non-image data; especially, they use historical wildfire incidents to make predictions. For example, methods such as logistic regression and support vector machine have stayed to use the detection of wildfire and analytical threat modeling as realized in [2,3] and "predicting fire occurrence patterns with logistic regression". Focusing mainly on images captured by the satellite in paper [1], they have exasperated to report the detection of wildfire using the DL method. In paper [4] work they have built DL models using the output of an identical influential "16-channel satellite" with the same granular temporal and spatial resolution to detect wildfires, i.e., Geospatial Operating Environmental Satellites-16. In "Environment-Agnostic Wildfire Detection with Satellite Imagery", also a DL model is used in the detection of wildfires based on satellite images. As a satellite imagery source, they used Landsat-8 which has a progressive resolution of each 16 days and a spatial resolution that varies between 30 and 60 m. There are 11 bands in the images of the Landsat satellite, 6 channels are used out of it, as per actual data. Three infrared bands and three RGB channels. Using over 40,000 satellite image actual data, an train data 86% and test data 87% accurate it was obtained with each image at $224 \times 224 \times 6$ [4].

14.3 Gaps in the Present Study

The temporal and spatial resolutions of Landsat are relatively poor and are free and easy to access. This might pointedly disturb the legitimacy of the model predictions. A better temporal and spatial resolution is provided by our model though we use the Sentinel satellite. Again, one more limitation of "Environment-Agnostic Wildfire Detection with Satellite Imagery" is that the training data set used for the detection of wildfire was obtained from Landsat's own computationally (statistically) estimated fire locations. The add "Environment- Agnostic Wildfire Detection with Satellite Imagery" limits the discovery of other convenient films or we also call layers which are accessible from satellites like Landsat or Sentinel. Additional to infrared, Sentinel also provides layers like normalized burn index, burned area index, moisture index, and normalized differential vegetation index, among others. Additional layers will be beneficial to developing models with better performance.

14.4 Proposed System and Algorithm

The wildfire detection system using DL proposes the trained model on pictures of ancient wildfire places from the satellite. This system will use CNN. We will use the transfer learning method to train our model. Window/block-based analysis will be used for capturing minute details such as smoke. In order to deal with wildfire detection, we walk through the applications of one main worldwide satellite Sentinel-2. Previous works are focused on the use of Landsat, whose satellite imagery service is less granular, and we are extracting different multiple features like vegetation index, true color, and moisture content via the Sentinel satellite for detection of wildfire using DL. Our typical model uses only actual true-color satellite pictorial film or layer with an easy sequential model of CNN on images for detection of wildfire through transfer learning.

14.4.1 Algorithm

Before going into an explanation of Adam optimizers let's understand some basic terms before that optimizers. *Optimizers* are used to alter the attributes of your neural network such as learning rate and weights in order to minimize the losses of model. Optimizer updates the weight parameters in an efficient manner to minimize the loss function of the model. The role of the optimizer is to find a suitable combination of weights so as to reduce the loss function. *Bias* can be imagined as an intercept which is present in an equation of line. It is an extra parameter in our neural network which is used to improve the weighted sum of the inputs to the neuron along with the output.

The neuron processing is thus denoted as:

Output=sum (weights * inputs)+bias

The given equation is similar to $y=mx+c$, where c=bias (intercept)

Bias allows you to shift the activation function of your model by adding a constant to the input. It helps the model to fit the given data.

Gradient descent is an ML algorithm to find and minimize the cost function. Gradient descents represent the direction of increase. We can go toward the opposite direction of the gradient in order to find the lowest point. Loss function directors the territory influence optimizer whether it is affecting the right area, to range the lowest point in the valley which is our worldwide minimum.

14.4.1.1 Adam Optimizer In-Depth

Now let's deep dive into the Adam optimizer. The individual adaptive learning rate is found by the Adam optimizer, the value for each factor from data points of the first and second gradient's moments. The Adam optimizer gears the exponential touching line, an average of the gradient's moment to scale the learning rate. The Adam optimizer relies on two important moments those are the mean and the variance first order and the second order, respectively. We can update the weights and the bias using moment estimates to get the appropriate step size or also it is called an error.

$$mt = \beta1 * mt - 1 + (1 - \beta1) * gt$$

$$vt = \beta2 * vt - 1 + (1 - \beta2) * gt * gt$$

where mt and vt are estimates of the first and second moments, respectively.

14.4.1.2 Adam Configuration/Hyper Parameters

$\beta1$ is the exponential decay of the rate for the first moment estimates, and its literature value is 0.9.

$\beta2$ is the exponential decay rate for the second-moment estimates, and its literature value is 0.999.

ε is a very small positive value which prevents division from zero error (10^{-8}).

mt and vt are estimates of the first and second moments, respectively.

The gt and gt^2 are gradient and squared gradient, respectively.

14.4.1.3 Window/Block-Based Analysis

As with the recent advancements in technology, high-resolution images of forest and wildlife is easily available. However, if we provide these images as an input to our model, there will be overheads for training. Common solutions involve reducing the quality of images, i.e., compressing the images to a lower resolution, which can cause loss of minute details such as smoke and can lead to wrong predictions. To overcome this problem, we divide our input images into small windows or blocks. We implemented this by detecting the smoke block by block.

The equations for the row (R) and column (C) are given as:

$$R = (Hi/Hb)$$

$$C = (Wi/Wb)$$

14.4.1.4 Binary Cross-Entropy Loss

The efficiency of an ML algorithm is measured by means of a loss function. If the prediction deviates too much, the loss function give a very large value indicating false results. A loss function penalizes the model according to the deviation from the ground or actual value. Since we are dealing with a classification problem, we will use a binary cross-entropy loss function for accurate prediction.

$$H_p(q) = -\frac{1}{N}\sum_{i=1}^{N} y_i \cdot \log(p(y_i)) + (1 - y_i) \cdot \log(1 - p(y_i))$$

14.5 Detailed Design

14.5.1 System Architecture

This is the basic system architecture of CNN training and testing flow. In the training phase, satellite images are used, in which labels are provided as a feature to the CNN, basically binary classification techniques are used to classify the fire and non-fire areas. In the testing phase, some test images can be provided to the trained model and the trained model will classify these images (Figure 14.1).

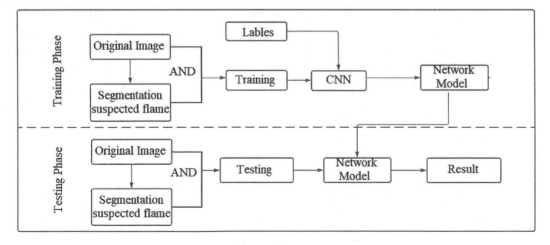

FIGURE 14.1
System architecture diagram is a flow of the system.

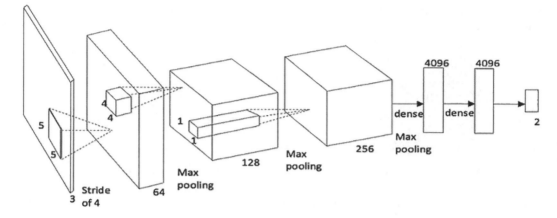

FIGURE 14.2
CNN model description (https://github.com/tobybreckon/fire-detection-cnn/blob/master/images/FireNet.png).

As shown in Figure 14.2, there are two ways for initializing a CNN, either by a sequence of layers or as a graph. Therefore, we are using the sequential model to initialize our neural network model as a sequential network. We are using Convolution 2D, in order to perform the convolution operation, i.e., the first step of a CNN, on the training images. In the next step of building a CNN, we have MaxPooling from the Keras library, which is used for pooling operations. For building this particular neural network, we are using a Max Pooling function. There are also other types of pooling functions like Min Pooling and Mean Pooling. Max Pooling is used for the maximum value of the pixel from the relevant region of interest. Flattening is the next step in which we are converting all the resultant two-dimensional arrays into a single extended steady linear vector. And finally, we are importing dense from the Keras library, for its functionality to perform the full connection of the neural network, which is an important step in the process of building a CNN [5,6].

14.5.2 Design Diagrams

We described our system architecture by using Unified Modeling Language diagrams which are used to understand archaeology and programs using an object-oriented paradigm. The design diagrams provide us with a way to visualize the program design process.
Below are the design diagrams for this model:

- Activity diagram (process view)
- Deployment diagram (physical view)

The *logical view* cares about the functionality by means of classes and methods that the framework gives to end clients. We are using the main three classes "Classifier", "Training" and "Prediction", where the "Classifier" class is the superclass, which contains the logic of creating a sequential model. "Training" class is using the model developed by the "Classifier" class to train the data test. "Prediction" class is using the trained model to make predictions.
Activity Diagram gives us the actual process view. The activity diagram shows the flow control, the image getting fed into the feature extraction model resulting in formation

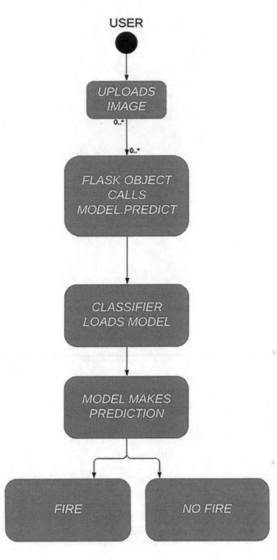

FIGURE 14.3
Activity diagram (original).

of fixed length vector and a match would be drawn corresponding to the database and accordingly, feature description will be fetched to the end user, as shown in Figure 14.3.

A *sequence diagram* depicts object communication sorted in time fashion. It portrays the involved object along with the flows of messages exchanged. In our project actor interact with the flask User Interface and uploads image for prediction, then flask User Interface interact with our model by using model object, and eventually our model makes predictions and return results.

A *deployment diagram* gives us the physical view. Physical or the deployment view delineates a framework from a developer's point of view and cares about programming the board. This view is furthermore alluded to as the usage see. It utilizes the Unified Modeling Language component chart to clarify framework segments (Figure 14.4).

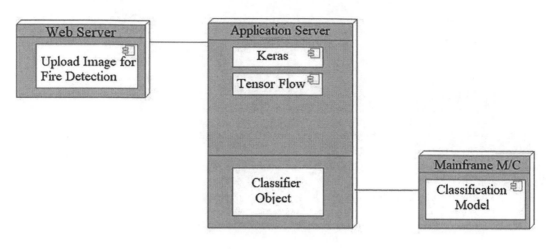

FIGURE 14.4
Deployment diagram (original).

14.6 Conclusion

Hence we can implement a DL detection of wildfire model that's training is done on pictures or images of ancient wildfire places from the Sentinel-2 satellite using window/-block-based examination technique and Adam analyzer algorithms. These algorithms are applied here to identify the fierce blaze through a convolution neural organization-based successive model by means of move learning. Window/block-based is applied methodology so it coordinates the high-goal pictures without playing out any down-inspecting. Down-examining may cause data misfortune and minuscule smoke tufts may get undetectable. Consequently, this window/block-based methodology doesn't experience the ill effects of down-examining, and it can help find the smoke areas, whereas Adam analyzer estimates the mean and variance.

References

1. D.Radke, A. Hessler and D. Ellsworth. Fire cast: leveraging deep learning to predict wildfire spread. *Proceedings of the Twenty-Eight International. Joint Conference on Artificial Intelligence*, 2019.
2. P. Cortez et al. A data mining approach to predict forest fires using meteorological data. *Proceedings of the 13th Portuguese Conference on Artificial Intelligence*.
3. E. J. S. Nhongo, et al. Probabilistic modelling of wildfire occurrence based on logistic regression. *Niassa Reserve, Mozambique, Geomatics, Natural Hazards and Risk*, 2019. 10(1), 1772–1792, DOI: 10.1080/19475705.2019.1615559.
4. N. T. Toan, P. T. Cong. N Quoc, V. Hong, J. Jo. A deep learning approach for early wildfire detection from hyper spectral satellite images. *2019 7th International Conference on Robot Intelligence Techn ology and Applications (RiTA)*, November 1–3, 2019, Daejeon, Korea.

15

Low-Resource Language Document Summarization: A Challenge

Pranjali Deshpande and Sunita Jahirabadkar

MKSSS's Cummins College of Engineering for Women

CONTENTS

15.1 Introduction

Among all the existing animal species on our planet, only humans possess a unique ability to express their thoughts and feelings via various modes of communication like written, speech, and gestures. With the advancements in digital technology doors of remote communication are also opened. Written communication is the most popular communication mode as people can express their ideas and share information in a much more convenient way by means of documents. Moreover, the documentation can be preserved in electronic form. Currently, the entire world is facing a difficult situation due to the COVID-19 pandemic. People have lost physical communication; so, remote communication is proving to be a boon to keeping people in a healthy mental condition. People from varied socio-economic backgrounds have started using e-communication to express themselves. Also, the textual e-communication is witnessing popularity in various domains like healthcare, business, banking, academia, and many more. Due to the use of various tools and techniques in the natural language processing domain, the support for the native language used by the people of the specific region has increased. There are more than 7,000 languages that exist in the world. Though English is not among the most spoken languages in the world, it has the highest internet presence. A large number of e-text resources are present in the English language. Whereas Indo-Aryan languages like Marathi, Hindi, and Kannada which have their origin in the Sanskrit language, many more such languages across the globe lack significant internet presence. All such languages which lack in large corpora are known as low-resource languages (LRL). It is a very challenging task to handle a different kind of ambiguities at various stages for such languages.

DOI: 10.1201/9781003283249-15

Every day a humongous amount of e-text is generated on the internet in varied domains. Any document is formed by some meaning-bearing sentences and some miscellaneous sentences. In the documentation of certain domains like legal and medical, it is observed that long documents are generated but actual contextual information is very less. In such cases, automatic document summarization proves to be extremely beneficial. Summary is a condensed piece of text produced from one or more documents. Summary contains contextually important information from the original document. Summary of a document should not be not more than half of the original document. Automatic summarization can be done using two approaches: extractive and abstractive. Extractive summary contains the key phrases or sentences, as they are written in the source document. Whereas in abstractive summarization the contextually important key sentences are rewritten by forming a new sentence in the summary. Extractive summarization is simpler than abstractive summarization as only the knowledge and techniques to address natural language understanding tasks are sufficient. In addition, abstractive summarization requires statistical applications for natural language understanding as well as natural language generation. One more level of complexity is added to the summarization task when the source documents are written in LRL. Every language is unique in its own sense. In any natural language processing application, right from the phonetics stage to the pragmatics stage, ambiguities of various forms exist. Generic summarization model building is an impossible task due to this linguistic diversity. In this context, the chapter focuses on the various constraints posed by LRL diversity. A literature survey about various approaches and techniques to handle LRL documents will be discussed in Section 15.2, followed by the probable approaches of summarization of LRL and the conclusion.

15.2 Literature Survey

As discussed in the introduction, in LRL there is a scarcity of manually crafted linguistic resources for building statistical applications. Keeping this in mind, the literature survey focuses on two broad domains. First is the linguistic domain, in which the survey has been carried out about the handling of various LRLs. The second domain includes various statistical approaches and techniques that researchers have adapted for solving the summarization problem.

In a survey of automatic text summarization systems for different regional languages in India [1] authors have proposed a survey of extractive summarization techniques for various Indian languages like Bengali, Tamil, Punjabi, and Hindi. The method has been proposed for automatic summarization of the Marathi language. The news documents are considered an input to the system. The headlines, the line next to the headline, identification of nouns and proper nouns, cue phrases, etc., are given importance in summary. The system consists of three phases: preprocessing, sentence ranking, and summary generation. The approach uses tf-isf scoring technique for Marathi keyword identification. The drawback of the system is that only an extractive summary can be generated.

In the paper [2], Marathi Extractive Text Summarizer is proposed using a graph-based model. The system is designed to generate an extractive summary. It uses the TextRank algorithm for a summary generation. The first step is preprocessing. In the second step, various extracted features are used to rank the document. Based on these ranks scores are assigned to the documents. A summary is obtained using the TextRank algorithm and weighted positional distribution of sentence score. The system is designed for the generation of extractive summaries only.

Regina Barzilay and Michael Elhadad [3] have designed the system using the approach of lexical cohesion. For generation of extractive summary, the technique of lexical chains is used. Three steps were proposed to generate lexical chains: In the first step, based on the noun entries mentioned in WordNet candidate words are selected. In the second step, based on the distance and their occurrence in WordNet, relatedness between the words is obtained. In the last step, the words are inserted into the chain, and the chain is updated. Once the chain is obtained, in the next phase sentence scoring is done. Finally, the summary is generated taking into account the following parameters: length of the sentence and homogeneity index. The limitation of this approach is summary length cannot be controlled. The second loophole is the ranking of the sentence depends majorly on the length of the sentence.

The system [4] works on the challenge of abstractive summarization of low-resource data of the responses from a student's feedback in the semester. Due to no availability of sufficient data for training it considers a news dataset for training. First, the approach of domain transfer is adapted for training a model using a news dataset. In the next step, the approach of the data synthesis method is carried out. In template-based data synthesis human summaries are used. Keywords are removed from the summaries and they are transformed into templates. These templates are used to create word embeddings. Bidirectional Encoder Representations from Transformers (BERT) is used for this purpose. The generated templates are later clustered and a summary is generated.

Kiyota and Sadao Kurohasi [5] have designed the method for summarizing Japanese language documents. The system is designed using three steps: first, the www text set is found using www spider; next, important sentences are extracted; and at the end, those are summarized. Japanese sentences consist of unclear word boundaries. The system uses morphological analyzer names such as JUMAN to separate the words. KNP parser is used to detect dependency relation between Bunsetsu: a linguistic unit in Japanese grammar.

The proposed work [11] focuses on designing an efficient system of extractive text summarization by combining multiple aspects of the text. The proposed graph-based approach is designed in three stages: preprocessing, graph builder, and summary generation. The authors have combined text rank, key phrase generator, and shortest path algorithm to get the crisp summaries.

15.3 Approaches for Automatic Summarization

From the literature survey it is clear that each language possesses unique features in itself. This section focuses on two approaches for building an automatic summarizer.

15.3.1 Lexical Chaining Approach

Lexical chain [3] is a legacy approach for document summarization. It works on the concept of lexical cohesion and uses WordNet for the summarization task. In this approach the words appearing as noun entries in an input document are chosen. In the first step all the candidate words are chosen. For each word, appropriate chain is found based on relatedness criteria. According to the relatedness found in the next words appearing as input,

TABLE 15.1

Lexical Chaining Approach [3]

Approach	Technique Used	Remarks
Lexical chains for text summarization (1999)	Step 1: POS tagging is done. Based on the noun entries mentioned in WordNet candidate words are selected.	Limited SynSets in WordNet
	Step 2: Based on the distance and their occurrence in WordNet, relatedness between the words is obtained.	
	Step 3: Sentences are scored. Summary is obtained by the parameters: Length of the sentence and homogeneity index.	Ranking is affected by length of the sentence Length of summary cannot be controlled

TABLE 15.2

BERT Approach [6]

Approach	Technique Used	Remarks
BERT for text summarization (2019)	Step 1: Tokenize the input text. Extract the sentences using NLTK. Remove the sentences starting with conjunctions and very small or too long sentences.	Removed sentences may affect centroids
	Step 2: Pass the tokenized sentences to BERT model for the embeddings. 10% to 15% words are masked. N (No of sentences) * W (tokenized words) * E (embeddings) matrix is generated. Pytorch pre trained BERT library is used.	Memory and computational requirements are more. Implemented on Google Co Lab
	Step 3: Cluster the embeddings with K-means and choose the sentences closest to centroids.	Need more clusters for long text to retain the context

the words are inserted and the chain is updated. The number of connections between the words indicates strong cohesion between the words.

Table 15.1 summarizes the approach of lexical chaining.

15.4 BERT Approach

BERT is an algorithm designed by Google Brains researchers in 2019 [6]. BERT uses a transformer neural network initially designed to solve the problem of language translation. As compared to long short-term memory networks, which are slow to train and with the second drawback of sequential processing, i.e. the words are processed sequentially so the meaning is lost. Even bidirectional long short-term memory will not help as the context is learnt right to left and left to right and then the results are concatenated. Transformer architecture is fast as words are processed simultaneously and context is better learnt as it is learnt simultaneously from both directions. BERT consists of two components: encoder and decoder. Encoder takes input words simultaneously and generates embeddings, encapsulating the meaning of the words. Decoder takes these embeddings and previously generated words. BERT consists of stacks of these encoders and uses them for understanding language. It also fine-tunes them to learn specific tasks.

Table 15.2 summarizes the approach of BERT.

Apart from the above two approaches there are other approaches like semantic triplet formation, domain transfer, and graph-based approach, which can also be used for building an automatic summarizer for LRL.

15.5 Conclusion

The chapter encompasses various aspects of the concept of automatic summarization of LRL documents. Daily humongous amount of text is generated due to the increasing use of the internet. To use this data wisely is the need of the hour. People are finding it comfortable to communicate in their mother tongue. Among the huge number of languages existing in the world, very few have a significant internet presence. These languages are known as low-resource languages. Building statistical applications using LRL data is a challenging task for all natural language processing applications. Automatic summarization is an important application for knowing the gist of the document and has many applications in various multidisciplinary domains. The chapter focuses on various approaches adapted by the researchers for handling various LRL tasks. It also discusses the statistical techniques to build an automatic summarizer for LRL documents.

References

1. S. Sheetal and S. Govilkar, A survey of text summarization techniques for Indian regional languages. *International Journal of Computer Applications* 165(11), 29–33, 2017.
2. V. V. Sarwadnya and S. S. Sonawane, Marathi extractive text summarizer using graph based model. *2018 Fourth International Conference on Computing Communication Control and Automation (ICCUBEA)*, Pune, India, 2018, pp. 1–6.
3. R. Barzilay and M. Elhadad. Using lexical chains for text summarization. *Advances in automatic Text Summarization* 3610, 111–121, 1999.
4. A. Magooda and D. Litman, Abstractive summarization for low resource data using domain transfer and data synthesis. *The Thirty-Third International Flairs Conference*, 2020, aaai.org.
5. Y. Kiyota and S. Kurohashi, Automatic summarization of Japanese sentences and its application to a WWW KWIC index. *Proceedings 2001 Symposium on Applications and the Internet*, San Diego, CA, 2001, pp. 120–127, doi:10.1109/SAINT.2001.905175.
6. D. Jacob, M.-W. Chang, K. Lee and K. Toutanova, BERT: pre-training of deep bidirectional transformers for language understanding. *Paper Presented at the Meeting of the NAACL-HLT* (1), 2019.
7. D. Miller, Leveraging BERT for extractive text summarization on lectures. arXiv preprint arXiv: 1906.04165 (2019).
8. Marathi WordNet: https://www.cfilt.iitb.ac.in/~wordnetbeta/marathiwn/wn.php.
9. K. Bellare, A. D. Sarma, A. D. Sarma, N. Loiwal, V. Mehta, G. Ramakrishnan and P. Bhattacharyya, Generic text summarization using WordNet. *The International Conference on Language Resources and Evaluation (LREC)* (2004).
10. J. Ouyang, B. Song, and K. McKeown, A robust abstractive system for cross-lingual summarization. *Annual Conference of the North American Chapter of the Association for Computational Linguistics (NAACL)* (2019).
11. A. Jeswani, S. More, K. Kapoor, S. Sheikh, R. Mangrulkar, Document summarization using graph based methodology. *International Journal of Computer Applications Technology and Research* 9(8), 240–245, 2020.

16

Eclectic Analysis of Classifiers for Fake News Detection

Vatsal Khandor, Yashvi Shah, and Krutik Shah
Dwarkadas J. Sanghvi College of Engineering

Nitin Goje
Webster University

Ramchandra Mangrulkar
Dwarkadas J. Sanghvi College of Engineering

CONTENTS

DOI: 10.1201/9781003283249-16

16.1 Introduction

Fake news is a sort of yellow press that deliberately spreads disinformation or hoaxes through conventional print news media as well as current internet-based social media [1]. Fake news for different political and commercial reasons has been surfacing in huge numbers and spreading in the internet world in recent years as a result of the blooming development of online social networks. The advent of the WWW and the rapid increased usage of social media platforms paved the way for unparalleled amounts of information transmission in human history. Fake news spreads misleading info and perpetuates a falsehood about a country's statistics or exaggerates the expense of particular services for a country, causing discontent and unrest in those countries [2]. In recent years, the spread of fake news has increased dramatically, especially during the 2016 US elections [3]. Such an increase in the number of people posting tales online that are not true has resulted in a plethora of problems, not only in governmental issues, but also in sports, health, and science [4,5]. The stock markets [6] is also one more sector affected by fake news, where a rumor may have devastating repercussions and even put the market to a standstill. One recent example is the transmission of the new coronavirus, which saw fake news stories regarding the virus's origin, biology, and behavior spread over the internet [7]. As more individuals learned about the false information online, the situation deteriorated [8]. However, finding and eliminating such news from the internet is a challenging problem. Concerns about author responsibility are being addressed by organizations such as the House of Commons and the Crosscheck initiative. However, because they rely on manual identification by humans, their application potential is severely limited. This is neither responsible nor feasible in a world where millions of items are deleted or published every minute. The establishment of a system that gives a reliable automatic index score [9], or rating, for the trustworthiness and news context of various sources might be a potential solution. This study offers a technique for developing a model that can determine if an article is genuine or not based on its words, phrases, sources, and titles, using supervised machine learning algorithms on a manually classified and guaranteed data set [10]. We suggest that several classification algorithms be used to build the model. The product model will test previously unknown data, and plot the findings, and, as a consequence, the product will be a model that identifies and classifies false articles that can be utilized and integrated with any system in the future.

16.2 Related Work

While there is a substantial rise in performance in the classification of fake news, this paper [11] presents a hybrid approach to deal with this issue. It uses a combination of a CNN–RNN-based approach. The authors use the ISOT dataset for the experimentation and deriving the conclusion. Their proposed model makes use of long short-term memory networks (LSTM) to learn long-term dependencies and CNN to extract local features. The authors use Glove for word embeddings and do the model implementation in Keras and achieve an accuracy of 0.60 0.007 on the FA-KES dataset and 0.99 0.02 on the ISOT dataset. The researchers think the deep learning models may work good when implemented on a particular dataset, but they do not generalize that well.

The approach in this work [12] is based on Count Vectorizer and the research intended here is to compare two different approaches. Firstly, they use the base model of many classifiers and then use an ensemble diversified using the Random Subspace method for the second one. BS Detector Chrome Extension users marked 13,000 texts as fake news. The results of the statistical analysis conclude that the proposed approach is more statistically important rather than the individual models.

The research in [13] uses Naive Bayes, support vector machine (SVM), and neural networks to classify believable and not believable messages from Twitter. Their experiment resulted in getting accuracies over 95% for all the three different models with the help of 22 attributes extracted from the tweets. The authors are unsure whether the method they adopted is applicable to real-world data.

The work in [14] analyses a few of the word embedding techniques with their performance on each machine learning model they perform. Overall, SVM performed the best for the word characterization technique with an accuracy of 89.34%. The research basically applies the inter-comparison and intra-comparison of the classifiers. On further implementation, cross-validation is done, TF-IDF and Count Vector gave the best results, and hence three different machine learning models were applied to these techniques.

As described in [11], a hybrid model may give better results. Similarly, instead of a CNN–RNN combination in [11], the authors in [15] use an ensemble of CNN and LSTM (bidirectional) along with attention mechanism to achieve highest accuracy of 88.78%. It also describes basic models such as logistic regression and SVM models that perform poorly. The paper describes their approach with different combinations of CNN and LSTM models. All the researchers in [11] and [15] conclude that simpler models do not work as good as ensemble architectures.

A similar approach as in [15] is used in [16] (CNN–LSTM architecture). The authors develop a series of four models. The highest accuracy was observed with the combination of Principal Component Analysis with CNN–LSTM reportedly 97.8%. Even after performing tenfold cross-validation, there was no much difference in the accuracies after taking the average that indicates the model is quite robust.

In research article [17], the authors used a Naive Bayes classifier to examine a basic approach for detecting fake news. Rather than online news publishers, they relied on Facebook news updates for their investigation. The article had a 74% accuracy rate during the classification procedure. In addition, the work assesses the fact, that very straightforward machine learning models like Naive Bayes can only help in achieving a decent degree of accuracy, and that to battle the issue of fake news in the future, more AI techniques should be used.

Authors in [18] explored how news may be identified as real or fake by concentrating on a few characteristics that are frequently seen in fake news. These features, according to them, are based on psychology, social theories, current algorithms from a data mining standpoint, assessment measures, and sample datasets. This work also examines the many obstacles that someone would face when researching this issue.

The work in [19] uses the realm of fake news, which is made up of ironic or satirical news. While fake news attempts to persuade viewers to believe a falsehood, satirical news must be recognized as jest. This study examines the characteristics of comedy and satire news, as well as the reporting style of the authors. The research looked at articles from 12 present-day news subjects from four different realms: science, civics, soft news, and business. The study presents an SVM-based method for detecting satirical news using characteristics such as humor, absurdity, punctuation, and grammar. The models had a 90% accuracy and an 84% recall.

Kelly Stahl's study [20] examines historical and present approaches for detecting false news in text forms, and also how and why fake news emerges in the first place. This study also includes a discussion of how a document's writing style might influence its classification. The study has used Naive Bayes Classifier and SVM techniques. The work also investigates the text's semantic analysis in order to classify it.

The authors of [21] state in their paper that they have developed an innovative machine learning fake news detection methodology that outperforms existing methods in the literature by up to 4.8% by combining news content and social context characteristics. Because they accomplished excellent accuracy when testing it on a chatbot for Facebook Messenger, the suggested model was then put to the test on a real-time application. On the real-time application, they obtained an accuracy of about 82%.

A study that uses unified key sentence information to detect fake news in published in [22]. The model isolates the article's key sentences relevant to the question and then combines the word vectors for each key sentence. The authors do their research using a Korean dataset. The model conducts an effective matching operations on the word vectors that are obtained using bidirectional LSTM. They were able to obtain an accuracy of 64%–69%. Their long-term goal is to create a more progressive model that can separately apply the model to each key sentence present in the dataset.

An extensive research is conducted utilizing n-gram and its comparison to various feature extraction methods is done in [23]. This research used a variety of feature extraction approaches as well as a number of machine learning techniques. The study produces the best results when it uses a feature extraction method and a classification technique as unigram and SVM, respectively.

The authors in [24] present a generalized framework for predicting tweet's trustworthiness in this study. First, they used the Twitter API to extract the main features and user features. A reverse image search is performed every time a tweet containing an image or Image URL is encountered. So the image or its URL is verified against the different sources of fake news in order to assess if it's a part of a dataset of fake news website. These characteristics are then wholly utilized by data mining algorithms to identify tweets as false or genuine.

Tweets were adjusted in real time in this research [25]. These tweets were background verified as they arrived to ensure that they were appropriately classified. After that, a classification algorithm was applied to the incoming tweets. Regardless of the fact that the dataset was noisy, a good result was attained.

The authors in [26] proposed a classification approach that may be utilized on live data generated collected on Facebook. Data generated by other social media giants like WhatsApp and Twitter can also use this classification approach. To classify the generated data as trustworthy or untrustworthy, he used a basic Naive Bayes classifier.

The study in [27] estimated several machine learning algorithms and conducted research on prediction percentages. Bounded decision trees, gradient enhancement, and SVM were used to test the accuracy of various prediction patterns. The patterns are calculated with 85%–91% accuracy using an unstable probability threshold.

16.3 Dataset Description

Around 70,000 articles within two datasets from [28] and [29], were included in the data corpus used in this study. There were 20,800 and 5,200 articles utilized for training and

TABLE 16.1

Dataset 1 Description

Id
Title
Author
Text
Label (1 or 0)

TABLE 16.2

Dataset 2 Description

Index
Title
Text
Subject
Date
Class (fake or real)

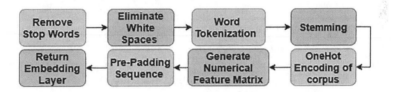

FIGURE 16.1
Steps for preprocessing.

testing, respectively, in Dataset 1. And 40,000 articles for training and 4,000 articles for testing were utilized in Dataset 2. The Kaggle datasets was noisy and needed to be cleaned. The following features were present in the dataset (Tables 16.1 and 16.2).

16.3.1 Preprocessing

To use machine learning or deep learning algorithms on text data, special preprocessing is required. To transform text data into a form that may be utilized for modeling, a variety of approaches are frequently employed. Both the headlines and the news articles are subjected to the data preprocessing methods outlined below in the following steps (Figure 16.1):

1. To begin, the string is cleaned of all sequences except English characters.
2. All characters in strings are then changed to lowercase to avoid false predictions or ambiguity with upper- and lowercase.
3. The sentences are then tokenized into words.
4. Stemming is performed on tokenized words in order to speed up processing. Stemming is the process of removing prefixes and suffixes from a word until just the stem remains. Thus, reducing inflectional and occasionally derivationally related variants of a word to a common base form by using stemming (Figure 16.2).

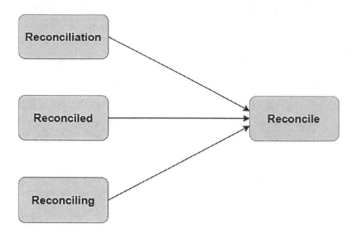

FIGURE 16.2
Illustration on how stemming works on tokenized words.

5. Following that, words are combined and kept in the corpus. After pre-processing,

1. In the vocabulary size=5,000 range, the pre-processed words are transformed to one-hot vectors. This is done so that a numerical feature matrix may be obtained.

   In NLP, a one-hot vector is a 1×N matrix which distinguishes each word in the vocabulary. With the exception of a single 1 in a cell that is required to uniquely identify the word, the vector is completely made up of 0s. For machine learning, larger numbers are not crucial because of one-hot encoding. For example, the number '6' is larger than the number '1,' yet this does not imply that '6' is more significant. The same is true for words: the value of 'laughter' is not greater than the value of 'laugh'.

2. Then, with sentence length=20, an embedding layer is built, which applies 'pre' padding to the one-hot encoded features. Padding is used to ensure that each sequence in the dataset has the same length.

3. Using the train_test_split method, the dataset is separated into training, validation, and testing data (ratio: 80/10/10).

16.4 Modeling and Evaluation

This section describes the usage of machine learning and deep learning algorithms such as Naive Bayes, Logistic Regression, K-Nearest Neighbors, Decision trees, Random Forest, XGBoost, CatBoost, and LSTM and their performance statistics using evaluation metrics such as accuracy, F1-score, precision, recall, and confusion matrix.

16.4.1 Performance Metrics

A variety of metrics have been utilized to assess algorithm performance. The confusion matrix is used by the majority.

16.4.1.1 Accuracy

One approach to assess how often a machine learning classification system successfully classifies a data point is to look at its accuracy. The number of accurate predictions out of the total predictions made for the data points is known as accuracy. The number of true positives and true negatives divided by the number of true negatives, true positives, false negatives, and false positives is how accuracy is defined more formally.

$$\text{Accuracy} = \left[\frac{TP+TN}{TP+TN+FP+FN} \right] \tag{16.1}$$

A model with a high accuracy value is certainly a good model. Since the work here involves training a classification model that will potentially detect a fake news article, if an article was predicted as genuine when it was actually fake then it can have adverse implications. Additionally, if an article was predicted as fake but had verifiable facts, it can lead to mistrust. As a result, it is important to make use three other metrics: recall, precision, and F1-score, to account for the erroneously categorized observation.

16.4.1.2 F1-Score

The F1-score represents the trade-off between precision and recall. F1-score calculates the harmonic mean of each precision as well as recall. As a result, it considers both observations: false positive and false negative. The following formula may be used to compute the F1-score:

$$\text{F1-score} = 2 \left[\frac{\text{Precision} \times \text{Recall}}{\text{Precision} + \text{Recall}} \right] \tag{16.2}$$

16.4.1.3 Recall

The total number of positive classifications out of true class is referred to as recall. It indicates the proportion of articles predicted to be true out of the total number of true articles in this scenario:

$$\text{Precision} = \left[\frac{TP}{TP+FP} \right] \tag{16.3}$$

16.4.1.4 Precision Score

Precision score, on the other hand, is the ratio of all observations that are truly positives to all true occurrences predicted. Precision in this context refers to the number of news articles that are actually true or genuine out of all the news articles that are positively predicted (or predicted as true).

$$h_\theta(X) = \left(\frac{1}{1+e^{-(\beta_0+\beta_1 X)}} \right) \tag{16.4}$$

16.4.1.5 Confusion Matrix

It's a $M \times M$ matrix that's used to assess a classification model's performance, where M is the total number of target classes. The matrix compares the actual target values to the predictions of the machine learning model. This gives us a clear view of how well the

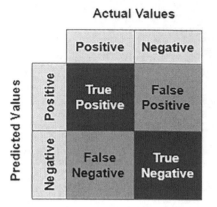

FIGURE 16.3
Confusion matrix for binary classification problem.

classification model is performing and what kinds of mistakes it makes. The chapter has a 2×2 matrix with four values for a binary classification issue like fake news detection, as shown in Figure 16.3.

16.4.2 Hyperparameter Tuning

The practice of tuning the parameters given as tuples when building machine learning models is known as hyperparameter tuning. These parameters are defined by the programmer and can be changed if desired. These parameters are never learned by machine learning algorithms. These have been fine-tuned to ensure that the model performs well. The goal of hyperparameter tuning is to identify the parameters that provide the model the best performance or the best performance with the lowest error rate.

16.4.2.1 RandomizedSearchCV

RandomizedSearchCV samples a predetermined number of hyperparameter settings from specified probability distributions. To decrease the amount of iterations and to utilize a random mix of parameters, RandomizedSearchCV is used. When you have a lot of parameters to try and your training time is longer, this is a good option. It aids in the reduction of computation costs.

16.4.2.2 GridSearchCV

Grid search is the process of fine-tuning hyperparameters to find the best values for a particular model. The value of hyperparameters has a major impact on a model's performance. There is no way to know ahead of time what the optimum values for hyperparameters are; therefore, one must attempt all conceivable values to find the best ones. Because manually tweaking hyperparameters would take a significant amount of time and resources, the authors' utilize GridSearchCV to automate the process.

16.4.3 Evaluation and Analysis

The main objective is to utilize a collection of classification techniques to create a classification model that can be used as a scanner for fake news. The classification algorithm used

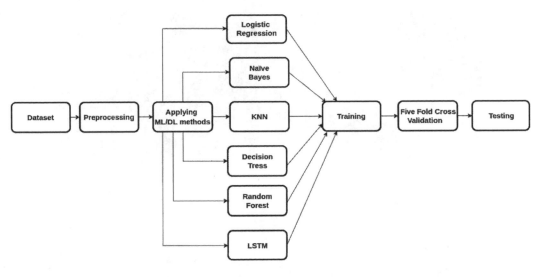

FIGURE 16.4
Flow diagram for the process of fake news detection.

are Logistic Regression, Naive Bayes, KNN, Decision Trees, Random Forest and LSTM. Figure 16.4 enunciates the flow of the entire process.

16.4.3.1 Model Implementation Using Logistic Regression

A logistic regression model is commonly used to classify textual content primarily based on a variety of aspects with a binary output (genuine article/fake article), because it gives an easy equation for classifying problems into binary or more than one classes. The hypothesis function for Logistic Regression can be described mathematically as follows [30]:

$$\cos t(h_\theta(x)), y) = \begin{cases} \log(h_\theta(x)), y = 1 \\ -\log(1 - (h_\theta(x)), y = 0 \end{cases} \quad (16.5)$$

The output of logistic regression is transformed into a probability value using a sigmoid function; the objective is to achieve the best probability by minimizing the cost function. The cost function is computed as follows:

$$P(c \mid x) = \left[\frac{P(x \mid c)P(c)}{P(x)} \right] \quad (16.6)$$

16.4.3.1.1 Classification Report

Since the model does not give satisfying results, it is not further hyperparameter tuned. Detailed analysis has been provided (Figure 16.5 and Table 16.3).

16.4.3.2 Model Implementation Using Naïve Bayes

The Naive Bayes machine learning model is based on conditional probability for labeling. The aim is to find a function *f: A B* that by utilizing an independent variables vector (*A*)

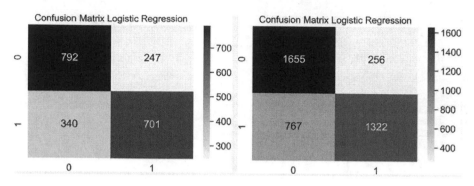

FIGURE 16.5
Confusion matrix logistic regression.

TABLE 16.3

Classification Report for Logistic Regression

	Dataset 1	Dataset 2
Accuracy	0.7177884615384615	0.74425
F1 Score	0.7048768225238813	0.7210253613307881
Recall	0.6733909702209414	0.6328386787936812
Precision	0.739451476793249	0.8377693282636248

to predict the class variable (*B*). The goal is to calculate *P*(*B A*), which is probability of *B* belonging to the given class *A*. *B* is a kind of variable, called as categorical variable which has having two or more discrete values, according to most definitions. In the testing set, when predicting the class of the next data item, it's mathematically straightforward to account for a variety of influences. The drawback of the Naive Bayes model is that it works on the assumption that all features are independent of one another. The Naive Bayes technique is based on Bayes' theorem as follows:

$$\text{Recall} = \left[\frac{TP}{TP + FN} \right] \tag{16.7}$$

where *P*(*x c*) is the likelihood, *P*(*c x*) is the posterior probability, *P*(*x*) is the predictor prior probability, and *P*(*c*) is the class prior probability.

16.4.3.2.1 Classification Report

Detailed analysis has been provided. See Figure 16.6 and Table 16.4.

16.4.3.3 Model Implementation Using KNN

The KNN algorithm is a decision-boundary-based classification algorithm that assigns a majority class to an input based on its k closest neighbors in space. It's a classification method that uses supervised learning. K denotes the number of closest neighbors in KNN. To begin, choose a k value and divide the data into k groups based on their resemblance (distance). At the end, the objects can be classified. The Euclidean distance can be used to calculate distance. There are several advantages to using KNN as a classification method

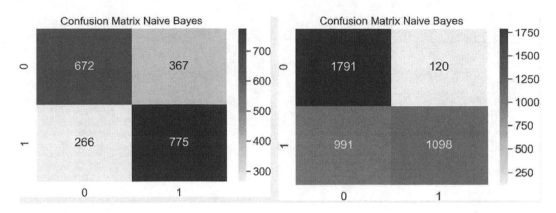

FIGURE 16.6
Confusion matrix Naive Bayes.

TABLE 16.4

Classification Report for Naive Bayes

	Dataset 1	Dataset 2
Accuracy	0.6956730769230769	0.72225
F1 Score	0.7100320659642693	0.6640459631085577
Recall	0.74447646493756	0.5256103398755385
Precision	0.6786339754816112	0.9014778325123153

in real applications. KNN is a non-parametric learning method that makes no assumptions about the input data's underlying distribution. There is not enough solid evidence to map the text of news items to a closed form probabilistic distribution for applications in natural language processing, especially classification of news articles as real or fake. Furthermore, because KNN is an instance-based algorithm, the only 'learning' required is to load the observations into memory, reducing training time substantially.

16.4.3.3.1 Classification Report

Detailed analysis has been provided. See Figure 16.7 and Table 16.5.

16.4.3.4 Model Implementation Using Decision Trees

A decision tree is a useful tool that is built on a flowchart-like structure and is mostly used to solve classification problems. Each decision tree internal node defines a condition or 'test' on an attribute, and branching is based on the test conditions and results. Finally, the leaf node has a class label that is determined once all attributes have been computed. The classification rule is represented by the distance between the root and the leaf. The fact that it can operate with both a category and a dependent variable is incredible. They are effective in identifying the most significant features and depicting the relationships between them. They are important in the creation of new variables and features that are beneficial for data exploration and accurately forecast the target variable. Predictive models that use supervised learning methods frequently use tree-based learning algorithms to achieve high accuracy. They excel at mapping nonlinear relationships. They are also known as CART and are very good at solving classification or regression problems.

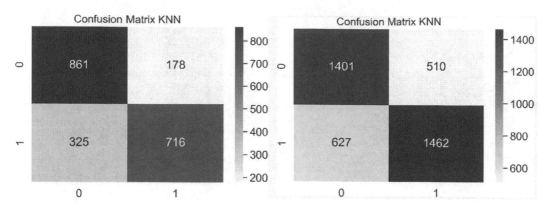

FIGURE 16.7
Confusion matrix KNN.

TABLE 16.5

Classification Report for KNN

	Dataset 1	Dataset 2
Accuracy	0.7581730769230769	0.71575
F1 Score	0.7400516795865634	0.720019699581384
Recall	0.6878001921229587	0.6998563906175204
Precision	0.8008948545861297	0.7413793103448276

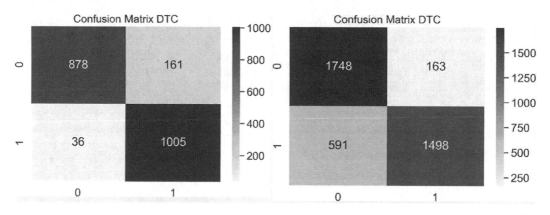

FIGURE 16.8
Confusion matrix decision trees.

16.4.3.4.1 Classification Report

Detailed analysis has been provided. See Figure 16.8 and Tables 16.6 and 16.7.

16.4.3.5 Model Implementation Using Random Forest

Random forest is a supervised learning model that is an enhanced version of decision trees. The class with the most votes is used to make the final prediction. Random forest is made up of a huge number of decision trees that collaborate to predict a class's outcome.

TABLE 16.6

Hyperparameter Values for Decision Trees

	Dataset 1	Dataset 2
criterion	entropy	Gini
max_depth	80	78
max_leap_nodes	95	85
min_samples_leaf	3	25
min_samples_split	25	14

TABLE 16.7

Classification Report for Decision Trees

	Dataset 1	Dataset 2
Baseline accuracy	0.894231	0.7915
Tuned accuracy	0.9052884615384615	0.8115
F1 Score	0.9107385591300409	0.7989333333333334
Recall	0.9654178674351584	0.717089516515079
Precision	0.8619210977701544	0.9018663455749548

Due to minimal correlation across trees, the error rate in random forest is low when compared to other models [31]. Random forest is most useful when applied to uncorrelated decision trees. The final outcome will be more or less comparable to a single decision tree if applied to similar trees. Bootstrapping and feature randomness can be used to create uncorrelated decision trees. The primary distinction between Random Forest and Naive Bayes is their model size. Because Naive Bayes models are not effective at capturing complicated behavior, they have a small model size and are only useful for a specific constant type of data. The model size for the Random Forest model, on the other hand, is quite big, which may lead to overfitting. When new data is entered, Naive Bayes is ideal for it since it can quickly be molded, but random forest may need a forest rebuild every time a modification is made.

16.4.3.5.1 Classification Report

Detailed analysis has been provided. See Figure 16.9 and Tables 16.8 and 16.9.

16.4.3.6 Model Implementation Using Boosting Ensemble Classifiers

Training weaker models to perform stronger for training is an ensemble approach called boosting. A forest containing of randomized trees is trained for this purpose, the final outcome or prediction of which is dependent upon each tree's majority vote outcome. This method employs an incremental approach to correctly classify data points that are frequently misclassified to assist the weak learners. To classify an issue, for all data points, an equal weighted coefficients are utilized at first. In subsequent rounds, the weighted coefficients are reduced for properly classified data points and increased for incorrectly classified data points [32]. Each round's subsequent tree learns to minimize the previous round's errors and enhance the overall accuracy by accurately predicting data points that were falsely predicted in previous rounds. Boosting ensemble may overfit to the training

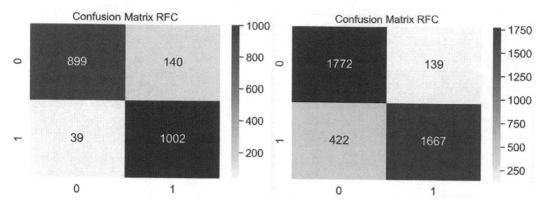

FIGURE 16.9

Confusion matrix random forest.

TABLE 16.8

HyperParameter Values for Random Forest

	Dataset 1	Dataset 2
bootstrap	False	True
max_depth	None	None
n_estimators	100	900
min_samples_split	6	5
min_samples_leaf	1	1

TABLE 16.9

Classification Report for Random Forest

	Dataset 1	Dataset 2
Baseline accuracy	0.909615	0.85625
Tuned accuracy	0.9139423076923077	0.85975
F1 Score	0.9180027485112231	0.85596919127086
Recall	0.962536023054755	0.7979894686452849
Precision	0.8774080560420315	0.9230343300110742

data, resulting in inaccurate predictions for unknown cases [33] which is one of the primary drawback. There are a variety of boosting techniques available that may be utilized for regression and classification problems. In the experiment, we employ XGBoost [34] and CatBoost [35] algorithms for classification of a news as real or fake.

16.4.3.6.1 XGBoost Classification Report

Detailed analysis has been provided. See Figure 16.10 and Tables 16.10 and 16.11.

16.4.3.6.2 CatBoost Classification Report

Detailed analysis has been provided. See Figure 16.11 and Tables 16.12 and 16.13.

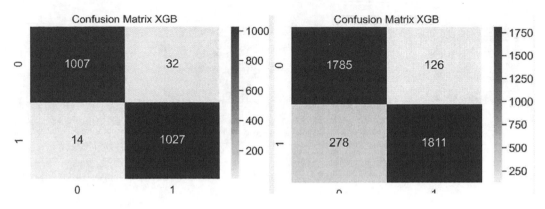

FIGURE 16.10
Confusion matrix XGBoost.

TABLE 16.10

HyperParameter Values for XGBoost

	Dataset 1	Dataset 2
colsample_bytree	0.5	0.5
learning_rate	0.12	0.1
max_depth	74	74
min_child_weight	1	1
n_estimators	850	850
subsample	0.5	0.5
verbosity	1	1

TABLE 16.11

Classification Report for XGBoost

	Dataset 1	Dataset 2
Baseline accuracy	0.910577	0.8115
Tuned accuracy	0.9778846153846154	0.899
F1 Score	0.9780952380952381	0.8996522603079979
Recall	0.9865513928914506	0.8669219722355194
Precision	0.9697828139754485	0.9349509550851832

16.4.3.7 Model Implementation Using LSTM

Recurrent neural networks (RNN) have a problem: vanishing gradient problem. This problem is basically when the gradient of the loss function tries to reach an optimum value which makes the neural network harder to train. This particularly happens due to change in the value of the sigmoid activation function which makes the derivative smaller. A solution to this could be using simply different activation function like ReLU because it does not cause a smaller derivative. Also, RNN suffers from memory loss. The vanishing gradient problem is solved by LSTM. Additionally, it addresses the memory issue

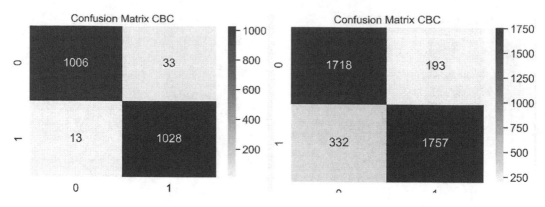

FIGURE 16.11
Confusion matrix CatBoost.

TABLE 16.12

HyperParameter Values for CatBoost

	Dataset 1	Dataset 2
border_count	200	110
depth	8	8
iterations	500	500
12_leaf_reg	10	2
learning_rate	0.2	0.3
thread_count	4	4

TABLE 16.13

Classification Report for CatBoost

	Dataset 1	Dataset 2
Baseline accuracy	0.975481	0.861
Tuned accuracy	0.9778846153846154	0.86875
F1 Score	0.978116079923882	0.8700173310225303
Recall	0.9875120076849183	0.8410722833891814
Precision	0.9688972667295005	0.901025641025641

and allows data to be persisted. The network uses an architecture of gates and does data handling. It is also capable of learning long-term dependencies, i.e., a network which can remember information for a longer period of time. LSTM are a kind of RNN that can learn long-term dependencies. A chain that consists of neural network modules which are repeated forms RNN. This repeating module in conventional RNN will have a very fundamental structure, for instance, a single tanh layer. The repeating module is different for LSTM, but they have a chain-like structure. Instead of a single neural network layer, there are four, each of which interacts in a unique way. Only the key sequences of words are remembered by LSTM, whereas unimportant words that do not contribute value to the prediction are forgotten. The three gates that make up LSTM are input gate, output gate, and forget gate. Based on the dropout value, these gates determine which information is relevant for classification and which information is forgettable. Previous input is saved in cell memory block CK, which is required for prediction. 30% of units are filtered out by a dropout layer and then go to the LSTM layer of 100 units. Post LSTM layer, another dropout layer is used and finally, a fully connected layer containing one unit with the sigmoid activation function is used binary classification, i.e., classifying the news. The following is involved in the model used:

1. The embedding feature vectors, which are target feature vectors for the embedding layer, have a value of 40.
2. A single 100-node LSTM layer is utilized.
3. The sentences are then tokenized into words.
4. Because this is a binary classification task, a Dense Layer with 1 neuron and sigmoid activation function is applied.
5. To avoid overfitting, the dropout technique is utilized, and the Adam optimizer is used to optimize the loss function.

16.4.3.7.1 Classification Report

Detailed analysis has been provided. See Figure 16.12 and Table 16.14.

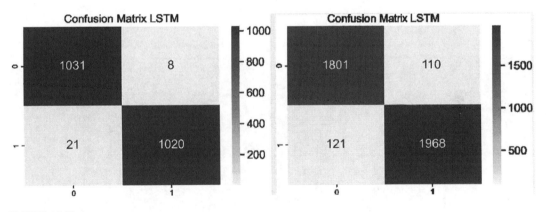

FIGURE 16.12
Confusion matrix LSTM.

TABLE 16.14

Classification Report for LSTM

	Dataset 1	Dataset 2
Accuracy	0.9860576923076924	0.94225
F1 Score	0.985983566940551	0.9445644348452124
Recall	0.9798270893371758	0.9420775490665391
Precision	0.9922178988326849	0.9470644850818094

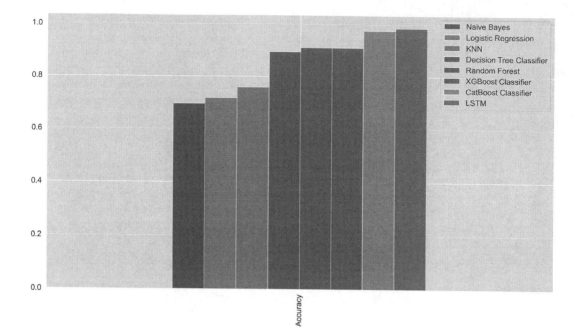

FIGURE 16.13
Model comparison for Dataset 1.

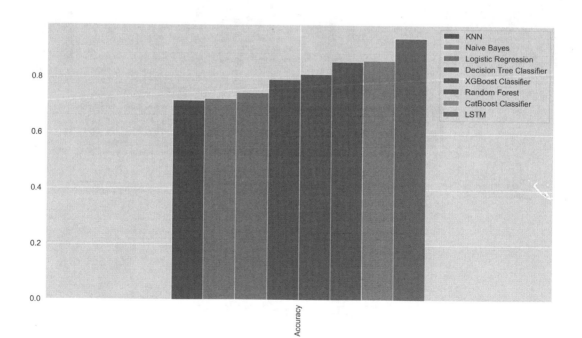

FIGURE 16.14
Model comparison for Dataset 2.

16.5 Conclusion, Limitations and Future Scope

Thus, the fake news problem possess a great threat to the society and thus with the techniques depicted, one can easily leverage these to use for the betterment of humanity. This yellow press tends to be so compelling that instead of abstaining it, a user just feels the urge of spreading it which can prove sometimes catastrophic. On analysis, it has been observed that LSTM model performs the best for both the datasets. Similarly, CatBoost follows the lead for both the datasets. But, for the rest of the classifiers, the accuracy varies. A model comparison graph for both the datasets is plotted in Figures 16.13 and 16.14.

The research thus concludes that the behavior of different classifiers and accuracies depends on the dataset. Hyperparameter tuning also can play a very important role in significant boosting the accuracies as seen in XGBoost.

One-hot encoding done in the preprocessing stages generates new matrix every time for the dataset and correspondingly the further part of the code changes due to the matrix which produces a minute difference in the accuracies for the classifiers which is one of the limitations.

Various machine learning and deep learning models are tried in this paper. However, in the future, depending on the datasets, a hybrid deep learning model combination like CNN–LSTM, CNN–RNN can be tried to give solutions with the same time an increase in accuracies.

References

1. Great Moon Hoax. https://en.wikipedia.org/wiki/Great Moon Hoax.
2. Nehinbe, Joshua Ojo. Statistical methods for conducting the ontology and classifications of fake news on social media. In: *Handbook of Research on Cyber Crime and Information Privacy.* edited by Cruz-Cunha, Maria Manuela, and Nuno Ricardo Mateus-Coelho, 632–651. Hershey, PA: IGI Global, 2021. http://doi:10.4018/978-1-7998-5728-0.ch029.
3. Lie Year Fake News. https://www.politifact.com/article/2016/dec/13/2016-lie-year-fake-news/.
4. Lazer, D.M., Baum, M.A., Benkler, Y., Berinsky, A.J., Greenhill, K.M., Menczer, F., Metzger, M.J., Nyhan, B., Pennycook, G., Rothschild, D. and Schudson, M., 2018. The science of fake news. *Science*, 359(6380), pp.1094–1096. https://doi.org/10.1126/science.aao2998.
5. Chavan, Pallavi and Dipti Jadhav, and Gautam M. Borkar. Challenges to multimedia privacy and security over social media. In: *Handbook of Research on Cyber Crime and Information Privacy.* edited by Cruz-Cunha, Maria Manuela, and Nuno Ricardo Mateus-Coelho, 118–131. Hershey, PA: IGI Global, 2021. http://doi:10.4018/978-1-7998-5728-0.ch007.
6. Kogan, S., Moskowitz, T.J. and Niessner, M., 2019. Fake news: Evidence from financial markets. Available at SSRN 3237763. https://doi.org/10.2139/ssrn.3237763.
7. Hua, J. and Shaw, R., 2020. Corona virus (Covid-19) "infodemic" and emerging issues through a data lens: The case of China. *International Journal of Environmental Research and Public Health*, 17(7): 2309. https://doi.org/10.3390/IJERPH17072309.
8. Salunkhe, Aditya Suresh, and Pallavi Vijay Chavan. An overview of methodologies and challenges in sentiment analysis on social networks. In: *Handbook of Research on Big Data Clustering and Machine Learning.* edited by Garcia Marquez, Fausto Pedro, 204–213. Hershey, PA: IGI Global, 2020. http://doi:10.4018/978-1-7998-0106-1.ch010.
9. Chavan, Pallavi, Prerna More, Neha Thorat, Shraddha Yewale, and Pallavi Dhade 2016. ECG-Remote patient monitoring using cloud computing. *Imperial Journal of Interdisciplinary Research*, 2(2): 368–372.

10. H. M. Mudia and P. V. Chavan, Fuzzy logic based image encryption for confidential data transfer using (2, 2) secret sharing scheme-review. *2015 International Conference on Advances in Computer Engineering and Applications*, 2015, pp. 404–408, doi: 10.1109/ICACEA.2015.7164738. https://doi.org/10.1109/ICACEA.2015.7164738.

11. Nasir, J.A., Khan, O.S. and Varlamis, I., 2021. Fake news detection: A hybrid CNN-RNN based deep learning approach. *International Journal of Information Management Data Insights*, 1(1): 100007. https://doi.org/10.1016/j.jjimei.2020.100007

12. Ksieniewicz, P., Chora's, M., Kozik, R. and Wo´zniak, M., 2019, November. Machine learning methods for fake news classification. In *International Conference on Intelligent Data Engineering and Automated Learning* (pp. 332–339). Springer, Cham. https://doi.org/10.1007/978-3-030-33617-2-34.

13. Aphiwongsophon, S. and Chongstitvatana, P., 2018, July. Detecting fake news with machine learning method. In *2018 15th International Conference on Electrical Engineering/Electronics, Computer, Telecommunications and Information Technology (ECTI-CON)* (pp. 528–531). IEEE. https://doi.org/10.1109/ECTICON.2018.8620051.

14. Mahir, E.M., Akhter, S. and Huq, M.R., 2019, June. Detecting fake news using machine learning and deep learning algorithms. In *2019 7th International Conference on Smart Computing Communications (ICSCC)* (pp. 1–5). IEEE. https://arxiv.org/ftp/arxiv/papers/2102/2102.04458.pdf.

15. Kumar, S., Asthana, R., Upadhyay, S., Upreti, N. and Akbar, M., 2020. Fake news detection using deep learning models: A novel approach. *Transactions on Emerging Telecommunications Technologies*, 31(2): e3767. https://doi.org/10.1002/ett.3767.

16. Umer, M., Imtiaz, Z., Ullah, S., Mehmood, A., Choi, G.S. and On, B.W., 2020. Fake news stance detection using deep learning architecture (CNN-LSTM). IEEE Access, 8, pp.156695–156706. https://doi.org/10.1109/ACCESS.2020.3019735.

17. Granik, M. and Mesyura, V., 2017, May. Fake news detection using naive Bayes classifier. In *2017 IEEE first Ukraine conference on electrical and computer engineering (UKRCON)* (pp. 900–903). IEEE. https://doi.org/10.1109/UKRCON.2017.8100379

18. Shu, K., Sliva, A., Wang, S., Tang, J. and Liu, H., 2017. Fake news detection on social media: A data mining perspective. *ACM SIGKDD Explorations Newsletter*, 19(1): 22–36. https://doi.org/10.1145/3137597.3137600.

19. Rubin, V.L., Conroy, N., Chen, Y. and Cornwell, S., 2016, June. Fake news or truth? using satirical cues to detect potentially misleading news. In *Proceedings of the second workshop on computational approaches to deception detection* (pp. 7–17). https://doi.org/10.18653/v1/W16–0802.

20. Stahl, K., 2018. Fake news detection in social media. California State University Stanislaus, 6, pp.4–15. https://www.semanticscholar.org/paper/Fake-news-detection-in-social-media-Stahl/b20 2b4b7124b774391109dc47a33e17224b12295.

21. Della Vedova, M.L., Tacchini, E., Moret, S., Ballarin, G., DiPierro, M. and de Alfaro, L., 2018, May. Automatic online fake news detection combining content and social signals. In *2018 22nd Conference of Open Innovations Association (FRUCT)* (pp. 272–279). IEEE. https://dl.acm.org/doi/10.5555/3266365.3266403.

22. Kim, N., Seo, D. and Jeong, C.S., 2018, November. FAMOUS: Fake news detection model based on unified key sentence information. In *2018 IEEE 9th International Conference on Software Engineering and Service Science (ICSESS)* (pp. 617–620). IEEE. https://doi.org/10.1109/ICSESS.2018.8663864.

23. Ahmed, H., Traore, I. and Saad, S., 2017, October. Detection of online fake news using n-gram analysis and machine learning techniques. In *International Conference on Intelligent, Secure, and Dependable Systems in Distributed and Cloud Environments* (pp. 127–138). Springer, Cham. https://doi.org/10.1007/978-3-319-69155-8-9.

24. Krishnan, S. and Chen, M., 2018, July. Identifying tweets with fake news. In *2018 IEEE International Conference on Information Reuse and Integration (IRI)* (pp. 460–464). IEEE. https://doi.org/10.1109/IRI.2018.00073.

25. Helmstetter, S. and Paulheim, H., 2018, August. Weakly supervised learning for fake news detection on Twitter. In *2018 IEEE/ACM International Conference on Advances in Social Networks Analysis and Mining (ASONAM)* (pp. 274–277). IEEE. https://doi.org/10.1109/ASONAM.2018.8508520.

26. Mar'ın, I.P. and Arroyo, D., 2019, May. Fake news detection. In *Computational Intelligence in Security for Information Systems Conference* (pp. 229–238). Springer, Cham. DOI https://doi.org/10.1007/978-3-030-57805-3-22.

27. Gilda, S., 2017, December. Notice of violation of IEEE publication principles: Evaluating machine learning algorithms for fake news detection. In *2017 IEEE 15th Student Conference on Research and Development (SCOReD)* (pp. 110–115). IEEE. https://doi.org/10.1109/SCORED.2017.8305411.

28. Kaggle Dataset 1. https://www.kaggle.com/c/fake-news.

29. Kaggle Dataset 2. https://www.kaggle.com/pnkjgpt/fake-news-dataset.

30. Mitchell, T.M., 2006. *The Discipline of Machine Learning, Vol. 9*. Pittsburgh: Carnegie Mellon University, School of Computer Science, Machine Learning Department. https://www.cs.cmu.edu/tom/pubs/MachineLearning.pdf.

31. Gregorutti, B., Michel, B. and Saint-Pierre, P., 2017. Correlation and variable importance in random forests. *Statistics and Computing*, 27(3): 659–678. https://arxiv.org/abs/1310.5726.

32. Schapire, R.E., 1999, July. A brief introduction to boosting. *IJCAI*, 99: 1401–1406. https://dl.acm.org/doi/10.5555/1624312.1624417.

33. Dos Santos, E.M., Sabourin, R. and Maupin, P., 2009. Overfitting cautious selection of classifier ensembles with genetic algorithms. *Information Fusion*, 10(2): 150–162. http://dx.doi.org/10.1016/j.inffus.2008.11.003.

34. Chen, T. and Guestrin, C., 2016, August. Xgboost: A scalable tree boosting system. In *Proceedings of the 22nd ACM SIGKDD International Conference on Knowledge Discovery and Data Mining* (pp. 785–794). https://doi.org/10.1145/2939672.2939785.

35. Catboost Documentation. https://catboost.ai/docs/concepts/about.html.

17

Data Science and Machine Learning Applications for Mental Health

Dhruvi Khankhoje, Pruthav Jhaveri, and Narendra M. Shekokar

Dwarkadas J. Sanghvi College of Engineering

CONTENTS

17.1 Introduction

Mental health is an issue which has come into the limelight in the recent past, given the current pace at which the world is progressing, the hectic lifestyle, workload and how societies have evolved, mental health has gained more importance as people have become aware of it. Mental health is defined as the state of well-being where an individual can keep up with their day-to-day life and the stress that comes along with it. It also means that they can work productively making a valuable contribution to society. According to WHO, mental health does not mean just the absence of a mental disorder, and it essentially means to ensure ongoing wellness and happiness. Almost anyone is prone to developing a mental health disorder irrespective of their age or gender. Mental health problems start from various sources of factors which are biological issues for example mental or psychological problems by family generation, life experiences, genetic, and brain [1]. Some of the most common mental disorders seen in individuals today are schizophrenia disorders, mood disorders, and anxiety disorders. These mental disorders and illnesses have become very common in the present and pose a great economic and social burden worldwide, yet there are no standardized biological diagnostic tests, and diagnosis still largely relies on the clinical expertise of trained individuals [2]. In recent years, advances in technology have enticed researchers to employ cutting-edge technology and try various approaches to improve the detection and treatment of mental disorders. Accurate diagnosis and timely treatment of mental illnesses can reduce their harmful effects and help the individual recover quickly before irreversible damage is done. Mental well-being has many health and social benefits, but an unstable mental state can have deleterious effects not only on the person facing it but also on the people around the individual.

Data Science is an emerging field that has gained immense relevance with the onset of the digital age. Data is found in copious amounts in almost every field, and this data holds information that can be analyzed and studied to gain insight and solve real-world problems, thus making data extremely valuable. Data Science may be defined as the area of study which combines domain expertise, concepts of mathematics, and statistics with programming to mine meaningful information from data. Data Scientists are practitioners of data science that apply machine learning algorithms to various data like images, numbers, text, and video to produce artificial intelligence systems to perform tasks that previously would require human intelligence. These systems are more efficient and accurate, and they produce findings that analysts can transform into valuable insights that can, in turn, be used to improve business profits, get a deeper understanding of a field or find a potential solution. In the field of mental health, the data collected has increased enormously in the last decade. The availability of large and quality datasets has helped researchers discover new methods of diagnosing and treating mental disorders. Through the data science approach, researchers have been able to detect previously unknown patterns and hidden information using techniques like machine learning, data mining, statistics, or time series analysis. This data-driven approach has contributed greatly to scientific knowledge in the domain, and it has not only improved the quality of public care but also greatly reduced the administrative cost of public mental health services.

This chapter aims to contribute to the research conducted in the field of mental health by focusing on how data science and machine learning methods can further improve diagnosis, treatment, and prevention of mental disorders. This chapter includes in-depth research of the various applications of data science and machine learning in this domain, and a careful analysis of the different approaches has been undertaken to identify which methods work most efficiently under the given conditions. The main impetus behind working in this domain is its relevance in today's world. According to WHO's statistics, around 800,000 people take their own life each year because of some mental illness and many more attempt suicide. These tragedies have a major impact and long-term consequences on the families and communities they leave behind. The majority of these cases are the result of some mental health condition that can be treated and brought under control if people had access to mental healthcare services, thus making it imperative to find accessible and cost-effective solutions, through which timely diagnosis and treatment of these illnesses can be done. Employing technologies like data science, machine learning and big data analysis will help solve this problem. Through this chapter, the various applications of data science in the field of mental health have been studied.

The contents of the chapter have been organized into the following sections: in Section 17.2, a detailed literature review of the domain has been conducted; in Section 17.3, the process of detecting mental illnesses through social media platforms has been discussed; in Section 17.4, two separate approaches to diagnose detection have been discussed; and in Section 17.5, a conclusion has been drawn and future scope has been discussed.

17.2 Review of Literature

In the last few years, there has been an immense growth in the amount of research work and surveys being done in the field of mental health using machine learning and data science. A review of the various methods and applications of machine learning in the domain of mental health is conducted, and it states that the three sub-domains within which extensive research is being done are (a) detection and identification, (b) predicting risks and understanding mental health disorders, and (c) treatment and support.

A convolution neural network-based approach is used in [3] to ascertain depression by employing a dataset consisting of motor activity of people primarily part of three groups namely, unipolar, bipolar, and people without depression. This chapter also classifies different levels of depression and trains a model to calculate MontgomeryÅsberg Depression Rating Scale scores. Their methodology achieved a mean squared error of 4.0 for score predictions and F1-score of 0.70 for detection of various groups of people. There exist several methods of input that can be utilized to detect mental health conditions [4,5] employs facial and vocal expressions as inputs for the detection of depression. Machine learning models like support vector machine (SVM) and logistic regression were used in [4]. An accuracy of 79% for active appearance modeling, 79% for voice patterns, and 88% for manual facts resulted in the conclusion that this model is feasible for automatic and accurate prediction of depression. In [5], useful information from dynamic factors such as audio and video data is extracted using the motion history histogram, and for each modality, the partial least square regression algorithm assisted in understanding the relationship between depression scale and dynamic factors. This ultimately aided in predicting depression scales. Authors of [6] implement a hybrid of logistic regression and decision trees to project the stress levels and recognize factors affecting the mental health of Indian patients. In their proposed approach, the data acquired, the Context Stress Pattern Detection Service will build rules using decision trees (ID3), with additional qualities from the dynamic components as antecedents and stress levels as consequent. The properties from frequently created rules are taken from the generated rules and can be further forecasted using logistic regression. Bayesian networks have been used in assisting the diagnosis of social anxiety disorder in [7] by creating the Bayesian network structure and the conditional probability tables. This achieves an 8.571% error rate. Another form of input for the diagnosis of mental health disorders or syndromes is neuroimages, which are images resulting from MRI, PET, and ERG scans. Machine learning algorithms like support vector machine, Gradient Boosting, Neural Networks, Random Forest Classifier, and K-Nearest Neighbor were applied in [8]. The results of these scans and all the algorithms produced an accuracy higher than 97 showcasing the reliability of these methods for early predictions of this disease. Table 17.1 displays the analysis of detection and identification of mental health disorders.

The colossal increase in usage of social media has led to a commensurate increase in research on its impact on humans. One major research sector is authenticated news. The authors of [9] study evaluate and analyze research on fake news and propose a detecting model for it. Additionally, in [10], the authors discuss authentication of news on social media using machine learning techniques. Reference [11] uses user-generated content from various social media communities like LiveJournal, along with their associated mood tags, and applies machine learning and statistical analysis methods to perform sentiment analysis. This is done to differentiate depressed posts from non-depressed posts in the context of social media analysis for clinical and psychological impact. The proposed

TABLE 17.1

Analysis of Detection and Identification of Mental Health Disorders

Paper Title	Mental Health Target	Approach/Method	Results
One-Dimensional Convolutional Neural Networks on Motor Activity Measurements in Detection of Depression [3]	Depression	(i) Motor activity measurements are used to detect depression using one-dimensional convolutional neural networks. (ii) Based on Montgomery-Åsberg Depression Rating Scale, the level of depression and MADRS score of participants is also predicted.	(i) Mean accuracy of 0.71 was achieved for leave one-participant-out experiment and mean accuracy of 0.98 for threefold cross-validation. (ii) For predicting levels, a mean accuracy of 0.72 was achieved for leave one-participant-out experiment and a mean accuracy of 0.991 for threefold cross-validation. A mean squared error of 31.40 was achieved for MADRS score prediction.
Detecting Depression from Facial Actions and Vocal Prosody [4]	Depression	Support Vector Machines were used to classify the FACS and AAM samples (SVMs). Audio signal processing with logistic regression was used to analyze the vocals.	(i) Through manual FACS coding, an accuracy of 89% was achieved. (ii) Accuracy for AAM and vocal prosody was 79%.
Depression Recognition based on Dynamic Facial and Vocal Expression Features using Partial Least Square Regression [5]	Depression	Motion History Histogram-based dynamic features are used, Edge Orientation Histogram and Local Binary Patterns are adopted and Partial Least Square (PLS) regression is implemented to predict depression.	Mean Absolute Error and Root Mean Squared Error were most optimal for the model using motion history histogram, Local Binary Patterns and Support Vector Regression for predicting depression. The values were 7.83 and 9.67 for MAE and RMSE, respectively.
Predicting Anxiety, Depression and Stress in Modern Life using machine learning algorithms [6]	Depression, Anxiety and Stress	Using the Depression, Anxiety and Stress Scale questionnaire, machine learning algorithms like Decision Tree, Random Forest Tree, Naïve Bayes, support vector machine and KNN were employed to detect anxiety, depression and stress.	The highest value of accuracy was achieved by Naïve Bayes with the values being 0.733, 0.855 and 0.742 for anxiety, depression and stress, respectively. The highest value of F1-score was achieved by Random Forest for Stress with the values being 0.711 and by Naïve Bayes for depression with the values being 0.836.
Bayesian Network Model for diagnosis of social anxiety disorder [7]	Social Anxiety Disorder	Bayesian Networks and Conditional Probability Tables are implemented to diagnose social anxiety disorder	An error rate of 8.751 was achieved for diagnosing social anxiety disorder.
Diagnosis of Alzheimer's Disease using machine learning [8]	Alzheimer's	SVM, Gradient Boosting, Neural Networks, KNN and Random Forest algorithms have been employed to diagnose Alzheimer's in its primitive stage using data obtained by neuroimaging technologies	Neural networks achieved the highest accuracy of 98.36% and KNN achieved an accuracy of 95.00%. All the other models achieved accuracy above 97%.

methodology achieved 90%, 95%, and 92% accuracy for the classification of depressive postings, depressive communities, and depression degree, respectively. The authors of [12] propose a Semi-Supervised Topic Modeling Over Time to keep track of symptoms of clinical depression from the tweets of Twitter users. By combining a lexicon-based strategy (top-down processing) with a method driven by data, the paper can determine the severity of depression exhibited in tweets for each user profile in our dataset (bottom-up processing). A depression vocabulary as per the clinical articulation of depression, which includes common depression symptoms from the recognized clinical assessment questionnaire, PHQ-9 is created. The terms are scored, and a list of useful and revealing lexicon terms for each user is constructed. This is utilized as a basis to uncover hidden subjects (depression symptoms) discussed in the subject's tweets (bottom-up processing). The Semi-Supervised Topic Modeling Over Time model is a partial supervision probabilistic topic modeling over user tweets and adds to the expressiveness of the Latent Dirichlet Allocation (LDA) model by introducing a preset set of seed terms to detect. With a precision of 72% and an accuracy of 68%, the automatic screening method can mirror the PHQ-9. The analysis of detection and identification of mental health disorders using social media is illustrated in Table 17.2.

The risks of not seeking help at the right time or not assessing the gravity of the mental state of an individual correctly can be very dangerous and at times even, fatal. To prevent such situations, research is also being conducted on the severity of the mental state. By analyzing natural language from a set of psychological evaluation records provided by the Centers of Excellence in Genomic Science Neuropsychiatric Genome-Scale and RDoC Individualized Domains (N-GRID) project of Harvard Medical School, [13] provides a novel method for determining the intensity of a patient's positive valence symptoms. The paper implements Pointwise Ridge Regression and Pairwise Random Forest classification for predicting the severity score. Both these models learn and use a distinct set of feature weights to determine how severe the symptom is. The pointwise method learns to make inferences about the severity score directly from a single psychiatric evaluation record, whereas the RF method sorts pairs of psychiatric evaluation data to infer severity

TABLE 17.2

Analysis of Detection and Identification of Mental Health Disorders Using Social Media

Paper Title	Mental Health Target	Approach/Method	Results
Analysis of user-generated content from online social communities to characterize and predict depression degree [11]	Depression	Data extracted from LiveJournal is employed to predict depressed posts and depressed communities using algorithms Random Forest Classifier and SVM. The Hierarchical Hidden Markov Model is used to define the degree of depression.	Random Forest performs best and achieved 90% and 95% accuracy in classifying the depressive posts and depressive communities, respectively. The accuracy of the proposed algorithm for the predicting degree of depression is 92%.
Semi-Supervised Approach to Monitoring Clinical Depressive Symptoms in Social Media [12]	Depression	For continuous temporal analysis of an individual's tweets, a semi-supervised statistical model which adds supervision to LDA can extract, categories, and track depression symptoms.	For recording depression symptoms per user, the accuracy was 68% and the precision was 72%.

score. To develop a more robust and accurate model, the paper also implements a hybrid model which is a linear combination of the inferred severity scores predicted by both models. These models predicted four severity levels: (a) absent, (b) mild, (c) moderate, and (d) severe. The mean absolute error (MAE) was most optimal for the hybrid model for mild, moderate, and severe with values 0.841, 0.869, 0.698, and 0.912, respectively. The optimal MAE for "absent" of 0.929 was achieved by pointwise ridge regression. In community mental health settings, social workers face a common and costly problem: rehospitalization of seriously and persistently mentally ill clients. The question of rehospitalization of mentally ill patients that have already been discharged is predicted with an accuracy ranging from 75% to 93% in [14]. In the first Axis I diagnostic category, the diagnostic profile of the subjects was as follows: schizophrenia (66%), affective disorder 43 (22%), organic disorder (4.1%), and other (7%). Thirty-two of the participants were diagnosed with an Axis II personality disorder (16%). The methodology adopted in this study is Bayesian Artificial Neural Networks to make predictions categorization judgments based on acquired knowledge and data from successfully resolved cases (correct decisions). The analysis of prediction of the severity of mental health disorders is depicted in Table 17.3.

The rise in the amount of research done in diagnosis and detection through machine learning applications in the domain of mental health causes a need to focus on how solutions, support, and treatment can be provided or improved. Most of the initial work that has been done focuses on supporting clients and promoting well-being, but professional counselors are the most effective way of treatment for any mental health ailment and due to a wide range of training and supervision quality, the effectiveness of motivational interviewing, a psychotherapy strategy that promotes behavior change, particularly for addiction and behavioral health issues in real-world circumstances can be quite diverse. In [15], a system is developed which focuses on the work of professional counselors, identifying strengths, improvement areas, and providing feedback on the quality of their service and their adherence to MI. The system is an automated artificial intelligence and machine learning-based evaluation and assessment tool which provides mental health counselors with a system that utilizes speech signal processing to convert a MI session's audio recording into a numerical representation of semantic and voice acoustic data and text-based and speech-based machine learning predictive models. The report drawn up through CORE-MI presents the professional with various metrics like percentage of MI adherence,

TABLE 17.3

Analysis of Predicting the Severity of Mental Health Disorders

Paper Title	Approach/Method	Results
Automatic recognition of symptom severity from psychiatric evaluation records [13]	Implements Pointwise Ridges · Regression and Pairwise Random Forest classification and a hybrid model combining both to predict severity of symptoms from psychiatric evaluation records.	MAE by the hybrid model for mild, moderate and severe was 0.841, 0.869, 0.698, and 0.912, respectively. MAE for "absent", was 0.929, achieved by pointwise ridge regression.
The Application of Artificial Neural Networks for Outcome Prediction in a Cohort of Severely Mentally Ill Outpatients [14]	Applies Bayesian Artificial Neural Networks to make predictions for rehospitalization of severely mentally ill outpatients.	Eight Bayesian ANN models achieved an accuracy ranging from 75% to 93%.

MI spirit and empathy ratings, quality of questions asked, and several more. Through [16], a paradigmatic shift from traditional services of mental health is initiated. Silby, a service based on artificial intelligence, proven science, and real-time assistance is a messaging platform aimed at providing digitally assisted guided self-help intervention and supportive coaching to assist individuals to improve their mental health and wellness. This paper has employed machine learning in their system to assess and improve adherence, giving real-time recommendations to increase the quality of our coaches' responses. Computerized systems are the most well-known and effective application of technology in mental health. The most relevant are websites called MoodGYM and Beating the Blues. The authors of [17] provide an application that provides methods for authoring a large number of interventions and matching them to people based on their personalities and current requirements, specifically for coping with stress in this fast-paced and competitive environment. The paper provides a strategy for creating micro-interventions that focuses on repurposing well-known web applications as stress management tools and a recommender system that over time understands how to tailor interventions to the needs of individuals and their temporal circumstances. To predict the expected reduction of stress if a certain intervention was performed ensembles of regression trees using the Random Forest algorithm were trained. Participants in the user study of this paper reported higher stress self-awareness, decreased depression-related symptoms, and having learned new basic techniques to handle stress after four weeks. Table 17.4 displays the analysis of applications of treatment and support for mental health disorders.

The elaborate and in-depth analysis and study of the diverse work being conducted in the field of mental health employing various data science and machine learning techniques reveal that quite a lot of the work being done uses a small dataset. To get an accurate overview of the impact and efficacy of all the research being conducted, it is imperative to use a considerably large sample space, this will allow us to conclude results that apply to a satisfactory size of the dataset. In the detection and identification segment, apart from features like vocal features and facial expressions, factors like physical activity, tiredness, and levels of concentration are also signs of depression, and sweating and trembling are symptoms of anxiety or stress. These factors can also be inculcated as additional features along with the aforementioned characteristics to include a broader list of symptoms. Additionally, on the diagnosis of these disorders, there can be a prediction of the type of

TABLE 17.4

Analysis of Applications of Treatment and Support of Mental Health Disorders

Paper Title	Purpose
"It's hard to argue with a computer": Investigating Psychotherapists' Attitudes toward Automated Evaluation [15]	An application that uses speech signal processing and speech/text-based predictive models to help mental health professionals evaluate their services and improve them.
Research driven: Sibly and the transformation of mental health and wellness [16]	An application aimed at guided self-help intervention and supportive coaching to help individuals improve mental health and well-being. The use of machine learning is employed in various features to make the system robust and examine the quality of the services.
PopTherapy: Coping with Stress through Pop-Culture [17]	An application that uses several intervention techniques to reduce the stress of humans, employs popular web applications as stress management interventions and an intervention recommender system based on machine learning that learns how to match interventions to persons and their temporal situations over time.

that specific disorder, if it exists. For example, if a user is detected with anxiety, the type of anxiety such as generalized anxiety disorder, social anxiety disorder (social phobia), specific phobias, and separation anxiety disorder can be predicted.

This chapter aims to study and analyze the application of data science and machine learning in the broad domain of mental health and review the various methodologies implemented.

17.3 Detection of Mental Health Disorders through Social Media

Social media refers to websites and programs that emphasize communication, community-based input, engagement, content-sharing, and collaboration. The number of social media websites and the functionalities available on these websites have augmented causing a commensurate increase in the users. Some platforms are used for pure information consumption, while some are for sharing content, thoughts, and feelings. As open and free communication platforms for problem-solving and information exchange, forums such as blogs and online discussion communities have grown in popularity. The vast amount of data available on the internet has corresponded with significant advances in computational algorithms capable of quantifying language and behavior into statistically relevant measurements. Harvesting social media activity has established itself as a reliable source for capturing customized and population data in the form of explicit remarks, patterns, and frequency of use, as well as linguistic nuances. Online activity may now be used to consistently monitor and predict health-related behaviors according to a new research, thereby increasing the amount of research being conducted on the utilization of social media for the detection, prevention, and treatment of various mental diseases. The following section explains research work carried out in the detection of mental health disorders like depression and schizophrenia through various social media forums like Twitter, Reddit, and many more.

Depression is a mood condition characterized by persistent sorrow and a loss of interest and it is essential to detect depression in a person before it reaches an extreme and dangerous stage. A model that combines SVM, and Naïve Bayes and leverages social networking sites such as Facebook, LiveJournal, and Twitter as a data source and screening tool to identify users based on user-generated content on social networking sites using artificial intelligence is implemented to predict mental health levels and depression in [18]. The model used in the paper consists of two datasets: seven main operators and several processes to test both the classifiers. The first set is the training dataset having a total of three columns. The first column is the binomial sentiment (depressed, not-depressed), the depression category (one out of the nine categories in case of depressed sentiment) is present in the second column, and the third column consists of manually trained 2,073 depressed posts and 2,073 not-depressed posts. The second dataset contains patient social networking site postings, which are altered for everyone to test the model's prediction. Select Attributes is the first operator and it determines which training dataset attributes should be maintained and which should be eliminated. Nominal to Text operators are the second and third operators, and they change the type of chosen nominal attributes to text and map all attribute values to matching string values. They are utilized in both the training and test datasets. The fourth and fifth are Process Documents that are utilized in training. Word vectors are generated from the dataset and the test set. It has four operators (Tokenize, Filter Stop-words, Transform Cases, and Stem) and has string properties. The Validation operator is the sixth operator, and it is applied to the training dataset, which is divided into two sections: training and testing. The classifier operator is found in the training section, and each time the patients are tested, the classifier model is switched from SVM (linear) to Naïve Bayes Classifier (kernel). The trained model is applied to the supervised dataset by the apply model, and the performance operator evaluates performance. These models make up the testing part. The apply model is the seventh, and the final operator, it gives the final result of the prediction using one of the classifiers in the patients. The proposed model achieved a precision of 100%, Recall of 57%, and accuracy of 63.3%. These results were compared with the results of [19] and [20] and have managed to receive a higher precision from both.

Users on Reddit freely share, seek advice and discuss issues related to mental health on various subreddits. The information and structure of these subreddits can be utilized for the detection of various mental disorders. The authors of [21] use data from the social media platform Reddit and leverage the American Psychiatric Association created and published DSM-5 (Diagnostic and Statistical Manual of Mental Disorders – 5th Edition) taxonomy and diagnostic manual along with SNOMED-CT, ICD-10, and DataMed, which are examples of domain-specific knowledge bases to provide a thorough examination of the nature of subreddit material from the perspective of a domain expert and through a novel approach enhance classification and mapping precision of subreddits to DSM-5 symptoms and categories. To begin with, DSM-5 lexicons consisting of n-grams associated with each of the DSM-5 categories are created using famous resources like DataMed, DAO, ICD-10, and SNOWMED-CT. Except for DataMed, all the medical information databases are stored and indexed in a graph structure, with each DSM-5 category being searched separately. For each mental health disorder first, the two-hop parents and four-hop children are looked for, then the search is extended using a Depth First Search graph traversal. It was established to empirically extract concepts that are contextually connected to the DSM-5 category in question. The automatic unsupervised mapping of the labor-intensive subreddit labels to DSM-5 categories is a novel contribution of the paper. The most common and collocated terms that have matches in the DSM-5 lexicon were extracted using the n-grams ($n=1,2,3$), which were generated by the SkipGram model and subsampling of frequent words, language model. LDA was used to conduct coherence analysis to determine the best representative subjects. The number of hits, which matches between n-grams in a subreddit main post and the DSM-5 vocabulary, both exact and approximate are calculated and combined with the number of hits for LDA with the n-grams and called "Normalized Hits". The proposed method only maps a subreddit to a DSM-5 category if the normalized hit score equals 1.0. The subreddit labels in the dataset are replaced with the subsequent DSM-5 category once the most prominent DSM-5 category for a subreddit has been discovered and this dataset is called a coarser dataset. After implementing logistic regression, SVM (linear and radial basis kernels), and Adaboost, and concluding that for a heterogeneous and unbalanced dataset they are of no use, the paper proposed an approach utilizing only Random Forest. Term Frequency and Inverse Document Frequency have also been used. Additionally, since there exists multi-class classification, Semantic weighting through Encoding and Decoding Optimization has also been utilized. The Balanced Random Forest model using features Horizontal Linguistic Features (HLF), Vertical Linguistic Features (VLF), Fine-Grained Features (FGF), and TF-IDF resulted in a precision of 0.60, Recall of 0.54, F1-score of 0.57, and False Alarm Rate of 0.14. Additionally, the Balanced Random Forest model using features such as HLF, VLF, and FGF resulted in a precision of 0.88, Recall of 0.83, F1-score of 0.85, and False Alarm Rate of 0.025.

Schizophrenia is a long-term mental illness that impairs a person's capacity to think, feel, and act rationally. Symptoms of schizophrenia include delusions, hallucinations, disorganized speech, difficulty thinking, and a lack of desire. If schizophrenia is left untreated, it can have a variety of severe effects (individually, socially, and economically). Suicide, homelessness, and incarceration are all elevated risks for people with schizophrenia. 6% of people with schizophrenia are homeless or live in a shelter, and another 6% are incarcerated. In [22], a framework is developed to distinguish people with schizophrenia from control individuals using Twitter data. Due to the heterogeneous presentation of this disease, its detection proved to be challenging. To begin with, several Twitter users were segregated as users having schizophrenia (cases) if the two or more of the following conditions were met: (a) user self-identifies in user description, (b) in status updates, the user self-identifies, and (c) the user follows "@schizotribe", a known Twitter community of users with schizophrenia and users who do not suffer from schizophrenia(controls). The age distribution group of both cases, user group and control user group, was matched. A set of 28 features were extracted from the user's profile and posting history to identify Twitter users with schizophrenia and distinguish them from controls. The features include the amount of time between tweets, emoticons, number of followed users, time of day when the user tweets, and the use of schizophrenia-related words. For each of the models, two transformations of the feature vectors in addition to the raw feature vectors: log scaling of the time between tweets and Principal Components Analysis (PCA) were analyzed. The classification models used in this paper were Naïve Bayes (NB), artificial neural networks (ANNs), and SVMs, and the model's feature set and hyperparameters were fine-tuned using fivefold cross-validation on the training data. The process of reduction of the number of principal components used did not improve the performance of the models implying that the models were able to adequately fit 28 features contained in the training data. With respect to F1-score and precision as evaluation metrics, SVM using PCA transformed data performed the best and achieved scores of 0.800 and 0.923. The recall and accuracy values recorded by this model are 0.706 and 0.893. The model implementing ANN using PCA transformed data attained a higher recall value of 0.765. The F1-score, precision, and accuracy achieved by this model are 0.788, 0.813, and 0.875, respectively. The Naïve Bayes model using the log-transformed data had considered the frequency of tweets with schizophrenia-related words, the time between tweets, happy emoticon usage, tweet time of day, and tweet frequency in the morning as the most integral features of the dataset. The values of F1-score, precision, recall and accuracy achieved are 0.667, 0.688, 0.647 and 0.803. Table 17.5 analyzes the Social Media-based Applications in the domain of mental health.

17.4 Study of Data Mining and Machine Learning Techniques for Diagnosing Depression

In this section, two approaches have been discussed to diagnose depression: a data mining approach and a machine learning approach. The benefits and drawbacks of both methods have been reviewed.

17.4.1 Data Mining Approach to Discover Association Rules to Diagnose Depression

Today's generation has seen a significant increase in the number of people suffering from depression. Given their daily life and workload, many people overlook the symptoms of melancholia and depression, this can prove to be very harmful over time and can produce

TABLE 17.5

Analysis of Social Media-Based Applications in the Domain of Mental Health

Paper Title	Purpose	Approach/Method	Results
Predicting Depression Levels Using Social Media Posts [18]	To classify user-generated content extracted from social media sites to enable early prediction of the mental health and depression level of the users.	A novel method using both support vector machine and Naïve Bayes with seven main operators.	The proposed system achieves accuracy, precision and recall of 63.3%, 100% and 57%, respectively.
"Let Me Tell You About Your Mental Health!" Contextualized Classification of Reddit Posts to DSM-5 for Web-based Intervention [21]	To provide crucial information to mental health advisors at a low cost by an algorithm that analyzes mental health subreddit posts and assesses their relevance to DSM-5 categories using a multi-class classification technique.	A novel method to automatically map unsupervised subreddit labels to DSM-5 categories and uses Random Forest.	The Balanced Random Forest model with HLF, VLF, FGF and TF-IDF resulted in a precision of 0.60, Recall of 0.54, F1-score of 0.57 and False Alarm Rate of 0.14. The Balanced Random Forest model using features HLF, VLF, FGF resulted in a precision of 0.88, Recall of 0.83, F1-score of 0.85 and False Alarm Rate of 0.025.
Mining Twitter Data to Improve Detection of Schizophrenia [22]	To identify schizophrenia, a rare but deadly disease from users of Twitter.	A sentiment analysis approach using models like SVM, ANN or NB paired with reduction or transformation methods like PCA or Log Transformation.	SVM with PCA reduced features resulted in precision of 0.923, Recall of 0.706, accuracy of 0.893 and F1-score of 0.800. ANN with PCA reduced features attained in precision of 0.813, Recall of 0.765, accuracy of 0.875 and F1-score of 0.788. NB+log-transformed data achieved in precision of 0.688, Recall of 0.647, accuracy of 0.803 and F1-score of 0.667.

serious complications within individuals. More research is needed to diagnose and treat melancholia and depression in its early stages before it can cause irreversible damage. In this section, a data mining method is discussed, following a questionnaire which was filled by patients data mining processes have been used to extract association rules [23]. The questionnaire aims to understand the physical and mental conditions of the patient by drawing a relationship between how a person feels and acts and the degree of depression he suffers from. The method reviewed advocates the use of Frequent Pattern (FP) tree algorithm over the Apriori algorithm, which reduces execution time; it discovers interesting relations without repeatedly generating candidate itemsets.

The FP tree has been constructed based on the evaluation of responses that were collected from the questionnaire. The questionnaire consisted of nine questions which were to be answered on a scale of zero to three depending on the degree to which one conforms to the stated condition. This survey is gathered and saved in the back-end which enables immediate analysis. Now in order to construct the FP tree the questions are numbered from one to nine (1–9) and the numeric scale is represented by the English alphabets where 0 corresponds to A and 3 corresponds to D.

Step 1: Scan the database to obtain the itemset that has a support value greater than the specified minimum support.

Step 2: After obtaining the itemset it is sorted in descending order, the itemset with most support is added first and the one with least support has been added last, as seen in Figure 17.1. It should be noted that 6C is the item, where 6 was the question number and C was the answer chosen. The colon (:) following the item separates the item from the support value. For example, in 6C:4, 6C is the item and 4 is the support associated with it.

Step 3: A virtual database is built with the reordered itemsets, in order to start building an FP tree first a root node is created.

Step 4: The ordered frequent itemsets get added to the tree and for all new transactions the prefix is checked with the existing path if they match the counter is increased otherwise a new branch is created. Figure 17.1 illustrates an example of an itemset and FP tree.

After the construction of the FP tree, the FP growth algorithm is designed to extract every frequent itemset from the tree. The algorithm searches the frequent itemsets in ascending order starting with the itemset with the least support value till it finds the itemset with the highest frequency. This has led to the development of various modules which can diagnose the level of depression as well as physical fitness.

Module 1: After analyzing the questionnaire filled out by the user, the score is displayed depending on which certain articles linked to depression are linked to help the user understand his situation and take the required action.

Module 2: In this, a simple and user-friendly mobile application has been developed where users can record their mood and upload it. The back-end server shall store this and after analysis a short message is sent to the user depicting the degree of depression.

Module 3: In this module, data mining has been used to discover insightful association rules from the answers to the questionnaire. Frequent itemsets obtained after applying varying thresholds of minimum support and confidence have provided

FREQUENT ITEMSET				
USER 1	6C	5B	2B	3D
USER 2	6C	5B	2B	9E
USER 3	6C	5B	2B	
USER 4	6C	5B	2B	3D
USER 5	3D	7C		

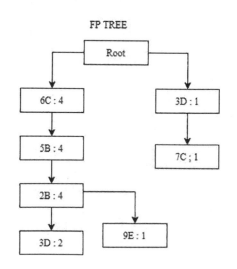

FIGURE 17.1

An example of an itemset and FP tree.

FIGURE 17.2
The data mining module for diagnosing depression.

useful information. Using this information psychiatrists and others can understand what are the common physical and mental conditions that are found in a person that suffers from depression. FP tree and FP growth algorithms have been used to discover the association rules. Further, the responses received are scored and have been divided into various groups to provide the users with comprehensive feedback so that they can understand their condition and take proper action. The groups that describe the condition of the individual are as follows: healthy condition, borderline condition, slight symptoms, medium symptoms, and heavy symptoms. Thus, depending upon the category the individuals fall in, they can make a proper plan of action, psychiatrists too can find similarities between behaviors that are a reflection of a serious mental disorder. For example, few people feel tired and drained but several cannot focus on what they are watching or reading. This shows that the majority of the people do not feel good and suffer from a serious mental condition. Similar relationships have been drawn between sleeping problems, lack of concentration, fun, and interest. Figure 17.2 outlines the overall functioning of this model.

The aforementioned methods can be incorporated into mobile phones with touch screens and users can easily fill out the questionnaires while sitting in the waiting lobby. The scores presented after evaluation and analysis can greatly assist psychiatrists in accurately diagnosing the degree of depression the patient is suffering from and treatment can be given accordingly.

The overall accuracy is satisfactory, however, there are certain drawbacks to the mentioned technique. The association rules sometimes fail to detect certain anomalies, if a patient is facing some unique or peculiar symptoms, the model might not consider them thus, resulting in a wrong diagnosis. Moreover, the questionnaires are filled by the patients themselves; thus, this technique relies on the honesty and integrity of the patient. Sometimes patients tend to fake their moods to avoid talking about their disorders. This calls for a technique that can be more accurate in detecting symptoms of depression in people and at the same time is free from human bias. Thus, recent research in the field of mental health is focused on employing machine learning techniques along with big data which has shown very promising results.

17.4.2 Machine Learning Approach to Detect Depression

In today's world, automation has taken over manual labor. Using various machines and programming them intelligently has simplified several tasks. To automate a process the machine must be first trained, just like a human brain, the machine then uses these past experiences to detect familiar patterns which provide valuable insight to users. This procedure of training, testing, and detecting are together known as machine learning algorithms. In the field of mental health, there are several complex parameters that have to be considered. In such a case, the possibility of human error is high, and automation of such

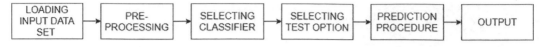

FIGURE 17.3
Overall procedure to predict depression.

a process can not only remove the factor of human error but also provide more accurate results within a short span of time. Recent developments in the field of machine learning and deep learning have brought a revolution in the field of medical diagnosis [24]. In this section, various machine learning classifiers have been reviewed to find the algorithm with the highest efficacy. The tool that has been used in the method under review is the WEKA tool, developed by the University of Waikato, New Zealand. This tool helps combine machine learning techniques to apply them to data mining problems like data pre-processing, forecasting, classification, prediction, and regression [25]. The various classifier models that have been reviewed: Bayes Net, Logistic, Multilayer Perceptron, sequential minimal optimization, and decision table; they have been used on different test options: training and testing set, cross-validation, and percentage split [26]. The overall procedure for the prediction of depression is demonstrated in Figure 17.3.

The individual steps followed in the procedure are:

Step 1: This is the initial step where the dataset is loaded.

Step 2: In the pre-processing stage select appropriate filters, here it is advisable to select the supervised filter attribute to select the optimized attributes.

Step 3: After the dataset has been loaded and the filters have been selected, classifiers are now chosen. The various classifiers are selected one after the other and the results of each are recorded.

Step 4: The test option that is selected will eventually determine the output of classification and prediction. There are three types of testing that have been used: training and testing, percentage split, and cross-validation.

Step 5: After selecting the appropriate classifiers and the testing option, now move on to begin the prediction procedure.

Step 6: After prediction has been completed, the output of various metrics related to the model is seen.

In the following paragraphs, the various classifiers and testing procedures have been discussed.

The various classifiers that have been used in this section are as follows:

1. **BayesNet Classifier**: A Bayesian network [27] is a probabilistic directed acyclic graph that consists of a set of nodes and a set of edges between them, the nodes represent random data whereas the edges signify the conditional dependency. The learning process is divided into two steps: learning network and learning relationship among data.

2. **Logistic Regression**: Since the dataset used for the prediction of depression has binary outputs linear regression cannot be used, hence logistic regression is used [28]. There are two sets produced, one is the positive set that has detected people suffering from depression and the other one is a negative set that represents

people that do not have depression. Each variable or attribute accounts for the prediction of the expected outcome.

3. **Multilayer Perceptron**: This model consists of weighted inputs and a single output. They accept a bipolar or binary input, but the output is always in a bipolar form [29]. The model consists of multiple layers as the name suggests, and each layer consists of a neuron. The input sum for each is calculated, and only if the total is greater than the threshold value, the output is activated or else it remains deactivated.

4. **Sequential Minimal Optimization**: This is employed for training SVM [30]. It provides a simple solution to train the SVM, and it breaks down the large problem into smaller ones and solves them individually. Not only does this make computation faster but also can handle large datasets.

5. **Decision Table**: This is a tree-based classifier used for predictive modeling [31]. It consists of two parts: an algorithm that designs the table and a visualization part that represents the graphical interface of the model. This algorithm chooses only the most important attributes set from the bigger dataset, thus reducing the chances of overestimation. Thus a smaller compact decision table is generated, from which the output decision is taken for the classification.

The various testing methods that have been used alongside the classifiers are as follows:

1. **Using Testing and Training Set**: Here the model is trained on a training set. After it has completed learning, it is tested on the testing dataset to verify the extent to which the model has learned to predict and classify the data.

2. **Cross-Validation**: Unlike training and testing, the two sets are not explicit. In fact, the test dataset is prepared from the practice dataset. The entire dataset is partitioned into training and testing sets over several iterations to ensure all permutations and combinations are covered. After all the iterations have been completed, the results from all the iterations are averaged and the final result is displayed. This method even considers errors for performance measurements, which makes the prediction results of unknown data more accurate.

3. **Percentage Split**: In this method, the training data is used for both training and testing. The amount of data used in testing is a percentage of the entire data which is taken as user input. For example, if there are a total of 100 samples and the split percent is 40, 40 samples will be used in testing and 60 will be used for training.

Among all the classifiers and testing methods, it has been found that the BayesNet classifier gave the highest accuracy of 95% and a precision of 0.95 when the percentage split testing technique was used. The decision table classifier showed equally promising results, however, when compared to root mean square error, the BayesNet classifier was less prone to errors.

17.5 Conclusion and Future Scope

Mental health has gained even more importance over the recent years. People that first ignored symptoms of mental disorders, now have become mindful of their mental illness. They now acknowledge their illness and seek to get medical help at the earliest. Given their lifestyle and work environment, there has been a significant increase in the number of people suffering from anxiety, depression, and other mental disorders. This calls for development in the way we diagnose and treat these mental disorders. Development in technology has paved the way to faster and more accurate diagnosis, and combining knowledge from the fields of data science, machine learning, big data, and artificial intelligence has helped develop self-diagnosing models, provide lines of treatment to patients and even assist psychiatrists with treating their patients.

This chapter reviews the various existing methods to detect mental disorders like depression, anxiety, and schizophrenia by collecting data from various social media platforms. Social media has become an outlet for not only information but also feelings, thoughts, and emotions. Due to this, a lot of work has been done in understanding mental health issues and detecting them through these platforms. Several novel methods employing machine learning techniques like SVM, Neural Networks, and Random Forest are being used to detect various mental health disorders like depression, stress, and schizophrenia by extracting data through social media websites like Reddit, Twitter, Facebook, and more. For detection of depression in particular, two methods have been studied: one is a data mining approach. In this, users are asked to fill out questionnaires, the responses are stored in the back-end server and association rules are discovered from them. They help classify the responses into different degrees of melancholia to provide users with insight into their condition. These questionnaires are also filled out by patients in the waiting area, and the results help the psychiatrist make a more informed and accurate diagnosis. The second method is the relatively newer method that employs various machine learning classifiers to predict depression. The input data is pre-processed and fed to different classifiers and various testing methods are employed. Various combinations of classifiers and testing processes have been used, and the metrics of each are carefully compared with one another to deduce the model that performs best. This technique is not only more efficient but also more accurate, and it is completely automated making it free from any human input or bias.

Given the development in technology, the applications of data science and machine learning can be further extended in the field of mental health. They can be used to overcome the hurdles faced by some of the techniques today which include poor efficiency of the model, restricted datasets, reliance on experts for final diagnosis and quality of treatment. In the future, the various models can be tested on larger datasets, deep learning models along with transfer learning can help improve the overall efficiency and accuracy of the model, and the detection, treatment, and prevention of mental disorders can be automated completely. This will improve the overall quality of healthcare provided to the patients.

References

1. Mentalhealth.gov. (2018). What Is Mental Health? | [MentalHealth.gov. online] Available at: https://www.mentalhealth.gov/basics/what-is-mental-health [Accessed 12 Oct. 2018].
2. Diederich, Joachim, Aqeel Al-Ajmi, and Peter Yellowlees. Ex-ray: Data mining and mental health. *Applied Soft Computing* 7, 3 (2007): 923–928.
3. Frogner, Joakim Ihle, Farzan Majeed Noori, Pål Halvorsen, Steven Alexander Hicks, Enrique Garcia-Ceja, Jim Torresen, and Michael Alexander Riegler. One-dimensional convolutional neural networks on motor activity measurements in detection of depression. In *Proceedings of the 4th International Workshop on Multimedia for Personal Health & Health Care*, pp. 9–15. 2019.

4. Cohn, Jeffrey F., Tomas Simon Kruez, Iain Matthews, Ying Yang, Minh Hoai Nguyen, Margara Tejera Padilla, Feng Zhou, and Fernando De la Torre. Detecting depression from facial actions and vocal prosody. In *2009 3rd International Conference on Affective Computing and Intelligent Interaction and Workshops*, pp. 1–7. IEEE, 2009.

5. Meng, Hongying, Di Huang, Heng Wang, Hongyu Yang, Mohammed Ai-Shuraifi, and Yunhong Wang. Depression recognition based on dynamic facial and vocal expression features using partial least square regression. In *Proceedings of the 3rd ACM International Workshop on Audio/Visual Emotion Challenge*, pp. 21–30. 2013.

6. Priya, Anu, Shruti Garg, and Neha Prerna Tigga. Predicting anxiety, depression and stress in modern life using machine learning algorithms. *Procedia Computer Science* 167 (2020): 1258–1267.

7. Estabragh, Zakiyeh Shojaei, Mohammad Mansour Riahi Kashani, Farnaz Jeddi Moghaddam, Simin Sari, and Koosha Sadeghi Oskooyee. Bayesian network model for diagnosis of social anxiety disorder. In *2011 IEEE International Conference on Bioinformatics and Biomedicine Workshops (BIBMW)*, pp. 639–640. IEEE, 2011.

8. Lodha, Priyanka, Ajay Talele, and Kishori Degaonkar. Diagnosis of alzheimer's disease using machine learning. In *2018 Fourth International Conference on Computing Communication Control and Automation (ICCUBEA)*, pp. 1–4. IEEE, 2018.

9. Bhoir, Smita, Jyoti Kundale, and Smita Bharne. Application of machine learning in fake news detection. In *Design of Intelligent Applications Using Machine Learning and Deep Learning Techniques*, pp. 165–183. Chapman and Hall/CRC, 2021.

10. Ambarkar, Smita Sanjay, Narendra M. Shekokar, Monika Mangla, and Rakhi Akhare. Authentication of broadcast news on social media using machine learning. In *Design of Intelligent Applications Using Machine Learning and Deep Learning Techniques*, pp. 185–194. Chapman and Hall/CRC, 2021.

11. Fatima, Iram, Hamid Mukhtar, Hafiz Farooq Ahmad, and Kashif Rajpoot. Analysis of user-generated content from online social communities to characterise and predict depression degree. *Journal of Information Science* 44, 5 (2018): 683–695.

12. Yazdavar, Amir Hossein, Hussein S. Al-Olimat, Monireh Ebrahimi, Goonmeet Bajaj, Tanvi Banerjee, Krishnaprasad Thirunarayan, Jyotishman Pathak, and Amit Sheth. Semi-supervised approach to monitoring clinical depressive symptoms in social media. In *Proceedings of the 2017 IEEE/ACM International Conference on Advances in Social Networks Analysis and Mining 2017*, pp. 1191–1198. 2017.

13. Goodwin, Travis R., Ramon Maldonado, and Sanda M. Harabagiu. Automatic recognition of symptom severity from psychiatric evaluation records. *Journal of Biomedical Informatics* 75 (2017): S71–S84.

14. Patterson, David A., and Richard N. Cloud. The application of artificial neural networks for outcome prediction in a cohort of severely mentally ill outpatients. *Journal of Technology in Human Services* 16, 2–3 (2000): 47–61.

15. Hirsch, Tad, Christina Soma, Kritzia Merced, Patty Kuo, Aaron Dembe, Derek D. Caperton, David C. Atkins, and Zac E. Imel. "It's hard to argue with a computer" Investigating Psychotherapists' Attitudes towards Automated Evaluation. In *Proceedings of the 2018 Designing Interactive Systems Conference*, pp. 559–571. 2018.

16. Wilbourne, Paula, Geralyn Dexter, and David Shoup. Research driven: Sibly and the transformation of mental health and wellness. In *Proceedings of the 12th EAI International Conference on Pervasive Computing Technologies for Healthcare*, pp. 389–391. 2018.

17. Paredes, Pablo, Ran Gilad-Bachrach, Mary Czerwinski, Asta Roseway, Kael Rowan, and Javier Hernandez. PopTherapy: Coping with stress through pop-culture. In *Proceedings of the 8th International Conference on Pervasive Computing Technologies for Healthcare*, pp. 109–117. 2014.

18. Aldarwish, Maryam Mohammed, and Hafiz Farooq Ahmad. Predicting depression levels using social media posts. In *2017 IEEE 13th International Symposium on Autonomous Decentralized System (ISADS)*, pp. 277–280. IEEE, 2017.

19. Hussain, Jamil, Maqbool Ali, Hafiz Syed Muhammad Bilal, Muhammad Afzal, Hafiz Farooq Ahmad, Oresti Banos, and Sungyoung Lee. SNS based predictive model for depression.

In *International Conference on Smart Homes and Health Telematics*, pp. 349–354. Springer, Cham, 2015.

20. De Choudhury, Munmun, Michael Gamon, Scott Counts, and Eric Horvitz. Predicting depression via social media. In *Seventh International AAAI Conference on Weblogs and Social Media*. 2013.

21. Gaur, Manas, Ugur Kursuncu, Amanuel Alambo, Amit Sheth, Raminta Daniulaityte, Krishnaprasad Thirunarayan, and Jyotishman Pathak. "Let Me Tell You About Your Mental Health!" Contextualized classification of Reddit Posts to DSM-5 for web-based intervention. In *Proceedings of the 27th ACM International Conference on Information and Knowledge Management*, pp. 753–762. 2018.

22. McManus, Kimberly, Emily K. Mallory, Rachel L. Goldfeder, Winston A. Haynes, and Jonathan D. Tatum. Mining Twitter data to improve detection of schizophrenia. *AMIA Summits on Translational Science Proceedings* 2015 (2015): 122.

23. Huang, Yo-Ping, Chao-Ying Huang, Shou-Ru Chen, Shen-Ing Liu, and Hui-Chun Huang. Discovering association rules from responded questionnaire for diagnosing geriatric depression. In *2012 ICME International Conference on Complex Medical Engineering (CME)*, pp. 343–348. IEEE, 2012.

24. Saraf, Vaibhav, Pallavi Chavan, and Ashish Jadhav. Deep Learning Challenges in Medical Imaging. In: *Advanced Computing Technologies and Applications*. Ed. by H. Vasudevan, A. Michalas, N. Shekokar, and M. Narvekar. Springer, Singapore, 2020, pp. 293–301.

25. Aksenova, Svetlana S. *Weka Explorer Tutorial*. School of Engineering and Computer Science, California State University, Long Beach, CA (2004).

26. Bhakta, Ishita, and Arkaprabha Sau. Prediction of depression among senior citizens using machine learning classifiers. *International Journal of Computer Applications* 144, 7 (2016): 11–16.

27. Bouckaert, Remco R. *Bayesian Network Classifiers in Weka*. Technical Report, Department of Computer Science, Waikato University, Hamilton, NZ 2004.

28. Komarek, Paul. *Logistic Regression for Data Mining and High-Dimensional Classification*. Carnegie Mellon University, Pittsburgh, PA (2004).

29. Mahajan, Manish, and Rajdev Tiwari. *Introduction to Soft Computing*. ACME Learning, New Delhi (2010).

30. Platt, John. *Sequential Minimal Optimization: A Fast Algorithm for Training Support Vector Machines*. In Technical Report MST-TR-98-14. Microsoft Research (1998).

31. Jena, Lambodar, and Narendra Ku Kamila. Distributed data mining classification algorithms for prediction of chronic-kidney-disease. *International Journal of Emerging Research in Management &Technology* 4, 11 (2015): 110–118.

18

Analysis of Ancient and Modern Meditation Techniques on Human Mind and Body and Their Effectiveness in COVID-19 Pandemic

Abhijeet Kushwah, Tirth Pandya, Prarthana Dhok, Prateek Koul, and Pallavi Vijay Chavan
Ramrao Adik Institute of Technology, D Y Patil Deemed to be University

Shreeraj Vijayan
Project Management Publicis Sapient

Vishal Shrivastava
Project Management CRG Solutions Singapore Pte Ltd.

CONTENTS

DOI: 10.1201/9781003283249-18

18.1 Introduction

During December 2019–January 2020, the World Health Organization picked up reports coming in from Wuhan about a cluster of pneumonia-related cases spreading in the People's Republic of China. On January 11, 2020, China reported its first death due to coronavirus disease (COVID-19) caused by the coronavirus (SARS-COV-2). On January 13, 2020, the first recorded case of COVID-19 outside the People's Republic of China was observed in Thailand. Soon after this, Japan and South Korea confirmed their first cases on January 15 and 20, 2020, respectively. This was the first time that the world was under the threat of a global pandemic. On January 23, 2020, China issued a lockdown to curb the spread of the virus in their country. Just one day later, the first COVID-19 case in Europe was recorded in France on January 24, 2020.

India's first reported case of COVID-19 was a 20-year-old student who had just returned to Kerala from Wuhan. Soon after this, the WHO declared COVID-19 a matter of international emergency. By February and March 2020, India observed a steep rise in the number of COVID-19 cases, with states like Maharashtra reporting about 100 daily cases. Schools and colleges were advised to stay closed, and a state of panic existed among citizens. In March, upon a call by Prime Minister Narendra Modi, a 14-hour-long voluntary lockdown called the 'Janta Curfew' was observed. However, looking at the rising number of cases, and with an intention to stop the spread of the virus, the government of India declared a nationwide lockdown from March 25, 2020 [1]. A national lockdown during the global pandemic was the need of the hour. However, it brought with it a lot of underlying problems such as unemployment, shutting down of shops and factories and huge pressure on Indian health infrastructure. It was during this time that people started noticing the effects of the global pandemic on their mental health, with a rise in anxiety, stress and pressure.

In month of April 2020, the government of Maharashtra, India, in association with the Brihanmumbai Municipal Corporation and MPower, a pioneer in Indian mental health care, had launched a toll-free 24×7 helpline number for people to reach out and seek help for any mental health concerns during the lockdown [2]. This helpline number received around 45,000 calls in just two months of its launch. These figures are evidence of the fact that we would feel low, with mixed emotions of anger, fear and anxiety because of the global pandemic.

One group of citizens whose mental health was particularly affected by the pandemic was the group within an age band of 17–22, particularly the students. This is because the national lockdown led to a closing of schools and colleges, crucial examinations were either canceled or postponed, and education shifted gears from offline to online teaching. Many students who had come to big cities for education moved back to their villages, from where attending online lectures was a distant possibility. While a lot of studies have been conducted in the past to understand the effects of mindfulness meditation on mental and physical health, and at the same time, many studies have also been conducted to understand the coronavirus, it is necessary to conduct a study that relates meditation and mindfulness and understand its impact during COVID-19.

All these factors combined led our team to undertake this study to determine if the simple techniques of meditation and music have an impact on the mental health of students and help them in reducing their stress, all during the time of the pandemic.

18.2 Meditation and Mindfulness

Meditation is a very ancient tradition. In many religions, meditation has been described as the medium to become one with the almighty 'paramatman'. As evident from ancient texts, meditation has been described as the path to self-knowledge and illumination, and a very important means to activate the chakras or energy centers of the body. Although meditation is an ancient art, not many people understand the impact of meditation and chanting on their mental health. The practice of meditation is usually divided into six types: mantra meditation, mindfulness meditation, spiritual meditation, focused meditation, movement meditation and transcendental meditation. Each technique has a unique way of execution: some simple and some complex.

Mantra meditation is one of the simplest forms of meditation. Mantra meditation is prominent in many teachings, including Hindu and Buddhist traditions. This type of meditation uses a repetitive sound to clear the mind. It can be a word, phrase, or sound, such as the popular 'Om' or the 'Mrityunjaya Mantra'. It doesn't matter if the mantra is spoken loudly or quietly. After chanting the mantra for Sometimes, one is more alert and in tune with one's environment. Some people enjoy mantra meditation because they find it easier to focus on a word than on their breath. This is also a good practice for people who don't like silence and enjoy repetition. At the same time, a newer, modern form of mindfulness meditation has developed that allows a person to be in a state of constant focus and be aware of their surroundings. Our study thus is concerned with getting to know the effect of both, the ancient form of chanting meditation and the newer form of mindfulness meditation during COVID-19. In order to conduct this study, the authors divided the process of the study into multiple phases as shown in Figure 18.1.

The authors first began the study by an extensive study of the available literature on the topic of meditation and mindfulness, and designed the experiment that has to be conducted. Then, we moved on to form the group of participants on whom the study was conducted for a month. As the study progressed, the authors collected data from the participants, and conducted data analysis and statistical tests to derive meaningful comparative results from the data. The authors then did a short time series modeling of the acquired data by using the Holt-Winters model. Finally, the authors went on to propose a system for effective meditation and analysis, called the MEDit application.

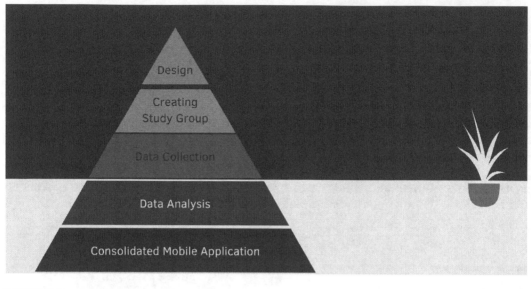

FIGURE 18.1
Flowchart of the study conducted.

18.3 Literature Survey

Many studies have been performed to understand the effects of meditation on the human mind and body. However, due to a constant change in the dynamics of the modern world, it is very important to keep up to date with the current mental health challenges. Therefore, before beginning our study, we did a brief survey of the present literature to understand all the past studies in this field. The findings of our literature survey are listed below.

A clinical intervention study with cancer patients conducted by Brown and Ryan (2003) shows that increases in mindfulness over time relate to declines in mood disturbance and stress [3]. A study conducted by Keng et al. (2011) suggests that mindfulness and its cultivation facilitate adaptive psychological functioning [4]. The findings of the study conducted by Stewart et al. (2018) supported their study hypothesis that choral singing is associated with enhanced health and well-being, in particular with the physical, psychological and social dimensions of well-being [5].

Findings by Adam Burke et al. suggest that meditation appears to provide an accessible, self-care resource that has potential value for mental health, behavioral self-regulation and integrative medical care [6]. There were significant reductions in anxiety and depressive symptoms from baseline to the end of treatment as reported by the study conducted by Susan Evans et al. [7].

Finally, as reported by Doug Oman et al., Research on the Mantram Repetition Program has documented reductions in posttraumatic stress symptoms, insomnia, hyperarousal and depression, as well as enhancement of quality of life, self-efficacy and mindfulness. Mantram repetition may possess comparative advantages for managing symptoms of various mental health conditions, including posttraumatic stress disorder, HIV/AIDS, cancer and chronic diseases [8].

18.4 Foundation of Study

After getting a final approval to conduct the study from our institute, and thoroughly analyzing the literature available, we moved on to design the experiment needed to conduct the study. For this, we decided to create a cohort study group by randomly dividing the total number of participants into two groups. The first group was to take part in mantra meditation and the second group would take part in mindfulness meditation. We decided to use music which is readily available in the public domain so that everyone could have access to it. We also finalized the Short Stress Overload Scale (SOS-S), the Brief Irritability Test (BITe) and the Scale of Positive and Negative Experience (SPANE) as a means of measuring stress, irritability and positive and negative emotions in participants for 30 days.

We first designed a WhatsApp message and after getting approval from our project guide and the department of our institution, we floated the WhatsApp message across five departments present in our college. The message was shared with the Heads of various departments in the college, who then shared the message with respective class counselors, who then shared the message with the students across the college. The message contained a detailed description of the study we were going to perform, and also included disclaimers regarding the duration of the study. 194 participants initially joined the WhatsApp group to take part in the study. Then, we conducted an online zoom meeting with all the participants and once again explained the course of this study to them. After the meeting, the participants were told to fill out a Google Form and data regarding their age, gender and phone numbers were taken for future reference. Out of the 194 participants who had joined the group, only 80 participants finally filled the form, and only they were included in the study. These 40 participants were then randomly assigned to one of the two groups: the ancient mantra meditation group and the modern mindfulness group by using a Python random number generator script.

By the end of the 30 days of the study, the number of participants who completed the study successfully was reduced to 20 participants in each group (40 total out of 80). Therefore, the final data analysis was only conducted on the data available from these 40 participants.

Figure 18.2 summarizes the flow of addition and removal of participants during the duration of our study.

Table 18.1 summarizes the demographic details of the 40 participants who successfully conducted the study and were included for final evaluation.

18.5 Data Collection

The participants participating in the study were briefed about both forms of meditation via an online zoom meeting. For the ancient group, we assigned the 'Maha Mrityunjay Mantra' chant to be chanted while meditation, which was obtained from the YouTube channel of Voices of Isha. Participants in the mindfulness group were assigned to a zen meditation music. Participants of both groups had to meditate by listening to the respective music assigned to them for 10 minutes daily for a period of 30 days. Participants in the ancient mantra meditation group were assigned IDs of a1, a2, a3, ..., a20; similarly, the

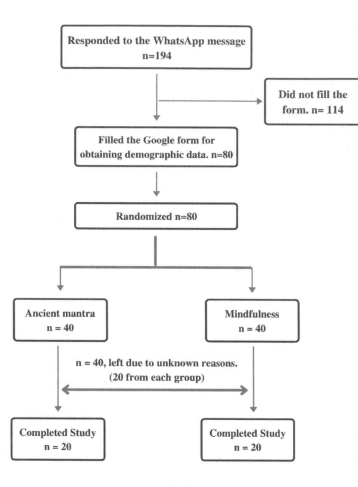

FIGURE 18.2
Flow of participants for the duration of the study.

TABLE 18.1

Demographic Details of Participants Completing the Study

Study Variable	Ancient	Modern
Age Band (n [%])		
18–20	14 (70%)	13 (65%)
21–22	6 (30%)	7 (35%)
Gender (n [%])		
Male	7 (35%)	5 (25%)
Female	13 (65%)	15 (75%)

participants in the modern mindfulness group were assigned the ID of m1, m2, m3, .., m20, respectively.

The participants were also made to fill out three forms daily. Before starting the meditation, the participants filled out the questionnaire on SOS-S. After ten minutes of meditation, participants from both groups filled the questionnaire on BITe. Finally, participants from both groups filled the questionnaire on SPANE, after around 5–6 hours of their meditation session.

18.5.1 SOS-S

Stress of the participants was measured using SOS-S, which basically looks for 'stress over-load', which is defined as a state that occurs when demands overwhelm the resources [9]. In this ten-item SOS-S scale, the respondents used a five-point Likert scale (1=not at all and 5=a lot) to record their subjective feelings over the past week. However, for the pur-pose of our study, we asked the participants to fill out the questionnaire daily before they start with their meditation.

Below is the questionnaire that was shared with the participants to be filled on the SOS-S scale before the beginning of their meditation session.

Q.1 In the past day, have you felt inadequate?

Q.2 In the past day, have you felt swamped by your responsibilities?

Q.3 In the past day, have you felt that the odds were against you?

Q.4 In the past day, have you felt that there wasn't enough time to get to everything?

Q.5 In the past day, have you felt like nothing was going right?

Q.6 In the past day, have you felt like you were rushed?

Q.7 In the past day, have you felt like there was no escape?

Q.8 In the past day, have you felt like things kept piling up?

Q.9 In the past day, have you felt like just giving up?

Q.10 In the past day, have you felt like you were carrying a heavy load?

Questions 1, 3, 5, 7 and 9 in this scale are items related to personal vulnerability while Questions 2, 4, 6, 8 and 10 in this scale are items related to Event Load. The maximum value for this scale is 50, and the minimum value is 10. The larger the total score, the larger the stress overload and vice versa.

18.5.2 BITe

BITe was used to measure the extent to which participants experienced irritation in their day-to-day life, on a daily basis. The BITe is a new five-item scale, suitable for use among both males and females [10]. The respondents of this scale use a six-point Likert scale (6=always, 1=never), and identify how frequently they associate with each statement of the questionnaire. The original scale asks the respondents to fill the questionnaire by look-ing at their experience over the past two weeks. However, for the purpose of our study, the participants were asked to fill out the questionnaire daily, after completing their medita-tion session. An average of all the values filled on the scale by the participants was aver-aged out to calculate their mean BITe score on a daily basis. The greater the value that is recorded on the BITe scale, the greater their irritability.

Below is the questionnaire that was shared with the participants to be filled on the BITe scale after completion of their meditation session.

Q. On a scale of 1–6, how would you answer the following questions:

1. I have been grumpy.
2. I have been feeling like I might snap.
3. Other people have been getting on my nerves.

4. Things have been bothering me more than they normally do.

5. I have been feeling irritable.

18.5.3 SPANE

SPANE was used to measure the levels of positive and negative emotions experienced by the participants over the course of the study. SPANE is a 12 item scale which contains 6 items to assess positive emotions and the other 6 items to assess negative emotions [11]. The respondent uses a five-point Likert scale (1=very rarely or never, 5=very often or always) to indicate how frequently they have experienced each item. The positive emotions, measured as SPANE-P ranges from 6 to 30, and the negative emotions range from 6 to 30, in a negative manner. The final balanced score, SPANE-B is calculated by subtracting the SPANE-N score from the SPANE-P score, which can finally range from –24 (unhappiest) to 24 (happiest). For the purpose of our study, the participants were asked to fill the SPANE questionnaire daily, after around 5–6 hours of the completion of their meditation session.

Below is the questionnaire that was shared with the participants to be filled on the SPANE scale after 5 to 6 hours of completion of their morning meditation session.

Q. On a scale of 1–5, how have you been thinking and experiencing the following emotions?

1. Positive

2. Negative

3. Good

4. Bad

5. Pleasant

6. Unpleasant

7. Happy

8. Sad

9. Afraid

10. Joyful

11. Angry

12. Contented

Finally, the data obtained from both ancient mantra meditation (a_i, i=1, 2, 3, ..., 20) and modern mindfulness (m_i, i=1, 2, 3, ..., 20) using the above three scales for a period of 30 days was analyzed and statistical tests on the obtained data were performed.

18.6 Data Analysis

For the sake of convenience and continuity, the ancient mantra group was labeled as 'a' group, and the mindfulness group was labeled as the 'm' group. Similarly, the final twenty participants of the ancient group are labeled as a1, a2, a3,..., a20, and the final twenty participants of the modern group are labeled as m1, m2, m3,..., m20, respectively. Also, 'aSOSS', 'aBITe', 'aSPANEP', 'aSPANEN' and 'aSPANEB' refer to the SOS-S score, the BITe score, the SPANE-P score, the SPANE-N score and the SPANE-B score of the participants of the ancient mantra meditation group. Similarly, 'mSOSS', 'mBITe', 'mSPANEP', 'mSPANEN' and 'mSPANEB' refer to the SOS-S score, the BITe score, the SPANE-P score, the SPANE-N score and the SPANE-B score of the participants of the modern mindfulness meditation group. All candidate data was analyzed using open source libraries like NumPy and SciPy in Python using the Jupyter Notebook tool.

18.6.1 Data Description

The describe() method in Python is used and applied on the data set to get a generalized description of the collected data sample. The results of the described method are listed below (Figures 18.3–18.12).

	a1	a2	a3	a4	a5	a6	a7	a8	a9	a10	a11	a12	a13	a14	a15	a16	a17	a18	a19	a20
count	30.000000	30.000000	30.000000	30.000000	30.000000	30.000000	30.000000	30.000000	30.000000	30.000000	30.000000	30.00000	30.000000	30.000000	30.000000	30.000000	30.000000	30.000000	30.000000	30.000000
mean	31.900000	32.533333	31.866667	30.566667	30.933333	28.200000	29.200000	32.066667	30.833333	28.80000	26.466667	30.10000	30.033333	30.233333	32.033333	30.066667	29.766667	32.200000	30.600000	29.633333
std	6.498541	5.733948	6.619372	5.529441	6.236341	3.305188	4.581823	5.125550	5.252804	4.55162	3.919301	3.72642	4.514218	4.665969	4.582450	4.898510	3.390487	4.475219	5.069177	4.206771
min	20.000000	23.000000	20.000000	20.000000	20.000000	23.000000	20.000000	20.000000	20.000000	20.00000	20.000000	20.000000	20.000000	20.000000	22.000000	22.000000	25.000000	20.000000	20.000000	20.000000
25%	25.250000	27.250000	25.250000	25.250000	25.250000	25.000000	25.000000	28.000000	26.250000	25.25000	25.250000	27.25000	26.250000	26.000000	28.250000	25.000000	27.000000	28.250000	27.000000	26.250000
50%	34.000000	34.000000	34.000000	32.000000	32.000000	28.500000	28.000000	34.000000	31.000000	28.50000	29.000000	30.50000	30.000000	32.000000	33.000000	30.000000	30.000000	34.000000	31.000000	30.000000
75%	37.750000	37.000000	37.000000	34.000000	35.750000	30.750000	33.000000	36.000000	35.750000	33.50000	31.750000	33.50000	34.000000	34.000000	35.750000	34.000000	32.000000	35.750000	35.000000	32.000000
max	41.000000	41.000000	41.000000	40.000000	41.000000	35.000000	39.000000	40.000000	40.000000	36.00000	36.000000	36.000000	37.000000	38.000000	39.000000	38.000000	36.000000	39.000000	39.000000	37.000000

FIGURE 18.3
Description of SOS-S data collected for ancient mantra meditation participants.

	a1	a2	a3	a4	a5	a6	a7	a8	a9	a10	a11	a12	a13	a14	a15	a16	a17	a18	a19	a20
count	30.000000	30.000000	30.000000	30.000000	30.000000	30.000000	30.000000	30.000000	30.000000	30.000000	30.000000	30.000000	30.000000	30.000000	30.000000	30.000000	30.000000	30.000000	30.000000	30.000000
mean	3.680000	3.545667	3.653333	3.406667	3.480000	3.493333	3.606667	3.486667	3.586667	3.366667	3.673333	3.193333	3.440000	3.093333	3.613333	3.493333	3.166667	3.600000	3.480000	3.326667
std	0.965044	0.798169	0.983636	0.830513	0.788688	0.814915	0.904370	0.789034	0.792968	0.739214	0.917994	0.602206	0.717062	0.562568	0.688694	0.698241	0.860093	0.584277	0.709735	0.613227
min	2.400000	2.200000	2.200000	2.200000	2.200000	2.400000	2.200000	2.200000	2.200000	2.200000	2.200000	2.400000	2.400000	2.200000	2.400000	2.000000	2.000000	2.600000	2.400000	2.400000
25%	2.800000	3.000000	2.800000	2.650000	2.800000	2.850000	2.800000	2.800000	3.000000	2.800000	2.800000	2.800000	3.050000	2.800000	3.050000	3.000000	2.600000	3.050000	3.000000	3.000000
50%	4.200000	3.500000	4.200000	3.100000	3.400000	3.000000	3.800000	3.600000	3.600000	3.300000	4.100000	3.000000	3.500000	3.000000	3.600000	3.700000	3.000000	3.400000	3.400000	3.400000
75%	4.400000	4.200000	4.400000	4.200000	4.200000	4.200000	4.200000	4.000000	4.000000	4.000000	4.400000	3.550000	4.000000	3.550000	4.000000	4.000000	3.800000	3.950000	4.000000	3.600000
max	5.200000	5.200000	5.200000	4.600000	4.800000	5.000000	5.200000	5.200000	5.200000	4.800000	5.000000	4.400000	4.000000	4.600000	5.000000	4.600000	4.400000	4.600000	4.800000	4.400000

FIGURE 18.4
Description of BITe data collected for ancient mantra meditation participants.

	a1	a2	a3	a4	a5	a6	a7	a8	a9	a10	a11	a12	a13	a14	a15	a16	a17	a18	a19	a20
count	30.000000	30.000000	30.000000	30.000000	30.000000	30.000000	30.000000	30.000000	30.000000	30.000000	30.000000	30.000000	30.000000	30.000000	30.000000	30.000000	30.000000	30.000000	30.000000	30.000000
mean	17.300000	16.933333	17.300000	17.766667	16.766667	17.633333	17.300000	17.033333	17.300000	17.233333	17.033333	17.166667	16.933333	16.20000	17.300000	17.466667	17.700000	17.600000	17.566667	17.833333
std	4.027064	3.628749	4.027064	3.892354	3.308123	2.525502	4.027064	2.894605	4.027064	3.673609	3.448971	3.639660	3.465295	2.75931	2.818045	3.115406	3.364623	2.964832	3.400642	2.937080
min	13.000000	13.000000	13.000000	13.000000	13.000000	13.000000	13.000000	13.000000	13.000000	13.000000	13.000000	13.000000	12.000000	13.000000	13.000000	13.000000	12.000000	13.000000	13.000000	13.000000
25%	14.000000	14.000000	14.000000	15.000000	14.000000	16.000000	14.000000	14.250000	14.000000	14.000000	14.000000	14.000000	14.000000	14.00000	15.000000	15.000000	15.000000	15.000000	15.000000	15.250000
50%	15.000000	15.000000	17.000000	17.000000	17.000000	17.000000	15.000000	16.000000	15.000000	15.000000	15.000000	15.000000	15.000000	15.50000	17.000000	17.000000	18.000000	17.500000	16.500000	17.500000
75%	21.000000	21.000000	21.000000	21.000000	19.750000	19.000000	21.000000	19.000000	21.000000	20.000000	19.000000	19.750000	19.000000	18.00000	19.000000	19.750000	20.000000	20.000000	20.500000	20.750000
max	24.000000	24.000000	24.000000	24.000000	23.000000	22.000000	24.000000	23.000000	24.000000	24.000000	24.000000	24.000000	24.000000	22.00000	23.000000	24.000000	24.000000	24.000000	24.000000	23.000000

FIGURE 18.5
Description of SPANE-P data collected for ancient mantra meditation participants.

	a1	a2	a3	a4	a5	a6	a7	a8	a9	a10	a11	a12	a13	a14	a15	a16	a17	a18	a19	a20
count	30.000000	30.000000	30.000000	30.000000	30.000000	30.000000	30.000000	30.000000	30.000000	30.000000	30.000000	30.000000	30.00000	30.000000	30.000000	30.000000	30.000000	30.000000	30.000000	30.000000
mean	16.166667	17.966667	17.333333	17.600000	17.600000	16.933333	16.400000	17.766667	18.033333	17.700000	16.066667	17.833333	18.30000	18.000000	17.700000	17.566667	18.533333	17.433333	16.600000	17.533333
std	3.639660	2.645634	3.345953	3.380639	2.283373	2.851900	3.654001	3.125902	3.145696	3.385058	3.258234	3.484778	3.26161	2.505167	2.692903	3.255565	3.308644	3.070250	3.244093	2.542512
min	12.000000	12.000000	12.000000	12.000000	12.000000	12.000000	12.000000	12.000000	12.000000	12.000000	12.000000	12.000000	12.00000	12.000000	12.000000	12.000000	12.000000	12.000000	12.000000	12.000000
25%	15.000000	16.000000	15.000000	15.000000	16.000000	15.000000	15.000000	15.000000	17.000000	15.000000	15.000000	15.000000	16.00000	17.000000	15.000000	16.000000	15.000000	17.000000	15.000000	15.000000
50%	18.500000	18.000000	17.500000	18.000000	18.000000	17.500000	16.000000	18.000000	18.000000	18.000000	16.000000	18.000000	18.00000	18.000000	18.000000	17.500000	19.000000	18.000000	18.000000	17.000000
75%	21.000000	19.000000	19.000000	20.750000	19.000000	18.750000	21.000000	20.000000	20.000000	20.750000	21.000000	20.750000	21.00000	20.000000	19.000000	19.750000	20.750000	19.750000	21.000000	20.000000
max	24.000000	23.000000	24.000000	24.000000	22.000000	22.000000	24.000000	24.000000	24.000000	24.000000	24.000000	24.000000	25.00000	25.000000	23.000000	24.000000	24.000000	24.000000	25.000000	22.000000

FIGURE 18.6
Description of SPANE-N data collected for ancient mantra meditation participants.

	a1	a2	a3	a4	a5	a6	a7	a8	a9	a10	a11	a12	a13	a14	a15	a16	a17	a18	a19	a20
count	30.000000	30.000000	30.000000	30.000000	30.000000	30.000000	30.000000	30.000000	30.000000	30.000000	30.000000	30.000000	30.000000	30.000000	30.000000	30.000000	30.000000	30.000000	30.000000	30.000000
mean	-0.866667	-1.033333	-0.033333	0.166667	0.000000	0.000000	-0.733333	-0.733333	-0.466667	-1.033333	-0.666667	-1.366667	-1.900000	-0.400000	-0.100000	-0.633333	0.166667	-1.033333	0.300000
std	7.281215	5.702236	6.769523	6.581496	4.528674	4.654103	7.288067	5.826945	6.612075	5.511175	6.552255	6.524950	6.183065	4.573904	5.021334	5.689373	6.201244	5.821640	5.945055	4.830265
min	-11.000000	-10.000000	-11.000000	-11.000000	-9.000000	-7.000000	-11.000000	-11.000000	-11.000000	-11.000000	-11.000000	-11.000000	-10.000000	-9.000000	-8.000000	-11.000000	-11.000000	-12.000000	-12.000000	-7.000000
25%	-7.000000	-6.750000	-5.750000	-4.000000	-4.750000	-3.000000	-7.750000	-5.000000	-6.000000	-5.750000	-6.000000	-5.000000	-6.750000	-5.000000	-4.000000	-5.000000	-5.000000	-3.750000	-5.750000	-4.000000
50%	-3.000000	-3.000000	-0.500000	-1.000000	-2.500000	0.000000	-3.000000	-1.500000	-3.000000	-2.500000	-3.000000	-3.000000	-2.500000	-2.000000	-1.500000	-0.500000	-1.500000	-1.000000	-2.000000	-1.000000
75%	6.000000	5.000000	6.000000	6.000000	4.000000	3.750000	6.000000	4.000000	5.750000	6.000000	4.750000	6.000000	3.250000	1.750000	3.750000	6.000000	4.500000	6.000000	3.750000	5.000000
max	12.000000	6.000000	12.000000	12.000000	6.000000	10.000000	12.000000	11.000000	12.000000	12.000000	12.000000	12.000000	9.000000	6.000000	9.000000	12.000000	11.000000	10.000000	10.000000	11.000000

FIGURE 18.7

Description of SPANE-B data collected for ancient mantra meditation participants.

	m1	m2	m3	m4	m5	m6	m7	m8	m9	m10	m11	m12	m13	m14	m15	m16	m17	m18	m19	m20
count	30.000000	30.000000	30.000000	30.000000	30.000000	30.000000	30.000000	30.000000	30.000000	30.000000	30.000000	30.000000	30.000000	30.000000	30.000000	30.000000	30.000000	30.000000	30.000000	30.000000
mean	31.400000	31.566667	29.000000	29.766667	30.966667	30.700000	31.633333	31.633333	31.933333	31.733333	29.166667	29.233333	29.033333	31.300000	30.700000	31.100000	26.733333	28.466667	29.233333	31.066667
std	5.116572	5.473324	4.205948	4.868501	5.798236	5.072917	4.766864	4.601970	5.016754	4.919563	4.009328	2.955806	3.614943	3.45563	3.196442	4.285903	3.741043	3.530491	2.541534	3.628749
min	23.000000	24.000000	23.000000	23.000000	23.000000	23.000000	25.000000	24.000000	26.000000	25.000000	23.000000	25.000000	23.000000	25.000000	26.000000	21.000000	21.000000	24.000000	26.000000
25%	27.000000	27.000000	26.250000	26.000000	25.250000	26.000000	27.000000	27.000000	27.000000	27.000000	26.000000	26.000000	26.000000	28.000000	28.000000	26.250000	25.250000	25.250000	28.000000	27.250000
50%	34.000000	33.000000	29.000000	28.500000	31.500000	30.000000	33.500000	32.000000	34.000000	34.000000	30.000000	30.500000	28.500000	33.000000	31.000000	32.500000	29.000000	29.000000	30.000000	31.500000
75%	35.000000	36.750000	32.750000	34.000000	36.000000	35.000000	35.000000	35.000000	36.000000	36.000000	33.000000	32.000000	31.000000	34.000000	33.000000	34.000000	31.000000	31.000000	31.750000	33.750000
max	39.000000	40.000000	39.000000	39.000000	40.000000	39.000000	39.000000	39.000000	39.000000	39.000000	36.000000	34.000000	36.000000	37.000000	38.000000	37.000000	36.000000	36.000000	33.000000	39.000000

FIGURE 18.8

Description of SOS-S data collected for modern mindfulness meditation participants.

	m1	m2	m3	m4	m5	m6	m7	m8	m9	m10	m11	m12	m13	m14	m15	m16	m17	m18	m19	m20
count	30.000000	30.000000	30.000000	30.000000	30.000000	30.000000	30.000000	30.000000	30.000000	30.000000	30.000000	30.000000	30.000000	30.000000	30.000000	30.000000	30.000000	30.000000	30.000000	30.000000
mean	3.473333	3.635333	3.626667	3.593333	3.693333	3.446667	3.473333	3.586667	3.513333	3.553333	3.060000	3.013333	2.906667	3.013333	3.126667	3.226667	3.173333	3.080000	3.306667	3.266667
std	0.732466	0.832252	0.897096	0.859002	0.910629	0.704044	0.697747	0.799885	0.795090	0.780245	0.268565	0.416664	0.359896	0.448548	0.440950	0.500496	0.532365	0.502682	0.529758	0.407967
min	2.200000	2.200000	2.200000	2.200000	2.400000	2.400000	2.400000	2.400000	2.400000	2.400000	2.600000	2.400000	2.200000	2.200000	2.200000	2.200000	2.200000	2.000000	2.400000
25%	2.850000	2.800000	2.800000	2.600000	2.800000	2.900000	2.800000	2.800000	2.800000	2.800000	2.850000	2.500000	2.400000	2.650000	2.800000	3.000000	2.800000	2.800000	2.900000	3.000000
50%	3.700000	4.000000	4.100000	4.000000	4.200000	3.500000	3.600000	3.800000	3.700000	3.800000	3.000000	3.000000	2.800000	3.000000	3.200000	3.200000	3.200000	3.000000	3.400000	3.300000
75%	4.150000	4.200000	4.400000	4.350000	4.400000	4.200000	4.200000	4.200000	4.200000	4.200000	3.200000	3.400000	3.400000	3.350000	3.400000	3.400000	3.550000	3.400000	3.600000	3.600000
max	4.600000	4.800000	4.800000	4.800000	5.000000	4.400000	4.400000	4.600000	4.600000	4.800000	3.800000	3.800000	4.200000	4.200000	3.800000	4.200000	4.400000	4.000000	4.200000	4.000000

FIGURE 18.9

Description of BITe data collected for modern mindfulness meditation participants.

	m1	m2	m3	m4	m5	m6	m7	m8	m9	m10	m11	m12	m13	m14	m15	m16	m17	m18	m19	m20
count	30.000000	30.000000	30.000000	30.000000	30.000000	30.000000	30.000000	30.000000	30.000000	30.000000	30.000000	30.000000	30.000000	30.000000	30.000000	30.000000	30.000000	30.000000	30.000000	30.000000
mean	17.466667	19.133333	17.200000	17.400000	17.233333	17.166667	17.066667	17.200000	17.300000	17.600000	17.566667	18.466667	17.800000	16.133333	17.000000	16.566667	17.200000	18.766667	15.500000	16.000000
std	3.234868	2.725782	3.556441	3.882765	3.490710	3.464779	3.372642	3.536997	3.611762	2.647867	2.884959	2.060009	2.618236	2.648791	3.028500	2.254242	2.496895	2.860954	2.738613	2.851072
min	13.000000	15.000000	13.000000	13.000000	13.000000	13.000000	13.000000	13.000000	14.000000	12.000000	14.000000	11.000000	12.000000	12.000000	13.000000	13.000000	12.000000	10.000000	14.000000
25%	15.000000	17.250000	14.000000	14.000000	14.000000	14.000000	14.000000	14.000000	14.000000	15.000000	15.000000	17.000000	16.000000	14.000000	15.000000	15.250000	15.250000	13.250000	16.250000
50%	17.500000	19.000000	15.000000	15.000000	16.000000	15.000000	15.000000	15.000000	15.500000	16.500000	17.000000	18.000000	18.000000	16.000000	16.000000	15.000000	16.500000	19.000000	15.000000	16.000000
75%	19.000000	21.000000	21.000000	21.000000	21.000000	21.000000	21.000000	20.750000	20.750000	20.750000	20.000000	20.000000	18.000000	19.750000	18.000000	19.000000	21.000000	17.000000	19.750000
max	23.000000	24.000000	28.000000	24.000000	23.000000	28.000000	29.000000	24.000000	24.000000	22.000000	23.000000	22.000000	22.000000	22.000000	23.000000	22.000000	22.000000	23.000000	21.000000	21.000000

FIGURE 18.10

Description of SPANE-P data collected for modern mindfulness meditation participants.

	m1	m2	m3	m4	m5	m6	m7	m8	m9	m10	m11	m12	m13	m14	m15	m16	m17	m18	m19	m20
count	30.000000	30.000000	30.000000	30.000000	30.000000	30.000000	30.000000	30.000000	30.000000	30.000000	30.000000	30.000000	30.0000	30.000000	30.000000	30.000000	30.000000	30.000000	30.000000	30.000000
mean	18.266667	17.000000	17.400000	16.666667	15.433333	18.666667	18.966667	19.233333	18.366667	16.633333	16.033333	17.366667	16.500000	16.366667	18.100000	17.900000	16.366667	17.166667	17.266667	16.900000
std	3.433439	3.026599	3.326042	3.457464	3.677609	3.262465	3.242852	3.158823	2.511811	2.769381	2.476283	1.902609	2.2705	2.484203	2.090207	1.988762	1.771096	2.478544	2.476357	2.233764
min	12.000000	12.000000	12.000000	12.000000	12.000000	14.000000	15.000000	15.000000	15.000000	14.000000	13.000000	12.000000	14.000000	13.000000	15.000000	12.000000	13.000000	14.000000
25%	15.250000	15.000000	15.000000	16.000000	15.000000	15.250000	15.250000	16.250000	16.000000	16.000000	16.000000	15.000000	15.000000	15.250000	17.000000	17.000000	15.250000	15.000000	17.000000
50%	19.000000	17.000000	18.000000	19.000000	18.000000	18.500000	19.500000	20.000000	18.500000	18.000000	16.000000	16.500000	16.000000	18.000000	18.500000	18.000000	17.000000	17.000000	19.000000
75%	21.000000	20.750000	20.750000	21.000000	21.000000	21.000000	21.000000	21.000000	21.000000	20.000000	16.750000	18.000000	18.000000	20.000000	19.000000	20.000000	19.000000	19.000000	20.750000
max	24.000000	24.000000	23.000000	24.000000	24.000000	24.000000	24.000000	23.000000	24.000000	24.000000	21.000000	21.000000	21.000000	22.000000	21.000000	22.000000	22.000000	22.000000	22.000000

FIGURE 18.11

Description of SPANE-N data collected for modern mindfulness meditation participants.

	m1	m2	m3	m4	m5	m6	m7	m8	m9	m10	m11	m12	m13	m14	m15	m16	m17	m18	m19	m20
count	30.000000	30.000000	30.000000	30.000000	30.000000	30.000000	30.000000	30.000000	30.000000	30.000000	30.000000	30.000000	30.000000	30.000000	30.00000	30.000000	30.000000	30.000000	30.000000	30.00000
mean	-0.800000	2.133333	-0.200000	-1.266667	-1.200000	-1.900000	-1.900000	-2.033333	-1.066667	-1.033333	-0.466667	1.100000	1.300000	-0.233333	-1.10000	-1.333333	-1.166667	1.500000	-1.766667	-0.90000
std	6.353929	4.960070	6.835543	7.096085	6.514791	6.516557	6.439908	6.498248	5.759151	5.255430	4.761435	3.376598	3.549782	4.199206	4.67827	5.707712	3.414809	4.613324	4.500447	3.65922
min	-11.000000	-5.000000	-9.000000	-11.000000	-11.000000	-11.000000	-11.000000	-11.000000	-8.000000	-8.000000	-9.000000	-5.000000	-8.000000	-7.000000	-9.00000	-8.000000	-7.000000	-7.000000	-10.000000	-7.00000
25%	-3.750000	-1.750000	-6.750000	-7.000000	-7.000000	-7.000000	-7.000000	-7.000000	-6.000000	-2.750000	-4.000000	-1.750000	-1.000000	-3.000000	-5.00000	-4.000000	-4.000000	-2.000000	-5.000000	-4.00000
50%	-2.500000	0.500000	-2.000000	-4.000000	-2.500000	-4.000000	-4.000000	-4.000000	-3.000000	-3.000000	0.000000	0.500000	2.000000	-1.000000	-1.50000	-2.000000	-1.000000	2.000000	-2.000000	-2.00000
75%	3.750000	6.000000	5.000000	6.750000	6.000000	5.750000	5.500000	5.000000	5.000000	4.750000	3.750000	4.000000	3.750000	3.500000	2.75000	0.750000	2.000000	6.000000	2.000000	2.00000
max	11.000000	12.000000	11.000000	12.000000	11.000000	7.000000	7.000000	8.000000	7.000000	7.000000	7.000000	7.000000	8.000000	6.000000	7.00000	7.000000	5.000000	8.000000	6.000000	6.00000

FIGURE 18.12
Description of SPANE-B data collected for modern mindfulness meditation participants.

```
               Ancient  Modern
   Male            7       5
   Female         13      15
   (0.11904761904761904, 0.7300697275800421, 1, array([[ 6.,   6.],
          [14., 14.]])))
   P-value : 0.7300697275800421
```

FIGURE 18.13
Contingency table and *p*-value for chi-square test of independence between groups and their gender.

```
               Ancient  Modern
   18-20          15      12
   21-22           5       8
   (0.45584045584045585, 0.4995743849807205, 1, array([[13.5, 13.5],
          [ 6.5,  6.5]]))
   P-value : 0.4995743849807205
```

FIGURE 18.14
Contingency table and *p*-value for chi-square test of independence between groups and their age band.

18.6.2 Chi-Square Test for Independence of Groups

The chi-square test was conducted to determine a relationship between the demographics of the groups and to test whether the two groups were similar in nature to each other.

18.6.2.1 *Chi-Square Test for Determining a Relation between the Groups and Their Gender*

The contingency table built for the test is shown in Figure 18.13. As the $p > 0.05$, we can conclude that the meditation groups and gender are independent of each other.

18.6.2.2 *Chi-Square Test for Determining a Relation between the Groups and Their Age*

The contingency table built for the test is shown in Figure 18.14. As the $p > 0.05$, we can conclude that the meditation groups and age are independent of each other.

18.6.3 Data Visualization for the Ancient and Modern Meditation

At first, we plot the progression in SOS-S values as recorded by the ancient mantra and modern mindfulness groups. Looking at Figures 18.15 and 18.16, we can observe that both the ancient and modern meditation groups display a decrease in SOS-S values which were recorded for a duration of 30 days. For both the groups, we can see that the values keep fluctuating for an initial phase, but both groups see a steady decline in the SOS-S values

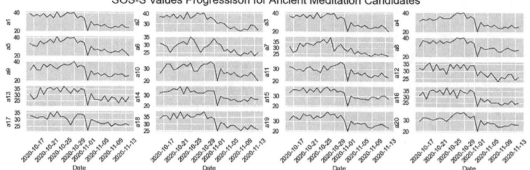

FIGURE 18.15
SOS-S value progression for ancient meditation participants.

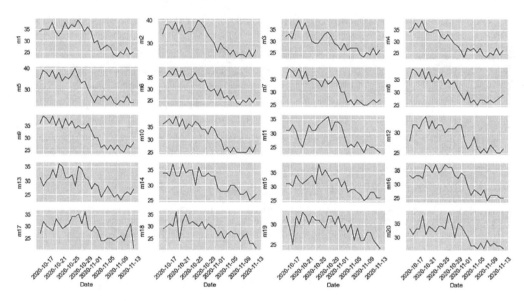

FIGURE 18.16
SOS-S value progression for modern meditation participants.

from around the third week of meditation. Although none of the groups follow a definite pattern. This indicates that even though the SOS-S values keep decreasing for both groups, their effect is different in each participant of the two groups.

Now, let us plot the progression of BITe score of participants in ancient and modern meditation groups for the duration of this study. As in Figures 18.17 and 18.18, we can see that the BITe score of participants in both groups shows a decreasing graph. This suggests that both meditation techniques were helpful in lowering the irritability of participants. However, we can also see from the plots that ancient meditation participants saw a gradual decrease in their BITe score; however, modern meditation participants showed a lot of fluctuations in their decreasing trend.

In Figures 18.19 and 18.20, we plot the progression of SPANE-P values in ancient and modern groups, respectively. Similarly, we plot the progression of SPANE-N values in

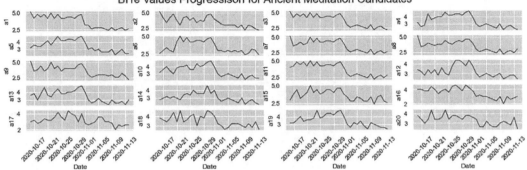

FIGURE 18.17
BITe value progression for ancient meditation participants.

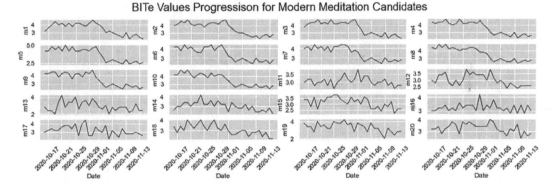

FIGURE 18.18
BITe value progression for modern meditation participants.

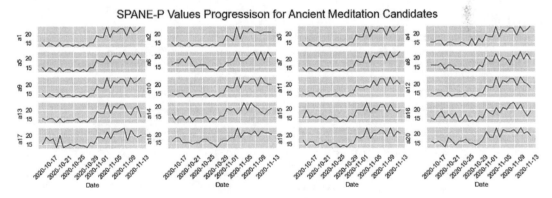

FIGURE 18.19
SPANE-P value progression for ancient meditation participants.

Figures 18.21 and 18.22 and SPANE-B values in Figures 18.23 and 18.24 for both the ancient and modern groups, respectively.

Looking at the SPANE-P, SPANE-N and SPANE-B plots, we can see that the SPANE-P values show a more gradual rise in value in ancient meditation groups than in modern meditation groups. Both groups also show a decreasing graph in SPANE-N values and an

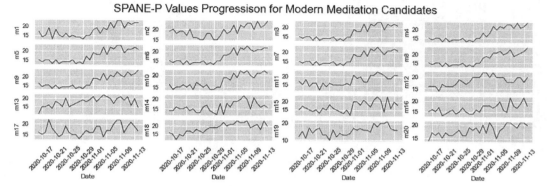

FIGURE 18.20
SPANE-P value progression for modern meditation participants.

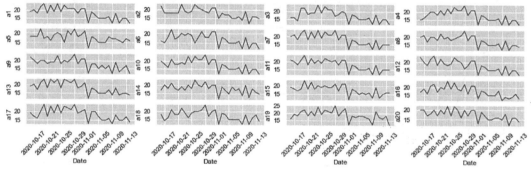

FIGURE 18.21
SPANE-N value progression for ancient meditation participants.

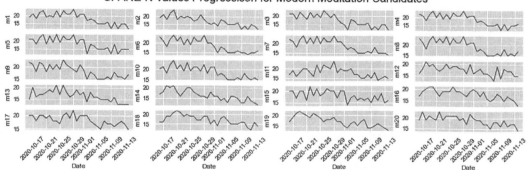

FIGURE 18.22
SPANE-N value progression for modern meditation participants.

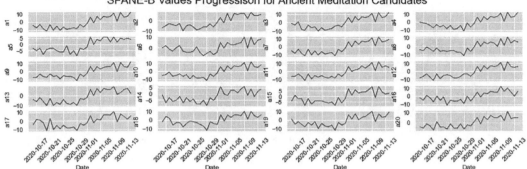

FIGURE 18.23
SPANE-B value progression for ancient meditation participants.

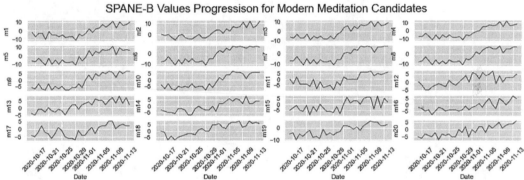

FIGURE 18.24
SPANE-B value progression for modern meditation participants.

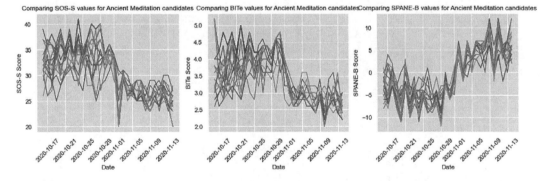

FIGURE 18.25
A combined plot of SOS-S, BITe and SPANE-B values of all participants in the ancient group.

increasing graph in SPANE-B values; however, there is no definite underlying pattern in the values.

To verify if there is an existing underlying pattern, we plotted a combined graph of all the participant's SOS-S, BITe and SPANE-B values. As shown in Figures 18.25 and 18.26, we can see that even though each participant has their own unique trajectory, the SOS-S score

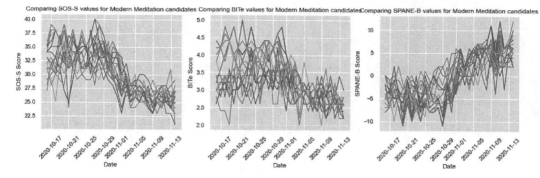

FIGURE 18.26

A combined plot of SOS-S, BITe and SPANE-B values of all participants in the modern group.

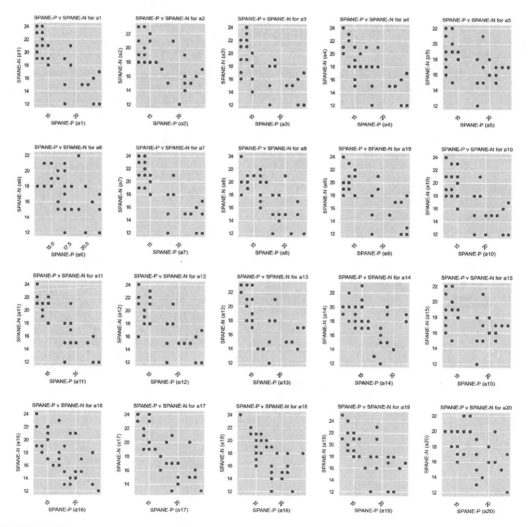

FIGURE 18.27

Scatter plot for SPANE-P vs. SPANE-N scores for participants in the ancient meditation group showing a negative correlation.

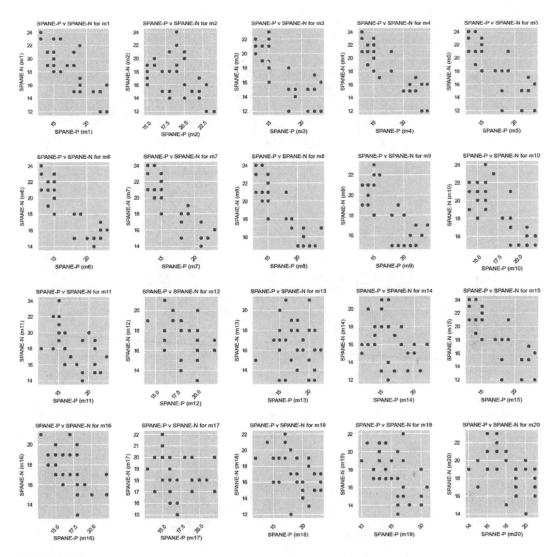

FIGURE 18.28
Scatter plot for SPANE-P vs. SPANE-N scores for participants in the ancient meditation group showing a negative correlation.

starts decreasing, the BITe score starts decreasing and the SPANE-B score starts increasing only after a continuous 2–2.5 weeks of daily meditation in both ancient and modern meditation groups. Before this threshold period, we see fluctuations in terms of increase and decrease in the scores. We thus would like to propose that our body needs a threshold amount of time to start reacting to any form of meditation and it is not an immediate effect. It was also observed that the ancient group saw a streamlined progress in their values as compared to the modern group, which was evidently more chaotic than the ancient group.

Figures 18.27 and 18.28 describe a scatter plot of SPANE-P vs. SPANE-N scores for ancient and modern groups, respectively. This is to understand whether the decreasing pattern of SPANE-N and the increasing pattern of SPANE-P are correlated to each other. To measure the extent of negative correlation between SPANE-P and SPANE-N scores for both groups,

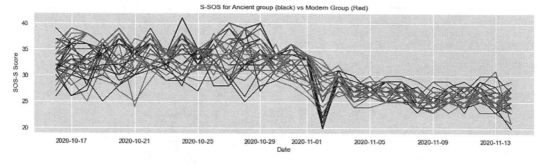

FIGURE 18.29
Plot of SOS-S values for ancient group (black) vs. modern group (gray).

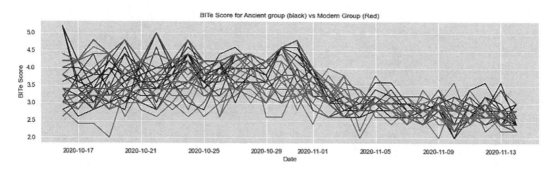

FIGURE 18.30
Plot of BITe values for ancient group (black) vs. modern group (gray).

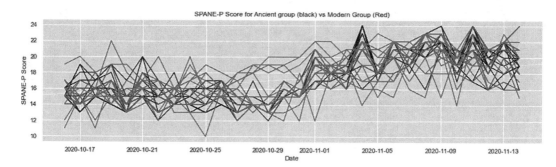

FIGURE 18.31
Plot of SPANE-P values for ancient group (black) vs. modern group (gray).

we measure Pearson's correlation coefficient for the groups in the section on Statistical Analysis. Figure 18.27 shows a small to moderate negative correlation between SPANE-P and SPANE-N scores of the ancient meditation group.

Figure 18.28 shows a small to moderate negative correlation between SPANE-P and SPANE-N scores of ancient meditation groups.

In Figures 18.29–18.33, we have plotted SOSS-S, BITe, SPANE-P, SPANE-N and SPANE-B values for ancient groups and modern groups on the same graph, so as to get a comparative picture of both the group scores. Black lines represent the participants of the ancient meditation group, and red lines represent the participants of the modern meditation group.

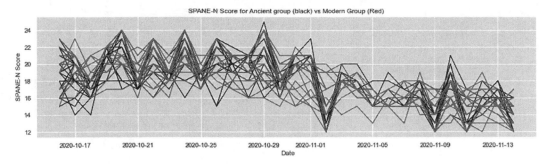

FIGURE 18.32
Plot of SPANE-N values for ancient group (black) vs. modern group (gray).

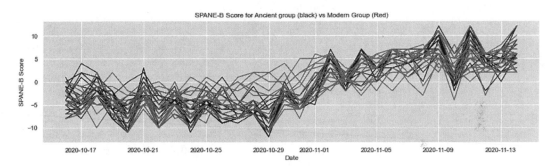

FIGURE 18.33
Plot of SPANE-B values for ancient group (black) vs. modern group (gray).

18.6.4 Statistical Analysis

In Section 18.6.3, while plotting the scatter plots, we observed a negative correlation between SPANE-P and SPANE-N scores of participants from both the ancient and the modern groups. Therefore to determine a quantitative correlation between the two scores, we found Pearson's correlation coefficient (r) for each participant in both the groups. Table 18.2 describes the resultant values of r for participants. The strength of correlation in Table 18.2 has been labeled with reference to the list posted by the Political Science Department at Quinnipiac University [12].

From the values in Table 18.2, we can confirm that SPANE-P and SPANE-N values in both groups are negatively correlated. Also, ancient meditation group participants majorly showed strong and very strong negative correlations with all their p-values less than 0.05, with just one participant showing a moderate negative correlation. Even though the modern meditation group had very strong negative correlations than the ancient meditation group, the modern group had a participant with negligible negative correlation, and four participants whose p-values were greater than 0.05, making their correlations insignificant.

18.6.4.1 Jarque–Bera Test for Goodness of Fit

The Jarque–Bera test was performed on the SOS-S, BITe and SPANE values of participants of both the ancient and modern meditation groups to check if they have the skewness and kurtosis matching that of a normal distribution. The null and alternative hypothesis for this test is as follows:

TABLE 18.2

Pearson's Correlation Coefficient (r) of SPANE-P vs. SPANE-N Scores for Participants in Ancient and Modern Meditation Groups

Participant	Ancient Mantra Meditation Group P		Strength	Participant	Modern Mindfulness Meditation Group P		Strength
at	−0.803	<0.005	Very strong negative relationship	m1	−0.81	<0.005	Very strong negative relationship
a2	−0.64	<0.005	Strong negative relationship	m2	−048	<0.005	Strong negative relationship
a3	−0.68	<0.005	Strong negative relationship	m3	−0.8	<0.005	Very strong negative relationship
a4	−0.72	<0.005	Very strong negative relationship	m4	−0.87	<0.005	Very strong negative relationship
a5	−047	<0.005	Strong negative relationship	m5	−0.8	<0.005	Very strong negative relationship
a6	−0.51	<0.005	Strong negative relationship	m6	−0.86	<0.005	Very strong negative relationship
a7	−0.8	<0.005	Very strong negative relationship	m7	−0.89	<0.005	Very strong negative relationship
a8	−0.68	<0.005	Strong negative relationship	m8	−0.88	<0.005	Very strong negative relationship
a9	−0.69	<0.005	Strong negative relationship	m9	−0.76	<0.005	Very strong negative relationship
a10	−0.7	<0.005	Very strong negative relationship	m10	−0.75	<0.005	Very strong negative relationship
a11	−0.81	<0.005	Very strong negative relationship	m11	−0.57	<0.005	Strong negative relationship
a12	−0.67	<0.005	Strong negative relationship	m12	−043	<0.005	Strong negative relationship
a13	−0.67	<0.005	Strong negative relationship	m13	−0.11	>0.05	Negligible relationship
a14	−0.37	<0.005	Moderate negative relationship	m14	−0.33	>0.05	Moderate negative relationship
a15	−0.66	<0.005	Strong negative relationship	m15	−0.65	<0.005	Strong negative relationship
a16	−0.59	<0.005	Strong negative relationship	m16	−0.52	<0.005	Strong negative relationship

(*Continued*)

TABLE 18.2 (*Continued*)

Pearson's Correlation Coefficient (*r*) of SPANE-P vs. SPANE-N Scores for Participants in Ancient and Modern Meditation Groups

Participant	Ancient Mantra Meditation Group *P*		Strength	Participant	Modern Mindfulness Meditation Group *P*		Strength
a17	−0.77	<0.005	Very strong negative relationship	m17	−0.25	>0.05	Weak negative relationship
a18	−0.67	<0.005	Strong negative relationship	m18	−049	>0.05	Strong negative relationship
a19	−0.6	<0.005	Strong negative relationship	m19	−048	<0.005	Strong negative relationship
a20	−0.55	<0.005	Strong negative relationship	m20	−048	<0.005	Strong negative relationship

H_0: The samples are normally distributed.

H_a: The samples are not normally distributed.

The result of the Jarque–Bera test was a deciding factor in choosing the statistical tests that could be performed on the data obtained. Table 18.3 describes the t statistic score, the *p*-value and the results of the Jarque–Bera test for both ancient and modern meditation groups, respectively.

Thus, SOS-S, BITe and SPANE-B scores of ancient meditation participants passed the Jarque–Bera test and therefore it could be concluded that the scores obtained from ancient meditation candidates do represent a normal distribution. Similarly, in modern meditation participants, the scores obtained from each participant for SOS-S, BITe and SPANE-B passed the Jarque–Bera test excluding the BITe score of participant 'm16' who failed the test.

18.6.4.2 Comparison of SOS-S Scores of Ancient and Modern Meditation Groups

Each meditation group, i.e., ancient or modern group, contained 20 participants whose SOS-S scores were collected for a duration of 30 days. Two separate lists were formed corresponding to each meditation group. The first list contained the monthly mean of SOS-S scores of each participant of the ancient meditation group and the second list contained the monthly mean of SOS-S scores of each participant of the modern meditation group. Levene's test conducted on the two groups (*p*=0.969) suggested that there is not enough evidence to say that the variances are significantly different between the groups. Thus, we moved on to conduct the two-sample T-test. The two-sample T-test conducted on the groups (statistic=0.11, *p*-value=0.911) suggested that there is no sufficient evidence to conclude that the two groups are different. Thus, we can conclude that after a month of meditation, both ancient and modern meditation groups had statistically similar SOS-S scores.

18.6.4.3 Comparison of BITe Scores of Ancient and Modern Meditation Groups

Each meditation group, i.e., ancient or modern group, contained 20 participants whose BITe scores were collected for a duration of 30 days. Two separate lists were formed corresponding to each meditation group. The first list contained the monthly mean of BITe

TABLE 18.3

Jarque–Bera Test Results for Goodness of Fit for Ancient and Modern Meditation Group

Participant	SOS-S			BITe			SPANE-B		
	t	p	Result	t	p	Result	T	p	Result
Ancient Mantra Meditation Group									
a1	2.93	0.23	H0 accepted	3.33	0.18	H0 accepted	2.55	0.27	H0 accepted
a2	2.51	0.28	H0 accepted	0.97	0.61	H0 accepted	2.7	0.25	H0 accepted
a3	2.71	0.25	H0 accepted	3.09	0.21	H0 accepted	2.03	0.36	H0 accepted
a4	1.46	0.48	H0 accepted	2.9	0.23	H0 accepted	1.64	0.43	H0 accepted
a5	1.78	0.4	H0 accepted	2.08	0.35	H0 accepted	2.24	0.32	H0 accepted
a6	1.19	0.55	H0 accepted	3.02	0.22	H0 accepted	1.34	0.51	H0 accepted
a7	2.04	0.36	H0 accepted	2.33	0.31	H0 accepted	2.57	0.27	H0 accepted
a8	1.19	0.55	H0 accepted	1.3	0.52	H0 accepted	1.42	0.48	H0 accepted
a9	1.72	0.42	H0 accepted	1.27	0.52	H0 accepted	2.43	0.29	H0 accepted
a10	1.4	0.49	H0 accepted	1.85	0.39	H0 accepted	2.18	0.33	H0 accepted
a11	0.74	0.69	H0 accepted	3.21	0.2	H0 accepted	2.18	0.33	H0 accepted
a12	1.63	0.44	H0 accepted	3.42	0.18	H0 accepted	2.19	0.33	H0 accepted
a13	1.61	0.44	H0 accepted	1.86	0.39	H0 accepted	2.39	0.3	H0 accepted
a14	1.33	0.51	H0 accepted	1.81	0.4	H0 accepted	1.5	0.47	H0 accepted
a15	1.3	0.51	H0 accepted	1.2	0.54	H0 accepted	1.67	0.43	H0 accepted
a16	2.65	0.26	H0 accepted	1.3	0.51	H0 accepted	0.72	0.69	H0 accepted
a17	0.8	0.66	H0 accepted	0.73	0.69	H0 accepted	1.47	0.47	H0 accepted
a18	2.36	0.3	H0 accepted	1.51	0.46	H0 accepted	0.7	0.7	H0 accepted
a19	1.66	0.43	H0 accepted	1.46	0.48	H0 accepted	1.36	0.5	H0 accepted
a20	0.42	0.8	H0 accepted	0.29	0.86	H0 accepted	1.69	0.42	H0 accepted
Modern Mindfulness Meditation Group									
m1	2.83	0.24	H0 accepted	2.53	0.28	H0 accepted	1.98	0.37	H0 accepted
m2	2.91	0.23	H0 accepted	2.94	0.22	H0 accepted	2.01	0.36	H0 accepted
m3	1.51	0.46	H0 accepted	3.26	0.19	H0 accepted	2.99	0.22	H0 accepted
m4	2.37	0.3	H0 accepted	3.34	0.18	H0 accepted	2.76	0.25	H0 accepted
m5	3.21	0.19	H0 accepted	3.32	0.18	H0 accepted	2.48	0.28	H0 accepted
m6	2.62	0.26	H0 accepted	3.09	0.21	H0 accepted	3.27	0.19	H0 accepted
m7	2.68	0.26	H0 accepted	3.26	0.19	H0 accepted	3.01	0.22	H0 accepted
m8	2.75	0.25	H0 accepted	3.25	0.19	H0 accepted	3.12	0.2	H0 accepted
m9	2.92	0.23	H0 accepted	3.34	0.18	H0 accepted	3.45	0.17	H0 accepted
m10	3.14	0.2	H0 accepted	2.98	0.22	H0 accepted	3.31	0.19	H0 accepted
m11	2.46	0.29	H0 accepted	2.65	0.26	H0 accepted	1.74	0.41	H0 accepted ·
m12	2.94	0.22	H0 accepted	2.03	0.36	H0 accepted	1.4	0.49	H0 accepted
m13	1.3	0.52	H0 accepted	1.38	0.5	H0 accepted	1.09	0.57	H0 accepted
m14	1.87	0.39	H0 accepted	0.36	0.83	H0 accepted	1.54	0.46	H0 accepted
m15	0.44	0.8	H0 accepted	1.69	0.42	H0 accepted	1.68	0.43	H0 accepted
m16	2.7	0.25	H0 accepted	11.6	0.002	H0 rejected	2.31	0.31	H0 accepted
m17	0.6	0.73	H0 accepted	0.97	0.61	H0 accepted	1.45	0.48	H0 accepted
m18	0.16	0.92	H0 accepted	0.67	0.71	H0 accepted	1.98	0.37	H0 accepted
m19	2.09	0.35	H0 accepted	1.25	0.53	H0 accepted	1.5	0.47	H0 accepted
m20	1.05	0.59	H0 accepted	0.89	0.63	H0 accepted	1.97	0.37	H0 accepted

scores of each participant of the ancient meditation group and the second list contained the monthly mean of BITe scores of each participant of the modern meditation group. Levene's test conducted on the two groups ($p=0.0007$) suggested that there is enough evidence to say that the variances are significantly different between the groups. Thus, we moved on to conduct Welch's T-test. Welch's T-test conducted on the groups (statistic$=1.90$, p-value$=0.06$, dof$=33.42$) suggested that there is no sufficient evidence to conclude that the two groups are different. Thus, we can conclude that after a month of meditation, both ancient and modern meditation groups had statistically similar BITe scores.

18.6.4.4 Comparison of SPANE-P Scores of Ancient and Modern Meditation Groups

Levene's test conducted on the two groups ($p=0.052$) suggested that there is not enough evidence to say that the variances are significantly different between the groups. Thus, we moved on to conduct the two-sample T-test. The two-sample T-test conducted on the groups (statistic$=-0.58$, p-value$=0.56$) suggested that there is no sufficient evidence to conclude that the two groups are different. Thus, we can conclude that after a month of meditation, both ancient and modern meditation groups had statistically similar SPANE-P scores.

18.6.4.5 Comparison of SPANE-N Scores of Ancient and Modern Meditation Groups

Levene's test conducted on the two groups (0.003) suggested that there is enough evidence to say that the variances are significantly different between the groups. Thus, we moved on to conduct Welch's T-test. Welch's T-test conducted on the groups (statistic$=-0.60$, p-value$=0.546$, dof$=28.27$) suggested that there is sufficient evidence to conclude that the two groups are different. Thus, we can conclude that after a month of meditation, both ancient and modern meditation groups had statistically different SPANE-N scores.

18.6.4.6 Comparison of SPANE-B Scores of Ancient and Modern Meditation Groups

Levene's test conducted on the two groups ($p=0.019$) suggested that there is enough evidence to say that the variances are significantly different between the groups. Thus, we moved on to conduct Welch's T-test. Welch's T-test conducted on the groups (statistic$=0.02$, p-value$=0.98$, dof$=28.49$) suggested that there is sufficient evidence to conclude that the two groups are different. Thus, we can conclude that after a month of meditation, both ancient and modern meditation groups had statistically different SPANE-B scores.

18.7 Time Series Modeling

In this section, we use the Holt-Winters model to model SOS-S, BITe and SPANE-B values for both ancient and meditation groups.

18.7.1 Modeling SOS-S Scores for Ancient and Modern Meditation Groups

Modeling of SOS-S scores for the ancient meditation technique as well as modern meditation technique is presented in this section. This modeling is performed using Holt-Winters. See Figures 18.34 and 18.35.

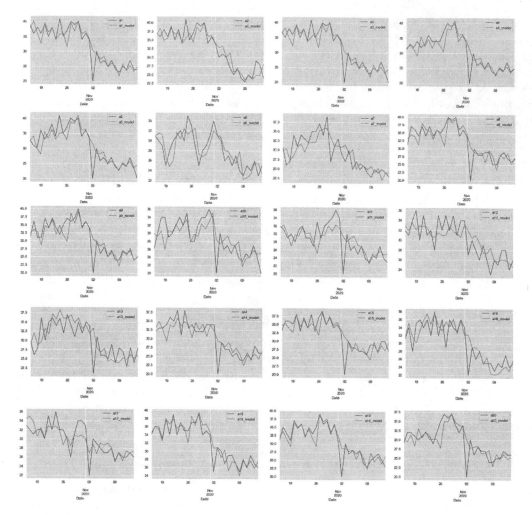

FIGURE 18.34

Modeling SOS-S values of ancient meditation using Holt-Winters model.

18.7.2 Modeling BITe Scores for Ancient and Modern Meditation Groups

Modeling of BITe scores for ancient and modern meditation techniques is presented in this section. See Figures 18.36 and 18.37.

18.7.3 Modeling SPANE-B Scores for Ancient and Modern Meditation Groups

Modeling of SPANE-B scores for ancient and modern meditation techniques is presented in this section. See Figures 18.38 and 18.39.

18.8 MEDit Architecture

In the course of this study, we saw that continuous meditation, either ancient or modern meditation, resulted in a decreasing trend in SOS-S, BITe and SPANE-N scores and an

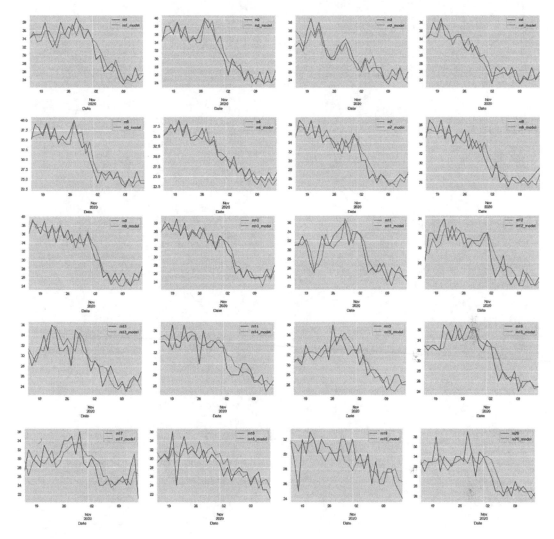

FIGURE 18.35

Modeling SOS-S values of modern meditation using Holt-Winters model.

increasing trend in SPANE-P and SPANE-B scores. Thus, the authors would like to propose the Meditate-Evaluate-Discover-it (MEDit) model, that simulates the conditions on which study is made and is presented in figure 18.40.

The proposed MEDit model contains three core components: meditation component, evaluation component and discovery component. All three components can be put together in the form of a mobile application or a web application.

18.8.1 Meditation Component

When the user first opens up the MEDit application, they are prompted to sign in for a better experience. The users can also complete the meditation without signing in; however, their scores would not be stored in the application database then. Signing in would allow

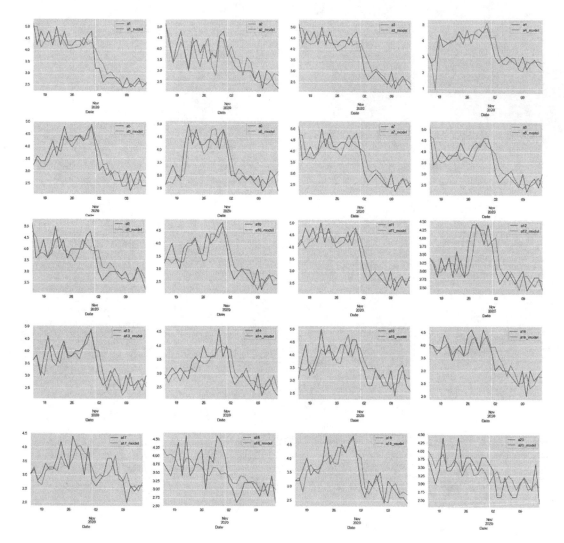

FIGURE 18.36
Modeling BITe values of ancient meditation using Holt-Winters model.

the application to track the user scores and analyze them. After signing into the all, the user has two options to carry out their meditation session. They can choose between a form of ancient meditation or a form of modern meditation. After selecting the meditation track, the user is taken to select the duration of their meditation session, which can range from 2 to 10 minutes. The track used by the user to meditate and the duration of meditation shall later be used to analyze the behavior of the user's post-meditation scores. Once the meditation track and duration are selected, the user is taken to the meditation screen where they can perform their meditation. After completion of the meditation session, the user is prompted to complete a questionnaire containing the SOS-S, BITe and the SPANE scales.

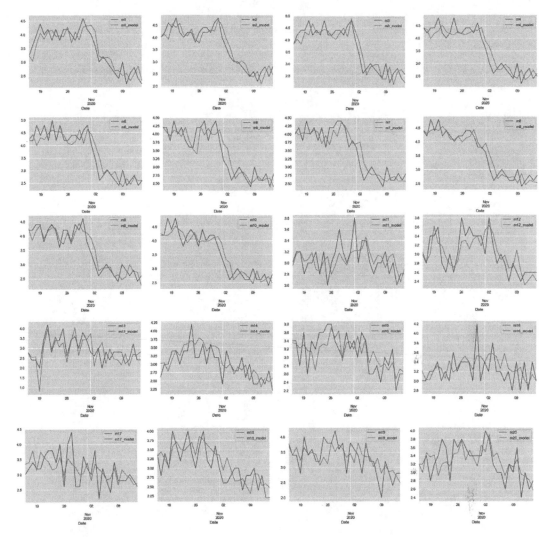

FIGURE 18.37
Modeling BITe values of modern meditation using Holt-Winters model.

18.8.2 Evaluation Component

A real-time database management system or a cloud-based database management system like Firebase forms a core component of the evaluation. The values obtained from the questionnaire filled by the user from the meditation component are recorded into the database along with details of meditation like the track selected and the duration of meditation and the corresponding SOS-S scores, BITe scores and SPANE scores are calculated.

18.8.3 Discovery Component

The scores calculated from the evaluation component are displayed to the user, along with the user's past records of meditation and an analysis of which track suits the user best, and what is the best duration for meditation for the user, based on the user's past meditation scores.

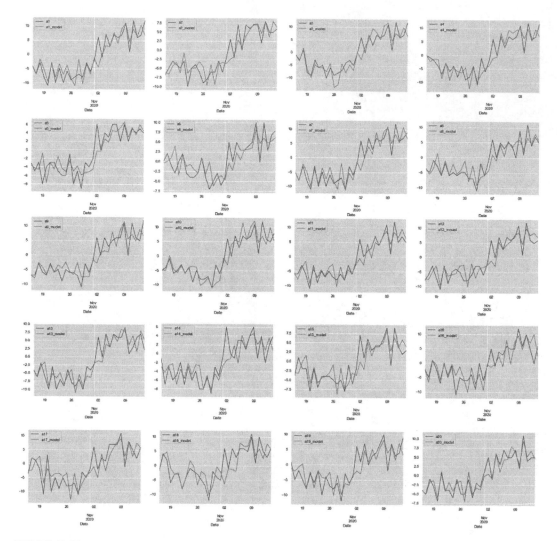

FIGURE 18.38
Modeling SPANE-B values of ancient meditation using Holt-Winters model.

18.9 Conclusion and Future Work

COVID-19 has presented itself as a devastating pandemic across the world and has already caused many deaths. The losses suffered due to this pandemic, either economic, social or psychological are incomprehensible. However, through this study, we intended to present some hope during these tough times. During the course of the experiments conducted and based on the meditation results evaluated, we come to a conclusion that both ancient and modern meditation tracks used by 40 participants (20 participants in each group) resulted in a decrease in their SOS-S, BITe and SPANE-N score which tested the stress overload, the brief irritability and negative experiences of the participants. Also, the participants showed a steady rise in their SPANE-P and SPANE-B scores, which measured the positive

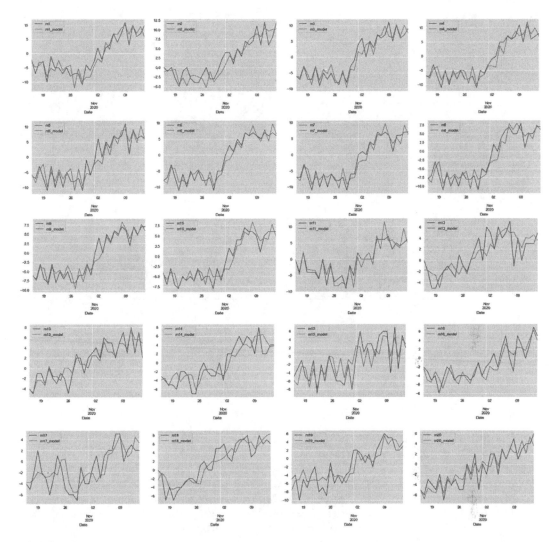

FIGURE 18.39
Modeling SPANE-B values of modern meditation using Holt-Winters model.

and balanced experiences of the participants. However, our experiments and study were based on a very small group of participants. It is therefore important to conduct a study on a larger scale in the future and then measure the results to see if they correspond with our study.

In this study, we have also proposed an easy MEDit architecture that will enable people to Meditate, Evaluate and Discover their stress overload, irritability and positive and negative experiences and analyze the effects of daily meditation on themselves in an easy manner, and thus improve their lifestyle and bring positive changes in their habits. A study also needs to be conducted in the future after the complete development of the MEDit application to test its efficiency with respect to the currently present mindfulness applications in the market like Headspace. The MEDit architecture can be integrated with smart devices like smartwatches and smart bands to work as a mobile application or a web application for tracking mindfulness levels of individuals as a part of future study.

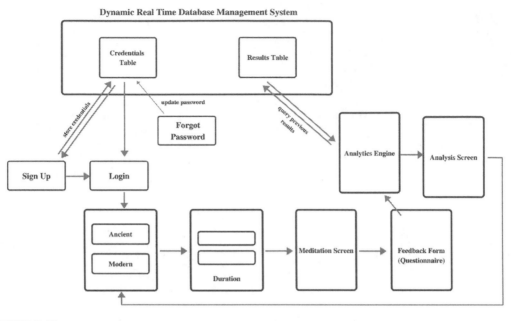

FIGURE 18.40
Proposed MEDit model.

References

1. Covid-19 India timeline: Looking back at pandemic-induced lockdown and how the country is coping with the crisis. *The Indian Express*, 23-Mar-2021. [Online]. Available: https://indianexpress.com/article/india/covid-19-india-timeline-looking-back-at-pandemic-induced-lockdown-7241583/. [Accessed: 25-Apr-2021].
2. Mishra, L. Coronavirus: Maharashtra, BMC, Mpower tie up to launch mental health helpline. *The Hindu*, 03-Apr-2020. [Online]. Available: https://www.thehindu.com/news/national/other-states/coronavirus-maharashtra-bmc-mpower-tie-up-to-launch-mental-health-helpline/article31248628.ece. [Accessed: 25-Apr-2021].
3. Brown, K. W., & Ryan, R. M. (2003). The benefits of being present: Mindfulness and its role in psychological well-being. *Journal of Personality and Social Psychology*, 84(4), 822–848.
4. Keng, S.-L., Smoski, M. J., & Robins, C. J. (2011). Effects of mindfulness on psychological health: a review of empirical studies. *Clinical 1592 Mindfulness* (2018) 9:1584–1593. *Psychology Review*, 31(6), 1041–1056. https://doi.org/10.1016/j. cpr.2011.04.006.
5. Holtzman, S., O'Connor, B. P., Barata, P. C., & Stewart, D. E. (2015). The brief irritability test (BITe). *Assessment*, 22(1), 101–115. https://doi. org/10.1177/1073191114533814.
6. Burke, A., Lam, C.N., Stussman, B., & Yang, H. (2017). Prevalence and patterns of use of mantra, mindfulness and spiritual meditation among adults in the United States. *BMC Complementary Medicine and Therapies*, 17(1), 316. doi: 10.1186/s12906-017-1827-8. PMID: 28619092; PMCID: PMC5472955.
7. Evans, S., Ferrando, S., Findler, M., Stowell, C., Smart, C., & Haglin, D. (2008). Mindfulness-based cognitive therapy for generalized anxiety disorder. *Journal of Anxiety Disorders*, 22(-4):716–721. doi: 10.1016/j.janxdis.2007.07.005. Epub 2007 Jul 22. PMID: 17765453.
8. Oman, D., Bormann, J.E., & Kane, J.J. (2020). Mantram repetition as a portable mindfulness practice: Applications during the COVID-19 pandemic. *Mindfulness (N Y)*, 16, 1–12 doi: 10.1007/s12671-020-01545-w. Epub ahead of print. PMID: 33224309; PMCID: PMC7667218.

9. Amirkhan, J.H. (2018). A brief stress diagnostic tool: The short stress overload scale. *Assessment,* 25(8), 1001–1013. doi:10.1177/1073191116673173.

10. Holtzman, S., O'Connor, B.P., Barata, P.C., & Stewart, D.E. (2015). The Brief Irritability Test (BITe): A measure of irritability for use among men and women. *Assessment,* 22(1), 101–115. doi:10.1177/1073191114533814.

11. Diener, Ed., Wirtz, D., & Tov, W. (2010). New measures of well-being: Flourishing and positive and negative feelings. *Social Indicators Research,* 39, 247–266.

12. Stephanie, G. Correlation Coefficient: Simple Definition, Formula, Easy Steps. From StatisticsHow To.com: Elementary Statistics for the rest of us! https://www.statisticshowto.com/probability-and-statistics/correlation-coefficient-formula/.

Index

Note: **Bold** page numbers refer to tables and *italic* page numbers refer to figures.